Dublin

The words of its writers are part of the texture of Dublin, an invisible counterpart to the bricks and pavement we see around us. Beyond the ever-present footsteps of James Joyce's characters, Leopold Bloom or Stephen Dedalus, around the city centre, an ordinary-looking residential street overlooking Dublin Bay, for instance, presents the house where Nobel laureate Seamus Heaney lived for many years; a few blocks away is the house where another Nobel laureate, W. B. Yeats, was born. Just down the coast is the pier linked to yet another, Samuel Beckett, from which we can see the Martello Tower that is the setting for the opening chapter of *Ulysses*. But these are only a few. Step by step, *Dublin: A Writer's City* unfolds a book-lover's map of this unique city, full of beautiful illustrations, inviting us to experience what it means to live in a great city of literature.

Chris Morash has published widely on Irish studies, with books on Irish Famine literature, Irish theatre history, media history, and spatial theory; he has collaborated with the Abbey Theatre, and chairs the judging panel for the Dublin Literary Award, one of the world's richest literary prizes.

Imagining Cities

Editor
Chris Morash, Trinity College Dublin

Imagining Cities is a series of books by leading literary scholars, each of which explores the ways in which writers have created cities of words that overlay the stones and pavements of the places where they lived and worked. Each book in the series is dedicated to an individual city – whether it be New York, London or Dublin – in which the words of its writers have shaped the experience of urban life.

Books in the series
Dublin: A Writer's City by Christopher Morash
New Orleans: A Writer's City by T. R. Johnson
London: A Writer's City by Matthew Beaumont
Cambridge: A Writer's City by Leo Mellor
New York: A Writer's City by Lisa Keller

Dublin
A Writer's City

Christopher Morash

CAMBRIDGE
UNIVERSITY PRESS

Shaftesbury Road, Cambridge CB2 8EA, United Kingdom

One Liberty Plaza, 20th Floor, New York, NY 10006, USA

477 Williamstown Road, Port Melbourne, VIC 3207, Australia

314–321, 3rd Floor, Plot 3, Splendor Forum, Jasola District Centre,
New Delhi – 110025, India

103 Penang Road, #05–06/07, Visioncrest Commercial, Singapore 238467

Cambridge University Press is part of Cambridge University Press & Assessment,
a department of the University of Cambridge.

We share the University's mission to contribute to society through the pursuit of
education, learning and research at the highest international levels of excellence.

www.cambridge.org
Information on this title: www.cambridge.org/9781108926942

DOI: 10.1017/9781108917810

© Christopher Morash 2023

This publication is in copyright. Subject to statutory exception and to the provisions
of relevant collective licensing agreements, no reproduction of any part may take
place without the written permission of Cambridge University Press & Assessment.

First published 2023

First published in paperback 2026

A catalogue record for this publication is available from the British Library.

ISBN 978-1-108-83164-2 Hardback
ISBN 978-1-108-92694-2 Paperback

Cambridge University Press & Assessment has no responsibility for the persistence
or accuracy of URLs for external or third-party internet websites referred to in
this publication and does not guarantee that any content on such websites is, or will
remain, accurate or appropriate.

For EU product safety concerns, contact us at Calle de José Abascal, 56, 1°,
28003 Madrid, Spain, or email eugpsr@cambridge.org

i.m.
Eavan Boland, Brendan Kennelly,
Thomas Kinsella and Derek Mahon,
all of whom passed away
as this book was being written.
'The names of the dead are like lightning'.

Contents

Series Preface ix
Chronology xi
Master Map xviii

Introduction: **The Imagined City in Time of Pandemic** 2
1 **Mapping the City** 12
2 **Baggotonia** 32
3 **Around St. Stephen's Green** 54
4 **Trinity College** 76
5 **Around the Liberties** 96
6 **O'Connell Street and the Abbey Theatre** 120
7 **The North Inner City** 142
8 **South Dublin** 164
9 **The South Coast** 186
10 **North Dublin** 208
11 **Riverrun** 230
Read On … 252

Notes 257
Bibliography 277
Acknowledgements 294
Index 296
A plate section appears between pages 144–145

A Writer's City:
Series Preface

This series of books grew out of a simple recognition: that the city I know best – Dublin – is a place in which there is more than meets the eye. Certainly, Dublin has some impressive old Georgian buildings, such as the Custom House along the quays; and in the city's recent surge of prosperity, some interesting new shapes have appeared in the old industrial docklands. And yet, Dublin has never been a monumental city, never been the sort of place where you go to gawp in wonder at architectural edifices. The things that really give the city its character are far more insubstantial than concrete, glass or Portland stone. Tourist literature about the city often speaks about a culture of talk, of the pubs, of the people – and none of that is inaccurate. But there is more to it. For me, truly experiencing Dublin means being able to read the city's collective memory in its streets and buildings; and having access to that memory from the inside means knowing the city's literature.

So, this series began, really, where this book begins: on the day I first arrived in Dublin in the mid-1980s, and began to recognize that the street on which I would be living was the one on which Oscar Wilde had been born, and was where part of James Joyce's *Ulysses* takes place. Once I began to associate a particular building, or street corner, or vista with a writer, with a novel, play or poem, that place was never quite the same again. Ghosting the city of the senses, with its diesel fumes and its roadworks, was another, more complex city, whose layers went back over centuries, and whose characters were many and fascinating. Over time, my map of this spectral, fictional city grew outwards from that single street to cover the entire expanding urban area of Dublin. By the time my editor at Cambridge University Press approached me with an idea for a book about Dublin and literature, the outlines of that map of the hidden city were already well sketched, at least in my own mind. At its simplest, this book is an attempt to share that experience of Dublin that is grounded in literary memory.

Like many people, whenever I travel, I have always tried to replicate something of what it means to know a city by its literature, by bringing a novel by Dickens with me to London, or a book by Pessoa to Lisbon. It is now apparent that what I have really been looking for was the equivalent of this book elsewhere: the one book that would show me the map of the unseen city. And so, just as this book grew from a single street to cover an entire city, so the idea grew beyond one city to become a series of books on writers' cities that will include New Orleans, New York, London, and more. However, for me, their starting point is always that moment on a street in Dublin.

Chris Morash
Dublin, 2022

Chronology

770	Irish annals record small army drowned at crossing of River Liffey
841	First record of Vikings overwintering where River Poddle meets River Liffey
1014	Battle of Clontarf
1337	*The Pride of Life* (play)
1352	(approx.) *Visitatio Sepulcri* (play; Church of St. John the Evangelist)
1498	Corpus Christi pageants recorded
1551	First book published in Dublin, *Boke of Common Praier*
1575	A third of Dublin population perish in plague
1592	Trinity College Dublin founded
1603	James I proclaimed king in Dublin
1610	John Speed maps Dublin; Dublin population: ca. 8,000–10,000
1635	Werburgh Street Theatre (probable date)
1640	Henry Burnell, *Landgartha* (play; Werburgh Street)
1662	Smock Alley Theatre built
1667	Dublin population: ca. 30,000
1669	Phoenix Park created
1680	St. Stephen's Green created
1685	First regular Dublin newspaper, the *News-Letter*
1700	William Philips, *St. Stephen's Green; or the Generous Lovers* (play, Smock Alley)

1710	Dublin's first literary magazine, *The Examiner*, begins publication
1721	Henrietta Street laid out
1726	Jonathan Swift, *Gulliver's Travels* (non-fiction prose)
1729	Jonathan Swift, *A Modest Proposal* (satire)
1729	Parliament Building, College Green
1732	Library of Trinity College
1750	Work begins on Sackville (later O'Connell) Street
1750	Dublin population: ca. 125,000
1754	*Mahomet* riots, Smock Alley Theatre (play)
1756	John Rocque's map of Dublin
1757	Edmund Burke, *A Philosophical Enquiry into the Origin of Our Ideas of the Sublime and the Beautiful* (philosophy)
1758	Wide Streets Commission
1791	Carlisle (later O'Connell) Bridge opens
1792	Grand Canal extended to Ringsend
1798	James Whitelaw, *Essay on the Population of Dublin*
1798	United Irishmen rebellion
1801	Act of Union; Ireland becomes part of United Kingdom
1803	Robert Emmet's rebellion
1804	Dublin population: 182,000
1812	Maria Edgeworth, *The Absentee* (novel)
1817	Completion of Royal Canal
1830	Jonah Barrington, *Personal Sketches* (memoir)
1833	*Dublin University Magazine* founded
1834	First urban rail line, Kingstown (Dún Laoghaire) to Westland Row
1839	Charles Lever, *The Confessions of Harry Lorrequer* (novel)
1842	*Nation* newspaper founded; suppressed, 1848
1845	Joseph Sheridan Le Fanu, *The Cock and the Anchor* (novel)
1845	First year of Great Famine
1848	Young Ireland rebellion

1849	James Clarence Mangan, *Autobiography* (memoir; written ca. 1849)
1851	Dublin population: 250,000
1854	Catholic University of Ireland founded (University College Dublin from 1882)
1859	*Irish Times* begins publication
1863	Lady Morgan, *Memoirs* (published posthumously)
1863	Sheridan Le Fanu, *The House by the Churchyard* (novel)
1890	National Library of Ireland opens on Kildare Street
1882	George Moore, *A Drama in Muslin* (novel)
1895	*Irish Homestead* begins publication with Æ as editor
1897	Bram Stoker, *Dracula* (novel)
1899	First production of Irish Literary Theatre, W. B. Yeats, *The Countess Cathleen* (play)
1901	Dublin population: 383,000
1904	Abbey Theatre opens
1911–1914	George Moore, *Hail and Farewell* (3 volumes; memoir)
1912	James Stephens, *The Charwoman's Daughter* (novel)
1913	Dublin Lock-Out; Church Street tenement collapse
1914	James Joyce, *Dubliners* (short stories)
1916	Easter Rising
1916	James Stephens, *The Insurrection in Dublin* (memoir)
1916	James Joyce, *A Portrait of the Artist as a Young Man* (novel)
1919–1921	War of Independence
1920	W. B. Yeats, 'Easter 1916' (poem)
1922	James Joyce, *Ulysses* (novel)
1922–1923	Irish Civil War
1923	Seumas O'Sullivan begins publishing *Dublin Magazine*
1923	W. B. Yeats, Nobel Prize for Literature
1925	G. B. Shaw, Nobel Prize for Literature
1926	Seán O'Casey, *The Plough and the Stars* provokes riot (Abbey Theatre)
1928	1,300 public houses built in new suburb of Marino

1929	Local Government Act makes Rathmines part of Dublin
1929	Censorship of Publications Act
1930	W. B. Yeats, *The Words Upon the Window-Pane* (play, Abbey Theatre)
1931	Housing Act facilitates clearance of tenements
1937	Oliver St. John Gogarty, *As I Was Going Down Sackville Street* (memoir)
1938	Samuel Beckett, *Murphy* (novel)
1939	Flann O'Brien, *At-Swim-Two-Birds* (novel)
1939	James Joyce, *Finnegans Wake* (novel)
1940	'Cruiskeen Lawn' column begins, *Irish Times*
1942	Elizabeth Bowen, *Seven Winters* (memoir)
1947	Patrick Kavanagh, *A Soul for Sale* (poems)
1949	*Envoy* (literary magazine, until 1951)
1950	Dublin population: 600,000
1950	Liam O'Flaherty, *Insurrection* (novel)
1951	Maura Laverty, *Liffey Lane* (play, Gate Theatre)
1953	Liam Miller founds Dolmen Press
1954	Brendan Behan, *The Quare Fellow* (play, Pike Theatre)
1955	Samuel Beckett, *Waiting for Godot* (play, Irish premiere, Pike Theatre)
1955	J. P. Donleavy, *The Ginger Man* (novel)
1958	Samuel Beckett, *Krapp's Last Tape* (play, Royal Court, London)
1958	Thomas Kinsella, *Another September* (poetry)
1960	Patrick Kavanagh, *Come Dance with Kitty Stobling* (poetry)
1962	Austin Clarke, *Twice Round the Black Church* (memoir)
1962	Paul Smith, *The Countrywoman* (novel)
1965	Iris Murdoch, *The Red and the Green* (novel)
1966	Lee Dunne, *Goodbye to the Hill* (novel)
1966	Austin Clarke, *Mnemosyne Lay in Dust* (poetry)
1967	Eavan Boland, *New Territory* (poetry)
1969	James Plunkett, *Strumpet City* (novel)

1969	Samuel Beckett, Nobel Prize for Literature
1970	Christy Brown, *Down All the Days* (novel)
1971	Mary Lavin, *Collected Stories* (short stories)
1971	John McGahern, *Nightlines* (short stories)
1973	Hugh Leonard, *Da* (play, Irish premiere, Olympia Theatre)
1975	Eavan Boland, *War Horse* (poetry)
1975	Brian Friel, *Volunteers* (play, Abbey Theatre)
1976	Anthony Cronin, *Dead as Doornails* (memoir)
1976	Seamus Heaney, *North* (poetry)
1980	Dublin population: 900,000
1981	*Poetry Ireland Review* begins publication
1984	DART light rail service begins operation
1987	Macdara Woods, *Stopping the Lights in Ranelagh* (poetry)
1987–1991	Roddy Doyle, *The Barrytown Trilogy* (novels)
1990	Thomas Kinsella, *Poems from the City Centre* (poetry)
1990	Eilís Ní Dhuibhne, *The Bray House* (novel)
1990	Dermot Bolger, *The Journey Home* (novel)
1993	'Celtic Tiger' first used to describe economic boom
1994	Eavan Boland, *In Time of Violence* (poetry)
1994	Roddy Doyle, *Paddy Clarke Ha Ha Ha* (novel)
1994	Paula Meehan, *Pillow Talk* (poetry)
1995	Seamus Heaney, Nobel Prize for Literature
1996	IMPAC Dublin Literary Award established (now Dublin Literary Award)
1997	Maeve Brennan, *The Springs of Affection: Stories of Dublin* (short stories)
1998	Good Friday Agreement ends conflict in Northern Ireland
1998	Paul Howard begins Ross O'Carroll Kelly column in *Sunday Tribune*
1999	Mark O'Rowe, *Howie the Rookie* (play, Bush Theatre, London)
2002	*Foreign Policy* ranks Ireland as most globalized country in the world

2004	Luas trams begin operation
2005	Sebastian Barry, *A Long, Long Way* (novel)
2006	Thomas Kinsella, *A Dublin Documentary* (poetry, memoir)
2007	Anne Enright, *The Gathering* (novel)
2008	Leland Bardwell, *A Restless Life* (memoir)
2008	Marian Keyes, *This Charming Man* (novel)
2008	Kevin Power, *Bad Day in Blackrock* (novel)
2010	Benjamin Black, *Elegy for April* (novel)
2010	Tana French, *Faithful Place* (novel)
2010–2014	*Monto Cycle* (site-specific plays, ANU Productions)
2010	Dublin designated fourth UNESCO City of Literature
2011	Christine Dwyer Hickey, *The Cold Eye of Heaven* (novel)
2013	Deirdre Madden, *Time Present and Time Past* (novel)
2014	Eavan Boland, *A Poet's Dublin* (poetry)
2015	Marriage Equality referendum recognizes same-sex marriage.
2018	Sally Rooney, *Normal People* (novel)
2019	Museum of Literature in Ireland (MoLI) opens on St. Stephen's Green
2019	Dylan Coburn Gray, *Citysong* (play, Abbey Theatre)
2020	Anne Enright, *Actress* (novel)
2020	COVID-19 pandemic begins
2020	Dublin population: 1.4 million
2020	Emma Donoghue, *The Pull of the Stars* (novel)
2021	Neil Jordan, *Lord Edward and Citizen Small* (novel)
2021	Peter Sirr, *Intimate City* (essays)

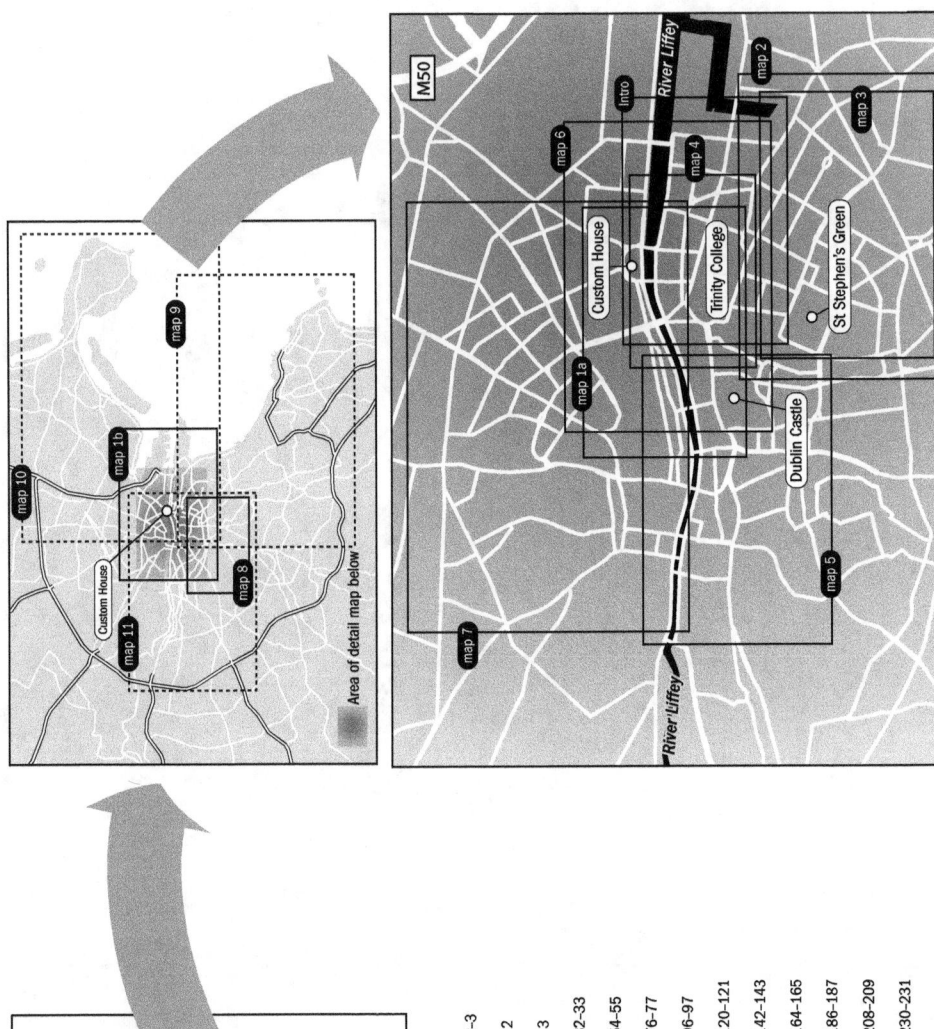

Intro	2–3
map 1a Lady Morgan	12
map 1b Brendan Behan	13
map 2 Baggotonia	32–33
map 3 St. Stephen's Green	54–55
map 4 Trinity College	76–77
map 5 Liberties	96–97
map 6 O'Connell St	120–121
map 7 North Inner City	142–143
map 8 South Side	164–165
map 9 South Coast	186–187
map 10 North City & Coast	208–209
map 11 Riverrun	230–231

1. Birthplace of Oscar Wilde (21 Westland Row)
2. Pearse Street Station (Westland Row)
3. Sweney's Chemists (1 Lincoln Place)
4. Antient Concert Rooms (42 Pearse St)
5. Finn's Hotel (1 South Leinster Street)
6. Grand Canal Docks

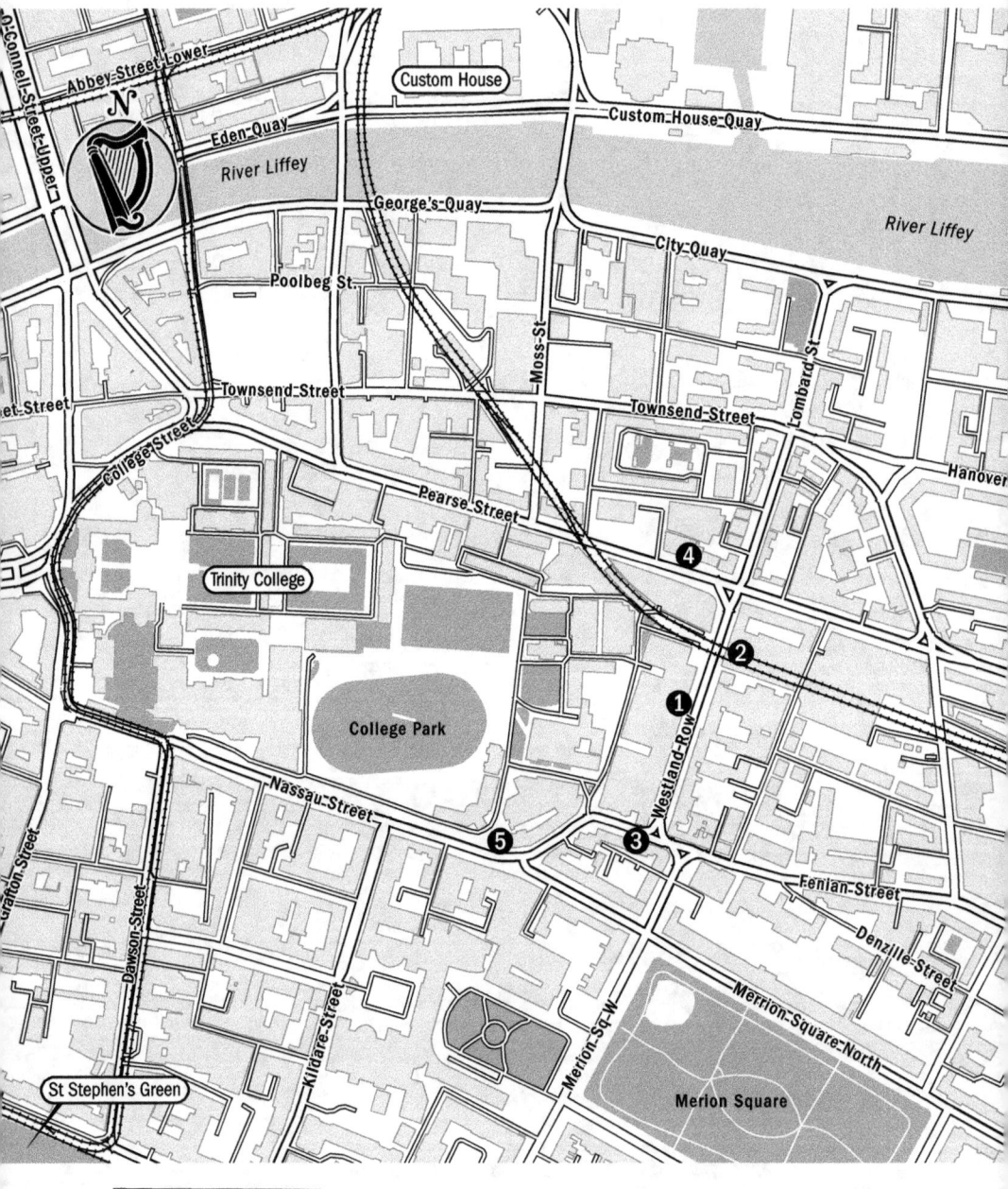

Introduction
The Imagined City in Time of Pandemic

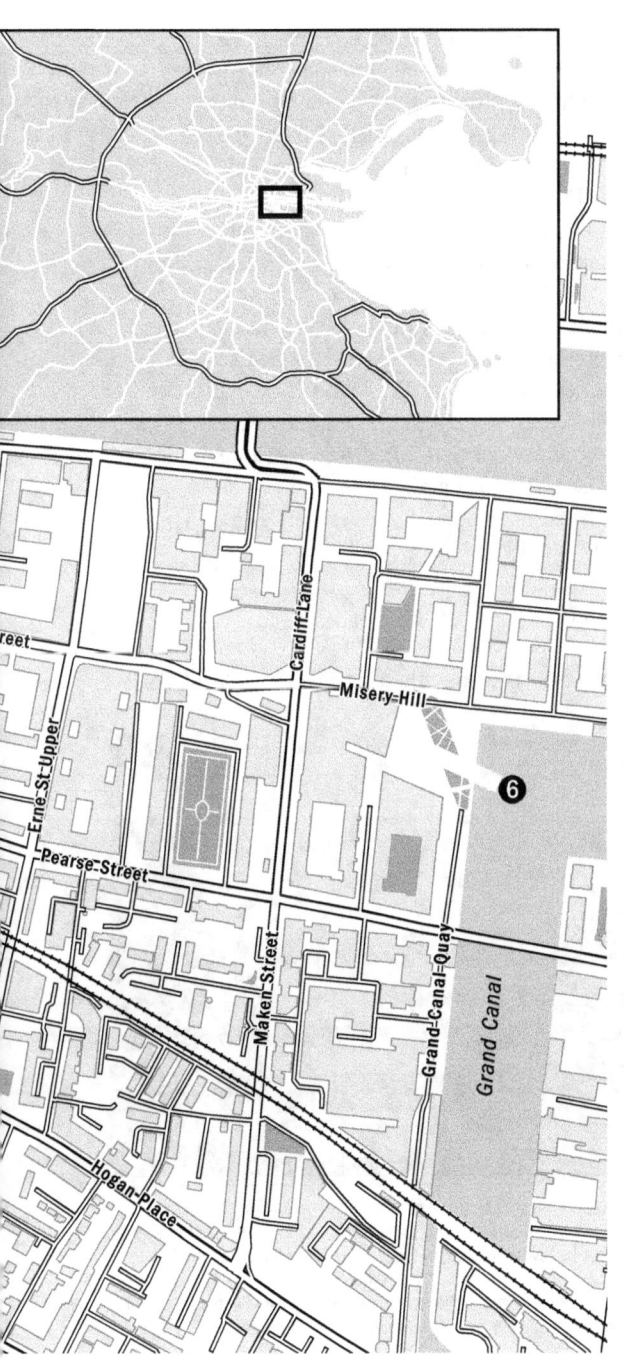

Cities of the imagination and cities of memory are close cousins. I live in a small village in County Meath, which in normal times is about a twenty-kilometre commute to my office in Trinity College, in the city centre. As I began to write this book in April 2020, exiled from the city by the first waves of the COVID-19 pandemic, I began to experience particularly vivid memories of Dublin as I had first encountered it thirty-five years earlier. 'Your first day in Dublin is always your worst,' wrote the American poet John Berryman, when he arrived in 1966.[1] It was otherwise for me when I first landed in the city in 1985 as a postgraduate student. In those initial few minutes in the city, I had a sense that there was something familiar about the address I gave to the taxi-driver on my way in from the airport: 15 Westland Row. At first I thought this was just the comforting thought that somewhere new already felt familiar. Then I remembered that I had been reading Richard Ellmann's biography of Oscar Wilde on the plane, where he mentions the house in which Wilde had been born – 21 Westland Row, only a few doors down from where I would be living.

After putting my bags in my room on that first day, I set out on jet-lagged search for aspirin. The first likely source was at the end of Westland Row, on Lincoln Place: Sweny's Chemist Shop. This, it

This apparently innocuous stretch of street – Westland Row – may not look particularly rich in literary associations; however, it features in works by Joyce, Beckett, Thomas Kinsella, and others; and the door of the house in which Oscar Wilde had been born, at 21 Westland Row, is just visible to the left. Photo from Fergus O'Connor Collection. *Courtesy of the National Library of Ireland.*

5 · THE IMAGINED CITY IN TIME OF PANDEMIC

turned out, was the setting for the 'Lotus Eaters' episode of James Joyce's *Ulysses* (1922), the shop in which Leopold Bloom buys his wife, Molly, a bar of lemon soap. 'Sweny's in Lincoln Place. [...] He waited by the counter; inhaling the keen reek of drugs, the dusty dry smell of sponges and loofahs.'² From the doorway of Sweny's I could see the brick building that had been Finn's Hotel, where Nora Barnacle had been working when Joyce first met her on 16 June 1904, the day on which they met and which he memorializes in *Ulysses*.

On my way back down Westland Row that morning, I decided to continue on past my building, conscious now that I was following Bloom's fictional footsteps, past the Westland Row train station where the tracks cross above the road, and where 'the engine departing hammered slowly overhead',³ as the poet Thomas Kinsella puts it in a poem set on the street. The end of Westland Row brought me to Pearse Street, where I encountered Belacqua, the fictional protagonist of Samuel Beckett's *More Pricks Than Kicks* (1934), who has a distaste for the parallel Nassau Street ('beset at this hour with poets and peasants and politicians'). Instead, he prefers 'long straight

Oscar Wilde (1854-1900). Although he would later reinvent himself in the context of a parodic version of fashionable London, Wilde was born on the edge of the Trinity campus, at 21 Westland Row; the family later moved around the corner, to 1 Merrion Square, and Wilde studied at Trinity. *Getty Images*.

James Joyce (1882-1941), more than any other single writer, has shaped the literary imagining of Dublin. 'If the city one day suddenly disappeared from the earth it could be reconstructed out of my book [*Ulysses*],' he once told his friend Frank Budgen. Pictured here in the rear garden of his friend C. P. Curran's house, at 6 Cumberland Place, Dublin, in 1904. *Getty Images*.

Pearse Street' with 'its vast Barrack of Glencullen granite [the police station], its home of tragedy restored and enlarged [the Queen's theatre], its coal merchants and Florentine Fire Brigade Station, its two Cervi saloons, ice-cream and fried fish, its dairies, garages and monumental sculptors [where Patrick Pearse worked], and implicit behind the whole length of its southern frontage the College.'[4]

Continuing my walk that first morning, across Pearse Street I noticed a building of diminished glamour, which turned out to have been the Antient Concert Rooms. This was where the Irish Literary Theatre – the forerunner of the Abbey Theatre, founded by W. B. Yeats, Lady Gregory, and Edward Martyn – staged its first production, *The Countess Cathleen*, on 8 May 1899. Inspired by what happened on Pearse Street on that night, Yeats wrote: 'The drama has need of cities that it may find men in sufficient numbers, and cities destroy the emotions to which it appeals, and therefore the days of the drama are brief and come but seldom.'[5] Yeats's comments on 'the days of the drama' have stuck with me over the years, and are not just limited to the theatre. As much as writers need somewhere quiet to write, it is the rare writer who does not also need the presence of other people – particularly other writers – and many thrive on being able to immerse themselves in the sensorium of the city, on living in a place rich with the lives of others. Precisely why Dublin might lend itself to this delicate balance of needs was something Elizabeth Bowen identified with her usual precision in 1936: 'Dublin's grandness, as a capital city, is anti-romantic,' she wrote. 'Her interest lies in her contrasts, in the expression she gives to successive different ideas of living.' Bowen went on to make an observation that I have found not only to be true, but to be increasingly true the better I have come to know Dublin. 'Emotional memory, here, has so much power that the past and present seem to be lived simultaneously.'[6]

Samuel Beckett (1906-1989) lived much of his life in Paris, and wrote some of his major works in French. However, he was born in Dublin, studied at Trinity College, and his earliest works are very much woven into the fabric of the city, while later works return to it in memory. *Getty Images*.

7 · THE IMAGINED CITY IN TIME OF PANDEMIC

Going back to that morning in 1985, I realize now that before I had even had a decent sleep, Dublin as a writers' city was taking shape for me. Many years later, when I came across Colm Tóibín's 2018 book on the fathers of Wilde, Yeats, and Joyce, *Mad, Bad, Dangerous to Know*, where he too writes about recognizing Westland Row's density of literary associations, I was not only thrown back to my own first hour in Dublin, but also felt a further accumulation of layers of association, so that my mental map now includes not just Yeats, Joyce, Wilde, and Beckett, but also Tóibín himself, and his memory of the street in the 1970s. Reading Tóibín's book during those strange displaced months of the spring of 2020, my own memories, the books I had read, and the books about books, all assumed a vividness that I might have missed had the actual city been present to insist on its noisy reality.

Over time, of course, that reality has altered. Sweny's stopped selling aspirin and filling prescriptions in 2009, and has since reinvented itself as a used bookstore and a place for literary readings. The Antient Concert Rooms looked like it was going to be demolished in the great property scramble of the late 1990s, but the façade was preserved, and the building has since been converted into hot-desk office space for new start-ups. And the house where Oscar Wilde was born is now part of the Trinity campus. It is, in fact, the building in which my office is located, in what is very likely the actual room in which Lady Jane Wilde gave birth. 'Cityful passing away, other cityful coming,' muses Leopold Bloom at one point in *Ulysses*; 'passing away too: other coming on, passing on. Houses, lines of houses, streets; miles of pavements, piledup bricks, stones. Changing hands.'[7]

There was also, however, something about the sheer strangeness of the images of an empty city that emerged from the pandemic lockdowns in 2020 and into 20201 that brought back Dublin as I had first seen it. In the Dublin of the 1980s, almost all the shops were closed on Sundays. Even the pubs closed for a period in the afternoon for what was known as 'holy hour'. As a result, fewer buses ran, fewer people were around, and the streets had a sense of in-drawn breath, of waiting. 'A man should clear a space for himself,' writes the poet Brendan Kennelly:

> *Like Dublin city on a Sunday morning*
> *About six o'clock.*
> *Dublin and myself are rid of our traffic then*
> *And I'm walking.*[8]

For me, those Sundays were a time when the hidden fabric of Dublin showed itself, and I would walk the derelict cobbles and empty quays around the Grand Canal Docks for hours, absorbing the sense of past lives lived.

Today, that area around the Grand Canal Basin where I used to walk is known as the Silicon Docks. An entirely new streetscape has emerged, and companies such as Google, Twitter, and Facebook are now based there. This is a Dublin that never existed before, mirrored across the River Liffey by the larger financial services district, zones of steel, glass, and fibre-optic cabling, in which business is not simply multinational in an older sense. It is a city within a city in which global connectivity itself is the main business. If it were possible to perform an MRI scan of twenty-first-century Dublin, showing flows of data, the docklands would radiate enough light to convince you not only that this was the new city centre but that it was a principal European data capital.

And yet, there is paradoxically a different quiet here now. This is not the quiet of dereliction of the 1980s, but the quiet of a place with no memories – or at least with no literary memories. If the writers and fictional characters who populated Westland Row chattered incessantly in my ear, this new city that has grown up in the midst of the old one – while often architecturally impressive – is strangely silent. The philosopher Edward Casey has written about what he calls 'place-thinning', the sense that 'certain habitual patterns of relating to places have become attenuated to the point of disappearing altogether'.[9] To walk through Dublin's Silicon Docks today is to understand what he means; the air is somehow both brighter and thinner here than it is elsewhere in the city. This is both an unwritten city and – paradoxically – one that is denser with information than any part of Dublin has ever been before. It is a place where it only takes a small effort of imagination to see the air buzzing with the constant feed of images and data that distract us from where we are. It not only feels like elsewhere; it is home to the industries that allow our attention to be where we are not. In the literary city it is otherwise: in the literary city, we are always – insistently – present.

There is a sense, then, in which this book is a double effort of recovery. At the time it was being written, in a kind of exile, immersing myself in the literature of Dublin became a means by which the words of Dublin's writers could become surrogates for the missing city. But this book is an act of recovery in another sense as well, stretching beyond the pandemic in which it was written. My experience of that first morning on Westland Row is constantly growing and changing: a line from a poem here, a reference there, an unexpected address from a novel. Piece by piece, over the years I have been assembling a never-to-be-completed mosaic of Dublin as a writer's city. And as a new piece of the mosaic falls into place, another corner of the city comes alive for me, and a previously innocuous building or street corner shines out with a new significance. Little by little, my sense of place becomes a bit thicker.

The design of this book is an attempt to impose some kind of pattern on that larger mosaic by dividing the city into interlocking (and sometimes overlapping) zones of memory. Those associations are, to some extent, necessarily partial and impressionistic. For instance, it is well beyond a book of this scope to do more than nod in the direction of Dublin's Irish-language literature, or the wealth of children's literature set in the city. With this in mind, after an initial historical chapter to sketch an outline of the city's history, the book moves chapter by chapter outwards from the city centre through a series of zones of varying sizes. These do not necessarily align with electoral wards or parishes and are not be found on standard maps. And yet, when you are in the city, these are areas in which you sense some definitional common quality – maybe it is the scale of the streets, or the smell of the air – that is palpable even if it escapes easy definition.

These distinctive emotional atmospheres in different parts of the city have produced writing that over the years has been in dialogue with itself – the working through of Bowen's 'emotional memory' if you like. It is as if Dublin's writers have been collectively reaching towards the elusive quality that makes the area around Huband Bridge over the Grand Canal in the south city, for instance, utterly different than that around Mayor Street Bridge over the Royal Canal in the north city, only a twenty-minute walk away. Dividing up a city in this way is not necessarily a tidy business. The zones are by no means absolute, the divisions are more pragmatic than dogmatic, and they vary considerably in territory, ranging from what is effectively the single city block occupied by Trinity College to the twenty-five-kilometre sweep from the north docks to Finglas. They also vary in historical depth, some resting on pre-Viking pathways, while others were fields within living memory. In the same way, the writers, novels, poems, and plays that I have used here to trace this provisional map are only one possible selection from the vast library of Dublin's literature. There are many,

many other ways to tell this story, and I expect that most readers will have suggestions for a favourite poem or novel that could or should have been included. In fact, I hope that they will – for those are the kinds of continuous conversations that a living city of literature has with itself.

In the end, perhaps the best way to understand *Dublin: A Writer's City* is to imagine its opposite: Dublin without its literature. Here I see once again the images of Dublin's Grafton Street during the worst of the pandemic, shops boarded up, emptied of people, with grass growing between the paving stones. This was the city that Derek Mahon evokes in one of his final poems before his death in October 2020, 'A Fox in Grafton Street':

> *Broad daylight, and on weed-grown cobblestones*
> *deserted by the pedestrian population*
> *a fox hunts for discarded edibles –*
> *fried chips, spare ribs or chicken bones;*
> *but everywhere from Bewley's to McDonald's*
> *is shut and shuttered for the duration.*

'Weed-grown cobblestones / deserted by the pedestrian population,' wrote Derek Mahon (1941-2020) in a late poem about a deserted Grafton Street (pictured here). When the pandemic that began in 2020 emptied the streets of the city, the extent to which Dublin owes its character to its people became apparent. *Photography by Seán Harrison.*

This, then, is a book born out of what Mahon calls later in the poem the 'shocked euphoria' of the 'enforced parenthesis'[10] of the pandemic. It is an attempt to repopulate a city from a collective imagination, acknowledging that the citizenry of Dublin includes not just the living and the dead, but also the remembered and the imagined.

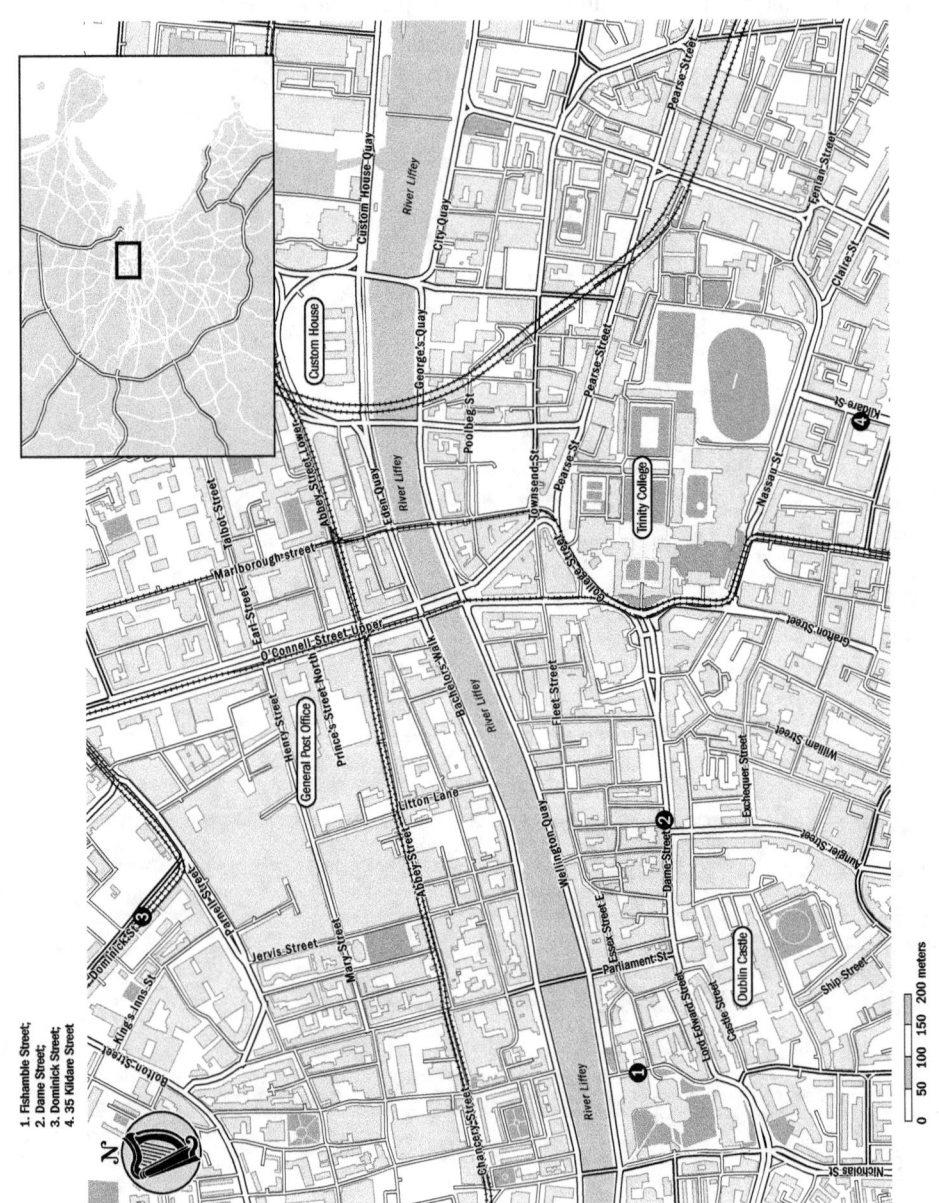

1. Fishamble Street;
2. Dame Street;
3. Dominick Street;
4. 35 Kildare Street

Mapping the City

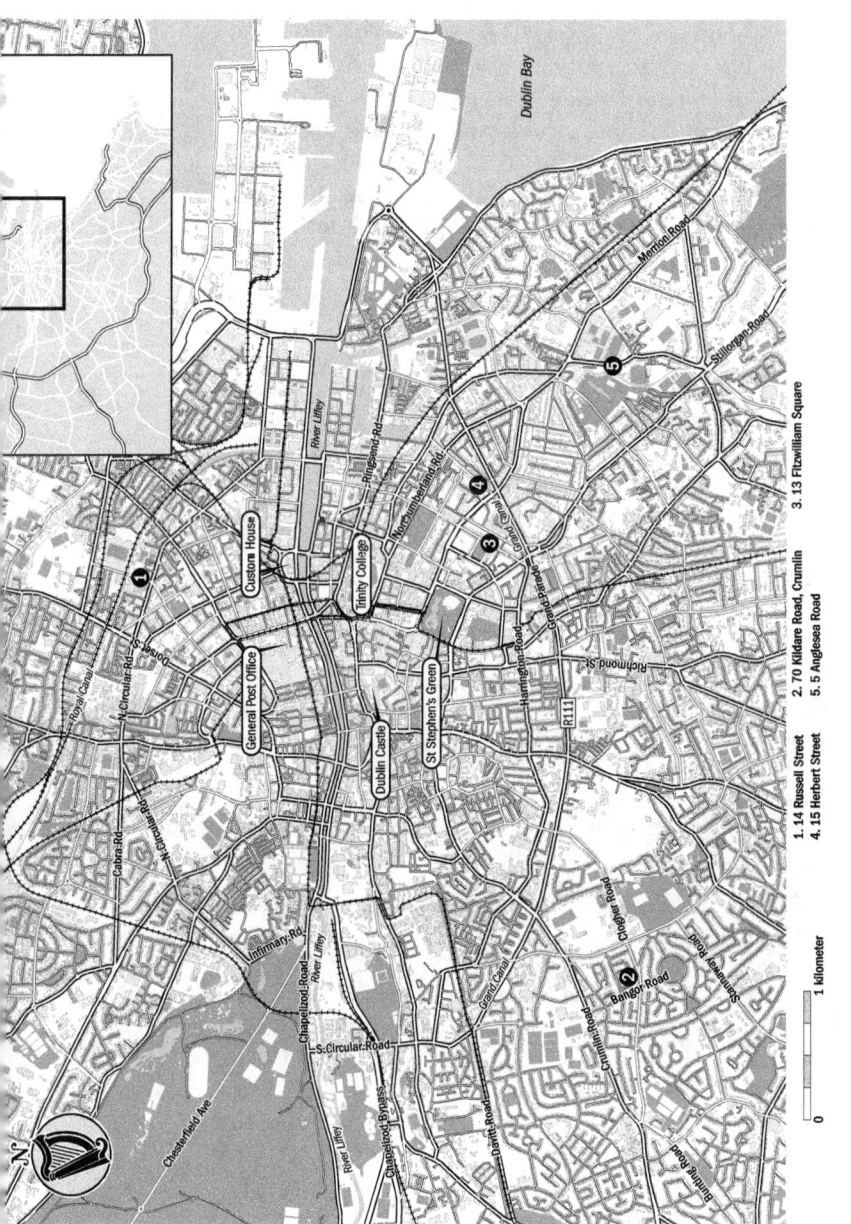

1. 14 Russell Street
2. 70 Kildare Road, Crumlin
3. 13 Fitzwilliam Square
4. 15 Herbert Street
5. 5 Anglesea Road

1

There is a poem in Eavan Boland's 1994 sequence, 'In a Time of Violence' entitled 'That the Science of Cartography is Limited'. The poem's opening line carries on the sentence that begins with the poem's title: ' – and not simply by the fact that this shading of / forest cannot show the fragrance of balsam'.[1] It is a useful reminder that while a series of maps can show the changing outlines of a city's streets over time, the experience and texture of change has a quality that goes beyond aerial views of streetscapes. Those experiences also leave their traces, the emotional memory that makes one street different from another, 'the fragrance of balsam' – or, in the case of a city, the feel of wet cobblestones, the dampness of a nearby canal, bullet holes in masonry, or the street corner where two people first met. So, if the science of cartography is indeed limited, a city's literature can be thought of as the missing words on the back of the map.

One of the great Dublin poems, Louis MacNeice's 'Dublin', works in just this way. MacNeice was not from Dublin (he was born in Belfast), but found himself in the city in 1939 just as World War II was breaking out. As he felt historical change rushing towards him like a great fireball, Dublin became a foothold from which to think about change itself:

> *Fort of the Dane,*
> *Garrison of the Saxon,*
> *Augustan capital*
> *Of a Gaelic nation,*
> *Appropriating all*
> *The alien brought,*
> *You gave me time for thought*
> *And by a juggler's trick*
> *You poise the toppling hour –*
> *O greyness run to flower,*
> *Grey stone, grey water,*
> *And brick upon grey brick.*[2]

The compact, almost conversational language of MacNeice's poem manages to condense into a very few short lines the layers of history that have built up – 'brick upon grey brick' – in the centre of Dublin. Apart from anything else, Dublin is a place in which historical change is inscribed in the city's fabric. One way to imagine the city is to picture the rings on the cross-section of a great tree: in the centre (or what had been the centre) is the old medieval core, surrounded by a grey-brick Georgian layer, which in turn is ringed by the two late-eighteenth and early nineteenth-century canals, beyond which is a redbrick nineteenth-century ring; beyond this, again, are successive layers of twentieth- and twenty-first-century growth, which are also dotted through the earlier rings, where the original wood has rotted or been cut away.

So, if we go back to the earliest detailed map of the city, John Speed's map of Dublin drawn in 1610, we see a small walled town with a population of somewhere between 8,000 and 10,000 people,[3] mainly clustered in a nest of streets on the south bank of the River Liffey between Dublin Castle and the narrow stretch of quays (see colour plate C1). To the south, outside the city walls, the main landmark is St. Patrick's Cathedral, but the land is mostly open fields. To the east of the Castle, apart from 'The Colledge' – Trinity College Dublin, founded in 1592 – there is only the odd scattered dwelling. A single bridge crosses the Liffey to a north bank that is much less densely settled than the south (the map shows about one hundred buildings), protected only by an incomplete stretch of wall. As Peter Sirr comments in his essay 'The Poet and the Mapmaker' (2021), in Speed's map 'the city looks frail and vulnerable, as if it might collapse at any moment, or be swallowed up by a modest invasion party'.[4]

The Dublin of Speed's 1610 map was MacNeice's 'Garrison of the Saxon'; however, at that point there had been a town on the site for almost eight hundred years. No one knows precisely when the very first human settlement took place at the mouth of the River Liffey, but there are mentions in early medieval annals of a people living in an area known as Áth Cliath, 'the ford of the hurdles' from at least AD770. There is also reference to a monastery, probably near where the very early Church of St. Michael le Pole stood, and where later again Dublin Castle would be built. There is some speculation that 'le Pole' referred to the deep pool where the River Poddle (which has since been completely covered over) joined the River Liffey, giving the settlement the name by which it would come to be known: Dubh Linn, or the 'dark pool'.

> *The River Liffey:* Dublin was first settled because of a river that begins unremarkably enough, in a bog between the hills of Kippure and Tonduff in the Wicklow mountains, and which runs for 132 kilometres through Wicklow, Kildare, and Dublin, before emptying into the Irish Sea. Originally its banks where it runs through the city were much more irregular, and parts of Dublin as far inland as Pearse Street were once marsh.

By the middle of the ninth century, Viking longboats were mooring in this pool, initially only during raiding sorties along the east coast of Ireland, but by at least 841 they were remaining for longer, until eventually they began building more permanent structures in the area of what is now Wood Quay. There are records of battles and skirmishes fought between the Danes and the Gaelic Irish, but by the early tenth century the Danes were well enough settled to begin constructing a fortified town. Sporadic fighting continued, however, most famously erupting in the great Battle of Clontarf in 1014, when an army led by a Munster king, Brian Boru, defeated an alliance between the Dublin Vikings and Máel Mórda mac Murchada, the King of Leinster. That battle has lodged vividly (and not wholly accurately) in Dublin folk memory as an Irish national victory over the Danish invaders. Stephen Gwynn tells a story in his *Dublin Old and New* (1937), of 'an old friend of mine, an ex-Fenian' confessing with some shame: 'I will tell you what I would not tell to many' – that his ancestors 'were on the wrong side at Clontarf'.[5] In fact, there were Gaelic Irish on both sides of the battlefield fighting for control of Dublin in 1014, which can remind us that (unlike most of the rest of Ireland) Dublin from the outset was ethnically hybrid, if not cosmopolitan – at least by the standards of the eleventh century. By the time of the Battle of Clontarf, the Vikings were long-term residents of Dublin, not temporary interlopers. What is more, when the site of the Viking settlement at Wood Quay was excavated in the late 1970s, it turned up bits of silk from Asia, walrus tusks from the Arctic, and coins from Samarkand. Old Norse was certainly spoken, but so, too, was Irish, English, and, later, Norman French.

As part of what one historian has called 'the evolution of a pirate base into a medieval city',[6] Dublin had already become a trading port by the time the last Danish ruler, Sitriuc Silkenbeard, died in 1042, and was well along the road to 'Appropriating all / The alien brought'. Initially, this was a slow process of intermarriage, as Gaelic Irish continued to migrate to the city. However, the situation changed much more dramatically in 1170, when a small (but effective) company of Norman knights surprised the city from the hills and woods of Wicklow to the south, capturing it for Richard de Clare, 'Strongbow', and thereby extending the Norman takeover of the neighbouring island that had begun in 1066. Over the next two centuries, Dublin Castle was rebuilt, with its huge circular towers. New streets were laid out, more quay walls built, and St. Patrick's Cathedral began construction in 1191. By the end of the middle of the thirteenth century, Dublin's population was triple what it had been before 1170. 'It is now possible to speak of Dublin as a *city*,' declares historian David Dickson. At the same time, it was as vulnerable as other European medieval cities to raiders, and its wooden buildings burned all too easily. Worse, along with much of the rest of the continent, it was

Just as the medieval city of Dublin developed around Dublin Castle, so the Castle grew in successive layers. This image shows the Record Tower, which dates from 1204, and is the oldest surviving element, with more recent additions clustered around it. The image is from a glass lantern slide, the crack in which is visible. *Courtesy of Royal Society of Antiquaries of Ireland.*

subject to famine, and to plague. In 1348, the bubonic plague – the Black Death – reached the city, as recorded by the contemporary Franciscan chronicler, John Clyn: '*ipsas civitates Dubliniam et Drovhda fere destruxit et vastavit incolis et hominibus*' (Dublin and Drogheda were almost destroyed and emptied of inhabitants and men).[7]

And yet Dublin survived. Seven years before Speed's map of 1610, Ireland had come under the control of the British crown, when James I was proclaimed king, making Dublin firmly the 'Garrison of the Saxon'. There then followed a period in which the institutions and apparatus of an early modern state began to be put in place. The first book printed in Dublin (indeed, in Ireland), an edition of *The Boke of Common Praier*, had already been produced by Humphrey Powell in Dublin in 1551; Trinity College had been founded (and its library started) in 1592. The Lords Deputy appointed after 1603 were keen to build up a viceregal court life in Dublin Castle, and this included, among other projects, sponsoring Ireland's first theatre, on Werburgh Street, just beside Dublin Castle, which was built around 1635. All of this activity was suspended with the English Revolution, or War of the Three Kingdoms in 1641; however, when the conflict subsided in the 1660s, the process of city-building resumed. The works of those years continue to define the outlines of the city's core.

'The Eighteenth Century lives on & on,' the poet John Berryman once wrote of Dublin.[8] There are many reasons that the eighteenth century continues to exert such a gravitational pull on the city, not the least of which is that the century had a head start in Ireland, and was effectively well under way by the early 1680s. Dublin in the 1590s, with a population of around 8,000, was still a small late-medieval city. By the time Jonathan Swift was born in Hoey's Court, an alley just off Werburgh Street, in 1667, it had swollen to around 30,000; by the mid-1680s, when Swift entered Trinity as a student, that population had doubled again, to more than 60,000.[9] In those years, as the original maze of streets around the Castle became ever more congested, it became apparent that the city needed to spread outwards. With land rapidly changing hands in the aftermath of war, the time was ripe for a major change.

By 1669, the Viceroy of the time, the Duke of Ormond, found himself tasked with the management of a large tract of land to the west of the city, on the north side of the Liffey, enclosed by seven miles of wall. It would become the Phoenix Park. 'It is hard to imagine such a park being created at any other time in the city's history,' comments historian David Dickson. Meanwhile, to the south and east of Dublin Castle, by 1680, St. Stephen's Green (named for a small nearby medieval Church of St. Stephen and its attached leper hospital) was transformed from a commonage for grazing animals into a formal public park. Houses then began to be built around its perimeter as wealthier citizens initiated what would become a repeated pattern in Dublin history, moving away from the increasingly congested older inner streets to the space and fresh air of the city limits – as odd as it is today to think of St. Stephen's Green as a greenfield site at the edge of the city.

In those same years, Dublin's print culture took hold. The first regular Dublin newspaper, *The News-Letter*, began appearing in 1685, and by the end of the century Dublin had a thriving publishing industry, given a boost in 1709 when the Copyright Act passed by the Westminster Parliament was not ratified in Ireland. It also helped that while other parts of Ireland had been convulsed by the Williamite War of the 1690s, there had been no actual fighting in Dublin, and, if anything, the political consequences of the defeat of Catholic power in Ireland had consolidated Dublin's place as what MacNeice calls the 'Augustan capital / Of a Gaelic nation'.

Here, as at other points in its history, Dublin stood out as anomalous in contrast to the rest of the island. The majority of the Irish population continued to be Irish-speaking throughout the eighteenth century. Indeed, in the hinterlands of Dublin, and throughout the city itself, large parts of the Catholic population were at the very least bilingual. And yet, this Irish-language culture had, as the cultural historian

Joep Leerssen once put it, 'no organisations to speak of, no Church infrastructure, no coffee houses',[10] and very limited access to print. In 1925, the writer Daniel Corkery memorably called this world 'the hidden Ireland'. And yet if Gaelic Ireland were in hiding in the century after 1690 – often in plain sight – English-speaking Dublin was the opposite, putting itself and its inhabitants on show. These were the years not only of building great public parks but also of laying out wide streets in which people could promenade and meet, of proliferating coffee houses and taverns, and of printing houses and theatres (most notably the Smock Alley Theatre, built in 1662). As Irish oral culture retreated around the island, Dublin blossomed into a world of print, public performance, and display.

Where the old medieval city had grown up without much real planning, the Dublin of the eighteenth century would be a planned urban environment with a strong sense of public culture, even if that sense of the 'public' was understood in a limited way. Following on from the great civic projects of the Duke of Ormond in the 1660s and 1670s, the early decades of the eighteenth century were a time of lasting public works, still to be seen – such as the magnificent Palladian Parliament House on College Green (1729) and the Library of Trinity College (1732). The establishment in 1758 of a Wide Streets Commission marked a further statement of intent. Although it took the Commissioners several decades to acquire real legislative power in the 1790s, even before that time they were managing traffic flows with new river crossings, and widening older streets such as Dame Street to create vistas and thoroughfares. Recently, the Dublin architectural writer and campaigner Frank McDonald referred to the Wide Streets Commission as 'Dublin's First Futurists'.[11] The architectural historian and poet Maurice Craig also puts it well in his poem 'Merrion Square': 'And those who built this city for a few / Laid out Wide Streets wider than they knew'.[12]

By the final decades of the eighteenth century, armed with new legislative powers, the Wide Streets Commissioners would be responsible for much of the civic planning that still defines the shape of Dublin within the canals. That final decade of the century also saw construction of the two great buildings that still dominate the riverscape: the Custom House (1791) and the Four Courts (1796). Knitting these monumental buildings together was a new network of streets, built and laid out by successive generations of private developers, from Joshua Dawson (for whom Dawson Street is named) in the early part of the century, to the two Luke Gardiners, father and son, the former developing Henrietta Street and what became Sackville Street (now O'Connell Street) in the 1720s, and the latter giving his name to Gardiner Street in the 1790s.

What is more, where for many centuries the two banks of the Liffey had been connected by a single bridge, by the end of the 1720s there were five bridges, opening up the north bank of the river to a total city population that would reach 125,000 by the middle of the century. Again, it was the attraction of space and clean air that attracted fashionable Dublin to the north city, to mansions on Dominick Street and Henrietta Street, where 'two giant terraces', as David Dickson describes these streets, 'of massive houses faced each other, their brick-faced façades (some as broad as sixty feet) in precise alignment, their flat parapets emphasising the cliffs of brick'.[13] Dublin would never quite have the grid of midtown Manhattan or Barcelona's l'Eixample, but John Rocque's map of 1756 does show a geometrical pattern of new streets laid out in sharp contrast to the tangled alleys of the medieval core (see colour plate C2). By the end of the eighteenth century, what the architectural historian Edward McParland has called a 'combination of enlightenment and power'[14] had indelibly shaped the physical fabric of Dublin's core, and today the phrase 'Georgian Dublin' immediately conjures up streetscapes in which principles of symmetry and balance highlight details such as the ornate fanlights over doors. They have become some of the most immediately recognizable images of the city.

At the same time, as the Georgian city was being built, the old medieval core continued to decline. For instance, what had been Skinner's Row (just

Perhaps the defining architectural image of Dublin is its Georgian streetscapes, in which the symmetry of the building highlights small details – such as the characteristic fanlight window over the door. This is the door to the house at 4 Ely Place, just off St. Stephen's Green, where the novelist, playwright and memoirist George Moore lived from 1901 to 1912. Courtesy of the National Library of Ireland.

beside Dublin Castle) had a claim to be the city's main street in the early part of the eighteenth century. It was here that you could find one of the city's main meeting places, Dick's Coffee House, as well as important printers and booksellers, including John Milliken, who in 1768 founded what would become Hodges-Figgis, which still operates today, making it one of the oldest bookshops in the world. However, by 1797 Milliken had moved to Grafton Street, just up from Trinity College. Within a few decades, the area around what had been Skinner's Row, which became Christchurch Place, was on its way to becoming one of the most dangerous parts of the city, notorious for prostitution and violent crime. Nearby, in his 1798 independent census of the city, the Rev. James Whitelaw came across 'the entire side of a house, in School-house Lane' that 'fell from its foundations. I observed with astonishment, that the inhabitants, above thirty in number ... had not deserted its apartments ... by the circumstance of the wall falling outwards.'[15]

If we know (or at least think we know) what we mean by eighteenth-century Dublin, the nineteenth century is more complicated. 'The nineteenth century in Dublin is so far an age without a name,' observed Elizabeth Bowen, in her history of the Shelbourne Hotel, built in 1824.[16] As always with Bowen, the observation is astute; there may be a 'Georgian Dublin' that conjures up a whole world, but the term 'Victorian Dublin' is largely restricted to architectural historians. The reasons for this go back to the way in which the eighteenth century ended, in one of those rare instances in which dates with round numbers line up with significant events. As the century came to a close, in 1798 a group known as the United Irishmen staged a rebellion founded on the republican ideals that had underpinned the revolutions in France and in the United States. Although the actual rebellion, in which more than 25,000 people were killed, took place largely outside of Dublin, notably in the north of Ireland and in the south-east, one immediate effect was felt in the heart of Dublin. Here, as historian Thomas Bartlett puts it, 'a further casualty was to be the Irish parliament; on learning that rebellion had broken out in Ireland, [British Prime Minister William] Pitt determined this was the opportunity he needed to push for a Union of the two parliaments'.[17] In May 1800, just as the new century dawned, induced by a combination of political pressure and bribery, the Irish parliament effectively voted itself out of existence. Henceforth, Ireland would become part of the United Kingdom of Great Britain and Ireland. There was a second, short-lived rebellion that did take place in Dublin in 1803. It was led by a Dubliner, Robert

Emmet, who was born on St. Stephen's Green, educated at Whyte's Academy on Grafton Street, and later went to Trinity. It ended in disarray; however, the memory of Emmet's rebellion (not least because of its continuous re-enactments in political melodramas in Dublin's theatres) meant that it had a long afterlife.

The effects of this sequence of upheavals would shape both the fabric of Dublin and the shape of Irish political and cultural debate well into the twentieth century – in both instances, in ways that were never simple. The group who perhaps felt the loss of an Irish parliament most directly were the former elected members of that parliament, many of whom had lived and socialized in the houses of the great Georgian squares. This produced a curious convergence, in that they shared with later nationalist writers (with whom they often shared little else) an interest in portraying Dublin after the Union as a kind of wasteland, a diminished provincial city. As a character in Maria Edgeworth's novel *The Absentee* (1812) puts it, there was a perception that the ink was barely dry on the Act of Union before 'most of the nobility and many of the principal families of Irish commoners, either hurried in high hopes to London, or retired disgusted and in despair to their houses in the country'.[18]

However, Edgeworth's novel as a whole presents a more nuanced view of the change, as one of her characters, Sir James Brooke, reflects that he, too, was at one point convinced that 'decorum, elegance, polish, and charm of society was gone' from Dublin after 1800. With hindsight, however, he has come to see that the shake-up of the old order produced a kind of filtering: 'You find a society in Dublin,' he says, 'composed of the most agreeable and salutatory mixture of birth and education, gentility and knowledge, manner and matter; and you see pervading the whole new life and energy, new talent, new ambition.'[19] Although *The Absentee* appeared in 1812, it was remarkably prescient as to the direction that the city would take over the next century, and the image of a ghost town, bemoaning past glories, is misleading. In part, this would be an effect of Catholic Emancipation in 1829, which activated the 'new talent, new ambition' of Irish Catholics who had been legislatively precluded from much of public life in the eighteenth century. In Dublin lore, when the Catholic church that took up residence in what had been the old Smock Alley Theatre – Saint Michael and Saint John – rang its bells in 1815 to mark the first opening of a Catholic church in the city since the Reformation, it not only anticipated Catholic Emancipation but also created one of its symbols (a century later, to mark the event, a cast of the bell was built into one of Dublin's bridges). In retrospect, the pealing of those bells signalled a turning of the tide, and by the end of the century what had been a predominantly Protestant city – politically and culturally – would become a city in which the Catholic Church was an inescapable force.

Even as the political tide shifted, Dublin continued to build and to grow. An impressive new theatre, the Theatre Royal, opened in 1821; the Shelbourne Hotel took in its first guests in 1824, and in 1854 a new university, which would become University College Dublin, opened on St. Stephen's Green, with John Henry Newman as its first Rector. On the map, there was not only growth but movement, as the city's centre of gravity also began to shift southwards and eastwards along the coast.

One way to trace Dublin's development after the Act of Union is to follow the moving van containing the possessions of the novelist Lady Morgan. Born Sydney Owenson, she was the daughter of an actor and theatre manager, Robert Owenson, who for a period ran a theatre in Fishamble Street, one of the oldest streets in the medieval city, originally the fish market. Born some time in the early 1780s (her memoirs are vague on this point), Sydney Owenson grew up at 60 Dame Street, not far from Dublin Castle. Around the turn of the century, she took a job as a governess in a 'fine, old-fashioned furnished house on Dominick Street',[20] in the fashionable north city. It was here that she wrote her first work (a collection of poems), which she followed with her best-known novel, *The Wild Irish Girl* (1806), subtitled 'A National Tale'. As her fame grew, she lived for a time outside of Ireland. However, when she returned to Dublin in 1835 as a celebrated novelist and centre of a literary salon that included the poet Thomas Moore (who had been born not far from her in the old city, at 12 Aungier Street), she avoided the now increasingly down-at-heels north side, where she had been a governess, and moved into the newly fashionable south side, at 35 (later renumbered as 39) Kildare Street (more or less opposite the National Library of Ireland today).

That Lady Morgan decided to call *The Wild Irish Girl* 'A National Tale' signals another of the lasting effects of the 1798 rebellion and the Act of Union. Over the course of the century that followed, to be an Irish writer increasingly meant contributing to a 'national literature', or else face questions as to why not. This would continue to be the case well into the twentieth, and, indeed, twenty-first centuries. In fact, the slow disentanglement of Irish writing from this nineteenth-century ideal has become an abiding concern for more than one contemporary writer. For instance, in her essay 'Becoming an Irish Poet' (2011), the poet Eavan Boland recalls that as a student in Trinity College in the 1960s, her walk home took her through Merrion Square, 'one of the old treasures of Georgian Dublin. An ambiguous gift of colony. [...] In the nineteenth century, this was the hub of a garrison city':

> The fanlights, then as now, spun off down the street, making a vista of semicircles. The topmost windows looked over chestnut trees. The demeanour of it all revealed a purpose. A deceptive grace closing its iron grip of class and dominion over an unreliable nation.

Here, in the heart of the 'garrison', Boland recalls that she always stopped outside No. 1 Merrion Square, the childhood home of Oscar Wilde. However, it was not Oscar that Boland recalled, but his mother, Lady Jane Wilde, who as 'Speranza' wrote poetry for the nationalist *Nation* newspaper in the years leading up to the rebellion of 1848, at the height of the Irish Famine. As much as she admires Speranza as a person, Boland has to admit that her poetry seldom goes beyond being 'bellicose and patriotic'. 'Through her,' Boland writes, 'I first came to realize that a national agenda could be an editor: I was less aware it could also be a censor.'[21]

Speranza's nineteenth-century Dublin, then, was one in which a literary world that increasingly (although never exclusively) fostered a literature framed in nationalist terms occupied a city built as the capital of a colony. And so, while Merrion Square may have retained its 'deceptive grace' right up to the time that Boland passed through it in the 1960s, and continues to do so today, in Speranza's lifetime large swathes of the Georgian city went into the same sort of decline that the medieval city had suffered a century and a half earlier. So, once again, the now familiar pattern repeated itself: as the Georgian city became congested, Dubliners with means began looking for fresh pastures (quite literally), and found them beyond Merrion Square to the east, and beyond the Grand Canal to the south. In this respect, Dublin in the middle of the nineteenth century makes a sharp contrast to the rest of Ireland – which is one of the reasons why a Dublin literature and a wider Irish literature do not always align. In the country as a whole, the population surged over the first half of the nineteenth century to a level it has yet to regain in the twenty-first century, reaching 8.2 million in the 1841 census. Rural Ireland was then decimated by the Famine of the late 1840s, and the population of the country as a whole fell to 6.6 million in the 1851 census and continued to drop in the decades after. Dublin, by contrast, grew steadily over the course of the century, and even increased by 6% over the decade of the 1840s to just under 250,000 by 1851.[22] By 1901, Dublin was a city of more than 380,000, whereas the population of the country as a whole had fallen below 4.5 million. If the image of the Irish countryside was increasingly dominated by derelict stone cottages and abandoned villages, in Dublin the picture was the exact opposite, with congestion, overcrowding and a burgeoning population.

Here again, the change shows up on maps. Maps of Dublin in the 1830s show a city still safely tucked inside the Royal Canal and the Grand Canal that ring the city to the north and south, respectively (see colour plate C3). By the end of the century, however, the footprint of the city is completely different. To the south of the city, rows of terraced houses now run from the canals all the way to the nearby villages of Ballsbridge, Rathmines, and Ranelagh, although they would continue to hold on to their individual municipal identities. Rathmines, for instance, would become large enough to be granted town status in 1847. The process of suburbanization was speeded up by rail, with five rail stations feeding into the city in 1876. The first of these opened in 1834, only five years after the first passenger line anywhere in the world, when a commuter line connected the city centre with the newly developed port of Kingstown (now called Dún Laoghaire) on the south coast. Initially, the area around Kingstown was a smattering of villages interspersed with private villas (such as the fictional one in Bray that provides much of the setting for Edgeworth's *The Absentee*). However, increasingly houses in this part of the city resembled the middle-class houses that had been built in places like Ballsbridge and Rathmines. 'It seems clear enough,' writes the historian Ciaran O'Neill, 'that we can identify the nineteenth century as the bourgeois century *par excellence* and that this is also true of Ireland, and the Irish bourgeoisie.'[23] If bourgeois Ireland had an epicentre, it was the new inner suburbs of south Dublin, spreading along the south coast, and their counterparts on the north side in Drumcondra and Phibsborough, as – to use the words of one of Edgeworth's characters – 'commerce rose into the vacated seats of rank'.[24]

If maps show this middle-class nineteenth-century city encircling the old Georgian and medieval core, what these maps do not show is the transformation that was taking place in the older streets. In the original city core, the three-storey, gable-fronted Dutch Billies, as they were known, which had housed generations of textile workers since the early eighteenth century, were giving way to rows of small artisan cottages, and in these streets a working-class culture took shape. Among the

Dubliners living here were many of the 2,000-strong workforce of the Guinness brewery, located along the quays at St. James's Gate, adjacent to the area known as the Liberties. The brewery would expand massively in the 1870s, and it still dominates the skyline in this part of the city. Similar workers' housing developments were being built in those same years on either side of the mouth of Liffey, in Ringsend and North Wall, for the workforce in the docks. Beyond those with solid industrial jobs, however, were increasing numbers of Dubliners who lived in real destitution, crammed into rooms in what had once been the city mansions of the wealthy.

So, by the end of the nineteenth century, most single families had long since moved out of the large houses on the great terraces of Henrietta Street and Dominick Street, including the one in which a young Lady Morgan had been a governess, and as property values dropped these vast buildings were divided and subdivided into tenements. In the case of Henrietta Street, for instance, by 1911 only No. 4 still housed a single family of three, while the building next door now housed 108 people from multiple families.[25] Moreover, this kind of grotesque overcrowding was neither unusual nor recent. Going back to the 1841 census, we find that fully 46.8% of Dublin's population lived in dwellings of a single room.[26] In other words, in the same years that the residential Victorian and Edwardian suburbs were taking shape, the suburbs in which so many Dubliners would live and continue to live, the city's medieval and Georgian core was deteriorating and becoming increasingly congested. The playwright Christine Longford puts it well in her 'biography' of Dublin published in 1936. 'In a play of Webster,' she writes, 'there is a character described as "an Italian nobleman, but decayed." Dublin is an eighteenth-century city, "but decayed".'[27] Eventually, the city's poverty would ignite: on 26 August 1913 a series of strikes began, culminating in a general strike and lockout that brought the city to a virtual halt. And, almost as a reminder as to what lay behind the strike, on 2 September, two tenements on Church Street collapsed, killing seven people.

It was conditions such as these, underpinned by a continuing sense of grievance at the loss of the Irish parliament, that fed into the sense that Ireland at the end of the nineteenth century was, as Yeats put it in his autobiographical writings, 'like soft wax',[28] not just ripe, but demanding to be formed into a new shape. As the century drew to a close, what Roy Foster has called a 'revolutionary generation' increasingly interrogated all aspects of the world they inherited 'in student societies, Gaelic League dances, and the front rooms of houses on those Dublin streets where comrades found lodgings close to each other and sat up late at night talking. The more one reads accounts, letters, and diaries and reflections of this generation, the more one gets the sense of an intimate but complex city, with certain areas defined by political subcultures.'[29] Those densely intertwined literary, cultural, and political subcultures were behind the military uprising that occurred at Easter in 1916, when groups of armed insurrectionaries occupied locations around Dublin, including the General Post Office on Sackville Street, a distillery in the Liberties, a biscuit factory a few blocks from Merrion Square, and St. Stephen's Green. From the perspective of thinking about Dublin as a literary city, part of the continuing fascination of the 1916 Rising revolves around the awareness that so many of its leaders – including its two principals, Patrick Pearse and James Connolly – were writers. As Fearghal McGarry puts it, 'the Rising was the product not only of Ireland's insurrectionary tradition but of the cultural-nationalist revival [...] Many of this "rising generation" graduated from learning Irish to fighting for Ireland'[30] – or, indeed, from staging plays to staging a revolution.

The week of the Easter Rising has probably exerted a greater hold on the historical imagination of Dublin than any other single event, and you can still walk down O'Connell Street and see the pockmarks made by bullets in the columns of the General Post Office. In the immediate aftermath of the Rising, to which the British army had responded by shelling rebel positions from a gunboat in the Liffey, large parts of the centre of Dublin were reduced to burnt rubble. However, unlike cities in the Netherlands, France, or Germany, for instance, where today planned streetscapes made up entirely of post-World War II buildings are often an indication that a city had been bombed flat, Dublin's main street was rebuilt after the Rising in a style that echoed what had been there before. In terms of the city's built fabric, the major casualty of the War of Independence that followed in 1919–1921, and of the Civil War that followed it in 1922–1923, was an explosion in the Four Courts that destroyed many of the city's oldest records, wiping clean, as it were, part of Dublin's memory. Deeper scars would be left by the particularly intimate warfare Dublin experienced, particularly during the Irish Civil War. While not anything like as destructive or extensive as the wider European experience of warfare in the middle of the twentieth century, Dublin's conflicts – such as the massacre of fourteen civilians in the Croke Park Gaelic Athletic Association stadium on 19 November 1920 – left deep scars because of their almost personal nature. 'I hope things are quieter with your world,' the Abbey Theatre director Lennox Robinson wrote to Lady Gregory, who was in Coole Park. 'Here they are very bad as you may imagine. [...] they were working up a strong anti-reprisal campaign. – Sunday has set all that back and no one ever mentions (in England) the little Amritzar at Croke Park in the afternoon.'[31] Once a city has had that experience, it lodges deeper than old bullet holes in the sides of buildings.

The Dublin that emerged from insurrection and civil war was a capital once again, with the new government eventually taking up residence in what had been the Duke of Leinster's old city address, Kildare House, across from where Lady Morgan had had her salon. However, in some respects, the city continued as it had been before, for better and for worse, and in the 1920s a new recognition that Dublin was now a large conurbation began to take hold. For one thing, the city expanded geographically, formally incorporating what had been independent townships such as Rathmines and Pembroke (in the Baggot Street area). At the same time, the tenement collapse in Church Street in 1913 had sparked a slow-burning enquiry that recommended the clearing of Dublin's slums. During the conflict, the ensuing report sat on a shelf, so it was not until the 1920s that the Dublin Corporation began to address a situation that had been festering for a century. By 1928, 1,300 new terraced houses in a planned development would be built in Marino, on the north of the city towards Dublin Bay, although these were initially out of the reach of the poorest tenement-dwellers. However, over the following decade, from 1930 to 1939, a further 6,000 suburban houses were built on greenfield sites outside the city, to which many of Dublin's former tenement dwellers were able to move, redrawing the map of the city by 1935 (see colour plate 4). This process would continue and accelerate into the 1960s; on the city's northern edge, the villages of Ballymun and Finglas grew into sprawling suburbs, while to the west the city crept outwards to take in Ballyfermot and Tallaght.

In some respects, Brendan Behan's story is the story of Dublin's development in those years. Behan was born in 1923, at the end of the Civil War, and was raised 'in a Georgian House that had gone to rack and ruin as a tenement', as he put it in a later memoir.[32] The house at 14 Russell Street was a three-storey stone townhouse that had been built in 1803, about a ten-minute walk from where Lady Morgan had been a governess on Dominick Street. By 1923, the Behans were one of fourteen families each living in a single room in the building, sharing a single toilet. In 1936, the building was condemned, and the family were allocated a newly built house at 70 Kildare Road, in the recently developed suburb of Kimmage. This was a classic piece of Irish modernist urban planning, with streets laid out in the form of a stylized Celtic cross, around a circular park bisected by crossroads. Here, the Behans' end-of-terrace house had its own toilet and a small garden. Behan hated the place, and spent as little time as possible there, often staying over with friends in a basement warren known as 'the Catacombs' at 13 Fitzwilliam Square, before settling in a small rented flat in a converted nineteenth-century house at 15 Herbert Street in what was then the respectable, but bohemian, Baggot Street area of the city. It was only in 1959, when Behan had a production of his play *The Hostage* about to open in Paris, and *The Quare Fellow* rehearsing in Berlin, that he and his wife Beatrice bought 5 Anglesea Road, in Ballsbridge, 'one of the most prestigious bourgeois addresses in suburban Dublin'.[33]

The Behan family's migrations in an outwardly expanding city tell us something about the continuing anomalousness of Dublin in an Irish context. In the half century or so between 1901 and 1961, the population of the island of Ireland as a whole continued its long post-Famine decline, losing 200,000 people to emigration.[34] Not surprisingly, much of the rural literature of this period revolves around themes of lethargy, depopulation, and general stagnation. However, in that same period the population of Dublin grew, and continued to shoot up sharply in the second half of the twentieth century, going from over 600,000 in 1950

Dublin's great outward sprawl in the middle of the twentieth century was characterized by large-scale public housing projects, like this one in the suburb of Kilbarrack, where Roddy Doyle grew up. One of the great challenges for recent Irish writers has been to find a way to write about parts of the city that have only been in existence for a generation or so. *Courtesy of Dublin City Library and Archives.*

to over 900,000 in 1980. Inevitably, as the city grew, there were periods during which its physical fabric – particularly the great Georgian squares – were ripped open in ways that caused many to despair, particularly during the 1960s and 1970s. 'First the city planners took away the old street,' writes the poet Gerard Smyth in his poem 'Taken' (2021), 'along with the neighbours who had seen tragedy and comedy. [...] They disturbed the dust / that lay on the handiwork of guilds, / pulled up foundations buried since / the first strangers put a name on what they saw.'[35]

The sense that the city was becoming one vast derelict building site intensified during the 1980s, at a time of economic stagnation throughout the country as a whole. Then, in the early 1990s, a variety of factors combined to produce an economic uplift that quickly mushroomed into a fully fledged boom – based to no inconsiderable extent on property speculation – in what became known as the Celtic Tiger. This would have a profound transformative effect on the fabric of Dublin, as older industrial areas became post-industrial office space, most notably around the docklands on either side of the Liffey. At the same time, the city's western and northern boundaries expanded outwards at an accelerated pace, repeating the process by which villages such as Rathmines and later Finglas had been absorbed into the larger urban area a few decades earlier. Iconic new postmodern buildings began to appear around the city, such as the swirling arcs of the Aviva Football Stadium, or the tilted cannister of the Convention Centre on the north quays. The economic collapse of 2008 put most of this development on hold; however, within a decade, the Dublin skies were full of cranes yet again, and, at the time of writing, a house on Anglesea Road where Brendan Behan used to live would not leave you much change out of €2 million.

As the old literary culture of pints spilt over sonnets gave way to gentrification, the literary culture of Dublin has changed. In some respects, it has become more professionalized. The city now plays host to half a dozen literary festivals every year, has a well-established theatre and fringe festival every autumn, and Dublin City Libraries sponsor the world's richest prize for a single novel, the Dublin Literary Award. In 2010, Dublin became the world's fourth UNESCO City of Literature, and in 2019 the Museum of Literature in Ireland (MoLI) opened on St. Stephen's Green. At the same time, as the economy grew so, too, did the population of the greater Dublin area, which now stands at just more than 1.4 million. For the first time since the end of the seventeenth century, when there was an influx of Huguenot migrants, a significant number of these new Dubliners were born outside of Ireland, attracted both by a growing economy and by the expansion of the European Union to include countries in Eastern Europe. In 2015, for instance, the Central Statistics Office counted 182 different languages spoken in Ireland, with the highest concentration in Fingal, North Dublin, where more than a fifth of the population spoke a language other than English at home. Polish is the most commonly spoken of these new languages of Ireland, but there is also a large number of Mandarin speakers. In fact, the 2016 Census shows that 'just over 17 per cent of the resident population of Dublin city were non-Irish with Polish, Romanian, UK nationals, Brazilian, Italian, Spanish and French making up more than half of the total 91,876 non-Irish in the city in 2016'.[36] As one historian puts it, in the twenty-first century Dublin has undergone 'the most significant demographic transformation in the modern history of the state'.[37]

This new multiculturalism has changed the experience of being in the city in very basic ways; to walk down O'Connell Street today is to hear a multitude of languages. Equally, it has multiplied the perspectives from which Dublin is now experienced. As the Greek-born Irish poet Natasha Remoundou writes:

> *On Grafton Street I noticed every single passer-by who looked foreign*
> *wondering if they could tell I was one of them,*
> *whether they know where I'm from,*
> *if I have good English*
> *if I have friends.*[38]

The built traces of these multiple Dublins, from the Viking trading settlement of the tenth century to the plurilingual conurbation of today, are layered on top of one another. In some cases, their physical traces have been erased, or are all but impossible to find. 'I walk the northside streets / that whelped me; not a brick remains / of the tenement I reached the age of reason in,' writes Paula Meehan in her poem 'A Child's Map of Dublin'. 'There is nothing there to show you, not a trace of a girl / in ankle socks and hand-me-downs, sulking.'[39] However, the great paradox of writing is that even when evoking what is gone, we conjure it into memory, so that a dead past becomes a living part of the present. When we remind ourselves that the tenement of Meehan's childhood no longer exists, we nonetheless call it into imaginary existence, where it becomes one of the layers of our experience of the city as we inhabit it.

1. Parson's Bookshop, Baggot Street Bridge
2. Pike Theatre, Herbert Lane
3. Brendan Behan's Flat, 15 Herbert Street
4. Patrick Kavanagh's Flat, 62 Pembroke Road
5. Raglan Road
6. Quirke's Rooms, Upper Mount Street
7. Catacombs, 13 Fitzwilliam Place
8. Merrion Nursing Home, 21 Herbert Street
9. Leland Bardwell's Flat, 33 Lower Leeson Street
10. Thomas Kinsella's House, 47 Percy Place
11. McDaid's Pub, 3 Harry Street
12. John Berryman's house, 55 Lansdown Park

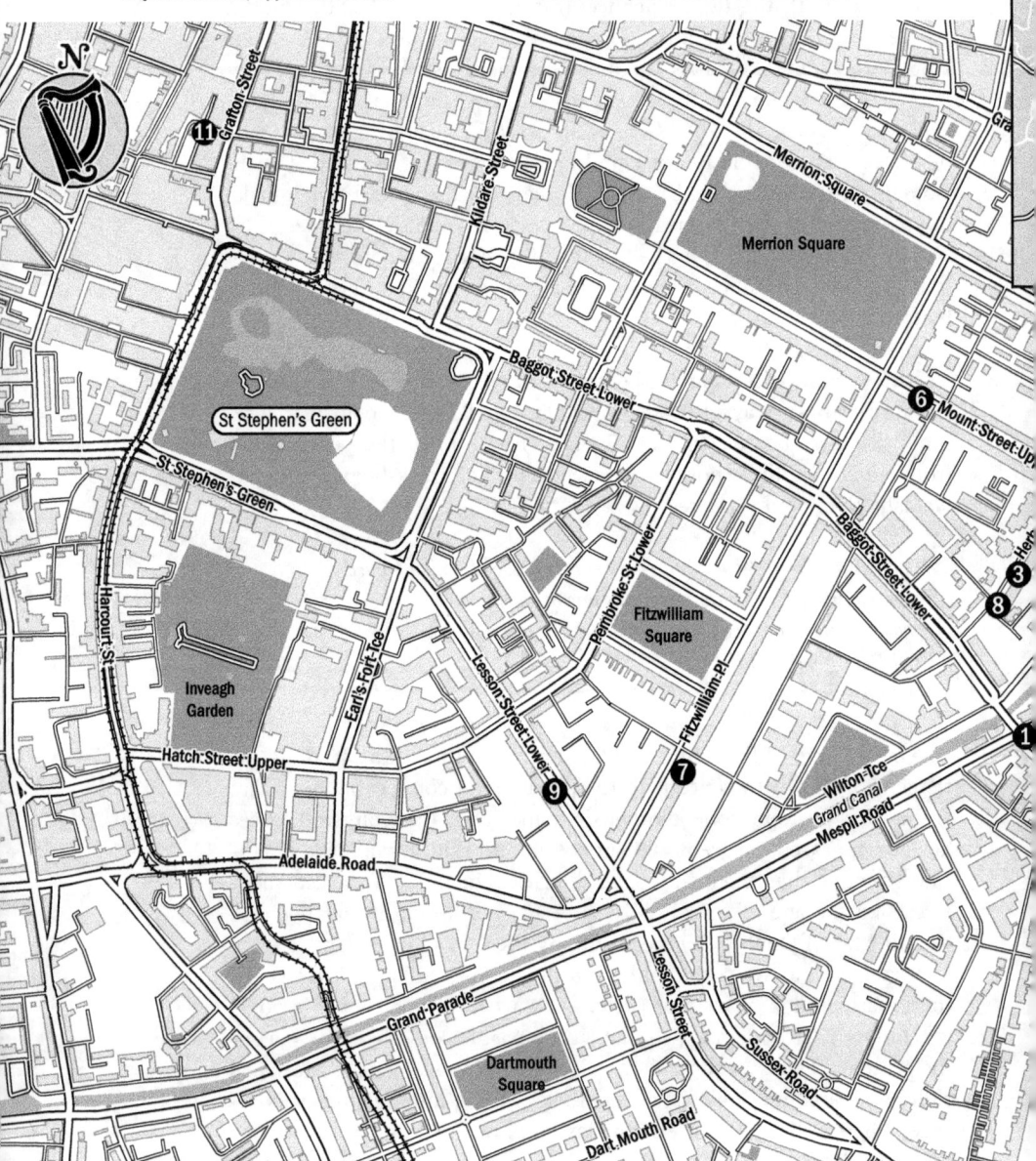

Baggotonia

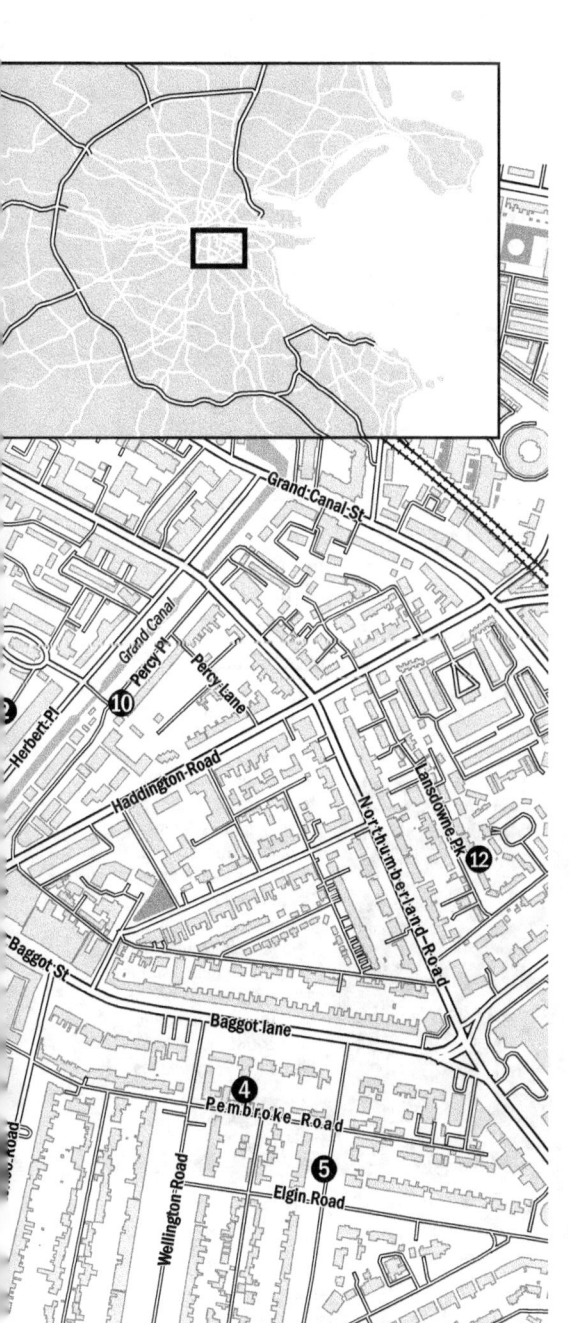

2

The search for Dublin as a writer's city could start in many places; however, a seat at the bar in McDaid's pub, just off Grafton Street, is as good a beginning as any. At least here you can be assured of a decent pint.

For a time in the middle of the twentieth century – from the mid-1930s until the early 1960s – any of Dublin's literary pubs would have been the obvious place to look for writers. In John McGahern's 1985 short story, 'Bank Holiday', set in a Dublin of thirty years earlier, the narrator meets a woman from Chicago who is visiting Dublin, and in the course of introducing her to the city, the conversation turns to literature. 'The standing army of poets never falls below ten thousand in this unfortunate country,' he tells her. 'Are these poets to be seen,' she asks. He laughs: 'They can't even be hidden.' And so, the following day, a Bank Holiday Monday, he brings her to the pub across the street from McDaid's, the Grafton Mooney (since renamed Bruxelles, and now best known for its statue to Thin Lizzy singer Phil Lynott). They sit for a while in 'the cool dark', listening 'in the silence to footsteps going up and down Grafton Street'. Then, 'into the quiet flow of the evening, the poet came, a large man, agitated, without a jacket, the shirt open, his thumbs hooked in braces that held up a pair of sagging trousers, a brown hat pushed far back on his head'. The poet bellows for a large whiskey – 'a Powers' – and 'a pint of Bass', before spotting the narrator, denouncing him as a 'cute hoar' and 'a mediocrity', and ordering him to run across the road to buy a packet of cigarettes – 'Ci-tanes. French fags. Twenty.'[1]

'If ever you go to Dublin town / In a hundred years or so, / Inquire for me in Baggot Street / And what I was like to know.' Poet Patrick Kavanagh (1904-1967) seated here in a characteristic location - a pub - with a small whiskey in front of him. This photograph is from 1966, shortly before his death. *Getty Images.*

The poet here is Patrick Kavanagh – the hat and trademark insult 'mediocrity' give him away – making a return appearance from an earlier McGahern story, 'My Love, My Umbrella' (from *Nightlines*, 1971), where the narrator, again in the company of a woman he is trying to impress, watches 'the poet' holding court in Mooney's, telling a table full of acolytes that he 'loved the blossoms on Kerr Pinks [potatoes] more than roses, a man could only love what he knew well'.[2] When McGahern's narrator and his companion in 'Bank Holiday' venture across the street to McDaid's and open the door of the pub, 'a roar met them like heat. The bar was small and jammed.' They do not stay, and once on the street again, the narrator admits that he 'always feels a bit apprehensive going in there'. His American companion is less daunted. 'Those places are the same everywhere,' she tells him. 'Mania, egotism, aggression ... people searching madly in a crowd for something that's never to be found in crowds.'[3]

McGahern's writing is so concise and precisely observed that we could unravel a number of threads from these little scenes: the pockets of chaotic bohemian life embedded in what was (and still is) one of the city's main shopping streets; the observation that writers in a crowd are searching 'for something that's never to be found in crowds'; and the role of women consigned to observers, but nonetheless showing the greatest insight as to what is taking place. That the author here should be John McGahern may come as a surprise, however, for he is best known for later novels, such as *Amongst Women* (1990) or *That They May Face the Rising Sun* (2001; published in the US as *By the Lake*) that are intimately woven into the rural life of County Leitrim, where he was born. Likewise, the (unnamed) figure of Patrick Kavanagh in these stories, rhapsodizing about potato blossoms, is now often remembered as a poet of the rural life of his native County Monaghan, where he grew up on a small farm. His earliest (and some would say best) poems are about that world: 'Shancoduff' (1937), 'Monaghan Hills' (1936), or 'Spraying the Potatoes' (1940). And yet, here we have two countrymen, one watching the other in a pub in the heart of the city. As Declan Kiberd once observed: 'Dublin was a centre dominated by the cultural values of the peasant periphery.'[4] This has become less true over time; still, in 1971, more than a quarter (26.3%) of the population of the city of 800,000 had been born in rural Ireland.[5]

A city full of country folk: it is a useful way to think of Dublin, at least starting in the 1920s (with a further burst of rural migration in the 1970s). It may also help to explain why the pub as a kind of small community hub was so much a part of Dublin literary life and a place for public performance. Pushing through the roar of McDaid's at its peak in the 1950s, one might find on any given night, as John Ryan recalls in his memoir, *Remembering How We Stood* (1975), 'a fight over the

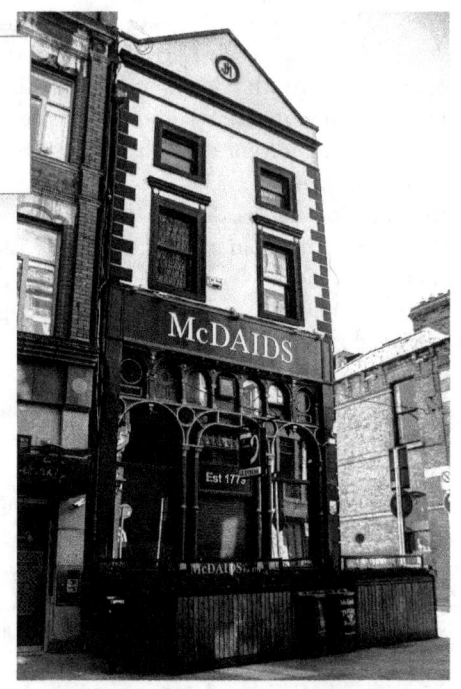

McDaid's pub on Harry Street, just off Grafton Street, was the heart of the hard-drinking literary culture of Dublin in the 1930s, 1940s, and 1950s. The offices of the magazine *Envoy* were next door, on the first floor. Photography by Seán Harrison.

use of spondees going on in one corner between two wild men in duffle coats, Brendan Behan standing on a table bawling his rendition of "I was Lady Chatterley's Lover", and Gainor Crist, [J. P.] Donleavy's Ginger Man, getting sick, evidently into someone else's pint.'[6] The poet John Montague adds to the chaotic picture: 'there was Kavanagh in his corner, coughing and snorting, Myles hunched over his whiskey before heading abruptly home, the artist Sean O'Sullivan discoursing in French.'[7] Myles was Myles na gCopaleen, one of the pen-names of Brian O'Nolan (he also published as Flann O'Brien), who grew up in the town of Strabane, County Tyrone, the same county from which Montague's family came. O'Nolan grew up in a household fluent in the Irish language, and would write in both languages. One of his brothers, Ciarán Ó Nualláin would later found the Irish-language newspaper, *Inniu*. In short, with the exception of Brendan Behan, the archetypal Dublin writer who once claimed the most land he had ever owned was a window box, but whose maternal grandmother nevertheless lived on a farm in County Meath, they were displaced countrymen all.

'McDaid's was never merely a literary pub,' another regular, the poet Anthony Cronin (from Wexford) recalls in his memoir of the period, *Dead as Doornails* (1976). 'Its strength was always in variety, of talent, class, caste and estate. The divisions between writer and non-writer, bohemian and artist, informer and revolutionary, male and female, were never rigorously enforced.'[8] The literary Dublin pubs of the 1940s and 1950s, then, were not simply places to drink (although they were that). They were places where writers met editors and publishers. But more than that, pubs were stages, on which it was possible to reinvent oneself before an audience. 'A poet has to have an audience,' admitted Kavanagh: ' – half a dozen or so'.[9] Their location, in the heart of the most fashionable area of the city, was no coincidence: it was centre stage. Flann O'Brien put it well when he said of Behan, that he was 'much more a player than a play-wright or, to use a Dublin saying, "he was as good as a play"'.[10] 'You could not in fact have a better companion in a day's idleness than Brendan,' Cronin adds. 'He was a kaleidoscopic entertainment.'[11] For others, simple public presence was a kind of statement. In his poem '"shiver in your tenement"', Derek Mahon evokes the journalist Cathal O'Shannon, artist Harry Kernoff, and poet Austin Clarke, 'long ago in the demure sixties / before the country discovered sex', strolling 'down Dawson or Grafton St. / thoughtful figures amid the faces, the laughter, / or sat among the race-goers and scroungers / in Sinnott's, Neary's, the Bailey, the Wicklow Lounge – / pale, introspective almost to the point of blindness / or so it seemed, living the life of the mind.'[12]

> *Censorship:* 'The moment we got rid of the tyranny of English rule,' George Bernard Shaw remarked in the 1920s, 'we rushed to enslave ourselves.' In 1929, the Irish government passed the Censorship of Publications Act, designed to battle 'evil literature'; it ended up banning most Irish writers of the time, including James Joyce, Kate O'Brien, and John McGahern, having a major impact on Irish writing until the late 1950s.

At the same time, the Dublin writer as a public figure needed more than the informal stage of the pub: many of them also wrote for the city's magazines and newspapers. Central to the literary culture of the time were a series of cultural magazines, the best-known of which was *The Bell* (1940–1954, with a break between 1948 and 1950). *The Bell* was published in Dublin; typically, its editor was not a Dubliner, but (in this case) the proudly Corkonian Seán O'Faoláin. Contemporary with *The Bell* was the journal *Envoy* (which ran from 1949 to 1951, initially designed to fill a gap left by *The Bell*), which 'spoke for a post-war generation' of 'Brendan Behan, Anthony Cronin, Aidan Higgins'[13] and others; it also published part of Samuel Beckett's novel *Watt*. If nothing else, it helped that *Envoy*'s offices were above a fish shop next to McDaid's, and that it was published by John Ryan, who owned the Bailey pub (which he accidentally bought at an auction where he had gone to buy a toaster). '*Envoy* was an annexe to the pub,' Cronin later recalled, 'or the pub to it. It had an air of gaiety, indeed of conspiracy about it.'[14]

The Bell, *Envoy* and others (notably *The Dublin Magazine*), and the writers associated with them did not, however, write only for a small coterie. They were public figures in a much wider sense, writing regularly for the major daily newspapers. For instance, shortly after he moved to Dublin in 1939, Patrick Kavanagh began writing a thrice-weekly column under the thinly veiled pseudonym 'Piers Ploughman' for the paper founded by Eamon de Valera, the *Irish Press*; he later contributed a weekly column to the Catholic weekly, *The Standard*, for which he became a staff reporter. Kavanagh even briefly edited his own newspaper, *Kavanagh's Weekly*, which ran for thirteen issues in 1952, and which contained a scurrilous, satirical gossip column, 'Graftonia'.

Likewise, Brendan Behan wrote a regular column for the *Irish Press* between March 1954 and April 1956, totalling almost one hundred items by the time he finished, all culled from the same seemingly inexhaustible store of comic routines and stories, much of it drawn from the life of the tenements, that he perfected in Dublin's pubs. His Dublin novel *The Scarperer*, which is made up of much of the same material, was serialized in the *Irish Times* in 1953, and appeared under a pseudonym that fooled no one, Emmet Street (which is an actual street, adjoining Russell Street, where he grew up). Its opening scene would have been instantly familiar to anyone who had seen Behan himself in action, shirt perpetually open, hilarious, roaring abuse. In the novel, characters with names such as Nancy Hand, Pig's Eye O'Donnell and the Shaky Man insult people from the countryside – 'Yous scruffy lot of bogmen. ... Culchiemocks'.[15] 'One of Brendan's special prides,' recalled Cronin, 'amounting almost to an obsession, was the fact that he was a Dubliner. All those who had the bad taste to be born elsewhere were "Kulchies" – called so of course after the town of Kiltimagh, pronounced Culchimah, in County Mayo.'[16]

The newspaper work of Behan and Kavanagh, however, pales beside that of Brian O'Nolan. Writing as Flann O'Brien, he published his first novel in 1939, the surreal, satirical *At Swim-Two-Birds*, which is now recognized

Perhaps few writers dominate the literary culture of Dublin at mid-century as forcefully as Brendan Behan (1923–1964). The hilarious, hard-drinking public persona has overshadowed the extent to which he was a serious writer. He is pictured here in 1952 in the National Library of Ireland on Kildare Street. *Getty Images.*

as one of the most innovative, funniest Irish novels of the twentieth century: a novel about a man who is writing a novel about a man who is writing a novel. It had the misfortune to appear just at the beginning of World War II, and as a result largely disappeared from view (not helped when some of the London stock was destroyed in a bombing raid), and only really began to find a readership when it was reprinted in 1961. It has never been out of print since. O'Brien followed *At Swim-Two-Birds* with *The Third Policeman*, which Longmans declined to publish (it would only appear posthumously in 1967; again, it has been in print ever since). Collectively, these novels, along with *An Béal Bocht* (1941; translated as *The Poor Mouth*) would form the basis of a posthumous reputation. However, in the 1940s and 1950s, Flann O'Brien was best known in the Dublin literary world not because of his novels, but because of his newspaper column. 'I have long had a hobby of provoking dog-fights in the newspaper here on any topic from literature to vivisection,' he confessed to his publishers in 1939.[17] That summer, he was responsible for a whole world of characters who took over the letters page of the *Irish Times*, with names such as Lir O'Connor, August Bandar-Ka-Bai, F. McEwe Obarn and Eoin T. MacMurchadha, who carried on a vigorous, if not always rational, debate. The editor, Bertie Smylie, finally called time, and hired O'Brien to write a regular column. And so 'Cruiskeen Lawn' began to appear in the *Irish Times* from 1940 under yet another pseudonym, Myles na gCopaleen; it would be a fixture in the paper (as often as three times a week) until the mid-1960s.

> **Newspapers:** Since the early eighteenth century, newspapers have been a force to reckon with in Ireland. For many years, there were more newspaper titles per capita in Ireland than almost anywhere else in the world, and by the late 1970s, almost 90% of the population regularly read a Sunday paper, a daily national paper, and, outside of Dublin, at least one provincial weekly paper.

Starting out in Irish, but increasingly written in English, 'Cruiskeen Lawn' introduced its own world of literary personae – the Brother, Keats and Chapman, and the often indignant, bemused figure of Myles himself. At their best, 'Cruiskeen Lawn' columns remain some of the funniest, most satirical, Irish writing ever. Often, the column was about the literary world itself. There is, for instance, a column headed 'The World of Books' that proposes a need for a professional 'book-handler' – 'a person who will maul the books of illiterate, but wealthy, upstarts, so that their books will look as if they have been read'. Often, an entire column will resolve itself in a hilarious, if improbable, pun. So, for instance, one column declares that (apart from Yeats and Joyce) all Irish writers should be classified as a kind of disease, 'an infestation of literary vermin, an eruption of literary scabies for which all the patience of scientists notwithstanding, no cure has yet been found. Call it, if you like, "type-phoid".[18]

Between them, then, these writers were known to Dubliners who might never pick up a book of poetry or a read a novel: but as journalists and public figures, they were read and seen everywhere in the city. In this respect, Brian O Nolan/Flann O'Brien/Myles na gCopaleen's multiple pseudonyms are an indication of the extent to which this group of writers were conscious of themselves as their own invention, even if they were never fully satisfied by it. In O Nolan's case, the multiplying personae spread across languages, notably in his novel *An Béal Bocht* (1941), a parody of the Irish-language memoirs such as Tomás Ó Criomhthain's *An tOileánach* (1929), subject of much official approval at the time (which made it a natural target for O'Brien's satirical ire). In Behan's case, the central character in almost all his work is some version of Behan himself. His major works – the plays *The Quare Fellow* (1954) and *The Hostage* (1958) or the autobiographical novel *Borstal Boy* (1958) – are less about plot or character, and more often frames for the kind of storytelling performances into which Behan himself would launch, aided only by strong drink, in the pubs of Dublin. As such, the public persona of their author is never far away.

The Quare Fellow, for instance, is set in Dublin's Mountjoy Gaol the night before an execution and was first performed in the tiny Pike Theatre in 1954. However, it became an international success after Joan Littlewood's Theatre Workshop in London reworked the play in 1956, where it became a major theatre event in almost the same week that *Borstal Boy* was published. As with most of Behan's work, the play's theatrical appeal resides less in the plot than in the stories that the prisoners tell one another. The success of the novel and the play turned Behan, and hence the figure of the Dublin pub raconteur, into a global phenomenon, as recognized on British or American television as he was on Grafton Street. Ultimately, the persona of the reckless drinker became more than a persona for Behan, and his subsequent work shows him struggling to rely on the sheer energy of his language to sustain his writing. 'The world loves the wild, uproarious fellow who is made in its own image,' observed Patrick Kavanagh in an essay with the wonderful title 'A Goat Tethered Outside the Bailey' in 1953. 'Display a touch of this kind of irresponsibility and you're home and dried.'[19]

Had Kavanagh written this essay only a few years later, he could well have been referring to the novel that has probably done the most –

internationally, at least – to consolidate the image of Dublin in the 1940s and 1950s as place in which writers roam the city in search of drink: J. P. Donleavy's *The Ginger Man*. While the novel's sexual politics have not aged well, part of its continuing appeal is the way in which the city itself emerges as the novel's real protagonist – to an even greater extent than its ostensible subject, the character of Sebastian Dangerfield (based on a real friend of Donleavy's at the time, the more improbably named Gainor Crist). *The Ginger Man* is rich with a sense of the energy of the city, accumulating detail and anecdote in a headlong rush at the expense of narrative. 'They went to the Green Cinema [at the top of Grafton Street] where they sat at a white table and golfed down platefuls of rashers, eggs and chips. When they came out the traffic was stopped. Heads out of cars and honking horns. Down the street a huge hulking man lay himself down in the road and went to sleep. Some said he had drink taken. Others that he was listening to see if he could hear the pulse of the city. Sebastian danced and yelped. Newsboys in the crowd asked him what he was doing. Dog dance, sonny.'[20]

Had Sebastian Dangerfield done his dog dance at the top of Grafton Street (where it meets St. Stephen's Green) a few years earlier, he might have run into the unnamed narrator of Flann O'Brien's *At Swim-Two-Birds* on one of his regular trips to the pubs in the area. If in *The Ginger Man* plot is less important than the texture of experience and the result is a twitchy, exuberant prose that is one of the novel's continuing attractions, in *At Swim-Two-Birds* the writing is like a parodic version of the civil service documents that O'Brien was producing in his day job. By contrast, the plot is like some unruly weed, multiplying and spreading. 'One beginning and one ending for a book was a thing I did not agree with,' his narrator tells us in his eminently reasonable tone. This is a novel about the writing of a novel with three interlocking stories-within-the-story, all of which wind their way back to a writer named Dermot Trellis (a fictional character in one of the unnamed protagonist's stories), whose own fictional characters break free and plan to kill him. The narrative does not so much develop as proliferate, before finally collapsing in much the same way that O'Brien's anecdotes in his 'Cruiskeen Lawn' column often collapse in an outrageous pun. And yet, in spite of all this, *At Swim-Two-Birds* is still grounded in a recognizable (if somewhat distorted) Dublin. Trellis, for instance, lives in an unlikely house 'by the banks of the Grand Canal, a magnificent building resembling a palace, with seventeen windows to the front and maybe twice that number to the rear'. There he spends most of his time in bed (oblivious to his fictional creations' designs upon his life), enjoying the park-like quality of the Canal outside his many windows, inhaling the air that 'had come down through Dundrum and Foster Avenue, brine-fresh from sea-travel, a corn-yellow sun-drench that called forth the bees at an uncustomary hour to their day of bumbling'.[21]

Those same banks of the Grand Canal where O'Brien's bees were bumbling was also where Patrick Kavanagh finally reconciled himself to Dublin. After years of writing poems of farm life in the city, Kavanagh had tried to find an urban verse form in satirical poems such as 'The Paddiad', or 'Bank Holiday' (from which McGahern's short story takes its title):

> *In the pubs for seven years*
> *Men have given him their ears,*
> *Buying the essence of his heart*
> *With a porter-perfumed fart.*[22]

As much as he railed against the city, Kavanagh nonetheless settled into one of its neighbourhoods, and from 1948 until 1958, he rented an apartment at 62 Pembroke Road, just off Upper Baggot Street, with the Grand Canal just right around the corner. John Ryan writes of calling to see him 'in his bed-sit, in a tall, late-Georgian building. [...] The main room was a desolation – ankle-deep in papers and typescript.'[23] This became Kavanagh's home turf. 'If ever you go to Dublin Town / In a hundred years or so,' he writes in the 1953 poem of that name, 'Inquire for me in Baggot Street / And what I was like to know.'[24] Even after he moved out of Pembroke Road in 1958, and lived variously in rented rooms at 19 Raglan Road, 110 Baggot Lane, 1 Wilton Place, 37 Upper Mount Street and 136 Upper Leeson Street, he never strayed far from the same stretch of the Grand Canal.[25]

It was in this patch of Dublin that Patrick Kavanagh created a distinctive urban pastoral, poems that have the same sense of wonder and simplicity as his earliest work about rural Monaghan, but which are still very much urban poems. Perhaps the best known is 'On Raglan Road' from 1946:

> *On Raglan Road on an autumn day I met her first and knew*
> *That her dark hair would weave a snare that I might one day rue;*
> *I saw the danger, yet I walked along the enchanted way,*
> *And I said, let grief be a fallen leave at the dawning of the day.*[26]

Kavanagh later met the Irish folk singer Luke Kelly (in whose memory there are now no fewer than two statues in Dublin), who recorded the song with The Dubliners, using the music of a traditional song, 'The Dawning of the Day'. The Dubliners had formed in O'Donoghue's pub, on Lower Baggot Street, not far from where Kavanagh lived; they would later work with Brendan Behan's brother, Dominic, who was also a playwright, novelist, and prolific songwriter. Between being sung and recited, the poem has become part of the memory of Dublin, and can be heard, for instance, bubbling up in Paula Meehan's poem 'Home' about a very different Dublin in 1996, where Kavanagh's line 'On Grafton Street in November we tripped lightly along the ledge' becomes: 'On Grafton Street in November / I heard a mighty sound: a travelling man with a didgeridoo / blew me clear to Botany Bay.'[27]

'I have been thinking of making my grove on the banks of the Grand Canal near Baggot Street Bridge where in recent days I have rediscovered my roots,' Kavanagh wrote in the essay 'From Monaghan to the Grand Canal', published in 1959 in the cultural journal *Studies*. 'My hegira was to the Grand Canal bank where again I saw the beauty of water and green grass and the magic of light.'[28] A year earlier, after having been released from hospital, Kavanagh had written two of his most enduring Dublin poems: 'Canal Bank Walk', and 'Lines Written on a Seat on the Grand Canal, Dublin' (which also appeared in *Studies*). Today, Kavanagh is remembered with a sculpted figure in bronze by John Coll, sitting on a bench beside the canal:

> *Leafy-with-love banks and the green waters of the canal*
> *Pouring redemption for me, that I do*
> *The will of God, wallow in the habitual, the banal,*
> *Grow with nature again as before I grew.*[29]

Certainly, the old bitterness returns in Kavanagh's later poems; however, his Grand Canal poems seem to contain the secret to a redeemed city, where it was possible to 'wallow in the habitual'. For this loneliest of gregarious writers, the canal as a kind of elongated park finally offered a way of being alone in the city that was not the same as being lonely; somewhere in which place itself was a sufficient consoling presence. What is more, that sense of some special quality about this little Dublin oasis would be passed on to the generation that followed Kavanagh, perhaps most memorably in one of Brendan Kennelly's most enduring poems, 'Begin': 'Begin again to the summoning birds,' the poem opens, 'to the sight of light at the window, / begin to the roar of morning traffic / all along Pembroke Road.' It then builds to a conclusion that must rank among the most quoted lines in recent Irish poetry:

> *Though we live in a world that dreams of ending*
> *that always seems about to give in*
> *something that will not acknowledge conclusion*
> *insists that we forever begin.*[30]

Kavanagh, Behan, and Flann O'Brien created their public personas of the Dublin writer in these streets around the Grand Canal and Pembroke Road with such clarity that the area acquired an unofficial name: Baggotonia. What is perhaps most remarkable about Baggotonia is that even though it was in the centre of the city, clustered around the centre of government, it had the feel of a village, although not one to be found on any municipal maps. 'The boundaries of Baggotonia are mysteriously fluid,' observed the novelist John Banville in his personal memoir, *Time Pieces* (2016). It is a matter of associations. So, says Banville (a one-time resident of this shifting neighbourhood), either end of Lower Mount Street, both near 'the leafier lower stretch of Percy Place', and the western end, where it runs into Merrion Square, are 'characteristic examples of Baggotonia Superba', but the street itself is not. 'Such are the enigmas of urban life.'[31]

> *Bookshops:* Dublin has been a city of bookshops since a loophole in copyright legislation in 1709 turned eighteenth-century Dublin into a kind of pirate's paradise, and the number of printers and booksellers mushroomed. One shop founded in 1768 – Hodges Figgis – still exists today. In the twentieth century, the city was also well supplied with second-hand bookshops, such as Greene's on Clare Street, and Webb's on the quays – both since gone the way of Parsons.

In general terms, however, Baggotonia follows the Grand Canal, running between Percy Place and Herbert Place (where, coincidentally, Flann O'Brien lived for a while as a child), spilling inland along Upper Mount Street as far as the edge of Merrion Square. Following the Canal, it runs past Baggott Street Bridge as far as Leeson Street Bridge. However, where Baggot Street cuts across the Canal, it forms a second axis, extending along Lower Baggot Street as far as (but not into) St. Stephen's Green, but certainly up to 13 Fitzwilliam Place, where there was once 'an infamous, bohemian warren' of basement flats known as the Catacombs, which feature prominently in *The Ginger Man*. Here, Anthony Cronin, Behan, and others, sometimes lived. It was on Fitzwilliam Square, as well, that one of the most important Irish painters of the past century (and an under-rated, but significant playwright), Jack B. Yeats, had his studio in the years before his death in 1957. Heading away from the city centre, Baggotonia runs past where Parsons Bookshop was situated on Baggot Street Bridge itself, and to where it turns into Pembroke Road (where Kavanagh lived and from where he edited *Kavanagh's Weekly*). Spokes run out from Baggot Street, particularly Waterloo Road and Raglan Road, reaching an outer limit with Herbert Park, eulogized by the American poet John Berryman, who lived in what he calls 'a trim suburban villa' at 55 Lansdowne Park. In one of his 'Dream Songs', he places his alter ego, Henry, here:

> [...] this most beautiful of parks since Bombay
> on this exquisite October Sunday,
> the great bright green spaces under the fine sun,
> children & ducks & dogs, two superb elms,
> the scene Henry overwhelms.[32]

While neither St. Stephen's Green nor Grafton Street are arguably part of Baggotonia proper, the cluster of pubs off Grafton Street – McDaid's, the Grafton Mooney (now Bruxelles), the Duke, the Bailey, and Davy Byrne's – most certainly are, like a colony that has become more like the homeland than the homeland itself.

Located on Baggot Street Bridge, Parsons Bookshop was a vital part of the literary culture of Baggotonia in the mid-twentieth century. Today it is an insurance office. *Photography by Seán Harrison.*

Apart from being supplied with a canal, a bookshop, and a quantum of pubs, Baggotonia had its own publisher. In 1951, Liam Miller opened what would become one of the most important Irish literary publishers of the twentieth century, the Dolmen Press, in an office at 23 Upper Mount Street (later moving around the corner to 8 Herbert Place). Miller himself lived nearby, at 94, Lower Baggot Street. 'Gaunt and bearded as a Talmudic scholar, Liam was a book designer and printer of genius,' John Montague later wrote.[33] Among Dolmen's many publications was an early series of the journal *Poetry Ireland*; when the title was revived in 1967 in the form in which it currently exists – as *Poetry Ireland Review* – it eventually settled in the basement of 44 Upper Mount Street, which also housed a library named for the poet Austin Clarke. Baggotonia at its peak also had two tiny but adventurous theatres: the Lantern Theatre Club, which ran from 1957 to 1967, mostly from a basement in Lower Mount Street; and the Pike, located on Herbert Lane, which runs parallel to Herbert Street, where Brendan Behan lived at No. 15, and the poet John Montague lived a few doors down. Much later, in the poem 'Herbert Street Revisited', Montague writes: 'A light is burning late / in this Georgian Dublin street: someone is living our old lives!'

So put back the leaves on the tree.
put the tree back in the ground,
let Brendan trundle his corpse down
the street singing, like Molly Malone.[34]

Montague later commented of the neighbourhood: 'It was said you couldn't shovel a load of coal into a basement without disrupting an avant-garde play.'[35]

Although it only lasted from 1953 to 1961, the Pike holds an important place in Irish theatre history. With a tiny performance space and only fifty-five seats crammed into a converted coach house (with the yard covered to make an auditorium), the Pike was the creation of Carolyn Swift and her husband, director Alan Simpson. 'It now seems,' Simpson

'A light is burning / late in this Georgian Dublin street: / Someone is leading our old lives!' John Montague (who wrote these lines) lived here, on Herbert Street, with Brendan Behan next door, and Patrick Kavanagh a few streets over. The division of these large Georgian houses into flats made affordable living places for writers in the mid-twentieth century. Photography by Seán Harrison.

wrote in retrospect, 'that we were in reality among the shock troops of a movement of change in the theatre, which was going on unknown to us throughout Europe.'[36] Swift later described the theatre itself, with its mixture of gilt and plaster cupids and Regency wallpaper as a 'weird cross between Covent Garden Opera House and a doll's house'.[37] This was the theatre in which Behan's *The Quare Fellow* was first performed on 19 November 1954, and it was here that the Irish premiere of Samuel Beckett's *Waiting for Godot* (1953) took place on 28 October 1955, only a few months after its English-language debut in London. 'Having run for two years in a Paris *"théâtre de poche"* that is little bigger than the Pike, it is ideally suited to our resources,' the *Pike Newsletter* told its readers.[38]

Although Beckett had been living in Paris for some time at that point, he had remained in contact with friends in Dublin. So, when Alan Simpson wrote late in 1953 asking if he could stage *Waiting for Godot* at the Pike, Beckett replied to say that he was still in the process of translating the play (originally written in French) 'into English, as literally as I could', but doubted it would be possible to stage in Dublin 'because of certain crudities of language'.[39] Taking this at face value, Simpson treated the marked-up translation that arrived in the post from Paris as a work in progress, and his 'immediate reaction was that the two tramps should be played as Dublin characters'.[40] Accordingly, he set about adapting it so that the two main characters, Vladimir and Estragon, could be played with working-class Dublin accents. So, when Vladimir speculates that if the (largely) mute character of Lucky 'got going all of a sudden' 'we'd be bollocksed', Simpson amended this to a uniquely Dublin word, 'bandjacksed' (which means more or less the same thing). Estragon's suggestion 'suppose we gave him a good beating' in Dublin became 'what if we wired into him'; likewise, the suggestion that finding new names for Lucky's master, Pozzo, would 'amusing' became: 'It'd be gas.'[41] By contrast, Simpson cast an actor with 'a rich, fruity Anglo-Irish voice' as Pozzo, who, dressed in a tweed jacket and cape, was played as 'an Anglo-Irish or English gentleman'.[42] A tree, a country road, evening; it may not have looked like Dublin, but in 1955 at the Pike, *Waiting for Godot* certainly sounded like Dublin.

'They seem to have done a good job in the Pike,' Beckett wrote from Paris to a Dublin friend, in spite of Simpson's 'minor improvements to the text'. 'The whole affair is so simple.' As well as being a kind of exemplary case of how to interpret Beckett – 'no symbols where none intended'[43] – the Pike *Godot* showed how the sound of the Dublin voice could make even the most challenging literature part of the city. Today, when *Godot* has become so firmly entrenched in the repertoire of world theatre, it is worth reminding ourselves that this play in which, as Vivian Mercier put it in the *Irish Times*, 'nothing happens, twice',[44] prompted puzzlement, outrage, and shock when it was first produced in London and New York. In Dublin, on the other hand, the quintessential Dublin comedian Jimmy O'Dea introduced Godot into his routines at the Gaiety Theatre, tramps 'waiting for Godot' began to feature in cartoons in the Dublin newspapers, and the Pike found itself with a hit on its hands – so much so that Swift and Simpson were able to rent the larger Gate Theatre the following March and embark on an Irish tour. Kavanagh praised the play in the *Irish Times*, 'because of its awareness of the peculiar sickness of society',[45] and Brendan Behan not only saw the play, but joined in one evening. Sitting in the back of the auditorium, having 'had a few jars, when one of the tramps in the play shouts out, "But when you're dead, who'll pull the rope?" I shouted back from the stalls, "I will".'[46]

The streets around the Pike Theatre also had a deeply personal significance for Beckett. 'I had two dreadful months in Dublin this summer,' he wrote to a friend in December 1950. 'I hope I shall never have to go back there. My mother died in July.'[47] May Beckett had suffered from Parkinson's disease, and her final months were spent in the Merrion Nursing Home, at 21 Herbert Street, six doors down from where Behan would live, backing on to Herbert Lane, where the Pike was located. The location appears in Beckett's 1958 play, *Krapp's Last Tape*, in which an elderly man (Krapp) sits listening to recordings he has made of himself every year on his birthday, flicking at random between moments in a life. At last he comes upon a tape in which he finds his younger self describing 'the house on the canal where mother lay a-dying'. The memory is tied to the experience of sitting on the 'bench by the weir from where I could see her window. There I sat, in the biting wind, wishing she were gone,' throwing a ball for a dog, waiting for the blind in her window to be lowered, as was customary when a person died:

> I happened to look up and there it was. All over and done with, at last. I sat on for a few moments with the ball in my hand and the dog yelping and pawing at me. [*Pause*] Moments. Her moments, my moments. [*Pause*] The dog's moments. [*Pause*] In the end I held it out to him and he took it in his mouth, gently, gently. A small, old, black, hard, solid rubber ball. [*Pause*] I shall feel it, in my hands, until my dying day. [*Pause*] I might have kept it. [*Pause*] But I gave it to the dog.[48]

'Think' writes the poet Harry Clifton in one of his *Portobello Sonnets* (2017), 'for instance, of Krapp / Outside his mother's window, on the canal, / Watching the blind come down. That hospital, / Does it still exist? That safe maternal lap, / Was it ever there to begin with?'[49] The answer to the first question is that it does not; the answer to the second question remains open.

In spite of having *Waiting for Godot* produced in the Pike in 1955, Beckett (who, admittedly, was seldom in Dublin in those years) distanced himself from a Dublin literary culture nourished on porter, whiskey, disappointment and internecine village warfare. Nor was he the only one. The novelist John Banville's first visits to Dublin from his native Wexford were to an aunt living in Percy Place, who later lived in Upper Mount Street. He would later stay with her. 'I arrived in Dublin towards the end of the McDaid Age, when the literary topers and talkers were on their last legs [...] Kavanagh, who by then was visibly dying would sit for hours on the steps outside the house where my flat was, and glare at the offices of the Dolmen Press across the road. [...] Flann O'Brien-Myles na Gopaleen-Brian O'Nolan I encountered only once, when on a twilit autumn eve I spotted him wobbling his way down a deserted Grafton Street with hat askew and coattails flapping in the October gale, a sad, drink-sodden figure.'[50] Within a few years of the young Banville's arrival in the city, many of the generation of Dublin writers as public figures would have died of alcohol-related illnesses: Behan in 1964, O'Brien in 1966, and Kavanagh the following year. What also becomes clear with the passage of time is that for all of their gregariousness, each was, in his own way, profoundly lonely. The last time he saw Behan, Anthony Cronin recalled, was in the Bailey pub; he had 'the same dried vomit still on his lapels' from the day before. 'Sounds, evidently words, came out of his mouth, but they were incomprehensible.'[51]

Looking back on this period, the writer Leland Bardwell observes in her 2008 memoir *A Restless Life* that 'writers, artists and composers do not self-destruct in the same way any more – or at least it's rare.' Bardwell arrived in the literary world of Dublin in the early 1960s, and after living in flats in Upper Mount Street and Pembroke Road ('where the fleas danced in the sunbeams like hayseed'), she settled in a basement flat at 33 Lower Leeson Street. 'In this deep Georgian basement, the main room, stone-floored and gritty, went the whole width of the flat. It ended in a gas fire with powdered burner. The entrance, a blackened porch, contained a leaking sink and a greasy gas cooker. [...]

As in every dungeon, the walls wept, but at least [...] for this vegetal apartment, we paid £2 a week.' Bardwell became close friends with Patrick Kavanagh in his final years, but also became a kind of mentor to a rising generation of poets, including Eiléan Ní Chuilleanáin, Paul Durcan, Michael Hartnett, and Macdara Woods. Bardwell's dripping basement flat became for a time what she calls, with more than a tinge of irony, a 'salon' – 'far from the kind of salon [...] in which Æ or Yeats participated fifty years previously'.[52] Looking back on that time in a late poem 'Leland: PS from Yalta', Macdara Woods writes:

> There was a house in Leeson Street
> and they called it 33 ...
> Keep it up for twenty years the poetry
> Kavanagh's words to me
> in your front room.[53]

The distance between that world of weeping walls and the same area today can be measured in property values. In 2018, a building a few doors down from the one Bardwell rented for £2 a week sold for €1.5 million. Part of the reason that the area had such a vibrant, if chaotic, literary culture in the 1950s and early 1960s was because it was still possible for a writer to live cheaply. Those writers who do live in this area today – such as Colm Tóibín, who has a house at 12 Upper Pembroke Street, off Fitzwilliam Square – are living in very different circumstances to Bardwell's damp basement.

However, well before the property boom began in the 1990s, the literary world of Dublin was changing. Overlapping both with the younger group of writers who first started publishing in the 1960s, and with the roaring generation who came before them, were a third group, who straddled both worlds. Keeping in mind that Behan was born in 1923, for instance, there were writers such as his Herbert Street neighbour, John Montague (born 1929, died 2016) and Thomas Kinsella (born 1928, died 2021) who, in retrospect, have come to seem like part of a later literary city, and not only by outliving their chronological contemporaries. 'I was not really part of the *Envoy* magazine crowd, which gathered in McDaid's,' John Montague later wrote, although he moved through that world.[54] Likewise, the letters of John McGahern (1934–2006) are filled with a wariness of the literary battles fought in McDaid's. 'One could circle that shindy forever but it's tiresome,' he confessed to friend in a letter; indeed, he would even go so far to make a more sweeping admission: 'I find literary people bore more almost to the point of violence' (in this case, rather oddly, after meeting Kate O'Brien in the Hibernian Hotel).

One of the people with whom McGahern did meet occasionally was Thomas Kinsella (although describing him privately as 'a bit unexciting').[55] Kinsella would live most of his life in the area around the Pepper Canister Church, first renting a room in Baggot Street, and then buying a house at 47 Percy Place, where he would live much of his life. He, too, largely kept his distance from the literary pubs. His poem 'Open House', begins in a Dublin literary pub:

> *an overcrowded sty,*
> *maroon in tone [...]*
> *six or seven, more or less,*
> *connected with the daily press,*
> *are gathered in the centre light*
> *debating the subject for the night*
> *– Drink and the High Creative Arts –.*

The poem ends with the poet 'On a fragrant slope descending into the fog / over our foul ascending city', where he has 'turned away in refusal'.[56] While not part of the literary pub scene, the streets around Baggot Street Bridge – the heart of Baggotonia – are firmly fixed in his imaginary landscape. His 1958 collection *Another September*, for instance, contains a haunting evocation of the area at night, 'Baggot Street Deserta'. He would revisit the area in later collections, such as *Poems from the City Centre* (1990), in poems such as 'The Stable' (about a stable that once existed in nearby Percy Lane) and 'The Bell', about the bell on the Haddington Road church, 'Disturbing the sanctuary lamp / – cup of blood, seed of light, / hanging down from the dark height'.[57] Indeed, Kinsella would name the poetry press he founded in 1972 after the Pepper Canister Church (actually St. Stephen's Church) that is one of the area's landmarks.

The streets around the canal and Baggot Street Bridge would also remain vivid for John Banville. 'I imagine we all have a particular place that is a kind of private Paradise,' he later wrote. For Banville, it is 'that stretch of placid water, rustling reeds and dark-umber towpath from Baggot Street down to Lower Mount Street'.[58] Dublin – and these streets in particular – appear in Banville's novels closely observed, but transfigured, like an old master painting under a thick glaze of shellac. So, in his 1986 novel *Mephisto* the narrator, Gabriel

Swan, spends time in Chandos Street, 'a decaying Georgian sweep with a Protestant church at one end and a railed-off green square at the other. I loitered there night after night, watching the house, one of a tall terrace, with worn granite steps and a black front door.' There is no Chandos Street in Dublin; but the streetscape is recognizably Upper Mount Street. The key to the transformation – and what happens to Dublin in most of Banville's writing – becomes clear later in the novel, after already murky events take a darker turn. 'The city I had thought I knew became transfigured now,' Gabriel realizes. 'Fear altered everything.'[59] Likewise, in *The Book of Evidence* (1989), the narrator, Freddy Montgomery (loosely based on the real-life convicted murderer Malcolm Macarthur) returns to the city after killing a maid while attempting to steal a painting. 'Here is Trinity, the Bank, Fox's, where my father used to come on an annual pilgrimage, with great ceremony, to buy his Christmas cigars. My world, and I an outcast in it.' The Dublin through which Freddy wanders, with its familiar shops, its pubs, 'its crooked alleyways and sudden broad, deserted spaces, and dead-end streets under railway bridges where parked cars basked fatly in the evening sun'[60] is at once recognizable and, at the same time, utterly strange, transformed by fear and guilt.

When in 2006, Banville created an alter ego, the crime writer Benjamin Black, responsible for a series of Dublin crime novels featuring a detective-pathologist, Quirke, he set these novels in the 1950s, and installed his protagonist in the apartment on Lower Mount Street in which Banville himself had stayed with his aunt when he first came to Dublin (although, Banville admits, 'I smartened it up considerably'[61]). To an even greater extent than in the novels he writes under his own name, Dublin is a brooding presence in the Benjamin Black novels. Early in the first Quirke novel, *Christine Falls* (2006), Quirke is walking along, 'admiring the rich light on the brick façades of the houses of Hume Street [just off St. Stephen's Green]', when he meets his adult daughter, Phoebe. 'They strolled along the Green towards Grafton Street. People were out promenading, enjoying the last of the fine day.' However, even in the thick autumn sunshine Quirke cannot repress an image of a dead body he had dissected earlier that day, the young girl Christine Falls (who gives the novel its title), 'waxen and wan on her bier'.[62] In the fourth novel in the Quirke series, *Elegy for April*, his daughter Phoebe, concerned that she has not heard from a friend (the eponymous April), decides to call at her flat in Herbert Place: a 'terrace of tall houses, their louring, dark brick exteriors shining wetly in the shrouded air'. Finding it empty, 'she walked up to Baggot Street and turned right, away from the canal. The heels of her flat shoes made a deadened tapping on the pavement. It was lunchtime on a weekday but it felt more like a Sunday twilight. The city seemed almost deserted, and the few people she met flickered past sinisterly, like phantoms.'[63] This is Quirke's Dublin, the dark mirror of the self-mythologizing, roaring dens of the literary pubs; an eerily quiet provincial city, holding close its dirty secrets.

1. St. Stephen's Green
2. Elizabeth Bowen's home, 15 Herbert Place
3. Teresa Deevy's flat, 16 Waterloo Road
4. Mary Lavin's house, 11 Lad Lane
5. Oscar Wilde's home, 1 Merrion Square
6. W.B. Yeats's house, 82 Merrion Square
7. Shelbourne Hotel, 27 Stephen's Green
8. Lady Morgan's house, 35 Kildare Street
9. George Moore's house, 4 Upper Ely Place
10. National Library of Ireland, 7-8 Kildare Street
11. University College Dublin (MOLI), 85 Stephen's Green

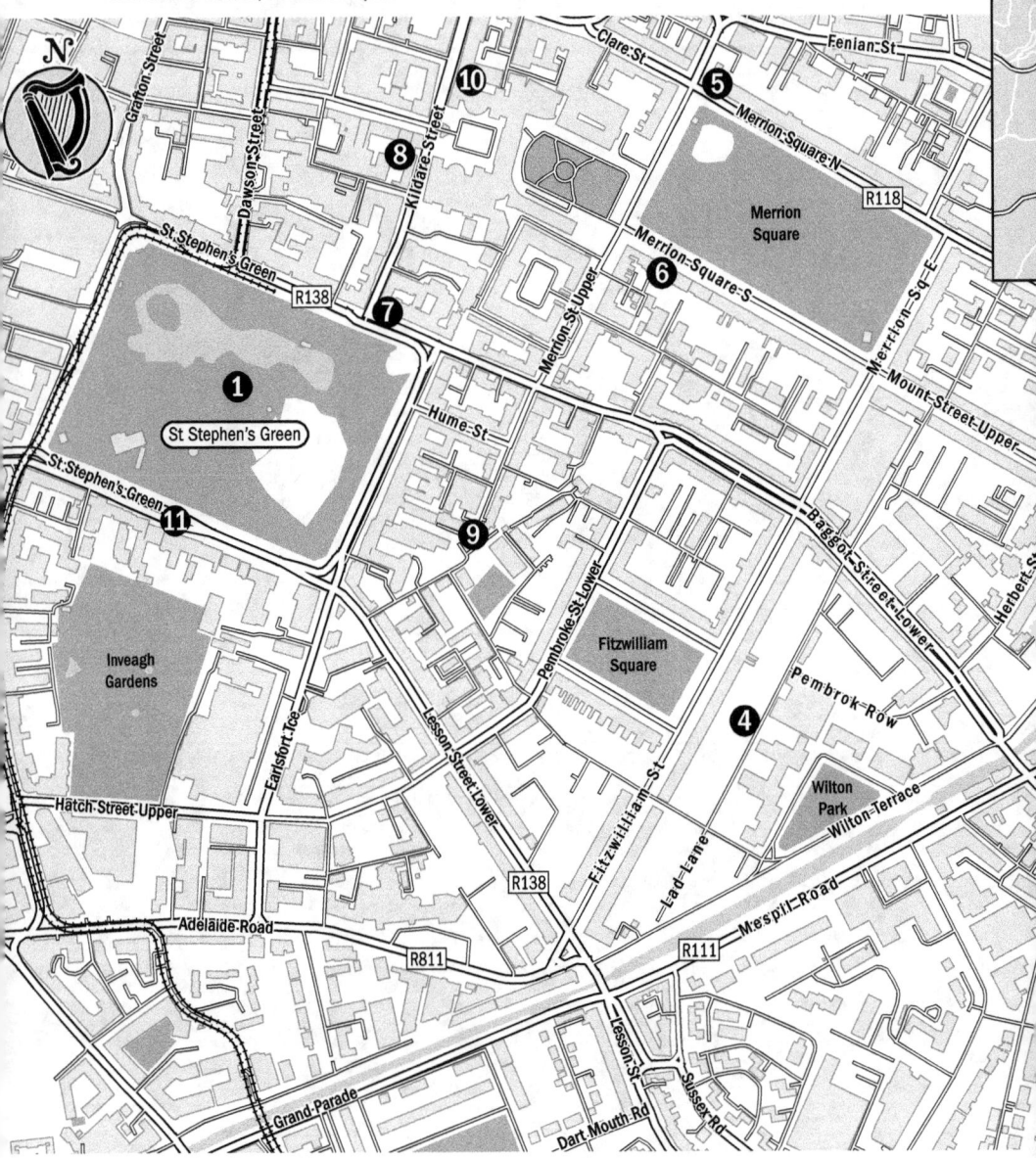

Around St. Stephen's Green

3

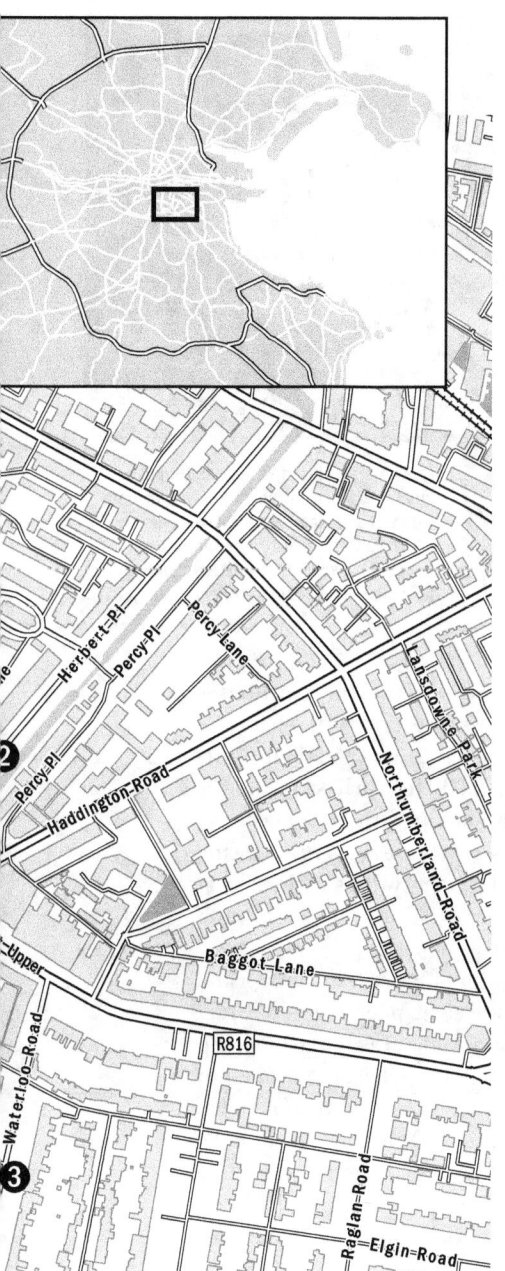

Although the area around Baggot Street Bridge was a kind of literary bohemia in the 1940s and 1950s, claimed by writers such as Brendan Behan (from a northside tenement) and Patrick Kavanagh (from Monaghan), the only writer to have actually been born in this part of Dublin was Elizabeth Bowen. The plaque on the house in which she was born, at 15 Herbert Place, often comes as a surprise to those noticing it today, for Bowen is not usually thought of as a Dublin writer at all. Instead, she is probably best known for her haunting novel of the final years of big country houses in *The Last September* (1929), or its autobiographical counterpart, *Bowen's Court* (1942), both written about her ancestral estate in County Cork, Bowen's Court. However, like many landed families, the Bowens had a Dublin address, and so in 1899 Elizabeth Bowen was born in one of 'that row of smallish, light-brown Georgian houses with high steps, fronting on the canal', as she describes it, where the rooms at the front of the house 'all had a watery quality in their lightness from the upcast reflections of the canal'.¹ Her earliest memories are of that light, and of walking through Dublin with her governess, vividly recalled in her Dublin memoir, *Seven Winters* (1942). 'On my walks through familiar quarters of Dublin,' she writes, 'I looked at everything like a spy.'²

No. 15 Herbert Place, facing the Grand Canal, was where Elizabeth Bowen was born and lived until she was seven years old, in 'that row of smallish, light brown brick Georgian houses with high steps, fronting on the canal'. *Photography by Seán Harrison.*

The Bowens' Dublin sits on top of the Dublin of Patrick Kavanagh and Brendan Behan in complex ways. For Bowen, Upper Baggot Street was not where one went to Searsons' pub for a steadying morning drink. It was where one went shopping, a place 'where everyone not only had manners, but time; we nearby residents made this our own village'.³ Her almost direct contemporary, Kate O'Brien (born in 1897, two years earlier than Bowen) knew this same Baggot Street area as a child, and records a memory of staying with an aunt on Mespil Road in 1907 on a visit from her native Limerick. 'The very wide, pale streets and sailing trams brought me a mood of something like concern and their far-off clang at night was sad. And there was last Mass at St. Mary's, Haddington Road, on Sundays. I did not like the church, and something about us all, young and old being so staggeringly well-dressed caused me uneasiness. I can still hear the starch in those summer dresses.'⁴

And yet, this Dublin neighbourhood of crinolined governesses and starched children occupies the same streets in which Brendan Behan (who would later live one street away from where Bowen was born) would come roaring home at dawn singing obscene ballads. Indeed, had the young Elizabeth Bowen been able to look out of her nursery window at the rear of the house into the not-too-distant future, she would have been looking down directly into Herbert Lane, where the Pike Theatre would be located in the 1950s. The building occupied by the Pike Theatre had been originally built as a coach house, offering stabling for the horses for residents of Herbert Street and of Herbert Place — such as the Bowens. It was here in 1955 that during the Pike's Irish premiere of Samuel Beckett's *Waiting for Godot*, the character of Pozzo (who addresses his servant Lucky as 'pig') dressed and spoke in the swallowed vowels of an Anglo-Irish gentleman — and so would have appeared very like Bowen's father. One might even imagine Elizabeth Bowen as a child, peering out her window one evening, and glimpsing Pozzo and Lucky, fifty years in the future.

> **Aristocratic Street Names:** Many of Dublin's streets, particularly in the Georgian and Victorian areas, still retain the names of the aristocratic families on whose estates they were built. So, for instance, Herbert Place, where Elizabeth Bowen was born, was named for the Herbert family, earls of Pembroke (and hence nearby Pembroke Road, where Patrick Kavanagh lived). There are also streets named for the eighteenth-century property developers who built the Georgian city, such as Joshua Dawson and Luke Gardiner, memorialized in Dawson Street and Gardiner Street, respectively.

Bowen's childhood world of governesses and country estates might seem like it belongs in a different century to Patrick Kavanagh's 'Adventure in the Bohemian Jungle', which ends with a competition between the poet and 'a group of Crumlin gurriers who are betting on a competition for who can urinate the highest'.⁵ In fact, Bowen was born in 1899, Kavanagh in 1904; her novel *The Death of the Heart*, for instance, appeared in 1938, the year before Flann O'Brien's *At Swim-Two-Birds*. And yet, even though she was technically their contemporary, she was separated from the literary world of McDaid's pub not only by class but also by gender.

We get a sense of Bowen's Irish literary world by turning to an evening in June 1939, when she was the guest of honour at the annual banquet of the Irish Women Writers' Club, held in the Gresham Hotel, on O'Connell Street. There she spoke to an audience, largely of women, of 'the vitality and fluidity which the English language assumes on the Irish tongue'.[6] The Irish Women Writers' Club had been founded five years earlier, on 7 September 1933, by the poet and playwright Blanaid Salkeld, initially from her home at 43 Morehampton Road. This address is less than a ten-minute walk from Kavanagh's flat on Pembroke Street, along the same leafy streets – but it was also a world away. With playwright and novelist Dorothy MacArdle as its first president, the Irish Women Writers' Club was a kind of parallel universe to the McDaidians, one that only partially intersected with the aggressively boozy hilarity of the male-dominated world of the literary pubs.

Unlike the pubs, which were often hostile assemblies of individualists united by stout, the Women Writers' Club had an organizational structure, with a president, secretary, and treasurer. Its activities revolved around monthly dinners in places such as the Gresham or Dolphin hotels, or in fashionable restaurants such as the Country Shop on St. Stephen's Green or Jammet's restaurant on Nassau Street. An annual banquet and award ceremony was the highlight of its year. And attendance could be large. For instance, more than 150 people sat down to the annual dinner to celebrate the novelist Kate O'Brien in 1946. What is more, as an organized group, the women writers could take collective stances on public issues (whereas the public comments of Kavanagh, O'Brien, and Behan were more often determinedly disorganized). For instance, honouring Kate O'Brien in 1946 was a political gesture because her novel *The Land of Spices* (which was about the life of a nun) had been banned in 1941 (on the basis of a single scene that hinted demurely at a gay relationship), and so had become a kind of touchstone for protests against the absurdities of the 1929 Censorship of Publications Act.

Once we begin to glimpse the world of the Women Writers' Club, their absence from memoirs of literary Dublin (such as Anthony Cronin's *Dead as Doornails* or John Ryan's *Remembering How We Stood*) becomes all the more remarkable. In fact, members of the Club often lived in the same streets as the McDaidians. The Waterford-born playwright Teresa Deevy, for instance, based most of her plays – such as *Katie Roche* (1936) – in small Irish cities or towns; however, she had a flat at 16 Waterloo Road throughout the 1940s and 1950s, and was friendly with the painter Jack B. Yeats, who lived around the corner at 18 Fitzwilliam Square, and who in turn was a neighbour of the great Irish naturalist writer, Robert Lloyd Praeger, who lived at No. 19. 'Went to [Liam] Miller's the other night' she wrote in 1953 to her close friend Patricia Lynch, herself an acclaimed children's author, and another active member of the Women Writers' Club. 'Celebrating [the Dolmen edition of David Marcus's translation of] *The Midnight Court* coming out! To-night we go to the "37"'[7] (yet another small theatre like the Pike, in this case located in an upper floor on O'Connell Street).

At the same time, Deevy's letters show that (at least partly because she was deaf in a society that made few accommodations for disability) she was always most comfortable in small groups of close friends, and was certainly not going to be found matching whiskies with Brendan Behan. As such, she was always both an insider and something of an outsider. And yet Deevy, too, was honoured by the Women Writers' Club, with an event at the Hibernian Hotel in 1949; and, as with Kate O'Brien, there was an edge to the gesture. By the mid-1940s, Deevy had become *persona non grata* with the Abbey Theatre, which had had a series of successes with her plays *The King of Spain's Daughter* (1935) and

Although often associated with her home in Bective, County Meath, Mary Lavin (1912-1996) kept a flat in Lad Lane, Dublin (just off Baggot Street) for much of her writing life. In 2021, a nearby park, at Wilton Square, was named for her. *Photograph by Paddy Whelan; Courtesy of Irish Times.*

Katie Roche (1936) in the 1930s. However, by 1941, the theatre had unceremoniously stopped staging her works, all of which feature strong (and enigmatic) female leads. As she wrote to a friend, the theatre one day returned a new script with a note making it abundantly clear that they had 'no use for my work – never asked to see any more'.[8]

For Deevy, who shuttled back and forth between Waterloo Road and her family in Waterford, geography was yet another factor that kept her on the edge of the teeming village life of literary Dublin. The same was true of the novelist and short-story writer Mary Lavin. Although she was educated at University College Dublin, and for a period lived in and around St. Stephen's Green, most of her life was spent on a farm in Bective, County Meath, from which her best-known collection, *Tales from Bective Bridge* (1943), takes its title. However, even after she moved to County Meath, Lavin kept a flat at 11 Lad Lane, just off Lower Baggot Street, and she often spent her days in the city. Colm Tóibín would later recall that 'in 1972, when I came to Dublin, you could see Mary Lavin in the city. In Bewley's in Grafton Street, or in the Country Shop [restaurant], or in the National Library.'[9]

A few of Lavin's stories are set in this area of Dublin, perhaps most evocatively 'In a Café', which first appeared in *The New Yorker* in 1960. Like so much of her work, Mary Lavin's 'In a Café' is about loss. It is a story in which a central character who has been widowed (as Lavin herself was in 1954) has a sudden recognition of absence, of what it means to be alone in the midst of others. It begins with the narrator, Mary, meeting a friend in a small café, where she notices original paintings on the walls, and the painter nursing a coffee at a corner table. Mary initially has a certain sense of liberation, telling herself that the café was the sort of place 'she would be unlikely ever to have set foot in' had her late husband, Richard, still been alive. When the friend leaves, however, she steps out into the street. 'She had reached Grafton Street once more, and stepped into its crowded thoroughfare. It was only a few minutes since she left it, but in the street the evasion of light had begun. Only the bustle of people and the activity of traffic made it seem that was yet day.' Reaching the top of Grafton Street, she crosses to St. Stephen's Green, where she imagines that were she to put her fingers between the railings 'it would

> **Parks:** While St. Stephen's Green and the Phoenix Park were originally laid out as public spaces, many of Dublin's parks – including Merrion Square, Mountjoy Square, and Dartmouth Square – were originally private grounds for the residents of the surrounding houses, but have since opened to the public.

be with a slight shock that the fingers would feel the little branches, like fine bones, under the feathers of mist' — and it is this that finally triggers her experience of profound aloneness. 'Oh Richard! she cried, out loud. [...] And as she cried out, her mind presented him to her, as she so often saw him, coming towards her.'[10] There are few moments in the writing of the city in which absence attaches itself so powerfully to the most incidental of places, particularly with such delicate tools as the phrase 'the evasion of light'. As Tóibín remarks, 'Mary Lavin is dealing here with the poetics of disappearance, walking on fictional ground that is deeply unstable.'[11]

If Lavin's Dublin was haunted by an intensely personal past, Bowen's Dublin in her memoir *Seven Winters* recalls an equally inward feeling for the city, channelling her own childhood sense that the façades of brick and stone radiated something like a human personality. So, as she goes on walks with her governess, the Georgian squares appear 'cryptic and austere' and 'even along the verges of St. Stephen's Green there were canyonlike streets' that produced 'a charnel fear, of grave-dust and fungus dust'.[12] At junctures, the child's sense of the city as somehow sentient merges with the mature writer's sense of historical change:

> Often I felt a malign temper at work. Stories of gloom would add themselves to the houses, till these shut out the sky. The street tautened and the distances frowned. Walking down Upper Mount Street or Lower Baggot Street, I at once had the feeling of being in the wrong, and Leeson Street became a definite threat. [...] The tyrannical grandness of this quarter seemed to exist for itself alone. Perhaps a child smells history without knowing it – I did not know I looked at the tomb of fashion.

Elizabeth Bowen (1899–1973), a writer more commonly associated with her family estate of Bowens Court, in County Cork, or with wartime London, about which she also wrote, has written movingly about her childhood in Dublin. Photographed here by Angus McBean ca. 1949. *Alamy Images*.

One defining detail captures for Bowen the eclipse of the world into which she was born: the appearance of the brass plaques on the doors of the Georgian houses, indicating that firms of solicitors or corporate offices now occupied what had once been private homes for families like her own. 'I know now,' she reflects, stepping back from the child's view for a moment, 'it did mark the end of an epoch when the first brass plate appeared in Merrion Square.'[13]

When they were first built, the buildings around Merrion Square were single-family houses on the very edge of the city, part of the slow migration of fashionable Dublin away from streets like Henrietta Street and Dominick Street on the north side of the Liffey. So John Rocque's map of 1756 (see colour plate 2) shows open fields in what is now Merrion Square, forming part of the vista from Leinster House, the Earl of Kildare's magnificent town house. And yet, even as Rocque was drawing his map, plans were already afoot to develop the site for fashionable townhouses for families with country estates. By the 1790s, the Square would be complete, marking the city's new outer edge. Part of Neil Jordan's novel about the earl's revolutionary son, Lord Edward Fitzgerald, is set in Leinster House at the time, told from the perspective of Fitzgerald's African American companion, Tony Small. On his first morning in Leinster House, Tony looks out over 'a view of fields and the city beyond. Every year, he [Fitzgerald] told me, it continued its slow crawl towards his father's mansion and would one day spread those new streets around it, streets of brown sandstone and tall windows of barely mottled glass.'[14] And, indeed, when Baggot Street Bridge was built in 1797[15] it would open up the area beyond the canal.

By the middle decades of the nineteenth century, Merrion Square had become one of the most desirable addresses in the city. The political leader Daniel O'Connell lived at 58 Merrion Square, and the gothic novelist and editor of the *Dublin University Magazine*, Joseph Sheridan Le Fanu, lived a few doors down, at 70 Merrion Square (in a building today bearing the brass plate of the Arts Council). The poet and editor of *The Nation*, Thomas Davis, lived (and died in 1844) around the corner at 67 Upper Baggot Street. Speranza, Lady Wilde, along with her husband, the physician and antiquarian Sir William Wilde, and their son, Oscar, lived at 1 Merrion Square. Today Oscar himself reclines luxuriously in Danny Osborne's multicoloured statue (on which opinions are sharply divided) in the bushes of the Square. Just off the north-east corner of the Square in Upper Mount Street is a house that features in Iris Murdoch's 1965 novel *The Red and the Green*, set during the 1916 Rising. This is what one character calls '"one of the better-class houses" of Dublin': 'Beneath its magisterial fanlight the door was a radiant newly painted rose pink, its brass knocker, shaped like a fish, polished as softly bright and smooth as Saint Peter's toes.'[16] In the opposite direction along the street, the often-forgotten co-founder of what would become the Abbey Theatre, the deeply religious Edward Martyn, lived in monastic austerity in rooms adjoining Lincoln Place. 'Is there another man in this world whose income is two thousand a year, and who sleeps in a bare bedroom,' marvelled George Moore.[17]

By the time W. B. Yeats and George Yeats rented 82 Merrion Square in 1922, however, the brass plates were well established. Indeed, the Irish Agricultural Organisation Society, where the poet George Russell (who wrote as Æ) worked for many years, was two doors down at No. 84. Yeats, however, was always alert to the symbolism of place, and his decision to live on Merrion Square was as much a symbolic gesture as had been claiming the converted Norman tower of Thoor Ballylee in County Galway a few years earlier. 'Do you know of a house that would suit us?', Yeats wrote to Oliver St. John Gogarty in February 1922. 'Nothing modern, no modern improvements, if possible, to ruin the servants with extravagance. Ancient names cut on the glass of the window panes if possible. Mountjoy Square, Rutland Square, Stephens Green, Ely Place.' After taking up residence a few weeks later, he wrote to Olivia Shakespear that 'the rooms are very large & stately. I feel very grand especially as I remember a street ballad about the Duke of Wellington. "In Merrion Square / This noble hero first drew breath / Amid a nations cheers".'[18] The family lived here while Yeats served as a senator in the 1920s, later downsizing to a flat a short distance away at 94 Fitzwilliam Square. What Yeats fails to mention to his correspondents in 1922, however, was that in order to pay the rent, the family rented out the top floor and the stables as flats. And it was precisely this change in use – the breaking up of single-family dwellings into flats – that within a decade would populate the area with Patrick Kavanagh, Brendan Behan, and John Banville's aunt.

It was from this perspective of the middle years of the twentieth century that Bowen's *Seven Winters* – first published in 1942 – looks back. By that point, what had been city mansions were almost all flats and offices. So, in Jack White's 1962 novel *The Devil You Know* the main character, who has just taken up a job in an unnamed institute on Merrion Square, looks at the street around him. 'National Board of This. National Association of That. Were there any real people at all left in these imposing houses, or were they all dead, a row of handsome filing cabinets?'[19] It is also a detail that Joe Joyce notes in *Echoland* (2013), the first of his trilogy of richly detailed spy thrillers set in neutral Ireland during World War II. Over the course of the novel, his protagonist, Paul Duggan, spends much of his time in a building with 'a polished plaque on the door' in Merrion Square, watching the movements of a German across the park, who may or may not be a spy. 'He went past the National Gallery and Leinster Lawn and turned left into the southern side of the square. [...] Through a gap in the bushes he caught a glimpse of a mound of earth. Another air-raid shelter, he thought.'[20] Ghosting Joyce's narrative here is the fact that World War II did, in fact, bring a notable figure to Merrion Square, the physicist Erwin Schrödinger, who for seventeen years from 1939 was based at the Institute for Advanced Studies, at 64 and 65 Merrion Square, where in 1944 he wrote the lectures that became his philosophical book *What is Life?* – an episode that provides the context for Neil Belton's 2005 thriller *A Game with Sharpened Knives*.

The other great square in the area, St. Stephen's Green, has a similar, if considerably longer, history. Like Merrion Square, the Green marked the southern limit of the city until well into the nineteenth century. Indeed, the main landmark beyond the park for many years was the public gallows, and in the eighteenth century a popular genre of lurid broadsheets kept the population informed of the final words of the never-less-than-garrulous condemned. 'I am entirely Innocent; [...] neither did I know any thing of the Matter, directly or indirectly, till I came and saw her Weltering in her Gore of Blood.'[21] However, proximity to the recently hanged did nothing to limit the popularity of St. Stephen's Green for well over a century; indeed, it may even have been an attraction.

First laid out as public space in the 1650s, initially as commonage, and then as parkland in 1664, with gravel walks added in the 1680s, it was 'a controlled space for polite society' as Dublin historian David Dickson puts it.[22] One of the earliest plays to be set in Dublin takes place here: *St. Stephen's Green: Or, the Generous Lovers,* by William Philips, which premiered in the Smock Alley Theatre in 1700. Set in what was known as the Beaux Walk, a broad promenade along the

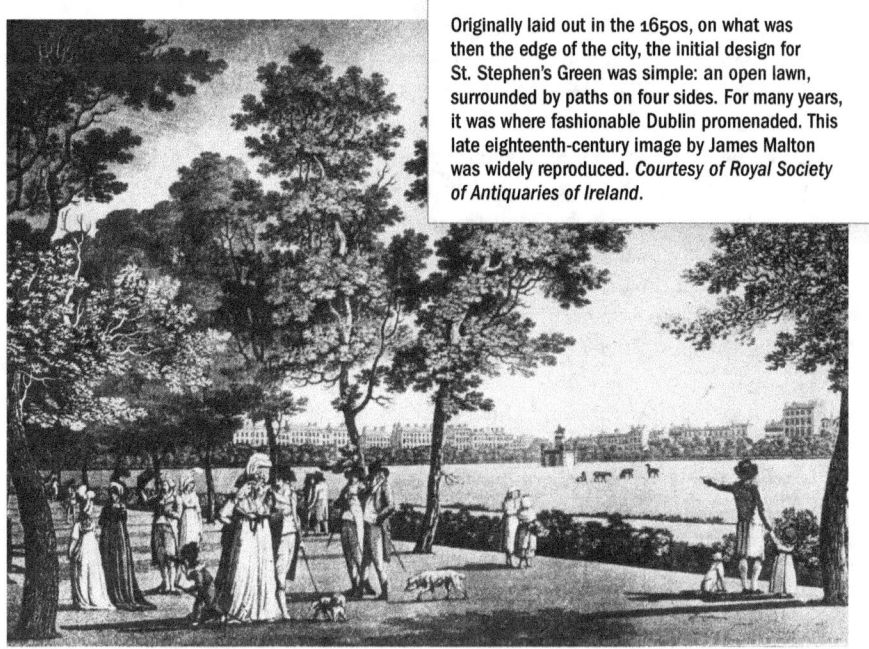

Originally laid out in the 1650s, on what was then the edge of the city, the initial design for St. Stephen's Green was simple: an open lawn, surrounded by paths on four sides. For many years, it was where fashionable Dublin promenaded. This late eighteenth-century image by James Malton was widely reproduced. *Courtesy of Royal Society of Antiquaries of Ireland.*

north side of the Green, Philips's play features a young Irish gentleman, Bellmine, and his English friend, Freelove (the names tell you all you need to know about the characters). Freelove expects to charm the Irish ladies with his London sophistication, but the steadier Bellmine warns him that Dublin is a very different place to London. 'In London, 'tis difficult to be known; here, impossible to be conceal'd. [...] I'll undertake you shall not be three days in Town, but every Body in Town will know you; nay, and know, whence you came, how long you stay, what's your Business, and if you have none, they will feign enough for you.'[23] By mid-century, the Green would amass its own literature of fashionable life, including Isaac Bickerstaffe's wonderfully titled *Stephen's Green: A Rhapsody, Exhibiting the Characters of the Belles, Beaux, Bucks, Bloods, Flashes, Fribbles, Jemmies, Jessamies, &c. of all Ranks and Professions that frequent the Beau-Walk.*[24] The poem is a mock-pastoral ode to Beaux Walk, where : "Mid trees of stunted Growth, unequal Roes, / On the coarse Gravel, trip the Belles and Beaus.'[25]

Hotels: While hotels such as the Shelbourne catered to visitors to the city, they also provided a city base for writers such as Lady Gregory, whose home was in Coole Park, County Galway. Many of her letters from Dublin are on the letterhead of the Nassau Hotel, on South Frederick Street, which is where she and Yeats first met James Joyce, inviting him to dinner there in 1902.

Elizabeth Bowen never lost the sense that places like St. Stephen's Green held traces of this older Dublin. Reviewing Stephen Gwynn's entertaining social history, *Dublin: Old and New*, in 1936, she cautioned that 'Dublin is so much more than purely spectacular; she is impregnated with a past that never evaporates.'[26] In 1951, Bowen carried out her own archaeological dig into that past when she wrote a history of the Shelbourne Hotel, which she describes as 'overhanging the ornamental landscape of trees, grass, water' of the Green, 'tall as a cliff, but more genial'. Largely dismissed by critics at the time, and ever since, *The Shelbourne* is much more than a history of the hotel, although it is that; it is really a history of Dublin seen through Bowen's well-polished lens. As Irish history flows around it, the Shelbourne Hotel becomes for Bowen a kind of still point, a splendid bow window through which the flux of time can be observed. While teaspoons clatter politely on fine bone china, outside there is the Great Irish Famine of the 1840s, the rise of nationalist politics, and the 1916 Rising, when more than 200 members of the Irish Citizen Army, among them Constance Markievicz, took over St. Stephen's Green. The hotel's initial response to the insurrection – transferring tea to the Writing Room at the rear of the building so as to take guests out of the direct line of gunfire – 'was met with disfavour'. Before long, however, guests were forced to take their tea elsewhere, as British snipers took up positions on the hotel roof from which to pick off members of the Citizen Army entrenched in the Green. 'One by one the wicked blue days burned through,' Bowen writes. 'As for nights, there were none, only a lurid dusk.'[27] What her biographer Victoria Glendinning calls 'the true Bowen note' can be heard in a later chapter, when the Irish Civil War swirls around the building in 1922, and the entire hotel is left in care of a lone assistant manager, 'apart from wild cats in the kitchen'. 'Leaping on and off the tables, glaring out from the cold blackness over the extinct ranges, these feline Maenads seemed to be chaos personified.'[28]

Venturing outside the Shelbourne, Bowen finds the neighbouring streets populated with the memories of those who lived around it. Around the corner she encounters Sydney Owenson, or Lady Morgan as she is better known, who in 1813 moved to 35 (later renumbered 39) Kildare Street, diagonally across from Leinster House. Writing to her friend, Lady Stanley, Lady Morgan describes her new home:

> We found an old, dirty, dismantled house, and we have turned our *piggery* into a decent sort of hut enough; [...] it is about *four inches by three*, and, therefore, one could afford to ornament it a *little*; it is fitted up in *gothic*, and I have collected into it the

The Shelbourne Hotel on St. Stephen's Green, is a landmark in the city. It was here, after the first production of Yeats's *Countess Cathleen*, that George Moore declared Dublin to be the new world centre of literary innovation. Moore lived around the corner, at Ely Place. *Courtesy of the National Library of Ireland.*

best part of a very good cabinet of natural history of Sir Charles [her husband], eight or nine hundred volumes of choice books in French, English, Italian, and German; some little miscellaneous curiosities, and a few scraps of old china, so that with muslin draperies, &c.. &c. I have made no *contemptible* set out.

In the same ironic tone, she continues: 'With respect to authorship, I fear it is over; I have been making chair-covers instead of periods; hanging curtains instead of raising systems, and cheapening pots and pans instead of cheapening philosophy.'[29]

In fact, far from spending her time in Kildare Street in 1813 and 1814 hanging curtains and scrubbing pots, Owenson was writing what would become her most acclaimed novel, *O'Donnel*, in which she continues her literary project of accommodating English and Irish cultures to one another. 'Literary fiction,' she writes in the novel's preface, 'has always in its most genuine form exhibited a mirror of the times in which it is composed; reflecting morals, customs, manners, peculiarity of character, and prevalence of opinion.'[30] For Owenson this meant that being a writer could never be a solitary activity;

she needed to be constantly surrounded with 'peculiarity of character' and 'opinion'. And so, 35 Kildare Street became a literary salon, one of the centres of cultural life in the Dublin of her time. 'Dublin required a Hostess,' writes Bowen: 'she was the woman. Her choice little dinners and just less exclusive *soirées* were soon talked of; she had the knack of collecting distinguished people,'[31] most notably the Dublin-born poet Thomas Moore, who sang his Irish melodies in her drawing rooms.

The other neighbour that Bowen encounters in the time-layered streets around the Shelbourne is George Moore, who from 1901 until 1911 lived at 4 Upper Ely Place – 'just the right perch for him,' comments his biographer, Adrian Frazier: 'quiet, central, and Georgian. It stood near the end of a cul-de-sac, just up the rise from the National Gallery [on Merrion Square] and National Library [on Kildare Street], and with a view from the upstairs window of a nunnery.'[32] Next door was the headquarters of the Irish Theosophical Society, whose members had included Yeats and Æ, who had rooms there in the 1880s. Moore's neighbours included the temperamentally similar Oliver St. John Gogarty, who lived at No. 15, and Sir Thornley Stoker, surgeon and brother to Bram Stoker. Like Bowen, Moore was from a landed family – the family estate, Moore Hall, was in County Mayo – and like the young Bowen, he observed the Dublin society around him 'like a spy'.

Before moving to Ely Place, George Moore's best-known Irish novel, *A Drama in Muslin* (1882), has a scene in the Shelbourne, among a group of young ladies who have come up from the country for the season, hoping to find husbands. 'Life in the Shelbourne is a thing in itself,' exclaims one of Moore's characters, in a line Bowen quotes, 'and a thing to be studied.'[33] On 11 May 1899, Moore himself was invited to speak at a dinner in the Shelbourne following the first performances of the Irish Literary Theatre (which was to become the Abbey), founded by Yeats, Lady Gregory, and Moore's friend, Edward Martyn. After watching Martyn's *The Heather Field* and Yeats's *Countess Cathleen* (which would generate protests) in the Antient Concert Rooms, about ten minutes' walk away on Great Brunswick (now Pearse) Street, the company repaired to the Shelbourne, where Moore told them he had spent the 1870s and 1880s in Paris (where he had been close to Manet, Zola, and Goncourt) because Paris was then the centre of the art world; he had gone to London in the 1890s, where he was associated with Whistler, among others, because the centre of creativity had shifted there. He was returning to Dublin, he announced, because the world had changed once again, and Dublin was now the cultural epicentre at the dawn of the new century.[34]

From the outset, Moore curated a kind of creative havoc in Ely Place. His literary reputation (he was 49 when he settled in Dublin) was based on novels showing the then-scandalous influence of Zola and French naturalism. He had no sooner taken up residence in Ely Place when the two sisters who lived next door bought a copy of his novel *Esther Waters* (about an unmarried maid who becomes pregnant) tore it to shreds, and posted the remains through his letterbox, along with a note reading 'Too filthy to keep in the house'.[35] Within a few years, he had fallen out, variously, with Martyn, Gregory and Yeats, generally for unwelcome attempts to rewrite their plays for them. And yet, for someone who was constantly quarrelling and scheming, he needed people around him. He became close to the painter William Orpen, who painted him as Manet had done in Paris twenty years earlier, and every week held regular 'Saturday Evenings' in Ely Place, with a shifting cast from the worlds of literature, journalism, and academia. One spring evening in May, 1902, he mischievously organized what he called a 'Gaelic Lawn Party', at which a play in Irish (Douglas Hyde's *An Tincéar agus an tSídheog*) was staged, and to which he invited the Catholic Archbishop of the time, with a letter beginning 'Cher Confrère'.[36] For language enthusiasts for whom the Irish-speaking peasantry of the west of Ireland were the unsullied spiritual bedrock of the language movement, the idea of a 'Gaelic Lawn Party' in the centre of fashionable Dublin was the sort of thing that fell somewhere between refreshing and deplorable. Moore fully understood that it would 'annoy Dublin society very much; which will add considerably to my pleasure.'[37]

What now appears in retrospect as Moore's major work was written in Ely Place: his three volumes of autobiography, published as *Hail and Farewell: Ave* (1911), *Salve* (1912), and *Vale* (1914). 'One half of Dublin is afraid it will be in it,' George Russell wrote to a friend in 1908, 'and the other is afraid that it won't.'[38] By the time the first volume appeared in print in 1911, Russell knew that it was time to leave Dublin. Much of the fascination of *Hail and Farewell* is in its shrewd (and often cutting) observations of the literary personalities in Dublin at the time, particularly of Yeats. Yeats in turn would respond in his autobiographical work, *Dramatis Personae*, countering Moore's jabs. 'He lacked manners,' writes Yeats, 'but had manner; he could enter a room so as to draw your attention without seeming to.'[39] However, beyond literary character assassination, Dublin itself comes alive in *Hail and Farewell* as a place of continual performance, seen through Moore's amused, sardonic eyes:

> We writers are always glad of any little excuse for an afternoon walk. [...] The Green tempted me, and I thought of Grafton Street [...] [*Daily Express* editor T. P.] Gill would be floating along there, lost in admiration of his own wisdom. Sir Thornley Stoker rarely misses Grafton Street between four and five; I should certainly catch sight of him hopping about a silversmith's, like an old magpie, prying out spoons and forks, and the immodest bulk of Lady Waldron, waiting outside for him, looking into the window. A hundred other odds and oddments I should meet there, every one amusing to see and to hear.

Among Moore's neighbours at Ely Place was Oliver St. John Gogarty, whom he describes in *Salve* as 'the arch-mocker, the author of all the jokes that enable us to live in Dublin; [...] a survivor of the Bardic Age he is, reciting whole ballads to me when we go for walks.'[40] Gogarty was a gregarious polymath, variously a surgeon, poet, playwright, novelist, founding member of Sinn Féin, and later a senator; and, like Moore, perhaps now best remembered for a memoir, *As I Was Going Down Sackville Street* (1937). 'Quaintly he came raiking out of Molesworth Street into Kildare Street,' it opens, 'an odd figure moidered by memories and driven mad by dreams which had overflowed into life, making him turn himself into a merry mockery of all he had once held dear.' He goes on to describe this figure (who is Gogarty himself), wearing 'a tail-coat over white cricket trousers which were caught at the ankle by a pair of cuffs,' carrying under his arm 'two sabres in shining scabbards of patent leather.' 'Dublin had accepted him,' Gogarty writes, 'as the present representative and chief of those eccentric and genial characters whom it never fails to produce every generation.'

Gogarty's Dublin is a city just large enough to accommodate eccentric characters, but not so large that individual character of any sort becomes lost in an anonymous crowd. No one in Gogarty's Dublin is unknown. So, the opening of *As I Was Going Down Grafton Street* brings Gogarty into the National Library of Ireland's Reading Room on Kildare Street, 'a large building roofed by a cylinder arch [with] two domes, the second being the bald head of its librarian, Lyster.'[41] This is Thomas William Lyster, director of the Library from 1895 until 1920, whom we meet in mid-sentence at the beginning of the 'Scylla and Charybdis' episode of James Joyce's *Ulysses* (1922): 'Urbane, to comfort

A haven for writers since it opened on Kildare Street in 1890, the National Library of Ireland houses one of the great collections of Irish literature. The building features at key points both in Joyce's *Ulysses* and *Portrait of the Artist*. Photography by Seán Harrison.

them, the quaker librarian purred: – And we have, have we not, those priceless pages of *Wilhelm Meister*?' The effect here, at the beginning of the chapter of Joyce's novel, is to throw the reader into the midst of an ongoing conversation, which will involve not only Joyce's alter ego, Stephen Dedalus, but also the character with whom the entire novel opens, 'stately, plump Buck Mulligan', based on Gogarty himself. 'A tall figure in bearded homespun rose from shadow and unveiled its cooperative watch. – I am afraid I am due at the *Homestead*.' This is George Russell (Æ), who maintained a firm belief in a spirit world (and hence his rising 'from shadow'), edited the *Irish Homestead* magazine, and helped run the Irish Agricultural Organisation Society (or cooperative movement – hence the 'cooperative watch') around the corner at 84 Merrion Square. '– Are you going, John Eglinton's active eyebrows asked. Shall we see you at Moore's tonight?'[42] Eglinton edited the journal *Dana*, in which Gogarty, Russell, and Moore all published, as did Joyce himself. In this little vignette from *Ulysses*, then, we glimpse the tightly knit literary world of Dublin in the early decades of the twentieth century. Describing a literary evening in Dublin in 1917, an English visitor to the city wrote: 'And what talk! [...] In Dublin I have never detected the faintest trace of the mental constipation from which England is suffering.'[43]

Partly because of their centrality, and partly because of their human scale, the streets around St. Stephen's Green would continue to be one of the main places in which Dubliners encountered one another, sometimes by chance, for long afterwards. It is this world that is annexed by the Baggotonians in the 1940s and 1950s, and it is here that Edna O'Brien sets a pivotal moment in her 1962 novel *The Lonely Girl*, about the relationship between a young country girl, Kate, and an older filmmaker. 'As usual I went to the bookshop at the bottom of Dawson Street where I had my free read every week,' she tells us. 'I read twenty-eight pages of *The Charwoman's Daughter* [by James Stephens] without being disturbed, and then came out, as I had an appointment to see Baba in O'Connell Street. Coming down the steps from the bookshop, I met him [the film-maker] point-blank.'[44] 'In a little city like Dublin one meets every person whom one knows within a few days,' writes James Stephens in the novel that Kate is reading, *The Charwoman's Daughter* (1912). 'Around each bend in the road there is a friend, an enemy, or a bore striding towards you, so that, with a piety which is almost religious, one says "touch wood" before turning any corner.'[45]

These streets also contain the greatest concentration of public buildings in the city. On Kildare Street, the National Library faces its mirror image in the National Museum of Ireland across the open space in front of Leinster House, which began as home of the Duke of Leinster, became headquarters of the Royal Dublin Society, and is now the seat of Irish government. As the area became an administrative district, many of its buildings were converted into government offices, occupied by figures such as the protagonist of Máirtín Ó Cadhain's richly satiric Irish-language novella, *An Eochar (The Key)* (1953), a Kafkaesque story of a civil servant who dies after being locked in his office because no one can determine the correct protocol for finding the key. Other buildings on these streets have cultural associations, such as the Royal Irish Academy on Dawson Street, or, on the Merrion Square side of the Kildare Street buildings, the National Gallery of Ireland, which continues to benefit significantly from an endowment from royalties from the works of George Bernard Shaw. Next door is the Natural History Museum, which is one of the landmarks in Paula Meehan's poem 'A Child's Map of Dublin':

> *The Natural History Museum: found poem*
> *of oriole, kingfisher, sparrowhawk, nightjar*
> *but the gull drew me strongest – childhood guide*
> *to the freedom and ecstasy of flight.*[46]

These streets, then, are a place of public memory. In one of her final poems, 'Statue 1916', Eavan Boland writes of the memorial in St. Stephen's Green to Constance Markievicz, whose bust now sits in the park she helped to commandeer in 1916:

> Stephen's Green. A half torso.
> Her head and shoulders framed
> by the coarse flowers of the boxwood shrub.[47]

Not far away is a haunting bust of the nineteenth-century poet James Clarence Mangan, while better hidden is Henry Moore's bronze sculpture of Yeats, which Colm Tóibín describes 'in its strange isolation, its purity, its odd nobility' as 'one of the most beautiful and powerful places in Dublin, full of a secret energy worthy of the great old ghost.'[48] Less shrouded by shrubbery is the monument to James Joyce, who peers myopically across the south side of the Green towards the building that once housed University College Dublin (UCD), where he had been a student.

Until it moved to a greenfield site on the outskirts of Dublin, the UCD campus was woven into the streets around the Green, with buildings in Earlsfort Terrace, Merrion Square, and its medical faculty at a slight remove in Cecilia Street, in Temple Bar. Initially, however, the main site was No. 86 St. Stephen's Green (which in 2019 was converted into the Museum of Literature, Ireland, or MoLI). As the university's first Rector, John Henry Newman worked here; and the poet Gerard Manley Hopkins taught, lived, and later died in the building in 1889. There was more than a touch of irony in the establishment of what was then Ireland's Catholic university

Henry Moore's statue of W. B. Yeats in St. Stephen's Green. 'This circle where the bronze stands,' writes Colm Tóibín, 'in its strange isolation, its purity, its odd nobility, is one of the most beautiful and powerful places in Dublin, full of a secret energy worth of the great old ghost.' *Photography by Seán Harrison.*

in what had originally been the home of a famous eighteenth-century gambler, Thomas 'Buck' Whaley. Whaley would posthumously become a successful author when his memoirs appeared, containing his lively account of what became known as his 'Jerusalem Wager'. In 1789, at dinner with his neighbour across the Green, the Duke of Leinster, he boasted that he was going to walk to Jerusalem (then under control of the Ottomans, and hence out of bounds to most Western Europeans) and return within two years. When he was laughed down, Whaley later wrote, it 'touched me in the tender point: the difficulty in an undertaking always stimulated me to the attempt,' and so 'I accepted without hesitation all wagers that were offered me.' By the time he left Leinster House that evening, he had more than 'twelve thousand pounds' (worth just over €2 million today)[49] wagered against him. Two years and some remarkable adventures later, Dubliners lined the streets as he triumphantly returned to collect his winnings.

The memory of Whaley floats up through Joyce's *A Portrait of the Artist as a Young Man* (1916) when Stephen Dedalus, who is a student in the university, walks up Grafton Street, and crosses St. Stephen's Green, where the trees 'were fragrant and the rainsodden earth gave forth its mortal odour, a faint incense rising upward through the mould from many hearts [...] and he knew that in a moment when he entered the solemn college he would be conscious of a corruption other than that of Buck Egan and Burnchapel Whaley.'[50] The memory of Buck Whaley here precedes what is probably one of the most resonant moments in Irish writing for the entire period of the Irish Literary Revival. This is the passage in which Stephen goes into the college building on the Green, and helps the English-born Dean of Studies to light an oil lamp. When the Dean directs him in the use of a 'funnel', Stephen replies:

– Is that called a funnel? Is it not a tundish?
– What is a tundish?
– That. The ... funnel.
– Is that called a tundish in Ireland? asked the dean. I never heard the word in my life.
– It is called a tundish in Lower Drumcondra, said Stephen laughing, where they speak the best English.

In spite of his laughter, the exchange continues to play on Stephen's mind: 'The language in which we are speaking is his before it is mine.

How different are the words *home, Christ, ale, master,* on his lips and on mine! I cannot speak or write these words without unrest of spirit. His language, so familiar and so foreign, will always be for me an acquired speech.'[51] No less than the ghosts of fashion that the young Elizabeth Bowen sensed in the brooding houses of Merrion Square, Joyce's Stephen here recognizes something about this area of Dublin. Here, even the simplest things can be weighted with multiple pasts, which can be both a snare and the stuff of literature.

1. Site of Thingmote, College Green (approx.)
2. Provost's House, 1 Grafton Street
3. Campanile
4. Front Square
5. Library Buildings
6. Botany Bay
7. Samuel Beckett's Rooms, 39 New Square
8. Queen's Theatre Royal, 212 Pearse Street
9. Birthplace of Oscar Wilde 21 Westland Row

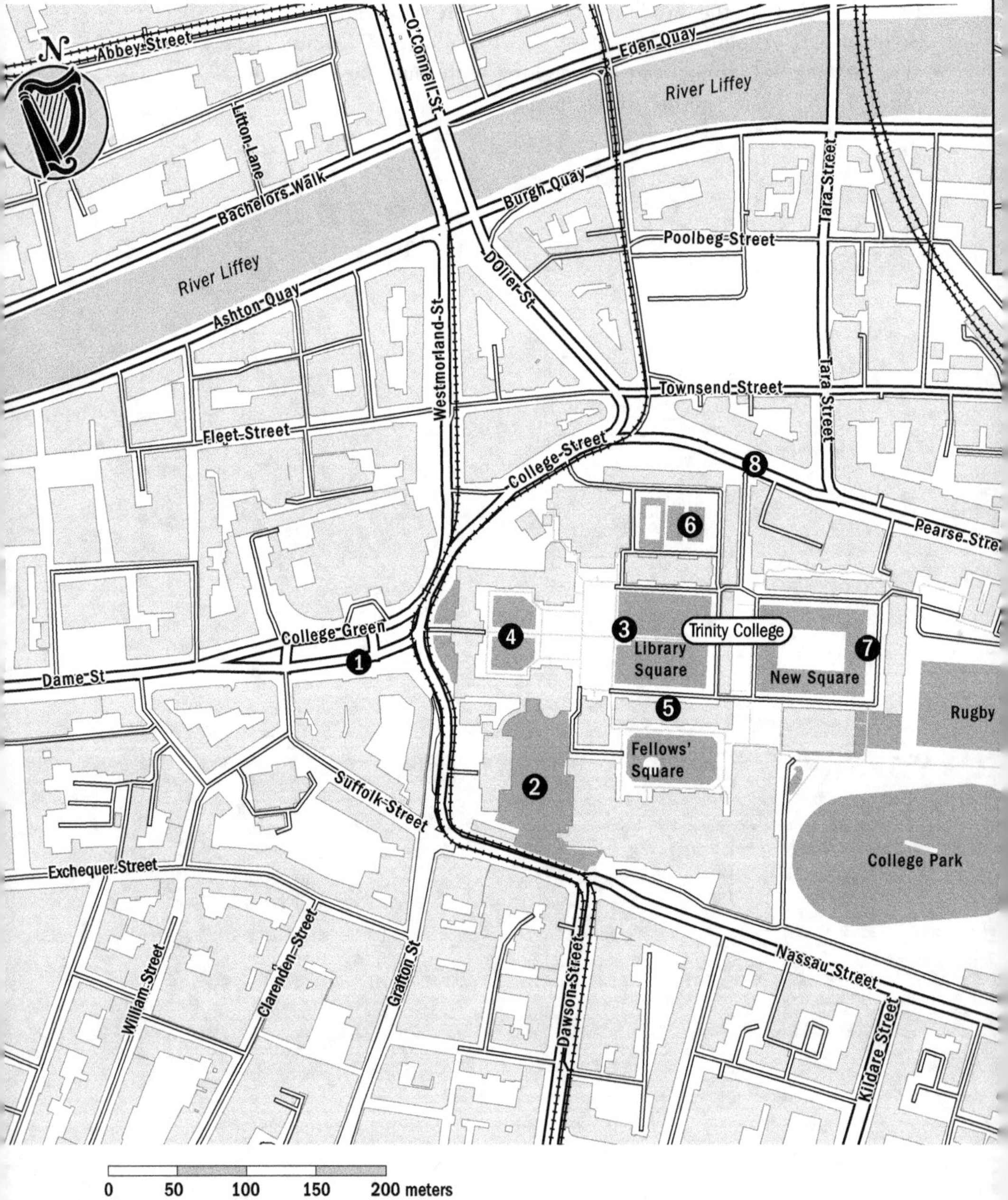

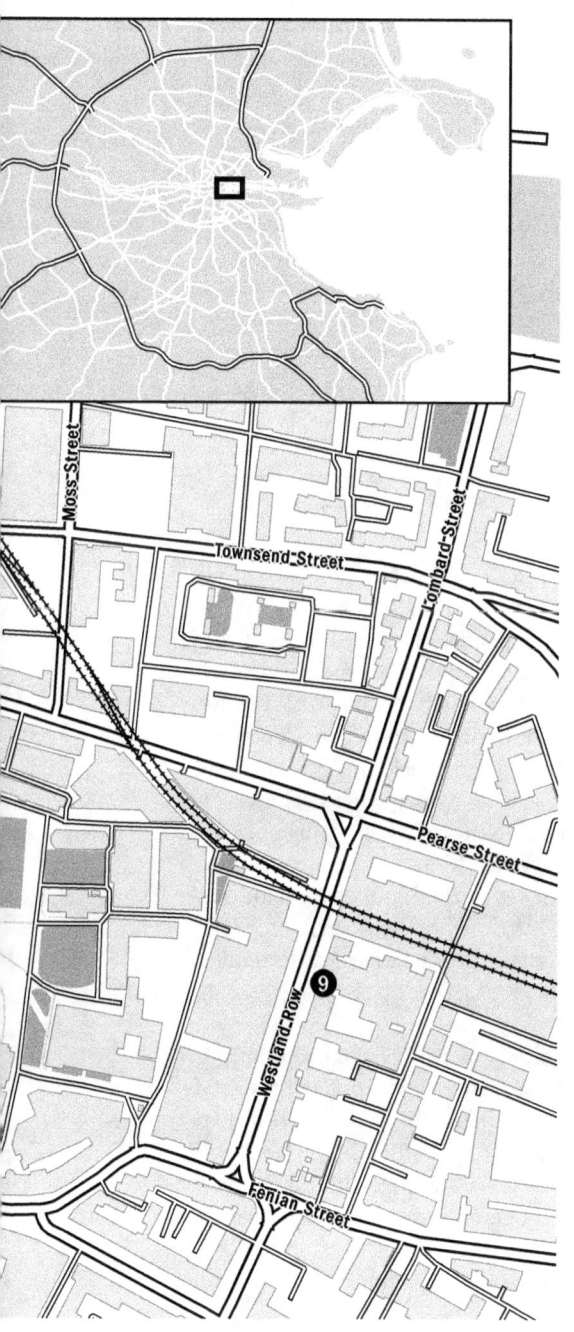

Trinity College

4

'This is perhaps the most interesting place in Dublin,' writes James Stephen of the junction of Grafton Street and Nassau Street in *The Charwoman's Daughter* (1912):

> Upon one vista Grafton Street with its glittering shops stretches [...]. On the left Nassau Street, broad and clean, and a trifle vulgar and bourgeois in its openness, runs away to Merrion Square, and on with a broad ease to Blackrock and Kingstown and the sea. On the right hand Suffolk Street, reserved and shy, twists up to St. Andrew's Church, touches gingerly the South City Markets, droops to George's Street, and is lost in mean and dingy intersections. At the back of the crossing Grafton Street continues again for a little distance down to Trinity College (at the gates whereof very intelligent young men flaunt very tattered gowns and smoke massive pipes with great skill for their years), skirting the Bank of Ireland, and on to the river Liffey.[1]

Stephens's novel filters its view of the city through the eyes of a young woman – Mary Makebelieve, the 'charwoman's daughter' of the title – who lives in a tenement on the city's northside. Mary finds herself in a relationship with a man from a wealthier background, and this brings her into unaccustomed parts of the city. As such, her view of Trinity College is telling: she sees no further than its front gate. 'Between the Trinity College railings and the start of Sackville Street [now O'Connell Street] from the bridge there is an opaqueness or blank in my memory,' writes Elizabeth Bowen in *Seven Winters*, seeing the city again through the eyes of her seven-year-old self. 'Through a thinning of the mist I just see the colonnades of the Bank of Ireland, that had been Our Own Parliament once.'[2] Where Stephens's narrator sees gates, the young Bowen (even though her own father had attended Trinity) sees railings.

This image of Trinity as gates and railings is part of the imagining of Dublin that goes back to some of the earliest visualizations of the city, such as John Speed's 1610 map of the city, where 'the Colledge' is drawn as a walled compound. Trinity had been first built in 1592, not long before Speed drew his map, on what had been the site of an Augustinian monastery facing a greenfield site, Hoggen Green, which was then at the outer edge of the medieval city. The architectural historian Niall McCullough, in his *Dublin: An Urban History*, reminds us that the

Although originally built on the periphery of the old city, from the eighteenth century onwards, College Green in front of Trinity became a centre point for Dublin, a place where roads and people meet. This image is from the 1920s. *Courtesy of Royal Society of Antiquaries of Ireland.*

medieval Hoggen Green occupied the ground of an even earlier site of importance in Viking Dublin, the Thingmote, or ceremonial assembly mound, located between what is now Suffolk Street and College Green. Here, the very first urban Dubliners gathered to hold meetings and pass the laws that shaped their city. A persistent sense that this is a point of convergence continues today, amplified by the criss-crossing here of so many of Dublin's north-south public transport routes. In the early twentieth century, it was where the original tramlines met; today, it is where major bus routes cross the Luas tramline. And it is here, at the nexus of intersecting flows of commuters and of history, that Trinity sits, surrounded by walls and entered through a gate, both part of, and apart from, from the city flowing around it.

'Very pleasant to be away from the noise of the streets, which makes but a dreamy hum in the distance,' observes an account of student life from 1892. 'The place, despite its gloominess of face, has the charm of stillness and seclusion in the heart of the city.'[3] Stephen Dedalus (who attends the rival University College Dublin, on St. Stephen's Green), passing the Front Gates in Joyce's *A Portrait of the Artist as a Young Man* (1916), registers 'the grey block of Trinity on his left, set heavily in the city's ignorance like a great dull stone set in a cumbersome ring.'[4]

His counterpart, Leopold Bloom, in the 'Lestrygonians' episode of *Ulysses* (1922), notes Trinity's 'surly front' as he passes by the Provost's House, well protected from the lower end of Grafton Street by a high wall. Bloom passes by the House on 16 June 1904, five months after the Provost of the time, George Salmon, had passed away in the house on 22 January. 'Provost's House,' thinks Bloom to himself. 'The reverend Dr Salmon: tinned salmon. Well tinned in there. Wouldn't live in it if you paid me' – after which his thoughts turn towards lunch in a more congenial public space, Davy Byrne's 'moral pub' on Duke Street (connecting Grafton and Dawson streets), where a glass of burgundy and a gorgonzola cheese sandwich await him[5] – not salmon.

The sense of Trinity's campus being defined by its walls and gates lingers in more recent writing, even though the grounds are now effectively public parks, where nearby office workers eat their lunches, and tourists photograph themselves on the cobbles. In Louise Nealon's campus novel *Snowflake* (2021), for instance, her narrator, Debbie, recalls that before becoming a student, when she would visit Dublin with her uncle Billy, from rural Kildare, he always 'pointed at the high

From the air, Trinity's plan, organized around a series of squares, becomes apparent, as does the way in which the campus is a kind of green oasis in the centre of the city. This aerial photo from 1954 is part of a series taken by Alexander Campbell Morgan. *Courtesy of the National Library of Ireland.*

stone walls and spiked railings at the side entrance on Nassau Street but we never went in. I don't think he realized that it was open to the public. I always thought of Trinity as a reverse *Shawshank Redemption* situation, where you had to bribe Morgan Freeman with cigarettes and tunnel your way in.'[6]

If for the city's *flâneurs* (whether Bloom, or Debbie and her uncle Billy), the granite bulk of Trinity acts like a rock in a stream, forcing them to flow around it, inside there is an oasis of quiet. All cities have these zones of quiet, where a revolving door seals behind you, or you step into the hushed, air-conditioned atrium of an office foyer. However, most are private spaces, accessible only to those with the right swipe card. Parks, of course, produce the same effect of crossing from one type of urban space into another. Step through the gates into St. Stephen's Green or Merrion Square, and you pass from the diesel roar of buses to the smell of moist earth and the rustle of birds in the bushes. Parks, however, are both fully public and places of leisure; the point of going into a public park is often precisely to do nothing: to sit, to lounge, perhaps eat a sandwich, read a book, watch the world go by. What makes the Trinity campus distinctive is that it is not fully private – it does not feel like stepping into someone's office foyer to eat your sandwich – and yet neither is it fully a public place of leisure; you are aware that people all around are teaching, working in labs, and writing books (such as the one that you are reading right now). And you are aware of conversations. This is a particular version of the oasis effect: a place quiet enough to converse, sometimes with purpose, sometimes just for the pure joy of it.

> **Trinity's Old Library:** Completed in 1732 after a period of political upheaval, the Old Library's most impressive feature is its Long Room, whose vaulted ceilings run almost the entire length of a building filled with some of the library's oldest books. The College's libraries have had legal deposit status since 1801, which means that they hold copies of all books published since 1801, not only in Ireland but also in the United Kingdom.

So, for instance, in one of the many of nineteenth-century novelist Charles Lever's works in which Trinity features, *The O'Donoghue* (1845), a character visiting a friend in college is struck, on stepping through the Front Gate, by the 'sudden change from the tumult and noise of a crowded city to the silence and quietude of these spacious quadrangles.'[7] George Birmingham's 1906 novel *Hyacinth* compares 'the material fabric, the actual stone and mortar' of Trinity to Oxford and Cambridge, where 'shops jostle and elbow colleges in the street. In Dublin a man leaves the city behind him when he enters the college, passes completely out of the atmosphere of the University when he steps on to the pavement. [...] The rattle of traffic, the jangling of cart bells, the inarticulate babel of voices, suddenly cease when the archway of the great entrance-gate is passed. An immense silence takes their place.'[8] Oliver St. John Gogarty, who studied medicine at Trinity, describes a similar effect of walking into the college from one of the busiest intersections in the city: 'The way through the Front Gate divides the great quad of Trinity College, which opens on a large cobbled space. In the lawn of each stands a great oak. Old grey houses with windows framed in lighter stone shelter the immense trees. In front, the graceful campanile stands between the Library and the Graduates' Memorial.'

Gogarty is writing this in 1937, in his memoir *As I Was Going Down Sackville Street*, and he goes on to imagine that, having passed through Front Gate, he sees a Provost of the College from earlier in the century, John Pentland Mahaffy, emerging from the discreet internal entrance to the Provost's House in the corner of the square, 'over six-foot and over seventy, unbowed, with head slightly inclined, I see him talking to some attentive Fellow.' The key word here is 'talking': Mahaffy was not only a famously witty and opiniated talker, he had written a serious academic treatise on the topic: *The Principles of the Art of Conversation* (1887). 'There can be no doubt,' begins this study by a scholar of classical civilization, 'that of all the accomplishments prized in modern society that of being agreeable in conversation is the very first.'[9] Mahaffy's world was one that took conversation seriously.

The Long Room in the Old Library in Trinity College, Dublin, is one of the great triumphs of eighteenth-century Dublin architecture. It still functions as storage for books, and occasionally as a film set. Photography by Seán Harrison.

Among Mahaffy's students in Trinity was Oscar Wilde, for whom conversation was more than simply an accomplishment; it was an art. Wilde had been born at 21 Westland Row, in a building that is now part of the Trinity campus, before the family moved around the corner to 1 Merrion Square. Wilde entered Trinity in 1871, won a gold medal for Greek in 1874, lived in rooms in the part of the campus known as Botany Bay, and later travelled to Italy and Greece with Mahaffy. In this respect, he could not be more of a Dublin writer. And, although he never wrote anything substantial about Dublin (nor, indeed, about Ireland for that matter), his contemporaries in Ireland saw Wilde as an Irish writer. When one of his earliest collections, *Lord Arthur Saville's Crime and Other Prose Pieces* was first published in 1891, W. B. Yeats, reviewing it in the newspaper *United Ireland*, observed that while English readers might misunderstand Wilde, 'we should not find him so unintelligible – for much about him is Irish of the Irish. I see in his life and works an extravagant Celtic crusade against Anglo-Saxon stupidity.'[10] When Wilde's play *Lady Windermere's Fan* (1892) appeared the following year, followed by *The Importance of Being Earnest* (1895) a few years later, it was clear that these works were open to multiple, coded readings – an effect that was amplified when it later became known that Wilde was gay. What to one audience might appear as the archetypal London drawing-room comedy could appear to another audience as parody, staging not so much a society as an attitude to that society. And the whole apparently effortless edifice of deceptive appearances on which the plays sit relies primarily on immaculately crafted conversation – which in turn brings us back to the Dubliner tutored by the author of *The Principles of the Art of Conversation*.

Around the corner from where Wilde had rooms is New Square, where Samuel Beckett lived as a student in a ground-floor room, to the left of the door of House 39. If Wilde's writing is often characterized by a provocative extravagance of language, Beckett might be thought of as his polar opposite, the writer for whom there was nothing left to say, and nothing with which to say it. However, this is something of an oversimplification, for Beckett's early works are, if anything, even more full of language tripping over itself than Wilde's. What is more, many of them take place not in the almost abstract wasteland of his better-known plays, but in a recognizable Dublin. So, for instance, the story 'A Wet Night' in *More Pricks than Kicks* (1934) begins in College Green, just outside the Front Gate of Trinity, proceeds by way of discussion of the philosopher Henri Bergson to a pub in Lincoln Place (just outside the rear gate of the campus), where the protagonist, Belacqua, encounters a poet, 'two banned novelists, a bibliomaniac and his mistress, [...], a chorus of playwrights, the inevitable envoy of the Fourth Estate, a phalanx of Grafton Street Stürmers and Jemmy Higgins.' Somewhat later, and a little the worse for wear after his exertions in the pub, Belacqua 'keyed up to take his bearings, issued forth into the unintelligible world of Lincoln Place. [...] He set off unsteadily by the Dental Hospital [which forms part of the southern side of the campus]. As a child he had dreaded its façade, its sheets of blood-red glass. Now they were brick, which was worse again, he having put aside a childish thing or two.'[11] The stories in *More Pricks than Kicks* were largely written at the time, just after he had graduated from Trinity, when Beckett worked for a short time in the offices of his father's surveying firm, which was located at No. 6 Clare Street, around the corner from Lincoln Place. Local lore has it that he also wrote much of the novel *Murphy* there. Whatever the case, Colm Tóibín, observing that Beckett did little of the work for which he was actually paid in the office, remarks: 'It would look good on a plaque: "This is where Samuel Beckett did nothing much."'[12]

Wilde and Beckett both, then, inhabit the Trinity campus and its environs, but in different ways. There is a danger here, however, of falling prey to a kind of competitive Irishness (or, indeed, Dublin-ness); is Beckett more Irish than Wilde because he wrote about the city, while Wilde was only born and educated here, and his sensibility has certain qualities that we can ascribe to Dublin? It is worth recalling here the conversational peril of what Mahaffy would have called 'a specialist subject'. And the danger with a specialist, writes Mahaffy in his *Principles of the Art of Conversation*, 'is that he will not leave his subject when it has been sufficiently discussed, as he will probably gauge the interest of others by his own preoccupation, and so may become not a blessing but a bore to his company.'[13] Debates over the Irishness of a given writer are particularly prone to the perils of the specialist subject. What is more, they tend to be magnified in the four acres or so of the Trinity campus.

There are good historical reasons for this, many of them arising out of the contradictions that inevitably attach themselves to a university dating back to 1592, founded by members of a ruling class in a colonial society, and located in the middle of a capital city. Throughout much of its history, Trinity was closely associated people such as Elizabeth Bowen's father, members of the Church of Ireland known as the Anglo-Irish, whose interests and sympathies were, to some extent, tied to England. For centuries, it was where soldiers (such as the playwright George Farquhar), Church of Ireland clergy (such as Jonathan Swift), civil servants (such as Bram Stoker, before he became a theatre manager), or members of the professional classes (such as Charles Lever or Oliver St. John Gogarty, both of whom were medical doctors) were educated. For instance, when W. B. Yeats was weaving the myth of his personal history of the Anglo-Irish in his poem 'The Seven Sages' (1932), all four names he invokes as his symbolic forebears were educated at Trinity, and each has a different relationship to what it means to be Irish, beginning with '[Oliver] Goldsmith and [Edmund] Burke, [Jonathan] Swift and the Bishop of Cloyne'[14] (the Bishop of Cloyne being the philosopher George Berkeley). There can be a tendency, then, to see the enclosed space of the campus as a kind of bastion of an older order, a sort of island of colonial culture left stranded by a rising tide of a Catholic nationalism, against which the gates act as a kind of flood defence. And, while there would have been periods where there was certainly truth to this perception, at the same time the flows back and forth between the campus and the city around it have rarely been so simple.

Sometimes, a single moment can capture these complexities like a sort of imaginary photograph. For instance, the northern edge of the campus, adjoining what is now Pearse (but was then Great Brunswick) Street shared street frontage with the Queen's Theatre, built in 1844 and demolished in 1969 (the newly opened student accommodation of Printing House Square now occupies the site). One evening in 1894, the Queen's

Although set off from the city, the Trinity campus has always been close to the centres of government. The Parliament House, opposite the Front Gate of Trinity on College Green, has been one of Dublin's finest buildings since it was built in 1729. It has been a bank since 1803, and part of it now houses a permanent exhibition on Seamus Heaney. *Photography by Seán Harrison.*

was offering the kind of play for which it was known, J. W. Whitbread's *Wolfe Tone*, a wildly popular patriotic melodrama of the time featuring a nationalist hero from Ireland's past. Plays about Tone (there were more than one) were particularly popular in the lead-up to the centenary of the 1798 rebellion, for not only had he been one of its leaders but his writings had laid the foundations for Irish republicanism and were widely read at the time. His relevance to understanding the space of the Trinity campus in the city, however, comes in the recognition that before he published his *Argument on Behalf of the Catholics of Ireland* in 1791, or helped to found the United Irishmen in 1794, Wolfe Tone had been a somewhat unwilling Trinity law student. As he admits in his autobiography, 'I began to look upon classical learning as nonsense; on a Fellowship in Dublin College as a pitiful establishment; and, in short, I thought an ensign in a marching regiment was the happiest creature living.'[15]

A century or so later, the stage character of Wolfe Tone who walked out on to the stage of the Queen's was an almost legendary hero to the audience, the ideal type of the republican revolutionary. This was particularly so for the lively, working-class audience of the Queen's, who talked and smoked during performances, and who cheered heroes like Tone and Robert Emmet, and hissed the informers who betrayed them. This audience also would have had a very clear sense of the class differences separating them from the students inside the walls only a few metres away, all of whom at the time would have been from the professional or landed classes. All of these factors played a role in what happened on a night in 1894 when Whitbread's play opened with Tone the Trinity student saving a College porter (played with a stage version of the same Dublin working-class accent of much of the audience) from being beaten by a gang of rowdy Trinity toffs. The stage directions read: *Enter* Shane, *a College Porter*.

(He sings quietly as he comes down. He looks R. and L., then up. Enter two STUDENTS. *One knocks his cap over his face.)*
SHANE: Murther alive! what's that? (*Other student hits him in the stomach*). Oh! I'm kilt. (*Dances about with hand on stomach*) Murther, thaves! (*Students laugh and exunt R. Enter* RUSSELL [Thomas Russell a United Irishman and colleague of Tone].
RUSSELL: Do you know Mr. Wolfe Tone?
SHANE: Is it Mr. Theobald Wolfe Tone? (RUSSELL *bows*). No one bether. Whether at larnin', dhrinkin' or larkin' wid the petticoats, he's always to the fore.[16]

What makes this otherwise ephemeral moment so evocative of Trinity's relationship to the city around it was the way in which it was staged. Rather than build a set that looked like Trinity on the stage of the Queen's, Whitbread simply opened the loading bay doors at the rear of the stage, so that the audience were looking straight through the theatre into the grounds of the College itself (into what would have been New Square, where Beckett would have his rooms), making it part of the set. The world of the Queen's audience, and the quiet of a College square at night were two very different places; but the distinctive intimacy of Dublin placed them not just side by side, but in a situation in which one literally framed the other.

We can hold this image in our mind for thinking about the campus's relationship to the city. For instance, few individuals did more in nineteenth-century Ireland to shape the idea of an Irish national literature than the poet and journalist Thomas Davis, one of the founders of the Young Ireland movement and author of the poem 'A Nation Once Again' (1844):

> *And then I prayed I yet might see*
> *Our fetters rent in twain,*
> *And Ireland, long a province, be*
> *A NATION ONCE AGAIN.*[17]

Like Tone, Davis had been a Trinity student, and in 1839 he gave an address to the College Historical Society (of which Tone had also been Auditor) entitled 'Patriotism': 'It is sweet to look back on those times when our country was great and free,' he told his listeners. As the historian James Quinn comments, 'looking back on the origins of Young Ireland, Davis identified the College Historical Society [...] as the cradle of the movement.'[18] The newspaper that Davis founded with another Trinity student, John Blake Dillon, and Charles Gavan Duffy, *The Nation*, whose offices were nearby at 12 Trinity Street, would become the centre of the Young Ireland movement, responsible for publishing vast quantities of patriotic poetry, which, when collected as *The Spirit of the Nation* (1844, and later expanded) became what is claimed to have been the best-selling Irish book of the entire nineteenth century. 'One of the very means of attaining nationality is securing some portion of that literary force which would gush abundantly from it,'[19] Davis had declared, ensuring that the poetic and political were inextricably entangled in Ireland for many years to come.

The Nation was not the only newspaper to be located in the streets around the Trinity campus over the years. In 1844, *The Nation* relocated to D'Olier Street, where in 1859 *The Irish Times* would begin publishing. Initially launched as a low-cost paper for the unionist middle classes, it began to reinvent itself after Irish Independence in 1922 as a newspaper of record, by the 1960s giving voice to a cultural pluralism that ran counter to the grain of the time. We see early intimations of this as early as 8 September 1913, for instance, when, in the middle of the Dublin Lock-out, the paper published Yeats's poem 'Romance in Ireland', which later became 'September 1913'. 'What need you, being come to sense, / But fumble in a greasy till / And add the halfpence to the pence / And prayer to shivering prayer [...]'.[20] The paper's importance in the literary world of Dublin rose under the editorship of Robert (known as 'Bertie') Smyllie, a larger-than-life (in every respect) figure, who edited the paper during decades (1934–1954, to be precise) in which writers such as Brendan Behan, Patrick Kavanagh, and Brian O'Nolan (whose 'Cruiskeen Lawn' column appeared in the *Times*) dominated Dublin literary life. For the writers in the *Irish Times* in those years, the Pearl Bar on Fleet Street, and the Palace Bar further along were effectively extensions of the newspaper office. Indeed, when one of the paper's former editors, Conor Brady, took up writing crime novels set in the 1880s, he has his detective regularly meet journalists for discrete assignations amid 'the fine mahogany counters and polished leather seating,'[21] of the Palace.

> **Irish Times:** One of the more interesting cases of adaptation to circumstances in post-Independence Ireland was made by the *Irish Times*. Founded in 1859 as a penny unionist newspaper, it famously denounced the Easter Rising in 1916; however, by the 1930s it had come around to a culturally pluralist editorial position, often critical of literary censorship, supportive of Irish writing, and providing an important place for literary reviewing.

If McDaid's pub formed one pole of the geography of literary pubs in the Ireland of mid-century, the Palace formed the other. What made the Palace and the Pearl so important in creating a public literary culture was the personal connection that formed between writers and journalists, so that the newspaper became, as Terence Brown writes in his history of *Irish Times*, 'a place where a post-Yeatsian generation of poets could see their work in print,'[22] working with editors and journalists they knew personally. In 1940, the paper published a cartoon by the caricaturist Alan Reeve, entitled 'Dublin Culture' (so popular that in June of that year it went on display in the window of Brown Thomas's department store in Grafton Street), showing the backroom of the Palace, with Smyllie front and centre, Patrick Kavanagh slouching, Flann O'Brien sitting near him, and around them forty or so other writers, artists, and journalists. What strikes us today looking at this image is both what is missing (there are no women in the room) and what is present: a culture in which talking and writing were part of a continuum.

This culture of conversation flowed back and forth through the gates of Trinity from the surrounding city in many different ways over the centuries. It was here that Máirtín Ó Cadhain spent his final years as Professor of Irish, best known for what is arguably the greatest Irish-language novel of the past century, *Cré na Cille*, of which a recent translator, Alan Titley, claims, 'talk is the principal character.'[23] However, there can be few writers associated with Trinity for whom the continuum of writing and speaking was as important as it was for Edmund Burke. Like Tone and Davis, in the 1740s Burke was Auditor (and, in his case, founder) of the debating club that would later become the College Historical Society. The intellectual historian Ian Harris has argued that in order 'to individuate Burke, we must turn to what he acquired from the Trinity syllabus.'[24] These roots go deep in several directions. However, there is a specific moment – and a specific place – that grounds Burke in Dublin even more firmly than his reading in the College Library. Apart from his extensive writings on political philosophy, Burke's major philosophical work was first written when he was only nineteen, and still a Trinity undergraduate, although it was published later. *A Philosophical Enquiry into the Origin of our Ideas of the Sublime and Beautiful* (1757) was to have a profound effect on writers

Alan Reeve's cartoon from 1940 shows the mingling of literary and journalistic worlds in the Palace Bar on Fleet Street. Brendan Behan is behind the waiter, while *Irish Times* editor Bertie Smylie is holding court, centre, in an all-male assembly. When it first appeared, it was so popular that the original was displayed in a shop window for a time. *Courtesy of the Irish Times.*

who came after him, giving shape to ideas that would underpin romanticism. Even today, if we ask whether art should shock or sooth, we owe a debt to Burke. The reason for its lasting influence is that Burke argued something that seems counter-intuitive, and yet which our experience tells us is true: that the pleasure of art can be produced not only from order and proportion, but also from 'whatever is in any sort terrible.' This, says Burke, 'is a source of the sublime; that is, productive of the strongest emotion which the mind is capable of feeling.'[25]

Luke Gibbons has argued that we can trace this radical and influential idea not only to Burke's precocious student reading of classical writers (such as Longinus, from whom he takes the term 'sublime'), but to his experience of living in Dublin at the time. In January 1745, Burke was staying in a house on Arran Quay when a torrential storm tore through the city, causing the Liffey to burst its banks, sending water, mud, and debris gushing through the streets. Burke was in an upper floor in the house, watching the city dissolve around him in a roar of water. His response was pick up his pen, and write to a friend:

> Tho' every thing around me conspires to excite in me a Contrary disposition, the melancholy gloom of the Day, the whistling winds, and the hoarse rumblings of the Swoln Liffy, with the flood which even where I write lays close siege to our whole Street ... yet the joy of conversing with my friend, can dispel the cloudiness of the Day, lull the winds and stop the rapid passage of the flood.[26]

We can trace a line between this experience of Dublin, and one of the most influential ideas in modern aesthetics: that art (including writing) can transform into pleasure things that should terrify us. As an idea, this will underlie everything from the terror of gothic and horror fiction, to a preference in the nineteenth century for wild, untamed landscapes over manicured gardens. For Burke in 1745, however, the idea was no abstraction. He had experienced 'the joy of conversing with my friend' while the world dissolved around him in a deluge of filthy Liffey water.

It may seem like a leap from Edmund Burke to the novelist Sally Rooney; however, if the title of her first novel – *Conversations with Friends* (2017) – allows us to make a fortuitous link, and that can be tethered to the fact that Rooney had been a champion debater in the college debating society that Burke had founded (becoming a European champion debater in 2013), it opens up an unexpected bridge across the centuries.

Rooney would later describe the experience of debating (and why she eventually gave it up) in terms that resonate with her characters. 'You hear yourself constructing syntactically elaborate sentences, one after another, but you don't necessarily have the sensation that you are the person doing it.'[27] That sense of distance permeates *Conversations with Friends*, written in an understated, emotionally detached prose that is nonetheless concerned with finding a place where conversation is possible between two people in the midst of a world that does not seem to make sense – much as Burke was intent on finding such a place as the Liffey broke its banks around him. For the character of Frances in *Conversations with Friends*, the Trinity library (named for the philosopher George Berkeley), with its austere modernist concrete and glass, becomes a kind of sanctum. 'I liked to sit in the library to write essays, allowing my sense of time and personal identity to dissolve as the light dimmed outside the windows. [...] I mostly forgot to eat on days like this and emerged in the evening with a fine, shrill headache.' 'When I couldn't make friends as a child,' she remembers, 'I fantasized that [...] I was a genius hidden among normal people. It made me feel like a spy'[28] – an echo of the words that Elizabeth Bowen used to describe her sense of herself as a child, being taken through the streets of Dublin, distanced and watching everything 'like a spy'.

The phrase 'normal people' also prefigures the title of Rooney's second novel, *Normal People* (2018), in which two students from a rural town in Sligo, Marianne and Connell, arrive in Trinity, each hoping to find the things that they cannot quite articulate, but which they know are missing from their lives. At one point in *Normal People*, the character of Connell is attending a literary reading in 'one of the big windowless halls in the Arts Building', and goes along afterwards to the Stag's Head pub (just off Dame Street). However, rather than finding the kind of literary world that he imagined existed in Dublin, he witnesses instead what he thinks of as 'culture as class performance, literature fetishized for its ability to take educated people on false emotional journeys, so that they might afterwards feel superior to the uneducated people whose emotional journeys they liked to read about.' And yet, as Connell makes his way home from the pub, 'he felt the old beat of pleasure inside his body,' as the idea for a new story takes shape, 'like watching a perfect goal, like the rustling of light through leaves, a phrase of music from the window of a passing car.' This, in some respects, is the crux of Rooney's writing: the deep suspicion that that writing may accomplish nothing, that people possibly never really communicate, and that there is no 'normal'. And yet, at the same time, characters in her novels keep on writing and continue having conversations, using words to create a space in the midst of the flood in which the world might just make sense. 'Life offers up these moments of joy despite everything.'[29]

Literature that centres on Trinity, for all of its questionings and misgivings, revolves time and again back to this idea of the sustaining power of 'conversing with my friend'. For instance, the poet Gerald Dawe (who taught in the college) juxtaposes the hard surfaces of the sculpture that sits in front of the Berkeley Library with the memory of talk in his 2019 poem 'Plinth, Berkeley Library, Trinity College':

> *Pomodoro's* Sphere Within Sphere,
> the classical *Printing House,*
> *the river-inflected sky,*
> *and then recall the chatter*
> *and everlasting laughter.*[30]

The library named for George Berkeley – or 'new' library – in which Rooney's characters lose themselves, and outside of which Dawe recalls 'the chatter' was built in 1966, the same year in which the poet Eiléan Ní Chuilleanáin started teaching in Trinity. In her poem 'Trinity New Library', she captures that something of what makes a university library different to other buildings: an awareness of the multiple worlds it contains, going back to Egyptian papyrus or the great illuminated medieval manuscript of the Book of Kells. 'You can have too much at once,' she writes. 'When I read *Arcadia* all other words / Became absurd and the library / Could blow up in the morning.'[31]

The Book of Kells: The Book of Kells is probably the most famous – and possibly the most beautiful – book in Ireland, although the origins of this ninth-century illuminated Latin Gospel with its elaborately illustrated pages and interlaced initial letters are still a matter of debate. It was presented to Trinity in 1661 by the Bishop of Meath at the time, Henry Jones, who was also Vice-Chancellor of the university. It has been in the College Library ever since.

Ní Chuilleanáin was both part of the 'salon' (as she ironically called it) who gathered in Leland Bardwell's damp basement at 33 Lower Leeson Street in the mid-1960s, and one of a generation of poets who taught or studied (or both) in the university at the time. At around the same time, the Kerry-born Brendan Kennelly, whose many collections of poetry began with *My Dark Fathers* (1964), completed his PhD in the college, and began teaching. In 1962, Eavan Boland entered Trinity as an undergraduate and published her first collection, *23 Poems*, later that year, followed by *New Territory* in 1967. The latter collection contains a poem dedicated to Kennelly, 'The Flight of the Earls', which opens with the line 'Princes it seems are seldom wise', and another dedicated to one of her fellow students at the time, the poet Derek Mahon – 'Belfast vs. Dublin':

We have had time to talk, and strongly
Disagree about the living out
Of life. There was no need to shout.
Rightly or else quite wrongly
We have run out of time, if not of talk.
Let us then cavalierly fork
Our ways, since we, and all unknown,
Have called into question one another's own.[32]

Mahon was originally from Belfast, as was Michael Longley, yet another dedicatee in *New Territory*, and also a student at the time; there he met Edna Broderick (later Longley), who would go on to become one of the most influential scholars of contemporary Irish poetry of her time. Mahon's first collection, *Twelve Poems*, appeared in 1965, the same year as Michael Longley's first collection, the slightly shorter *Ten Poems*.

The title of Boland's collection – *New Territory* – captures in two words what was taking place on the campus in this time of first collections: this was a generation of Irish poets who would map out new territory, not so much by rejecting the generation who had come before them, but by looking past them. Michael Longley would later recall

Brendan Kennelly (1936-2021), just inside the College Green gates of Trinity. Kennelly was among of generation of poets who met in Trinity in the 1960s. Kennelly continued to teach in the university until 2005, and over the years became very much a poet-as-public-figure. *Courtesy of the Library, Trinity College Dublin and the Brendan Kennelly Private Collection.*

student evenings in rooms in College: 'We inhaled with our untipped Sweet Afton cigarettes MacNeice, Crane, Dylan Thomas, Yeats, Larkin, Lawrence, Graves, Ted Hughes, Stevens, Cummings, Richard Wilbur, Robert Lowell, as well as Rimbaud, Baudelaire, Brecht, Rilke – higgledepiggledly, in any order. We scanned the journals and newspapers for poems written yesterday.'[33]

Forty years later, in Barry McCrea's novel *The First Verse* (2005) set in these same rooms, when his protagonist climbs the stairs in the student residences known as Botany Bay for the first time, the novel captures a strangely parallel sense of potential and transformation, two generations later. 'My third-floor room was large and bright, furnished with a desk, single bed, and bookshelf, a sink in the corner and two old windows looking out onto the tennis courts and the gothic Graduate Memorial Building. I looked at the bookshelf and the bare walls, and up at the high, white ceiling, and I thought I will furnish this room with a life.' In McCrea's novel, this involves becoming entangled with a cult-like group of students who shape their lives by concentrating on a question, and then 'pull a book at random from the shelf, open it at a random page and begin reading a random sentence' – from which 'the right answer' invariably emerges.[34] For the generation of Irish writers of the 1960s, furnishing their college rooms with a life did not quite mean interpreting books at random; however, there was an intense sense of discovery to their reading, given an urgency by a pressing awareness that there were new territories to explore everywhere, and a need to create not just a new historical map, but a new chart of Irish experience.

Boland's writing in particular in those years took shape against the background of growing unrest in Northern Ireland and wider campaigns for equality internationally, which can be seen as setting the groundwork for her lifelong project of resituating the place of women in Irish culture, culminating in the magisterial poem she published just before her death in 2020, 'Our Future Will Become the Past of Other Women'. Equally, for Longley, the classical literature he studied in the 1960s would become a resource that he would draw on throughout a writing career that coincided with the worst years of the conflict in Northern Ireland. Looking back in his 1995 poem 'River & Fountain', he finds in the college's Front Square covered in snow an image of time folding in on itself:

> *I am walking backwards into the future like a Greek.*
> *I have nothing to say. There is nothing I would describe.*
> *It was always thus: as if snow has fallen on Front*
> *Square, and, feeling the downy silence of the snowflakes*
> *That cover cobbles and each other, white erasing white,*
> *I read shadow and snow-drift under the Campanile.*[35]

The sense of stillness in Longley's poem ('There is nothing I would describe. / It was always thus') captures something that still defines the experience of stepping through the Front Gate of Trinity College from the roar of College Green; the Front Square, with its cobbles, symmetrical pillars and centrepiece campanile, backed by the seventeenth-century red brick of the Rubrics, all evoke an uncanny sense of time suspended, which may be the key to its sense of separateness, of stillness in the midst of flux. Deirdre Madden perhaps best sums this up in her 2002 novel *Authenticity*, in which her middle-aged protagonist, William, who had been a student in the College, walks through the campus, and 'as he walked past the Rubrics into Front Square, he thought of how little it had changed over the years unlike other places he had known in Dublin, and how he liked that, because it meant that he could pretend that time had not passed.'[36]

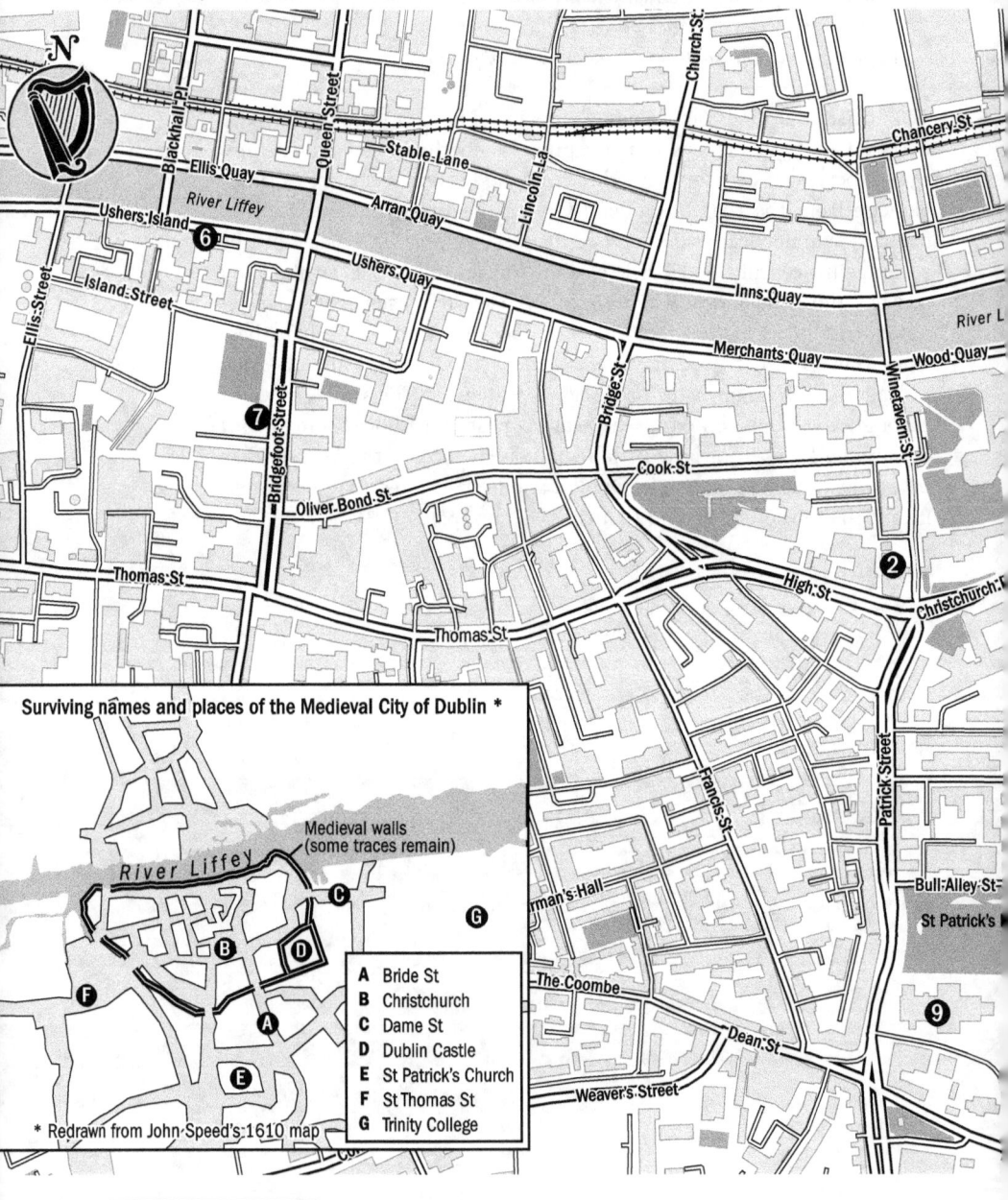

Around the Liberties

5

The awareness of differing scales of time in Dublin is not the same everywhere in the city. Sometimes, the past opens up before us in a vista that seems to stretch away from the contemporary city of builders' cranes and data centres. One such moment occurred in the spring of 2020, when archaeologists excavating a site on Ship Street, beside Dublin Castle, found themselves looking down a pit into the source of the city: what had once been a dark pool, the Dubh Linn, that gave the city its name. The original Irish name for the area at the mouth of the Liffey had been Áth Cliath, 'the ford of the hurdles', named for a site probably located where the river narrows, near what is today Islandbridge. Over the centuries, the land around this river crossing became cross-hatched with paths that snaked out into the surrounding countryside, converging on the hill that forms the south bank of the river: one such path, the Slige Mohr, followed the course of present-day Thomas Street; Slige Data ran along what is now the Coombe; Slige Chualainn inscribes the line of Francis Street; and running down to the river, Slige Midluacha was a path that is now Bow Lane. Where these early routes met, they formed what architect Niall McCullough calls 'a shadowy urban trading entity',[1] somewhere in the vicinity of the present-day intersection of Kevin Street and Bishop Street. By the sixth century, there was a church and monastery in the vicinity – the Church of St. Michael le Pole – located near where the nearby River Poddle flowed into the River Liffey.

The major streets around Christchurch and the Liberties follow the lines of older tracks, predating the Viking settlement. For instance, Thomas Street, pictured here, follows the line of the Slige Mohr, the ancient road running inland parallel to the south bank of the Liffey. Photography by Seán Harrison.

It had been in the deep pool at the confluence of these two rivers that Viking raiders had begun to moor their longboats in the ninth century. One account has as many as two hundred ships summering in Dubh Linn in 841.[2] By the end of the tenth century, there was a permanent Viking settlement next to where Christchurch Cathedral would be built, and by about 1026 Dublin was an important enough part of the Viking world for the Icelandic poet Óttar *svarti*, writing in Old Norse, to include Ireland in a poem of praise to the Danish king, Cnut the Great: 'Skal svá kveðja / konung Dana, / Íra ok Engla / ok Eybúa, /at hans fari /með himinkröptum, / löndum öllum / lof viðara' ['I will greet the king of the Danes, the Irish, the English and the Islanders; so his praise may travel through all the lands under heaven.']³ As the original Viking settlement of wattle huts grew into the medieval town, what would become Dublin Castle was built on the site beside the Poddle basin, eventually covering the river and its dark pool completely – until its site was uncovered by 2020 excavations. In the layers that had accumulated over the riverbed, archaeologists found remains of the city's oldest prison cells, and a punishment grave containing a body from which the hands and feet had been severed.⁴

In the streets radiating out from the site of the old Viking settlement between Dublin Castle and Christchurch Cathedral, the past is always just beneath the surface. There are so many layers of the past buried here – Viking, medieval, seventeenth- and eighteenth-century – that no one of them dominates: rather, it is the past as such that haunts these streets, what Peter Sirr calls (writing of Thomas Street) 'a brooding, dark-eyed presence living on the ghosts of lost or forgotten riches'.⁵ The poet Gerard Smyth, who lives in the area, observes in his 2020 collection *The Sundays of Eternity*: 'A Dane still haunted the parish. / In the junkyard things were given a second chance.'⁶ In *In the Dark River* (2018), Conor Brady's historical crime novel set in Dublin in 1889, workmen digging a drain find themselves in the subterranean channels of the old Poddle, where they discover a body. 'Even to the untrained eye this was no Viking or Norman. The two rows of teeth in the jaw were complete and perfect, still in their sockets. This was a young person, no relic from medieval times but someone whose life had been much more recently, and probably violently, brought to an end.'⁷

> **Liberties:** Originally, the 'liberties' were areas adjacent to the old medieval city, but outside its jurisdiction, and hence falling under the governance of a large property owner (sometimes a religious organization). The largest of the original liberties, the Manor of St. Sepulchre, used to run as far as Donnybrook. Today, however, the term is used more loosely to designate the area that corresponds to the old liberties of Thomas Court and Donore, which had been granted to the earls of Meath, running around the edge of the old city walls – more or less, an area surrounding and just west of St. Patrick's Cathedral.

Likewise, Tana French's 2010 crime novel *Faithful Place* is set in the (fictional) Faithful Place, in the (very real) Liberties of Dublin, just south of Christchurch. 'The Liberties grew on their own over centuries, without any help from urban planners, and the Place is a cramped cul-de-sac tucked away in the middle like a wrong turn in a maze. It's a ten-minute walk from Trinity College and the snazzy shopping on Grafton Street, but back in my day,' says French's narrator, detective Frank Mackey of the Dublin Murder Squad, 'we didn't go to Trinity and the Trinity types didn't come up our way.' French chooses her location here precisely. *Faithful Place* is a novel that revolves around past crimes refusing to stay hidden, and this is a part of the city in which the past never quite goes away. At one point, Mackey muses: 'I went looking for the parts of my city that have lasted. I walked down streets that got their names in the Middle Ages, Copper Alley, Fishamble Street, Blackpitts where the plague dead were buried.' Looking around him at 'the shoddy new apartment blocks and neon signs', he reflects on 'the truth of ruins': 'It's the old stuff, the stuff that's endured, that might just keep enduring.'[8]

French is not alone in sensing in these streets the uncanny presence of old time. When the conflict in Northern Ireland was effectively a civil war in the mid-1970s, two writers – both originally from Northern Ireland – turned to the traces of Viking Dublin for what Yeats had earlier called 'befitting emblems of adversity':[9] Seamus Heaney and Brian Friel. One of the definitive collections of poetry from a time when bombings and sectarian killings in Northern Ireland were making the conflict seem increasingly intractable was Seamus Heaney's *North* (1975). Born in the townland of Bellaghy, in County Derry, Heaney opened his first major collection, *Death of a Naturalist* (1966), with a poem that established what would be a guiding metaphor in his writing: 'Digging': 'Between my finger and my thumb / The squat pen rests; snug as a gun.'[10] *North* pushes the metaphor of writing as digging further, as Heaney tries to burrow down into the roots of communal violence in a series of poems that take as their guiding image the mummified bodies of Iron Age sacrificial victims that have turned up in bogs from Denmark to Ireland, often with their hands bound, their throats slit. For Heaney, these figures open a route to understanding 'the exact / and tribal, intimate revenge'[11] of warfare within a tightly knit community.

One of the pivotal poems in *North* is 'Viking Dublin: Trial Pieces', first published in June 1974, less than a month after three no-warning bombs on 17 May had killed thirty-three people and an unborn child in the centre of Dublin, in what would be the largest loss of life in a single day in the course of the Troubles:

*Like a long sword
sheathed in its moisting
burial clays,
the keel stuck fast*

*in the slip of the bank
its clinker-built hull
spined and plosive
as* Dublin.[12]

The keel of the Viking longboat, the sword, and the carved pieces of bone that Heaney imagines being excavated from the site of the first Viking settlement in Dublin are all 'trial pieces', in more than one sense. On a literal level, they are practice pieces for artisans to try out their craft, and in this respect (as with the blacksmiths who populate Heaney's poetry) they are metaphors for the poet's craft – 'the craft's mystery / improvised on bone'. However, these pieces of carved bone are also 'trial pieces' in two other senses: they are objects produced through hardships endured – by 'trial'. Finally, they result from ceremonial proceedings – trials – whose verdicts resulted in weapons and bodies buried in the mud. These pieces of carved bone thus become

In the 1970s, more than one writer found in the archaeological remains of Viking Dublin an image of the present. This scene is from Brian Friel's play, *Volunteers* (Abbey Theatre, 5 March 1975), with actors Raymond Hardie and Donal Donnelly in the foreground, considering a Viking skeleton. *Photograph by Fergus Bourke. Courtesy of the Abbey Theatre Archive.*

images for understanding violence as something other than random acts of carnage. The word 'plosive' is precisely resonant here: it is both a term from phonetics for the sudden puff of air produced by consonants 'd' and 'b' in the word 'Dublin', as well as carrying a suggestion of the word 'explosion' in a city where the rubble from the explosions of a few weeks earlier had yet to be cleared.

The Viking excavations in Dublin also provided the playwright Brian Friel with a way of exploring the Northern Ireland conflict in his play *Volunteers*. Dedicated to Heaney, it was first performed 5 March 1975, three months before *North* was published. Friel's 'volunteers' are a pair of IRA prisoners who have been sentenced to death *in absentia* by their colleagues for volunteering to join a work detail at the Wood Quay archaeological site where the play is set. Although the stage directions simply specify 'a city', it is clearly Dublin, where the excavations reach 'from early Viking down to late Georgian', becoming, as one character puts it, 'an encapsulated history, a tangible precis of the story of Irish man'.[13] On a set otherwise made up of tables and buckets, the audience members are constantly aware of the skeleton of a sacrificial victim, with a leather thong around his neck and a precise hole in the centre of his skull, discovered during the excavations. 'Was the poor eejit just grabbed out of a crowd one spring morning,' wonders one of the IRA men, Keeney, 'and a noose tightened around his neck so that obeisance could be made to some silly god. Or [...] maybe the poor hoor considered it an honour to die – maybe he volunteered.'[14] As with Heaney's bog poems, there is no suggestion in any literal way that the causes of the conflict of the 1970s can be traced back to Viking (or Iron Age) Ireland; instead, these bodies from the past provide ways of thinking about the dynamics (and legitimizing) of communal violence per se.

When Friel's *Volunteers* opened across the Liffey at the Abbey Theatre in 1975, it was part of a theatre tradition in Dublin whose origins can be traced back to the Church of St. John the Evangelist, which had been built in the twelfth century directly over the site of the Viking settlement on Wood Quay, between present-day Winetavern Street and Fishamble Street. Although there were performances of various sorts earlier in Gaelic Ireland, the theatre historian Alan Fletcher has shown that the oldest surviving script of a play performed anywhere in Ireland was written to be performed in this particular church at some point in the middle of the fourteenth century (and no earlier than 1352).[15] Known as the *Visitatio Sepulcri*, this Latin text formed part of the liturgy at a time when all across Europe clergy were beginning to extract passages from the Bible, breaking them into speaking parts, and shaping the movements of performers to the architecture of the church. 'Quem queritis ad sepulcrum o cristicole?' ['Whom do you seek at the Sepulchre, O worshippers of Christ?'], a priest playing an Angel asks the Three Marys as they approach the altar. When they reply 'Jesus of Nazareth', the angel responds: 'Surrexit non est hic sicut dixit uenite et uidete locum positus fuerat' ['He has risen and is not here, as he told you. Come and see the place where he was laid.']¹⁶ If we bracket for moment its religious content, this long-lost performance uncannily prefigures a motif that will recur again and again in the literature from this part of the city, from Friel's *Volunteers* to French's *Faithful Place*: the prospect that in certain places, the dead can rise.

There is also something powerfully resonant in being able to identify so precisely a site of origin for theatre in a city where theatre has been so much part of its fabric for so long. For the centuries immediately following the staging of the *Visitatio*, a form of open-air theatre became part of the civic life of Dublin in the form of processional plays, which progressed around the old city walls that extended from Dublin Castle to the Liffey. The Great Chain Book (a set of municipal records) for 1498 records the details of 'the pagentes of Corpus Christi day made by an olde lawe', during which in the course of a June day the various trade guilds would parade through the city streets, performing scenes from the Bible. So, for instance, that the 'maryners, vynters, shipcarpynderis & samoun takers' would all have paraded through the streets performing the story of 'Noe [Noah] with his ship', while the 'ffishers' were responsible for 'Þe xij apostelis [the twelve apostles]'.[17] In each case, the pageants were, as historian Susan Beckwith puts it, 'part of the material organization of public life',[18] placing the ordinary day-to-day labour of Dubliners in the frame of a greater biblical story. When a ship's carpenter set to work each day with his hammer, he was doing the work of Noah; so, too, with fishermen doing the work of the apostles, and so on. In short, the performances in the streets of Dublin in these plays involved a way of thinking about time in which the past (particularly the biblical past) was a living part of the present.

Other tantalizing fragments exist of this earliest Dublin theatre culture. The oldest surviving morality play in English (Middle English, to be precise), *The Pride of Life* (ca. 1337) exists now only as interpolations in other manuscripts (the original was destroyed in 1922). However, it was probably associated with one of the Augustinian priories in the area around Christchurch. Likewise, there is mention in another manuscript that 'the Comedy of Cæres, Goddess of Corne, was acted by the Bakers'[19] at a Christmastide festival in 1528 on Hoggen Green (which would later become College Green, after the establishment of Trinity College in 1592). However, it would be a full century later in the 1630s before Dublin would have its first purpose-built theatre, on Werburgh Street, probably located opposite St. Werburgh's Church, at the side of Dublin Castle, on which it depended for patronage.

It was here that the first play both set and written in Ireland was performed, *St. Patrick for Ireland* (1639) by the English playwright James Shirley, who came to Ireland in November 1636 when the London theatres were closed by plague. This is effectively the beginning of a secular theatre culture with regular performances, in which surviving prologues to plays begin to address, for the first time, a Dublin theatre audience. It was also in the Werburgh Street Theatre in 1640 that there is the first production of a Dublin play (and the oldest surviving play in English by an Irish-born writer), Henry Burnell's *Landgartha*. In one scene, two 'foolish Coxcombes' from the countryside, Cowsell and Radgee, discuss the attractions of Dublin in ways that suggest what life was like in the city:

> For you see, when we come to Towne, we doe
> Nothing but runne from Taverne to Taverne;
> Oft to blind Ale-houses, to visit the fine
> Wenches, of purpose there plac'd, to draw custome;
> Now and then to see a Play.[20]

However, by the time Burnell published his play in 1641, the unstable ground on which this little theatre world existed was ready to collapse, and, as the earliest historian of the Irish theatre, Robert Hitchcock, wrote in his *Historical View of the Irish Stage* (1788), 'rebellion breaking out in October of 1641 involved the whole kingdom in confusion. The drama naturally shared the fate of the state, with which it was so intimately connected.'[21] By the end of the year, what had been the Werburgh Street Theatre became a military stable for the Castle on which it had depended for patronage.

The next theatre to be built in Dublin was also, initially, connected to the court in Dublin Castle. However, it would quickly grow beyond those origins to become one of the most important theatres of its time. In the 1990s, a team of archaeologists was surveying the recently deconsecrated Church of St. Michael and St. John on Essex Street East, about

Opened in 1662, the Smock Alley Theatre (on what is now Essex Street East) was the first purpose-built post-Restoration theatre in Ireland or England, and would remain for the next century as one of the most important theatres in Europe. The original building was rediscovered, hiding in plain sight as a converted church, in the mid-1990s. *Photography by Seán Harrison.*

100 metres from where the *Visitatio* had been performed in the Church of St. John the Evangelist in the fourteenth century; as they removed the decaying plaster from what they thought was an eighteenth-century church, they uncovered an odd diagonal line of joist holes, not corresponding to any obvious feature of a church, and in exploring the building further they discovered, as archaeologist Linzi Simpson later wrote, 'that most of the existing structure [of what had been the church] is, in fact, the Smock Alley Theatre building',[22] which had been built in 1662 but which had closed in 1788. It soon became apparent that the original theatre had not been torn down, as everyone had long believed; it had simply been converted into a church, with minor modifications. Even for a part of the city in which the past insists on re-emerging, the discovery of a seventeenth-century theatre hiding in plain sight on a busy street, disguised as a church, was remarkable.

It was in Smock Alley, shortly after it opened in October 1662, that the first public production anywhere of a play in English written by a woman was staged, when Katharine Philips' *Pompey* (a translation of Corneille) was produced on 10 February 1663. In that same year, Richard Head published *Hic et Ubique; Or the Humours of Dublin*, 'acted privately', a bawdy play set largely in the Dublin tavern of Alderman Thrivewell, where he encounters a group of characters freshly arrived from London whose names tell us all we need to know about them: Bankrupt, Contriver, and Trustall. This would be the first in a series of plays that tell us something about the rivalry of Dublin and London, where the comedy arises from landing London characters in Dublin, or vice versa. Later, after a brief closure during the war that brought William of Orange to the throne in the 1690s, a former Trinity student and soldier in William's army, George Farquhar, began his theatre career on the Smock Alley stage, before he turned to writing plays. His earliest play, *Love and a Bottle*, opened in London, in Drury Lane, in 1698, featuring an Irishman, Roebuck, newly arrived in London. In 1700, William Philips' *St. Stephen's Green*, would reverse the trope for Smock Alley audiences, by following an English character, Freelove, newly arrived in Dublin.

Over the course of the next century, the area around the Smock Alley Theatre (in what is today the western end of the Temple Bar area) also became the heart of a dynamic print culture, bounded by Trinity College on one end and Christchurch on the other. Initially, Irish printers and booksellers were given a boost when Ireland slipped through a loophole in the British Copyright Act of 1709 (8 Anne cap. 19), which meant that Irish publishers could print editions of London works relatively cheaply. However, once a thriving print world was established, it developed its own momentum,[23] and over the ensuing decades there were hundreds of printers, engravers, bookbinders, and booksellers operating in the streets around Smock Alley and Dublin Castle. So, for instance, George Faulkner, the printer and bookseller who would become known as 'the prince of the Dublin printers' in a career that stretched from 1724 to 1765, and who published many of Jonathan Swift's works, operated at different times from premises in Christchurch Yard, Skinner's Row (which ran from present-day Castle Street, south of Christchurch), Essex Street, and Parliament Street, all a few minutes from both the theatre and Dublin Castle.

It was here, too, that Dublin's periodical culture began. Ireland's first literary magazine, *The Examiner* (1710–1712) was printed here by the publisher Cornelius Carter, in Fishamble Street. This was followed by the *Dublin Weekly Journal* (1725–1752), published in Dame Street, and, later in the century, the major literary magazine of the period, *The Hibernian Magazine*, also published in Dame Street. Later again, the first Irish literary magazine aimed at women appeared, in 1795, *The Parlour Window*, with offices in Exchange Street. 'Female Authors have so many discouragements to encounter,' declares its first editorial, 'it is no wonder they so rarely appear in Print; the general opinion is against them.'[24]

This world of print was not a world of solitary reading. For instance, the printer and publisher Stephen Powell, who operated from 1697 to 1722, and whose son and grandson were still in the trade in 1775, published books from 'the back of Dick's Coffee House, Skinner's Row', and later 'over against the Crown Tavern, Fishamble Street'.[25] To put it simply, the world of polite literature was often far from polite, and authors and readers expected to encounter one another in the literary taverns or coffee houses of the city. A poem from 1747, *The Gentleman*, describes the scene in those streets:

> *Lords, ladys, show-boys, gentlemen, and whores,*
> *Dogs, horses, chairs, parsons, bullys, proctors,*
> *Old men and widows, quacks, madmen, doctors;*
> *Pimps, statesmen, pocket pickers, poets, fools,*
> *Coaches and chariots, flams and chairmen's poles;*
> *All mix'd confusion, noise, tumults, curses,*
> *Swearing, breaking shins, and picking purses.*[26]

There was a distinctively urban energy in these streets, where the gossip of the taverns and coffee houses, amplified by newspapers and pamphlets, became a kind of public performance.

The results could be volatile, particularly when they were channelled into the confined space of the theatre. For example, not long after a young Trinity student, Thomas Sheridan, made his debut as an actor in Smock Alley in 1743, he became embroiled in controversy with a more senior actor, Theophilus Cibber, stemming from a missing costume. Where today the antagonists might have aired their differences on social media, in 1743 the actors and their respective supporters turned to the eighteenth-century equivalent, churning out a series of pamphlets, prologues to be spoken at the theatre, and satirical poems and essays that were quickly printed and sold in the shops surrounding the theatre and posted up on walls. As these piled up, they were collected in a work whose title tells the whole story: *Cibber and Sheridan: Or the Dublin Miscellany Containing all the Advertisements, Letters, Addresses, Apologies, Verses, &c. &c, &c. lately publish'd on Account of the Theatric Squabble, To Which are Added, Several Prologues and Epilogues, spoke at the Theatre in Smock-Alley, this Summer, by Mr. Cibber.*[27] Sheridan survived that particular row, however, and by 1745 he was managing Smock Alley.

In the Dublin of the eighteenth century, these literary and theatrical battles could escalate, and more than once in those years disputes boiled over from satiric poems and pamphlets to become full-blown theatre riots (they also often ended in duels – but that is another story). In 1754, for instance, a pamphlet war over a political matter (a dispute as to whether Irish tax revenues should be sent to London) erupted into a theatre riot during a production of a play entitled *Mahomet*, when the audience insisted that an actor repeat a line condemning those 'Vipers', who, 'singled out by the Community / To Guard their Rights' would, 'for paltry Office, sell them to the Foe!'.[28] When Thomas Sheridan tried to calm the audience, he was first of all pelted with 'a Volley of Apples and Oranges', followed by 'Glass Bottles, and Stones', and the evening ended with some of the audience ransacking the theatre. There then followed a fusillade of satirical pamphlets and newspaper pieces. The *Dublin Journal* published what purported to be a recipe for making a tragedy ('Take the Words Liberty, Patriot, Country, Tyranny, Oppression [...] Divide into Five Equal Parts, between each Part let there be a Chorus of Groans in the Upper Gallery').[29] Other satirical pamphlets purported to be written by Sheridan himself appeared, including *The Sighs and Groans of Mr. Sh——n*, and *Mr. Sh——n's Apology to the Town*, in which he tells the audience 'O Ye Sons of Liberty and Turbulence, I will make you swallow such Stuff as I please to ram down your Throats.'[30] Sheridan's response, typically, was to publish his own response, culminating in a lengthy pamphlet in which he argued for the theatre as a model of the state, 'wherein no Man shall be refrained from

Even as the city around it has changed, St. Patrick's Cathedral, where Jonathan Swift was Dean, continues to dominate the skyline around it. At the same time, as was the case in the eighteenth century, it is very much connected to the streets around it. *Photography by Seán Harrison.*

saying or doing any thing that is consistent with Reason and Truth; nor be compelled to do any thing contrary to the Conviction of his Mind.'[31]

This part of Dublin in the eighteenth century was a world of ferocious intimacy, a kind of overheated urban village where debates over 'Reason and Truth' could be punctuated by fusillades of rotten fruit. The figure whose spirit in many ways presides over it, even after his death in 1745, was Thomas Sheridan's godfather: Jonathan Swift. Although he was born in what was then the very centre of Dublin, and once jokingly described himself as 'an absolute Monarch in the Liberties, and King of the Mob'[32] Swift has sometimes been painted as a reluctant Dubliner. 'The Account I have frequently heard the Dean give of himself,' wrote his friend Lætitia Pilkington, 'was that he was born in [No. 7] Hoey's-Alley, in Warburgh's Parish,'[33] next to where the Werburgh Street Theatre had been located. When his early career was on the rise, Swift established himself in London, but a change in the political tide in 1713 resulted in his being appointed Dean of St. Patrick's Cathedral, which lay just south of the old city walls. However, it was while he was Dean that Swift wrote his most famous work, *Gulliver's Travels* (1726), claiming to be the work of a sea captain, Lemuel Gulliver, recounting his voyages to a series of clearly allegorical lands – Lilliput, Brobdingnag, and the Land of the Houyhnhnms. Indeed, a section involving Gulliver's journey to Lindalino, originally omitted by his friend, the publisher George Faulkner, but included in all modern editions, is a satire about Dublin politics ('Lindalino' being a play on the word 'Dublin').

Swift's work on *Gulliver* was interrupted in 1724 and 1725 when he became involved in the uproar that followed plans to issue new Irish coinage in what were believed to be inferior metals. Swift responded to the controversy by creating yet another literary persona, and as M. B. Drapier, a Dublin shopkeeper, he laid out with escalating preposterousness 'the Plain Story of the Fact'[34] in a series of pamphlets that were again published by George Faulkner. The voice here – as in *Gulliver's Travels* – is that of the reasonable person following the logic of a mad world. And this is the voice that Swift would push even further a few years later in his *Modest Proposal* of 1729. 'It is a melancholy Object to those, who walk through this great Town, or travel in the Country,' he begins, 'when they see the *Streets*, the *Roads*, and *Cabbin-doors* crowded with Beggars of the Female Sex, followed by three, four, or six Children, *all in Rags*.' If the problem, Swift's literary persona reasons, is that there are too many children in Dublin, and not enough food, the solution is obvious: 'A young healthy Child, well nursed, at a Year old, [is] a most delicious, nourishing, and wholesome Food; whether *Stewed, Roasted, Baked*, or *Boiled*; and, I make no doubt, that it will equally serve in a *Fricasie*, or *Ragoust.*'[35]

While Swift's *Modest Proposal* is read all over the world today as a classic example of satirical writing, it was very much a product of the kind of literary city that Dublin was – and, to some extent, still is. The same tightly knit community of readers and writers that fuelled pamphlet wars in Smock Alley makes possible the games with authorship that Swift plays here. When authors, printers, booksellers, and readers all live, drink, and work in the same streets, literature is not simply a solitary pleasure, and this makes satire – particularly savage satire – possible. Few who read *A Modest Proposal* in 1729 were unaware of its authorship (even if it was published anonymously); and no one seriously thought that the Dean who officiated at religious services in St. Patrick's Cathedral on Sundays was an advocate of cannibalism.

When literary works feed off the conversations in the coffee houses, taverns, and on the streets, and the resulting publications feed back into those conversations, one of the effects is to make literature into something fluid and dynamic, of which the printed word is only a part. There is a vivid glimpse of this world in which writing and talking were intertwined in the *Memoirs* of Lætitia Pilkington, one of Swift's close friends. 'My Evening's Chat with the Dean furnished me with Matter of Speculation on the most amazing Faculty of the human Mind, Memory,' she writes in a typical passage; 'which, according to my usual Custom, I threw into Rhime.'[36] A conversation becomes a poem, which in turn fuels more conversation, recorded in a memoir; the poem, then, is subsequently published, sparking more conversation; and so on. Indeed, in one of his own greatest poems, 'Verses on the Death of Dr. Swift, D.S.P.D.' (1731/39), Swift adopts what is perhaps the ultimate form of assumed authorship – his own dead self:

> *Suppose me dead; and then suppose*
> *A Club assembled at the Rose [a tavern];*
> *Where from Discourse of this and that,*
> *I grow the Subject of their Chat.*[37]

Even after (his supposed) death, Swift was still provoking conversation.

In a world in which talk and print spill over one another, it was possible to say the most outrageous things and not be taken literally; or to publish anonymous works where everyone knew the author. In the end, when the whole town was in on the joke, and when the joke had a serious point, it could often be the most effective way of saying something of consequence. If we think about the situation in this way, Swift may well have been imagining a kind of anti-Dublin in *Gulliver's Travels* in the Land of the Houynhnms, which is populated by talking horses (possibly a joke in itself, given the Irish rural gentry's obsessive interest in horses). The Houynhnms have a very unambiguous view of language as communication, and their language has no word for fiction: 'The Use of Speech was to make us understand one another, and to receive Information of Facts; now if any one *said the Thing which was not*, these Ends were defeated.'[38] The point for Swift is that this utterly logical literalism does not prevent the Houynhnms enslaving the Yahoos. In fact, the real subversive power of language is precisely the ability to say '*the Thing which was not*'.

The comedy of Swift's satire is shot through with a genuine anger at the stupidity of the world, which seems to intensify with age. And so, the image of Swift in his old age, infuriated by injustice, isolated by tinnitus that produced a constant ringing in his ears, and struggling with his mental health, was given a lasting physical monument when he left his estate to St. Patrick's Hospital, on Bow Lane (which continues to provide mental health services today). Typically, he forever memorialized the gesture in an addition to his 'Verses on the Death of Dr. Swift, D.S.P.D.':

He gave the little wealth he had
To build a house for fools and mad;
And show'd by one satiric touch,
No nation wanted it so much.[39]

Swift continues to haunt Dublin's literature, often as a tormented figure. In his long poem *Mnemosyne Lay In Dust* (1966), about his own time in St. Patrick's after a mental breakdown, the poet Austin Clarke refers to 'The Mansion of Forgetfulness / Swift gave us for a jest'. In a later poem, his 'Sermon on Swift', Clarke announces: 'Here is his secret belief / For sure: [...] a voice proclaiming / The World's mad business – Eternal Absolution.'[40] In Yeats's play *The Words Upon the Window-Pane* (1930), the spirit of Swift is conjured up during a seance, where his memory is summed up in Yeats's own translation of Swift's Latin epitaph: 'He has gone where fierce indignation can lacerate his heart no more.'[41]

In order to understand Swift's 'fierce indignation', we need to picture him in the crumbling streets around St. Patrick's, where traces of the original tanning, brewing, and weaving industries still lingered in overcrowded alleys. The population of the medieval city had been, as one historian reminds us, 'packed into a small space',[42] but by Swift's time, after centuries of dilapidation, the situation had worsened considerably. By the end of the century, more or less anyone who could afford it had decamped to the new Georgian terraces of Henrietta Street or Dawson Street, leaving behind poverty, congestion, and industry, bequeathing an increasingly industrial character to an area that had long had tanneries and distilleries, and would be increasingly overshadowed by the massive Guinness brewery. Even today, we can sense that world. The poet Gerard Smyth, who grew up in the area, writes in his poem 'The Hot Bread of St. Catherine's' (2010): 'It's an old parish, an inner-city labyrinth. / And there behind the shine of glass / are ribbons of meat hanging on hooks.'[43]

Guinness: The Guinness brewery continues to dominate the skyline between Christchurch and Heuston Station. However, it is only the last survivor (along with some new distilleries that have been revived in the area) of what was an eighteenth-century industrial zone. In addition to brewing, there were extensive tanneries where it stands, as well as weaving and cloth-making, much of it associated with the Huguenots who settled in the area in the late seventeenth century.

As the area declined in the eighteenth and into the nineteenth century, however, it became a place where new arrivals to the city could find lodgings. The most notable of these must have been the Roscommon-born Irish-language writer Seán Ó Neachtain, one of Swift's near-contemporaries, who settled not far from St. Patrick's Cathedral, and set up a school on Thomas Street that would become one of the most important centres for Irish-language culture in the country. Ó Neachtain himself not only transcribed earlier manuscripts but also translated into Irish from English, Latin and Italian, as well as writing original poetry and prose, most notably the quasi-autobiographical prose fiction *Stair Éamoinn Uí Chléirigh*, which follows its fictional protagonist's struggles to become a schoolteacher, providing occasions for commentary on the relations between the English and Irish languages. His son, Tadhg, who lived on South Earl Street in the Liberties from 1709, picked up his work, writing (among many other things) a poem of more than 2,000 lines that traced the history of Ireland from the beginning

Medieval Street Names: Some traces of old descriptive street names survive in the medieval city: Winetavern Street, Fishamble Street, and Blackpitts Lane (variously said to refer to plague pits or to run-off from the nearby tanneries). Others have been replaced by names less objectionable to modern ears: Fleshamble, Skinner's Row, or the self-explanatory Dunghill Lane, which has become Island Street, while the equally self-explanatory Dirty Lane (which ran into it) has become part of Bridgefoot Street, so named because it connected with the city's oldest bridge.

of time. The irony here is that the Ó Neachtains, and the wider circle of Irish-language writers of which they were a part, nurtured a thriving manuscript and oral literary culture in the same streets that housed one of the greatest concentrations of printers and booksellers that the city has ever known. But because they were writing in Irish, not English, they had almost no access to the world of print. *Stair Éamoinn Uí Chléirigh*, for instance, did not appear in print until 1918.[44]

A century after the Ó Neachtains, the Tyrone-born novelist and short-story writer William Carleton (best known for his accounts of Irish peasant life) describes in his *Autobiography* his own arrival in Dublin some time around 1820. After only a few days, he spent all of his scant savings on lodgings in Bridgefoot Street (back when it was still called 'Dirty Lane') and found himself forced to sleep in a nearby cellar full of beggars:

> I should think that the entrance into Dante's Inferno was paradise compared to it. [...] It resembled nothing I ever saw before or since. The inmates were mostly in bed, both men and women, but still a good number of them were up, indulging in liquors of every description, from strong whiskey downwards. [...] There were the lame, the blind, the dumb, and all who suffered from actual and natural infirmity; but in addition to these, there was every variety of imposter about me – most of them stripped of their mechanical accessories of deceit, but by no means all. [...] Crutches, wooden legs, artificial cancers, scrofulous necks, artificial wens, sore legs, and a vast variety of similar complaints, were hung upon the walls of the cellars.[45]

As Dublin moved eastwards and northwards, the historic core around Christchurch became increasingly dilapidated. This photograph from the early twentieth century shows the remnants of much older dwellings, as well as the precarious state of the streets. Bridgefoot Street, where this photo was taken, was originally called 'Dirty Lane', and led into the self-explanatory 'Dunghill Lane', where the city's animal waste was piled. *Courtesy of the Royal Society of Antiquaries of Ireland.*

Whether or not Carleton's account is entirely factual, it is consistent with a theme that will run through literature from this part of the city throughout the nineteenth century: a horrified fascination with levels of dilapidation and poverty that are almost grotesquely unreal. So, for instance, in Joseph Sheridan Le Fanu's 1845 historical novel *The Cock and the Anchor*, set in the early eighteenth century, there is a passage in which a character leaves the tavern that gives the novel its title, which is located 'in one of those sinuous and narrow streets which lay in the immediate vicinity of the castle'. He quickly finds himself in a 'broken lane', lit only by moonlight 'revealing every inequality and pile of rubbish upon its surface, and throwing one side of the enclosure into black, impenetrable shadow.'[46] Le Fanu also set one of his most haunting short stories in this area, 'An Account of Some Strange Disturbances in Aungier Street' (1853), in which two students move into an ancient house, which 'had seen years and changes enough to have contracted all that mysterious and saddened air, at once exciting and depressing, which belongs to most old mansions.' It is not long before one of the students begins to have visions of an old man's face materializing in the window, 'sinister and full of malignant omen'.[47]

It was also in these streets that the most celebrated nineteenth-century Dublin street poet, Zozimus (real name: Michael J. Moran), lived until his death in 1846, and wrote his ballads of poverty. 'I live in Faddle Alley, / Off Blackpitts near the Coombe; / With my poor wife Sally, / In a narrow, dirty room.'[48] Particularly at night, some of these winding alleys still exude menace, helped, perhaps, by the popular belief that the name 'Blackpitts' came from the burial of plague victims here in the fourteenth century (although other accounts attribute the name to nearby tanneries). In her poem 'Night Walk' (1990), Paula Meehan evokes the sense of menace that some of these small streets exude at night:

> *You take Fumbally Lane*
> *to the Blackpitts, cut back by the canal.*
> *Hardly a sound you've made, creature*
> *of night in grey jeans and desert boots,*
> *familiar of shade. Listen.*[49]

It seems appropriate, somehow, that it was here, in the city's oldest library, in the shadow of St. Patrick's Cathedral, that Bram Stoker did some of the reading that would later feed into *Dracula* (1897). Marsh's Library, which opened to the public in 1707, granted a reader's ticket

Founded in 1707, Marsh's Library is Dublin's oldest public library; much of the fabric of the library remains as it was in the eighteenth century. The library's rarest holdings, including most of the books that Bram Stoker would have consulted, are kept in special cages, seen here. *Courtesy of Dublin City Library and Archives.*

to the young Stoker (then working as a civil servant nearby in Dublin Castle) in 1866, and the records of books he consulted show him reading not only antique atlases, depicting the lands at the edge of Europe where he would set *Dracula*, but also books such as John Foxe's *Acts and Monuments* of 1684, with its gruesome accounts of the decapitations and dismemberments endured by early Christian martyrs.[50]

Another of the readers in Marsh's Library in the nineteenth century was the poet James Clarence Mangan, whose nineteenth-century biographer, D. J. O'Donoghue, records him making extensive use of 'its wonderful collection of old and curious literature. Here Mangan worked, surrounded by the worm-eaten tomes in which are treasured the thoughts of all the philosophers and poets of antiquity, unjostled by clamorous moderns.'[51] Mangan had been born at No. 3 Fishamble Street, and later lived at No. 6 York Street, where his neighbour at 41 York Street was the novelist and playwright Charles Robert Maturin, author of one of the great behemoths of nineteenth-century gothic fiction, *Melmoth the Wanderer* (1820). Today, not far away there is a Clarence Mangan Road, an extension of the old Blackpitts Lane, where for a time in the 1960s and 1970s a small poetry publisher, New Writers Press, found a home. However, the address of which Mangan has left the most vivid account in his *Autobiography* is the house to which he had moved when he was sixteen years old, made up of 'two rooms, or rather holes, at the rear of a tottering old fragment of a house, or, if the reader please, hovel, in Chancery Lane [about mid-way between St. Patrick's and Dublin Castle]':

> These dens, one of which was over the other, were mutually connected by means of a steep and almost perpendicular ladder, down which it was my fortune to receive many a tumble from time to time upon the sloppy earthen floor beneath. Door or window there was none to the lower chamber – the place of the latter in particular being supplied, not very elegantly, by a huge chasm in the bare and broken wall.[52]

Mangan's *Autobiography* was written in 1849, while he was lodging with a priest, Fr. C. P. Meehan on Fishamble Street, near where he had been born in 1803; he would die of cholera shortly after writing it, a victim of the disease that killed so many during the Irish Famine of those years. So, on the face of it, Mangan's *Autobiography* seems to be a testimony from one of the most harrowing moments in Irish history.

However, a closer look suggests that not all is as it seems in Mangan's *Autobiography*. At one point, he describes how, when he was sixteen, the 'cold, heat, hunger, and fatigue' in which he lived produced a fever, and he ended up in hospital, 'introducing into my blood the seeds of a more virulent disease than any I had yet known – an incurable hypochondriasis.'[53] The reader is suddenly tripped up here: 'incurable hypochondriasis'? Does he mean that this was all imagined?

It is known that Mangan was born in relative poverty, almost certainly an alcoholic, and probably an opium user; his prose in particular – such as 'A Sixty-Drop Dose of Laudanum' – circles around the compulsions of addiction. In his poem 'The Nameless One', Mangan writes:

> *Tell how this Nameless, condemned for years long,*
> *To herd with demons from hell beneath,*
> *Saw things that made him, with groans and tears, long*
> *For even death.*[54]

Mangan was also very much part of Dublin, an unmistakeable figure, usually glimpsed at night, whom one contemporary describes as always wearing green eyeglasses, a cloak, a 'broad-leafed, steeple-shaped hat', carrying 'a large, malformed umbrella'; and yet 'this eccentricity in costume and manner was not affected.'[55] 'No one can thoroughly realise Mangan's life,' wrote the poet Lionel Johnson in an introduction to his collected prose, 'without some knowledge of Dublin. [...] He wanders about the rotting alleys and foul streets, a wasted ghost.'[56] There was also genuine poetic achievement, and he was a prolific contributor to *The Nation*, edited by Thomas Davis, and to the *Dublin University Magazine*, edited by Le Fanu.

And yet, while there was real poverty and real addiction in Mangan's life, there was also myth, much of it of Mangan's own making, and an element of game-playing with reality. In one of his prose works, 'An Extraordinary Adventure in the Shades' (1833), he recounts an afternoon in 1832 when he was 'in College Green, in the Shades Tavern', and as he drinks, he becomes convinced that the man sitting opposite to him is in fact a sorcerer named Maugraby. As he watches horrified, Maugraby's nose begins to grow. 'Eventually the entrance to the tavern would be blocked up; [...] Extending itself through College Green, through Dame Street, Westmoreland Street, and Grafton Street, it would by regular degrees occupy every foot of vacant space in this mighty metropolis.'[57] Convinced he is seeing a catastrophe overcoming Dublin as it is swallowed up in a giant nose, the poet collapses; when he regains consciousness, he is informed that the man opposite him was not a magician at all, but another writer. It is a typical Mangan moment: unsettling, perhaps not entirely serious – or perhaps deeply serious in its refusal of seriousness.

Like Swift, the memory of Mangan continues to haunt Dublin's literature. In an early poem from 1892, Yeats wrote in 'To Ireland in the Coming Times': 'Nor may I less be counted one / With Davis, Mangan, Ferguson' (Ferguson is Samuel Ferguson, a poet and translator).[58] Thomas Kinsella's first collection from 1956 contains a poem entitled 'Clarence Mangan', in which he writes of being 'stretched with terror by only a word a mouth had uttered';[59] and Brian Moore's novel *The Mangan Inheritance* (1979) involves a young American travelling to Dublin in the belief that he is descended from the poet. Michael Smith's poem 'Long Lane' (2009), named for a street a few hundred metres behind St. Patrick's, imagines the poet as a continuing presence: 'Long Lane, one of Dublin's back-streets, / just such a street as Mangan struggled down, / the winter darkness and pitchy dampness.'[60] James Joyce wrote about Mangan twice, once in 1902, and again in 1907, in what was supposed to have been a lecture in Trieste (but which was never delivered). 'His dwelling was a dark and dingy room in the old city,' Joyce wrote, 'a quarter of Dublin that even today has the significant name "The Liberties". His nights were so many Stations of the Cross among the disreputable dives of "The Liberties", where he must have made a very strange figure in the midst of the choice flower of the city's low-life – petty thieves, bandits, fugitives, pimps and inexpensive harlots.' And yet, Joyce goes on: 'So lived and died the man that I consider the most significant poet of the modern Celtic world, and one of the most inspired singers that ever used the lyric form in any country.'[61]

What is curious here is that Joyce praises Mangan as a 'singer'. While not utterly unusual as a synonym for 'poet', Joyce is always one to choose his words with care. We can put this in context. As a student at University College Dublin, Joyce had spoken to the Literary and Historical Society about Mangan. Later, when he was in Trieste between April and September of 1907, he set about turning his student work into a publishable essay, while at the same time he was completing his novella-length short story, 'The Dead', the final story in *Dubliners* (1914). He was also recovering from a bad bout of rheumatic fever at the time, and his biographer Richard Ellmann speculates that the circumstances of its composition 'probably helped him to see more clearly the ending of the story in an atmosphere of fatigue, of weariness, of swooning.'[62] We know from Joyce's other work that particular locations in Dublin were like a dictionary of associations for him; places are never random, and this practice would become ever more engrained through the composition of *Ulysses* (1922) and ultimately *Finnegans Wake* (1939). So why did Joyce locate 'The Dead' at 16 Usher's Island, on Dublin's quays, just a few hundred yards along the river from where Mangan had been born and had died on Fishamble Street?

Joyce's essay on Mangan begins with a meditation on death and remembrance (Joyce wonders if Mangan's 'spectral quiet' would be 'disturbed by a countryman in exile') and ends with the reflection that 'in the vast courses of the multiplex life that surround us, and in the vast memory which is greater and more generous than ours, probably no life, no moment of exaltation is ever lost.'[63] The story he was writing at the same time, 'The Dead', follows Gabriel Conroy and his wife, Gretta, as they make their way to 'the dark gaunt house on Usher's Island' for an annual Christmas evening of singing. The songs trigger in Gabriel a sense that the past can be redeemed through memory, and when he remembers a letter he once wrote to Gretta, 'like distant music these words that he had written years before were borne towards him from the past.' Later, back in their room at the Gresham Hotel, Gretta seems distracted, and Gabriel learns that a particular song sung that evening in the house on Usher's Island has conjured up for her a 'delicate' boy she used to love back in Galway, who died young. Gabriel suddenly feels as if 'his own identity was fading out into a grey impalpable world: the solid world itself which these dead had one time reared and lived in was dissolving and dwindling.'[64] In that moment – one of the iconic passages in Irish writing – we have, perhaps the echo of Mangan's presence, and through him the lingering sense that the dead are near on Dublin's oldest streets.

1. General Post Office, O'Connell Street
2. Spire, O'Connell Street (also site of Nelson's Pillar)
3. Percy Bysshe Shelley's rooms, 7 O'Connell Street
4. Moore Street
5. Abbey Theatre, Middle Abbey Street
6. Offices of Freeman's Journal, Prince's Street North

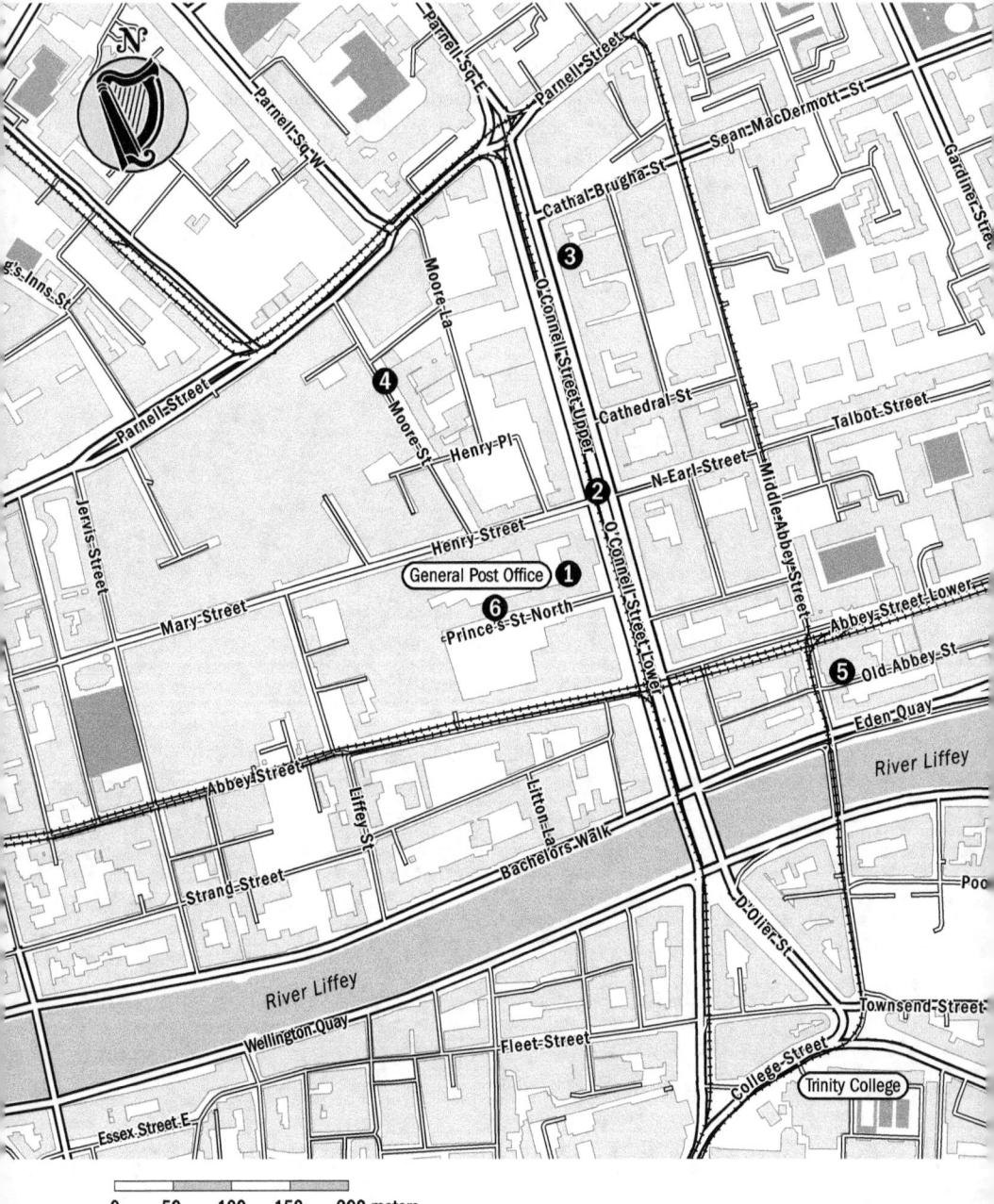

O'Connell Street and the Abbey Theatre

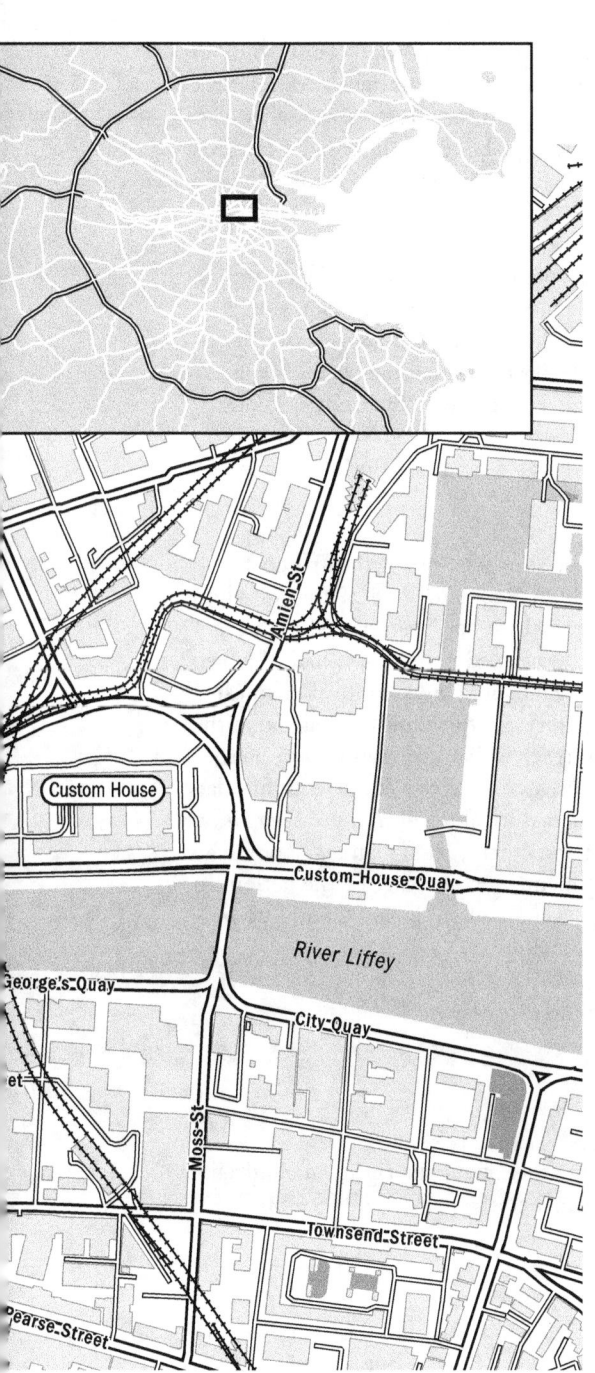

6

When the avid theatregoer and diarist Joseph Holloway set out to attend a matinee in the Empire Theatre on Dame Street on Easter Monday, 24 April 1916, he found the theatre closed, and the streets strangely quiet. 'No trams, no cars, and but a few people about.' As he walked towards Carlisle (now O'Connell) Bridge, a poster he first mistook for a theatre advertisement 'caught my eye at once':

> It had a Gaelic heading and went on to state that Ireland was now under Republican Government, and they hoped with God's help, etc. etc. to do justly by their own countrypeople. It was signed by seven names including T. J. Clarke (who headed the list), Thomas MacDonagh, Joseph Plunkett, P. H. Pearse of St. Enda's, James Connolly, and two others [Seásn Mac Diarmada and Éamonn Ceannt] in Gaelic characters. It was a long and floridly worded document full of high hopes.[1]

What Joseph Holloway had in fact seen was not a theatre poster at all, but the 'Proclamation of an Irish Republic', one of the founding documents in modern Irish history, which had been pasted up around the streets of Dublin after some 1,200 armed nationalists had occupied parts of the city that Easter Monday morning. Few political manifestos have such a consciously literary quality: 'In the name of God and of the dead generations from which she receives her old tradition of nationhood' it begins, 'Ireland, through us, summons her children to her flag and strikes for her freedom.'[2] In his historical novel *A Star Called Henry* (1999), Roddy Doyle places his fictional hero, Henry Smart, a boy who had grown up in the nearby tenements, in the heart of the action. In Doyle's novel, Henry is the first person to whom James Connolly hands a copy of the freshly printed Proclamation:

> – What do you think? He [Connolly] asked.
> – It's the stuff, I said.
> – Is it perfect?
> – Well, I said.
> – Go on, said Connolly.
> – There should be something in there about the rights of children.
> He looked at me. He saw my pain, and the pain of millions of
>   others. And his own.[3]

'This has taken everyone by surprise,' begins the Dublin-born novelist and poet James Stephens in his eyewitness account of the Easter Rising of 1916, *The Insurrection in Dublin* (1916). 'To-day, our peaceful city is no longer peaceful; guns are sounding, or rolling and crackling from different directions, and, although rarely, the rattle of machine guns can be heard also. Two days ago war seemed very far away.'[4] Earlier that Easter Monday in 1916, members of three organizations – the Irish Volunteers, the Irish Republican Brotherhood, and the socialist Irish Citizens' Army, supported by a women's auxiliary, Cumann na mBan, and a youth movement, Na Fianna Éireann – took up positions in St. Stephen's Green, occupied a biscuit factory near Mount Street Bridge, garrisoned themselves in the Four Courts on the north quays, and south of the Grand Canal took possession of the South Dublin Union poorhouse and the adjoining Jameson distillery. However, the command centre for the insurrection, and the building that most indelibly holds the memory of Rising in Dublin's streetscape, is the General Post Office (or GPO) in the centre of what is now O'Connell Street, but which in 1916 was still called Sackville Street. As was true of the other locations seized by the rebels, the GPO, with its wide façade full of windows, was 'of little strategic value' as historian Fearghal McGarry puts it. At the same time, McGarry continues, it would 'prove ideal for what would become a symbolic insurrection, [...] an act of armed propaganda rather than an attempt to seize power.'[5]

Walking down O'Connell Street today, it is difficult to imagine that it was all but destroyed by shelling during the Easter Rising. In this photo taken in the immediate aftermath in 1916, only the tramlines and Nelson's Pillar are (curiously) intact. *Courtesy of the National Library of Ireland.*

There is a delicate balance to be struck here. There was nothing fictional or poetic about the violence that occurred in Dublin in 1916. More than five hundred people, many of them civilians, and including children, lost their lives. Stephens describes seeing a man who had been shot on the first day of the Rising: 'There was a hole in the top of his head, and one does not know how ugly blood can look until it has been seen clotted in hair.'[6] There is a particularly vivid and disorienting account of the Rising in Sebastian Barry's novel *A Long Long Way* (2005), told from the perspective of Willie Dunne, a Dubliner in the British Army who has just returned from the trenches of World War I:

> It was the most astonishing thing Willie Dunne ever thought he would see in his native place. It was one of those dragoon regiments, with all the old plumage of the last century in place. But this was just Dublin in the modern day with all of modernity raging peaceably there in the principal street of the country, the second most important street in the entire three kingdoms. [...] Then, even more bizarrely, rifle shots crackled out from the General Post Office, in a most queer moment of ill-fitting likelihood, and then horses and riders started to go down [...][7]

By the end of the week, 'the second street in the entire three kingdoms' would be reduced to rubble. In Jimmy Murphy's documentary drama, *Of This Brave Time*, staged in 2016 at the Abbey Theatre, and made up entirely of verbatim eyewitness testimonies from the archives, a combatant describes the moments before the surrender. 'The appearance of O'Connell Street and the GPO was an unforgettable sight. On both sides of the streets the buildings were mostly burned out. The bodies of some civilians shot during the week were lying around, also a few horses about O'Connell Bridge. The heart of the city presented a picture of utter desolation.'[8] It would stay that way for some years. In Emma Donoghue's 2020 novel *The Pull of the Stars*, set during the Spanish Flu pandemic of 1918 and, by strange coincidence, published just as the COVID-19 pandemic that began in 2020 took hold, her protagonist, a nursed named Julia Power, is on her way to work in a Dublin hospital when she passes 'the charred carapace of the post office, one of half a dozen spots where the rebels had holed up for their six-day Rising. A pointless and perverse exercise.'[9] The history that was symbolized by this building would remain contentious for many years to come. As the speaker in Máire Mhac an tSaoi's poem 'Fód an Imris: Ard Oifig an Phoist 1986' ['Trouble Spot: General Post Office 1986'], asks: 'Anso, an ea, 'athair, a thosnaigh sé? / Gur dhein strainséirí dínn dá chéile? / Anso, an ea?' ['Here, father, is this where it started? / Here we became strangers to each other? / Was it here?']¹⁰

From a strictly military point of view (coloured by the character having a brother who fought in World War I), Donoghue's Nurse Power is historically accurate as to the Rising being 'pointless and perverse'; 1,200 volunteers entrenched in a park, a post office, a distillery, and a cookie factory were never going to defeat 20,000 soldiers equipped with artillery and naval support. In Iris Murdoch's novel set the week before the Rising, *The Red and the Green* (1965), two members of the same Anglo-Irish family, one a British army officer and one a Volunteer, contrive to keep each other away from the fighting, both arriving on O'Connell Street after the Post Office has been occupied. Here they find the street possessed of a 'sudden utter emptiness. [...] The Post Office had a strange look. The glass in all the windows had been broken and the spaces barricaded with piles of furniture. The building already had a huddled, beleaguered appearance, the air weirdly of a fortress.'¹¹

The events of 1916 and their legacy need to be put in the context of the raids and killings that took place a few years later, in the Irish War of Independence that began as a guerrilla war in 1919; and, perhaps even more traumatically, of the Irish Civil War that followed in 1922–1923, when Irish soldiers fought one another on the same ground over which they had fought the British Army only months earlier. These complex and sometimes contradictory layers of resonance emerge in one of the earliest pieces of fiction to deal with the Civil War, Liam O'Flaherty's first short story, 'The Sniper' (1923):

> The long June twilight faded into night. Dublin lay enveloped in darkness, but for the dim light of the moon that shone through fleecy clouds, casting a pale light as of approaching dawn over the streets and the dark waters of the Liffey. [...] On a roof-top near O'Connell Bridge, a Republican sniper lay watching. Beside him lay his rifle and over his shoulders were slung a pair of field-glasses. His face was the face of a student – thin and ascetic, but his eyes had the cold gleam of the fanatic. They were deep and thoughtful, the eyes of a man who is used to look at death.

The story concludes with the sniper killing a Free State Army sniper on the roof opposite; when he goes down into the street to see who he has shot, 'he turned over the dead body and looked into his brother's face.'¹²

Even as Dublin became a lethal battlefield in those spring days of 1916, there was a quality of the carnivalesque in the streets. Lia Mills captures this in her 2014 novel *Fallen* as her protagonist (who, like Emma Donoghue's Nurse Power, has a brother who fought in the War) witnesses the looting that followed the seizure of the Post Office. 'When we turned on to D'Olier Street, we saw a crowd on O'Connell Bridge', she says, 'it was like entering a fairground. [...] People thronged in all directions, pushing carts, wheelbarrows, prams piled high with goods. Children staggered past, their mouths stained with confectioners' sugar. A boy had become a jewellery tree, hats stacked on his head like upside-down nests, watches on the branches of his arms.'[13] A century earlier, James Stephens had also puzzled over this paradoxically festive aspect of the Rising. 'The people in the streets are laughing and chatting,' he writes. 'Indeed, there is gaiety in the air as well as sunshine, and no person seems to care that men are being shot every other minute, or bayonetted, or blown into scraps or burned to cinders.'[14] Liam O'Flaherty opens his 1950 novel set during the Rising, *Insurrection*, with a chapter in which his protagonist, Bartly Madden, finds himself awakening on Easter Monday, 1916, with a poisonous hangover in the midst of a crowd of inner-city Dubliners whose general view of the rebellion is that it is 'just jig-acting [...] They should all be shot without trial.' When the Proclamation is then read out from beneath the portico of the occupied Post Office, the characters in O'Flaherty's novel are described as 'now like an audience at a theatre, tensely waiting for the climax of the play's first act. Even the windows and roofs of the houses on either side of the street were thronged with spectators. Seagulls were soaring overhead on sunlit wings. The hoarse rattle of machine-gun fire came from beyond the river.'[15]

Feeding into the sense that the Rising was both real and a performance was the detail that initially misled Joseph Holloway that spring morning when he recognized four of the seven signatories of the Proclamation as established writers: Thomas MacDonagh, Joseph Plunkett, Pádraic Pearse, and James Connolly. In 1908, MacDonagh had written and staged a play, *When the Dawn is Come*, set 'fifty years hence, in Ireland, in time of insurrection'.[16] MacDonagh had also worked with another of the signatories, Joseph Mary Plunkett, to create an experimental theatre, the Theatre of Ireland, on Hardwicke Street, about a ten-minute stroll north of the Post Office; Plunkett in turn had dedicated his 1911 collection of mystical poetry, *The Circle and the Sword*, to MacDonagh.[17] Pearse had established a school (St. Enda's, which Holloway mentions) in Rathfarnham, on the southside of Dublin, in which theatre featured prominently in the curriculum, and for which he had written plays, short stories, and poems. One such poem proclaims: 'O King that was born / To set bondsmen free, / In the coming battle, / Help the Gael!'[18] Yet another signatory, James Connolly, who had founded the socialist Irish Citizen Army, had written and staged a play, *Under Which Flag?*, whose plot hinges around the main character's decision to join a rebellion. 'You will never have to blush for the boy you sent to fight for Ireland,' his mother is told at the play's conclusion.[19] *Under Which Flag?* was staged in Liberty Hall, just down the quays from O'Connell Bridge, on 26 March 1916, only a few weeks before the Rising. Seldom has there been a revolution so comprehensively imagined by its instigators beforehand. As theatre historian James Moran writes in his provocatively titled book *Staging the Easter Rising: 1916 as Theatre*: 'In 1916, it was easy for Dubliners to mistake the Easter Rising for an Easter dramatizing.'[20]

From the outset, then, the 1916 Rising had the dual quality of being a military conflict with very real consequences, and a literary event. It would also have a long literary afterlife. W. B. Yeats was in London that Easter, from where he wrote to his sister Elizabeth. 'I have no new news but what everyone has,' he confessed. 'I know most of the Sinn Fein leaders & the whole thing bewilders me for Connolly is an able man & Thomas MacDonagh both able & cultivated. Pearce [*sic*] I have long looked upon as a man made dangerous by the Vertigo of self sacrifice.'[21] Shortly after, he wrote one of his best-known poems, 'Easter 1916'. This is also one of relatively few of Yeats's poems set in Dublin, opening with a powerful image of the city's ordinary men and women 'at close of day / Coming with vivid faces / From counter or desk among grey / Eighteenth-century houses,' before moving to its resounding conclusion, in which the citizens of the city are transformed by an event whose suddenness changes everything:

> *And what if excess of love*
> *Bewildered them till they died?*
> *I write it out in verse –*
> *MacDonagh and MacBride*
> *And Connolly and Pearse*
> *Now and in time to be,*
> *Wherever green is worn,*
> *Are changed, changed utterly:*
> *A terrible beauty is born.*[22]

The 1916 Rising not only prompted one of the best-known Irish poems of the twentieth century, in Yeats's 'Easter 1916', but also provided the material for one of the most enduring Irish plays, Seán O'Casey's *The Plough and the Stars* (1926). *The Plough and the Stars* is the third of O'Casey's *Dublin Trilogy* – along with *The Shadow of a Gunman* (1923) and *Juno and the Paycock* (1924) – which are set, respectively, during the War of Independence of 1919–1920, the Irish Civil War of 1922–1923, and the 1916 Rising. In each, the fighting and the politics are almost all off stage, seen from the perspective of ordinary Dubliners living in the tenements of the north inner city. So, for instance, we hear of an attack on the GPO in *The Plough and the Stars* from the comic character of the Covey, who describes British cavalry 'throttin' along, heads in th' air, spurs an' sabres jinglin' an' lances quiverin', an' lookin' as if they were assin' themselves, "Where's these blighters, till we get a prod at them?" when there was a volley from the Post Office that stretched half o' them, an' sent th' rest gallopin' away wondherin' how far they'd have to go before they'd feel safe.'[23]

The Plough and the Stars provoked riots in the Abbey Theatre when it was first staged in 1926, led by Republicans (including relatives of those who had died) who felt that its attitude to the events of 1916 was not reverential enough. At the time, a play in which characters pledging to die for Ireland are also flirting with a prostitute and determinedly drinking pints of Guinness in a pub seemed to some like patriotic blasphemy. In retrospect, however, we can see O'Casey setting the tone for many writers who would come after him. Over time, the tendency

'There's a statue there / To mark the place / By Oliver Shepard done' – so ends Yeats's final play, *The Death of Cuchulain*. This is the same statue against which a character tries to knock himself senseless in Beckett's novel *Murphy*. This photo was taken by the Irish tourist board in 1956. *Courtesy of Dublin City Library and Archives.*

for Dublin's writers to undermine the mythologization of the Rising would overtake the mythology itself.

For instance, if you go inside the GPO, you will see a bronze statue of the mythological Irish warrior, Cuchulain, by the Dublin sculptor Oliver Sheppard. Although cast before 1916 (it actually dates from 1911), Sheppard's statue has become emblematic of the General Post Office as a kind of sacred space in Irish history, the site where ordinary Irish women and men in 1916 were 'changed, changed utterly' into the heroes of myth, such as the warrior Cuchulain. This mythic version of history was largely created by literature in the first place, in poems such as Pádraic Pearse's 'I am Ireland', which contains the line: 'Great my glory / That I bore Cuchulain the valiant.'[24] Likewise, in one of his great later poems, 'The Statues', from his *Last Poems* in 1939, Yeats asks:

> When Pearse summoned Cuchulain to his side,
> What stalked through the Post Office? What intellect,
> What calculation, number, measurement, replied?[25]

And yet it would be through literature that this myth would be unravelled as well. In the same months he was writing 'The Statues', Yeats was at work on his final play, *The Death of Cuchulain* (1939), in which, after the death of his weakened hero, the stage is taken over by a balladsinger, who asks: 'What stood in the Post Office / With Pearse and Connolly?' His answer: 'A statue's there to mark the place, / By Oliver Sheppard done. / So ends the tale that the harlot / Sang to the beggarman.'[26]

The year before Yeats's *Death of Cuchulain*, Samuel Beckett's novel *Murphy* (1938) appeared, which contains a (very funny) scene in which a character named Neary is 'recognized by a former pupil named Wylie, in the General Post Office, contemplating from behind the statue of Cuchulain. Neary had bared his head, as though the holy ground meant something to him. Suddenly he flung aside his hat, sprang forward, and seized the dying hero by the thighs, and began to dash his head against the buttocks, such as they are.' Neary is about to be detained by the not-terribly-bright policeman on duty, who calls out 'Howlt on there, youze', but, 'happily Wylie, whose reactions as a street bookmaker's stand were as rapid as a zebra's, had already seized Neary round the waist, torn him back from the sacrifice, and smuggled him halfway to the exit.'[27] Today, it is difficult to see the statue without also seeing Neary preparing to make his parodic 'sacrifice'. For anyone who has

Looking up O'Connell Street (then Sackville Street) at around the turn of the twentieth century, from Carlisle Bridge, the street is alive with multiple forms of traffic – not least, pedestrians. Nelson's Pillar is to the right, and the General Post Office just opposite.
Courtesy of the National Library of Ireland.

read Beckett, it is Cuchulain's buttocks that are of the greatest interest, not the aura of sacrifice that hangs around the building:

> The bronze hero [...]
> faces the tourist regiments, the banners
> and flags of old politics,
> raised fists and effigies, schoolchildren
> who cannot tell Parnell from O'Connell.'[28]

So writes Gerard Smyth in his 2020 poem 'Cúchulainn in the GPO'. From O'Casey's *Plough and the Starts* to Beckett's buttock-bashing hero or Smyth's 'tourist regiments', Dublin's writers have long been attuned to a distinctive, paradoxical quality of this part of Dublin: a tendency for the carnivalesque to erupt on what should be holy ground.

On the face of it, O'Connell Street should be Dublin's ceremonial centre, its Mall or Pantheon, a streetscape whose sense of a majestic expanse

> **Streets Renamed:** While the Georgian and medieval streets retained many of their original names, some of Dublin's major thoroughfares were renamed for national heroes after Irish Independence in 1922. The renaming of Sackville Street had been proposed as early as 1885, but was not changed to O'Connell Street (after Daniel O'Connell, who had won Catholic voting rights in 1829) until 1921; in 1923, Great Brunswick Street became Pearse Street (after Pádraig Pearse), while Gloucester Street (running parallel to O'Connell) became Seán MacDermott Street (after another of the signatories of the 1916 Proclamation) in 1932.

was by design. Originally called Drogheda Street (before it became Sackville Street in the 1750s), it was named for Henry Moore, Earl of Drogheda, whose name was literally inscribed in the map of the city, with the surrounding streets still known as Henry Street, Moore Street, and Earl Street; there was once even an Of[f] Lane (to complete the topographical signature, Henry Moore, Earl *of* Drogheda).²⁹ 'I never looked up Sackville Street without pleasure,' writes Elizabeth Bowen in her childhood memoir, *Seven Winters*, 'for I was told it was the widest street in the world.'³⁰ And yet, for at least the past century, O'Connell Street has always had something of the giddy air of a circus. It is a streetscape whose scale commands a certain ceremonial grandeur inhabited by Dubliners who refuse to act solemnly. Writing in 1962 in her travelogue *My Ireland*, the novelist Kate O'Brien lamented that 'sometimes now when I consider the pitiful mess of rebuilt O'Connell Street from the Bridge to Nelson's Pillar, I smile back sadly to that other time, when this present stretch of absolutely comical commercial vulgarity was a huge, swept-away arena of tragedy in black and white.'³¹

In the second novel in Joe Joyce's espionage trilogy set in Ireland during World War II, *Echobeat* (2014), his protagonist Paul Duggan is on his way to meet someone who works on O'Connell Street who he hopes will spy on a group of Germans who meet in a nearby café, when he gets stuck with his bicycle on Henry Street. 'He realized his mistake: he shouldn't have come this way on Christmas Eve. The street was crowded with shoppers who had taken over the roadway as well, reducing traffic to less than their own walking pace. He abandoned his attempt to cycle through them and walked with the bike up past the raucous shouts from Moore Street. He was almost at the side of the GPO when the crowds thinned enough and he threw his leg over the saddle and pedalled up to the Pillar.' A few chapters later, he attends a New Year's Eve dance in the Gresham Hotel, emerging after midnight to an O'Connell Street full of taxis, only to hear 'the flat crump-crump of explosions' as two Luftwaffe bombs fall on the South Circular Road.³² This is also the nightlife, a generation later, into which Kate and Baba in Edna O'Brien's *The Country Girls* (1960) arrive with such initial euphoria, 'the neon fairyland of Dublin. I loved it more than I had ever loved a summer's day in a hayfield. Lights, faces, traffic, the enormous vitality of people hurrying to somewhere.'³³ A few more generations later, a

> **Trams:** As Dublin's suburbs expanded in the 1870s, a system of commuter trams developed to meet the demand. Between 1872 and 1879, five companies opened eleven different routes, connecting the city centre with Sandymount, Donnybrook, Dartry, Rathmines, Rathfarnham, Glasnevin, Drumcondra, and Clontarf. The trams remained a feature of the Dublin streets until they were replaced by buses; the last Dublin tram ran in 1949.

character in Roddy Doyle's novel *Love* (2020) tells us: 'O'Connell Street was wild. There was fight at the [taxi] rank outside the Gresham. There was blood on the ground, and a tooth. There was a screaming girlfriend and another girl who was trying to get at her hair.'[34]

Today, O'Connell Street still has that same energy and motion (or 'comical commercial vulgarity', if you prefer), compounded by an untidy mixture of burger joints, donut shops, and sports stores, Luas trams, Dublin buses, and shoppers from the adjoining streets, particularly from Henry Street and Talbot Street. There always seems to be someone selling something on O'Connell Street. Dublin's main street market for fruit and vegetables is just around the corner on Moore Street, while the flea market known as 'the Cobbles' is nearby on Cumberland Street North, and street-sellers often spill over into the main thoroughfare. Moreover, as the population of Dublin has diversified in the first decades of the twenty-first century, and significant populations of new Irish people, particularly from South-East Asia and West African countries, have moved into many of the streets around O'Connell Street, they have embraced the street market culture of the area, and now shops selling African hair extensions and traditional Chinese medicine share

While Admiral Nelson may not have been universally popular in Dublin, the vantage point from the top of his Pillar – which could be accessed for ten pence – was. This is the view of the crowds below on O'Connell Street in 1921. *Courtesy of the National Library of Ireland.*

'Look: the spire's a spindle or axis and while it's not vinyl the city is a record of all that has happened to us, is happening, or will' – so begins Dylan Coburn Gray's play, *Citysong* (2019). The Spire, erected in O'Connell Street in 2003, continues to divide opinion, with some critics pointing to its complete lack of context in a street rich with historical resonance. *Photography by Seán Harrison.*

Moore Street with the stalls of Dublin women selling apples or prams full of wrapping paper.

For many Dublin writers over the years, the tension between the street's imposing ceremonial quality and its combustible street life was given a focus in the forty-metre-high pillar, surmounted by a statue of Horatio Nelson, which was both the street's architectural centrepiece, and which, from the 1880s onwards, functioned as the city's main tram terminus. James Joyce, always alert to the pulse of his city, captures the city's more than slightly ironic attitude to the Pillar in the 'Aeolus' episode of *Ulysses* (published in 1922, but set in 1904). This episode is set in the offices of the *Freeman's Journal* newspaper, just around the corner from the GPO. Each chapter in *Ulysses* is written in a different style, and this chapter mimics the form of a newspaper, broken into small sections with headlines – beginning with the one captioned 'In the Heart of the Hibernian Metropolis':

> Before Nelson's pillar trams slowed, shunted, changed trolley, started for Blackrock, Kingstown and Dalkey, Clonskea, Rathgar and Terenure, Palmerstown, part and upper Rathmines, Sandymount Green, Rathmines, Ringsend and Sandymount Tower, Harold's Cross. The hoarse Dublin United Tramway Company's timekeeper bawled them off.
> – Rathgar and Terenure!
> – Come on, Sandymount Green!
> Right and left parallel clanging ringing a double-decker and a singledecker moved from their railheads, swerved to the down line, glided parallel.
> – Start, Palmerstown Park![35]

Later in the chapter, the character Stephen Dedalus tells a tale of two Dublin ladies, 'elderly and pious' from 'Fumbally's lane' (in the Liberties) 'who want to see the views of Dublin' from the top of the pillar (it had a viewing platform at the top). They struggle up the narrow, winding staircase, but once at the top, they only have the energy to 'settle down on their striped petticoats, peering up at the statue of the onehandled adulterer', spitting plum pits down at the people below.[36] He calls it 'The Parable of the Plums', and if nothing else it tells us something about Dubliners' reverence for heroes of all stripes.

The Admiral Nelson who stood atop his pillar in an independent Ireland was no longer the hero of the Battle of Trafalgar commanding a view of Dublin's central thoroughfare as he had once commanded the seas; he is reduced to the 'onehandled adulterer' (he had lost a hand in the battle), marooned by history atop his pillar. In his poem 'The Three Monuments' (1927), Yeats uses Nelson on his pillar to take a similar swipe at post-Independence politics. He imagines Nelson conferring with the statue of Charles Stewart Parnell (erected in 1910), at the top of O'Connell Street, and that of Daniel O'Connell (erected in 1882), on the Liffey end of the street: 'They hold their public meetings where / Our most renownèd patriots stand / [...] among the birds of the air.' Yeats's monuments preside over an Ireland in which 'popular statesmen say / That purity built up the State', to which, Yeats retorts: 'The three old rascals laugh aloud.'[37] In 'Dublin', written at the onset of World War II, in 1939, Louis MacNeice refers to 'Nelson on his pillar / Watching his world collapse',[38] while at around the same time, Oliver St. John Gogarty, in his memoir *As I Was Going Down Sackville Street* (1937), captures this same sense of the hero abandoned by the retreating empire: 'That pillar marks the end of a civilization, the culmination of the great period of eighteenth-century Dublin, just as the pillar at Brindisi marks the end of the Roman road.'[39]

It was not simply the sense of being stranded by the falling tide of history that made the statue of Nelson so irresistible for Dublin's writers; it was equally the contrast between the kind of po-faced imperial patriotism that the statue represented, and the irrepressible street life around it. In his autobiography, Seán O'Casey writes of 'the dark form of Nelson looming up before him, thrusting his haughty head into

> **Nelson's Pillar:** While it stood, Nelson's Pillar was the most visible monument in Dublin. Built in 1809 from money raised by public subscription, it stood just over forty metres high; Katharine Tynan claimed it was visible from Belgard, ten kilometres away. For an initial cost of ten pence, it was possible to climb the 168 steps to the viewing platform at the top, until the pillar was finally dynamited by the IRA in 1966.

the purple sky, looming like a rod of discipline over the people, out of the dark, in Dublin, Ireland's sailor boy, one arm missing and one eye gone; but watching with that one eye the slum kid rolling in the mud; [...] the bobby bringing the drunk safe home to the police station; the bloated, blossom-faced whores waiting for randy men to go with them to the stews to see the sights.'[40] Later, in his 1957 poem 'Nelson's Pillar, Dublin', Austin Clarke sees Nelson as a fitting figure to stand over the 'Capital for the few' in an independent Ireland still rife with inequality: 'No, let him watch the sky / With those who rule. [...] Let him stand / There, imagining our land.'[41] In the end, it is perhaps Richard Murphy in 'Nelson's Pillar' (1985) who best captures the contradictions of the Pillar by giving Nelson a voice: 'I never controlled the verminous / Poor beggars round my plinth, schooled to rebel. / I was loved well as a tramway terminus.'[42]

'In March 1966,' writes John Banville in his memoir, *Time Pieces* (2016), 'in the small hours of the morning I was jolted out of sleep by a distant thud that was not so distant that it did not make the panes of bedroom window rattle. [...] *The isle is full of strange noises*, I thought dreamily, and fell back to sleep.'[43] He later awoke to find that Nelson's Pillar had been blown up by Republican activists to mark the fiftieth anniversary of the 1916 Rising. However, Nelson had barely been dynamited off his pillar when it became apparent that the street looked empty without some kind of vertical feature to offset its width – that his function had been architectural as well as commemorative. In 1988, the Pillar was replaced by an elongated fountain designed by sculptor Éamonn O'Doherty, based on the figure of the river as a woman, Anna Livia Plurabelle, from James Joyce's *Finnegans Wake*. After too many incidents of creative vandalism (filling the fountain with soap suds was a favourite), it was replaced in 2003 by a more invulnerable 120-metre pure spike of graffiti-proof stainless steel, designed by Ian Ritchie Architects. Even with Anna Livia gone, however, the Joycean trace remains, in a statue of Joyce at street level across from the Spire, of which Caitriona Lally's protagonist in her novel *Eggshells* (2018) muses: 'I cross the Spire onto North Earl Street, passing the statue of James Joyce with his legs crossed. He looks easy to topple and, if I had to read *Finnegans Wake*, I'd probably try to topple him.'[44]

Unlike Nelson's Pillar or the Anna Livia Fountain, the Spire's complete lack of any historical resonance has made it a blank slate for the city's writers. For instance, Dylan Coburn Gray's play *Citysong*

(2019), in which the voices of the city form a sort of urban symphony, begins with the Spire. 'Look: the spire's a spindle or axis and while it's not vinyl the city is a record of all that has happened to us, is happening, or will. It spins as the world does and a godlike needle could read its spaces, how it bumps and juts and dimples and cavities, as pages or notes in the book or the symphony of us.'[45] In Christine Dwyer Hickey's 2011 novel *The Cold Eye of Heaven*, her elderly protagonist, Farley, wanders around Dublin, lost in a modern city constantly shadowed by the older city he remembers. 'And now here he is, standing in the island in O'Connell Street, looking up at the glint of the giant needle that used to be Nelson's Pillar. And thinking about the junkies again and trying to pull the two ends of the same idea together; the junkies and the giant needle.'[46] Pat Boran's poem 'The Spire (10 Years On)' celebrates Dubliners' irreverent propensity for giving civic monuments satirical nicknames: 'Stiletto in the ghetto, / Monument of blight, / The nail in the coffin, / The "we" reduced to "I".[47]

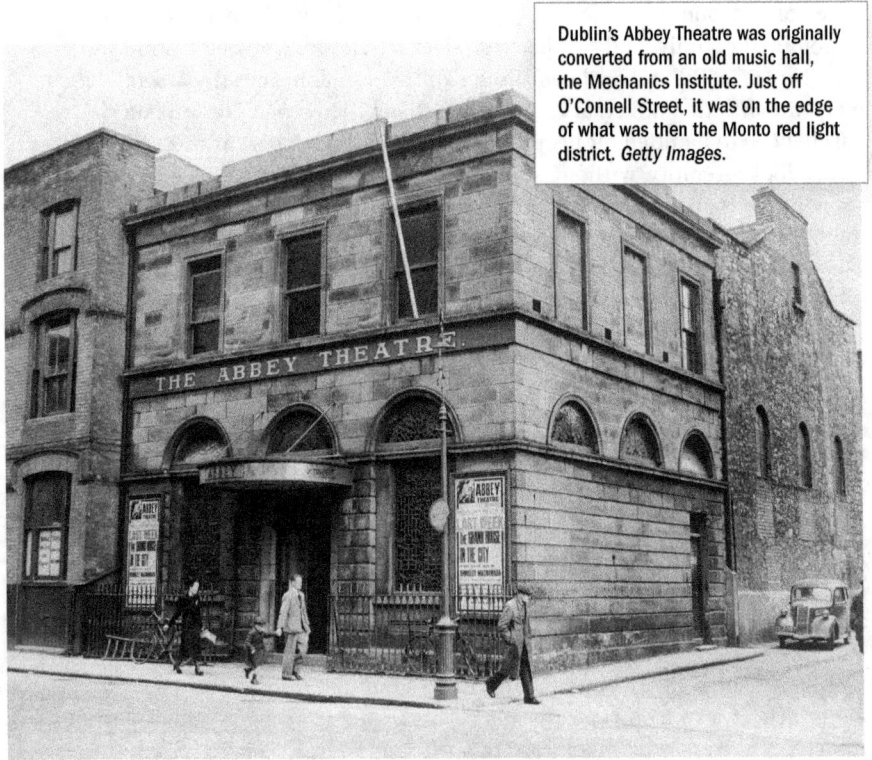

Dublin's Abbey Theatre was originally converted from an old music hall, the Mechanics Institute. Just off O'Connell Street, it was on the edge of what was then the Monto red light district. *Getty Images*.

In Sally Rooney's 2021 novel *Beautiful World, Where Are You*, one of the characters, Alice, observes that Dublin is, 'literally and topographically, flat – so that everything takes place on a single plane':

> Other cities have metro systems, which add depth, and steep hills or skyscrapers for height, but Dublin has only short squat grey buildings and trams that run along the street. [...] It gives the sky a position of total dominance. Nowhere is the sky meaningfully punctuated or broken up by anything at all. The Spire, you might point out, and I will concede the Spire, which is anyway the narrowest possible of interruptions, and dangles like a measuring tape to demonstrate the diminutive size of every other edifice around.[48]

A century earlier, in one of the most extraordinary passages in George Moore's memoir *Hail and Farewell* (1911–1914), Moore captures what can be the reverse effect of the still determinedly low-rise scale of the city's centrepiece: the revelation of sky, the sudden sense of openness. Crossing O'Connell (or Carlisle, as it was then) Bridge with Yeats, Moore is suddenly almost supernaturally aware of 'the houses on the other side, the quays themselves, the gulls floating between the bridges, everything seemed to have put off its habitual reality, to have sloughed it, and to have acquired another – a reality that we meet in dreams.'

Moore is here walking with Yeats in 1904 on their way to the Mechanics Institute on Middle Abbey Street, which housed a small library where Moore notices 'twenty or more shabby genteel scholars who sat reading ancient books under immemorial spider webs.'[49] The building also had a theatre space, in which a young Seán O'Casey had acted in popular melodramas as a young man, 'strutting the stage there before a rough-and-randy crowd who came to while away the time, but who put great pass on the suffering and rollicking that shivered and shone on the stage.'[50] On the day that Moore accompanied him, Yeats had been negotiating the purchase of the Mechanics Institute as a home for the Irish Literary Theatre he had founded with Lady Gregory and Edward Martyn a few years earlier, and this dusty old theatre would become the Abbey Theatre. 'It is extraordinary what conviction they can put into their dreams,' Moore thought to himself that afternoon as he crossed the bridge over the Liffey.[51]

The Abbey's founders were not content simply to found a theatre; they also wanted to rewrite Irish cultural history around it. 'I was asked the other day to tell when the Irish Theatre had come into being,' writes Lady Gregory in her memoirs. 'I said I could tell the very day, almost the moment, and that was true in a sense – I was as it were present at its birth.' She then dismisses (not entirely fairly) most of what had taken place on Irish stages in previous centuries – 'The nineteenth century was a chilly and scanty one where Irish literature was concerned' – before dating the beginning of modern Irish literature to the death of the Irish Parliamentary Party leader Charles Stewart Parnell (whose statue stands at the top of O'Connell Street) in 1891. 'Parnell's death,' she writes: 'That was the unloosing of forces, the disbanding of an army. In the quarrels that followed and the breaking of hopes, the imagination of Ireland had been set free, and it looked for a homing-place.'[52] While there is an element of creating a personal mythology to these recollections, it pales beside that of her collaborator, Yeats, the master self-mythologizer. In the section of his autobiographies entitled 'After Parnell', Yeats declares that 'the sudden emotion that now came to me, the sudden certainty that Ireland was to be like soft wax for years to come, was a supernatural insight.'[53] And yet, both of these accounts capture something of the retrospective wonder at the sense of being part of an abrupt, once-in-a-lifetime cultural reimagining that took place in Dublin at the turn of the twentieth century, akin to James Stephens opening his account of 1916 with the words: 'This has taken everyone by surprise,' or Yeats's own 'changed, changed utterly.'

Something truly remarkable happened in the theatre in Dublin in the early years of the last century, and it appropriate that it should have found a home only a few hundred metres from the site of the 1916 Rising. There was, in those, years, a conviction (a 'supernatural insight', in Yeats's case) that sudden transformation was possible, and that it could occur in the most unlikely of places – such as a converted music hall on the edge of what was the red light district. 'I would not be trying to form an Irish National Theatre,' Yeats wrote in an essay published to accompany the opening of the new theatre in 1904, 'if I did not believe there existed in Ireland, whether in the minds of a few people or of a great number I do not know, an energy of thought about life itself, a vivid sensitiveness to the reality of things.'[54] What is more, not only did this 'revolutionary generation' (to use Roy Foster's phrase) believe sudden, radical change was possible, both in politics and in the arts, they also believed in a cause-and-effect relationship between culture and politics, in which a transformed theatre or new forms of fiction or poetry would lead to a transformed nation. As Foster reminds us, the revolutionary (and later playwright) Kathleen O'Brennan wrote in

1906: 'Through the drama, our people can be [...] taught that what we need most is the power of concentrating through ourselves.'[55]

This utopian sense of possibility runs deeply through this part of the city as a kind of counterpoint to the carnival, from which it is nonetheless inextricable. Between them, the General Post Office on O'Connell Street, and the Abbey Theatre on Middle Abbey Street – separated by less than three hundred metres – are like two galvanic poles of a battery at a time when politics and literature inhabited the same neighbourhood in more than a strictly topographical sense. Indeed, this axis sits over an even deeper deposit of transformative dreaming. In February 1812, when the poet Percy Bysshe Shelley arrived in Dublin, attracted by the non-violent potential of the embers of the 1798 rebellion, he lived at 7 Sackville Street, roughly midway between the two. Here he wrote his *Address to the Irish People*. 'Think and talk, and discuss,' he exhorted. 'The only subjects you ought to propose, are those of happiness and liberty. Be free and be happy, but first be wise and good.'[56] Much later, in 1974, Brendan Kennelly imagined Shelley overwhelmed by the sheer poverty of Dublin, in his long poem 'Shelley in Dublin', where he has the English poet say: 'I close my eyes at night / And walk the drunken streets / Of Dublin and of hell.'[57]

It is in light of this sense of utopian possibility that we can understand the famous theatre protests of the Abbey's early years. It was not that Irish audiences were not somehow uniquely rowdy. Quite the opposite: on the occasions that Abbey audiences rioted, it was because they took theatre seriously, and when the utopian failed, the carnivalesque burst through the doors. So, when during its first week in January of 1907 John Millington Synge's *The Playboy of the Western World* ended with one half of the audience singing 'God Save Ireland', and an equally energetic part of the audience in the more expensive stalls singing 'God Save the King', it was not simply bad manners; it was a kind of public debate about serious questions of allegiance, identity, and freedom, given a form that came from the city streets around the theatre. Likewise, when Seán O'Casey's *The Plough and the Stars* opened there on 11 February 1926, the play spoke to what had taken place in the streets and pubs just outside the stage door. 'You have disgraced yourselves again,' Yeats told the rioters in a carefully prepared speech from the stage. 'The news of the happenings of the last few minutes here will flash from country to country.'[58] From the stalls, a Republican activist, Hanna Sheehy-Skeffington responded: 'The Free State Government is subsidising the Abbey to malign Pearse and Connolly. We have not come here as rowdies. We came here to make a protest against this defamation of the men of Easter Week.'[59] At the time, the protest appeared to be yet another piece of unfinished business between competing Civil War parties; in retrospect, it may appear like another chapter in the ongoing tug of war between national reverence and the messy energy of the streets that inhabits this whole area of Dublin.

At the same time, there were periods of real violence when the theatre could not contain what was happening in the streets. As Yeats admitted in his Nobel acceptance speech in 1923, 'audiences grow thin when there is firing in the streets.'[60] Indeed, the firing did not always remain in the streets. 'We're through the worst now I hope,' the long-serving Abbey theatre director and playwright Lennox Robinson wrote to Lady Gregory in July 1924, in a letter now in the New York Public Library. 'A few stray shots came into the Abbey through the windows over the stage, probably they came from the National troops who were on the roof of Trinity trying to get snipers who were on Hopkins roof. Also on some day, Monday possibly, the National troops broke into the Mechanics Institute and barricaded some of the upper windows with old books.'[61]

And yet, just as the Proclamation of 1916 with its injunction to 'cherish all the children of the nation equally' left its utopian trace in the politics of the Irish state so, too, has the Abbey's foundational belief that theatre is more (or other) than simply entertainment created a set of expectations that is triggered every time the curtain rises. At many points over the decades, when that potential has not been realized, criticism of the Abbey has been no less harsh than that levelled at the Irish state itself for failing to live up to its founders' ideals. And so, we find Flann O'Brien's helpful suggestion in his 'Cruiskeen Lawn' column in the *Irish Times* in the 1950s that whiskey should be piped directly to each seat in the Abbey by means of rubber tubes, 'through which our middle-aged sucklings could draw their golden pap without leaving their seats.' 'How is it so few can stand a play cold sober,' he wondered.[62] Likewise, Patrick Kavanagh once blamed the quality of Abbey plays in the 1950s for the decline in Dublin conversation. 'If the plays at a particular theatre are persistently bad, the people who come to talk in the foyer will stay away. And this is the best part of any play.'[63]

At the same time, the opposite is also true, and there continues to be a kind of invisible red line, just about visible in the cracks in the pavement, connecting the Abbey Theatre to the utopianism of 1916 in the

General Post Office. And every so often it lights up on the Abbey stage. This happened on the night of 20 February 1973, when Brian Friel's play based on the 1972 shooting of Civil Rights marchers in Derry, *The Freedom of the City*, opened; and again on the evening of 29 September 1983, when during a play set in the dingy office of a quack therapist, Tom Murphy's *The Gigli Concert*, it was possible to glimpse theatre as a place of transformation; or, once again, in October 1994, when Frank McGuinness's play about Northern Irish unionists in World War I, *Observe the Sons of Ulster Marching towards the Somme* (1985) was revived just weeks after the IRA declared a ceasefire in Northern Ireland, and a new understanding seemed possible. Or on the night of 1 February 2014, when Panti Bliss, a self-described 'drag queen and accidental and occasional gay rights activist' (and, indeed, playwright) gave her 'Noble Call' speech from the Abbey stage after a production of *The Risen People*, a stage version of James Plunkett's Dublin novel *Strumpet City*. That speech, on homophobia and its effects, would later be seen as pivotal in the vote for marriage equality the following year:

> Have any of you ever been standing at a pedestrian crossing when a car drives by and in it are a bunch of lads and they lean out the window as they go by and they shout 'Fag!' and throw a milk carton at you? It doesn't really hurt. It's just a wet carton, and, anyway, they're right – I am a fag. So, it doesn't hurt, but it feels oppressive. And when it really does hurt is afterwards, because it is afterwards that I really wonder, and worry and obsess over, what was it about me, what was it they saw in me? [...] It feels oppressive.[64]

At such moments, we once again see how Dublin is still a city in which words are important, and in which words spoken in the street can be refashioned by the city's writers and performers on stage in ways that channel the street's energies into the possibility that all can be changed, changed utterly.

1. Séan O'Casey born, 85 Dorset Street
2. R.B. Sheridan born, 12 Dorset Street
3. Henrietta Street
4. James Joyce Street (Monto)
5. J.S. Le Fanu born, 45 Lower Dominick Street
6. Austin Clarke born, 83 Manor Street
7. Séan O'Casey's rooms, 35 Mountjoy Square
8. Brendan Behan born, 14 Russell Street
9. Iris Murdoch born, 59 Blessington Street
10. Bloom residence in Ulysses, 7 Eccles Street
11. James Joyce residence, 17 North Richmond Street

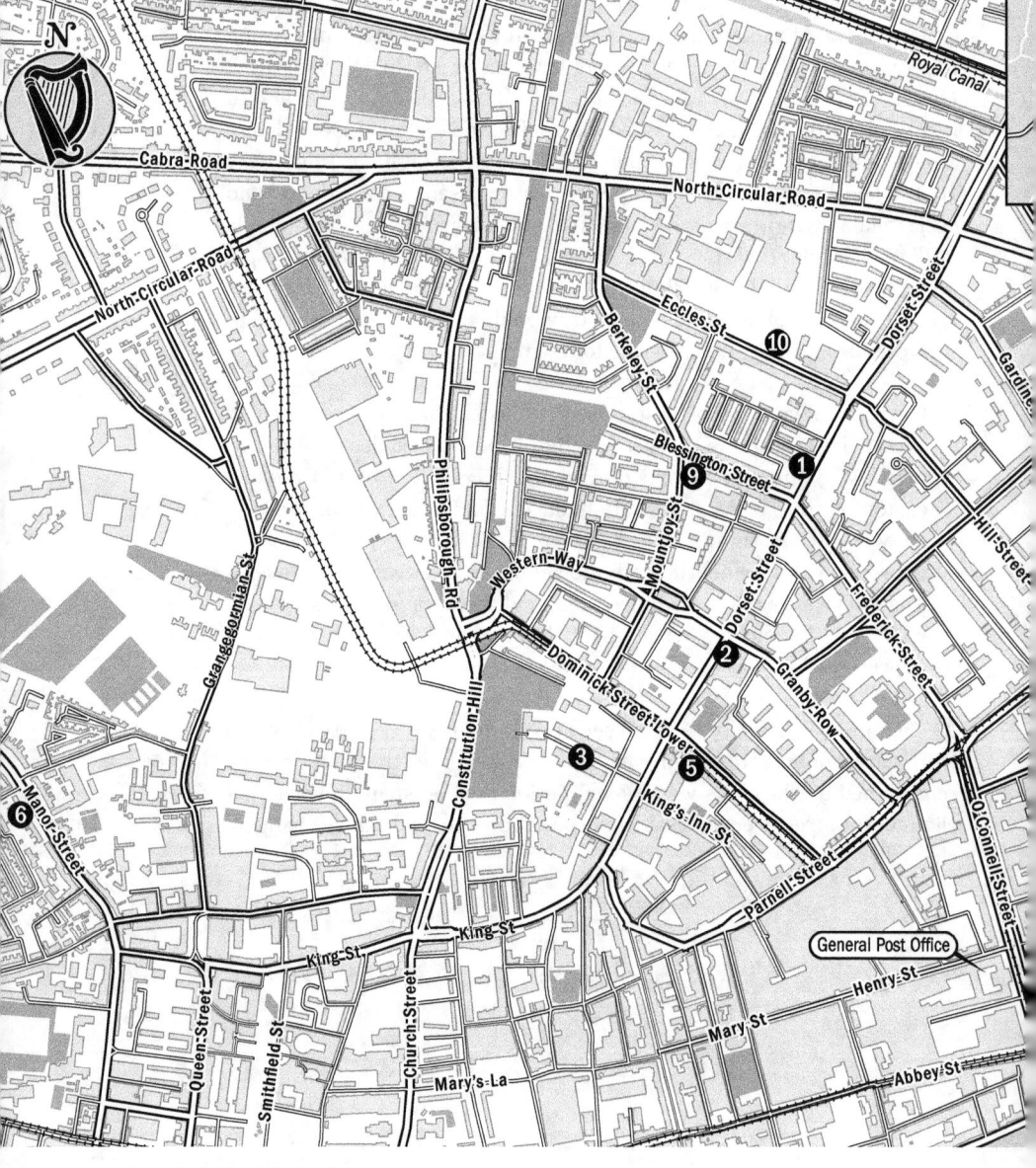

The North Inner City

7

Part elegant and part slum
Skies cleared by rain,
Plum-blue hills for a background;
Dublin, of course.
The only city that has lodged
Sadly in my bones.[1]

If O'Connell/Sackville Street is the ceremonial spine of the north city, the streets that frame it on three sides are where we find the starkest instances of the contradictions that define Dublin, so concisely captured in Sheila Wingfield's short poem 'A Melancholy Love' (1974): 'part elegant and part slum'. 'My childhood city was the north inner city,' Paula Meehan told Eavan Boland in a dialogue published in Boland's *A Poet's Dublin* (2014): 'Sean Mac Dermott Street where we lived in one of the Corporation tenement flats, the Gloucester Diamond, Mountjoy Square.' She also had a family connection to the nearby area known as 'The Monto': 'My great-grandmother Anna Meehan was a madame at the turn of the century when the Monto was the biggest red-light district in Europe. A hidden history in our family.'[2] 'In them days the whole area was call the "Monto",' seventy-two-year-old Tommy 'Duckegg' Kirwan told social historian Kevin C. Kearns in his oral history of the Dublin tenements. 'See, it was Montgomery Street when the English was here, and that's how it was called 'Monto' for short. It got a bad name. These places were called kip houses, the red-light houses,' Tommy said, going on to recall how when he was a child the prostitutes would 'let down a can with a string on it to go off and get them gargle at the pub, to get the stout, and hand the can up agin.'[3]

Duckegg Kirwan was born in the year that James Joyce published *Ulysses*, 1922, and he grew up in the same streets in which Joyce sets the novel's 'Circe' episode. The episode takes place at night, as a disoriented Stephen Dedalus and Leopold Bloom, after unwittingly crossing paths all day, meet in Bella Cohen's brothel in the Monto, which Joyce calls 'nighttown'. This is an hallucinogenic chapter, in which characters from throughout the novel appear and then vanish as if in a drunken dream: 'The Mabbot Street entrance of nighttown, before which stretches an uncobbled tramsiding set with skeleton tracks, red and green will-o'-the-wisps and danger signals. Rows of flimsy houses with gaping doors. Rare lamps with faint rainbow fans.'[4] The brothels in the Monto were closed down shortly after *Ulysses* was published, and Mabbot Street has since been renamed James Joyce Street. It is now home to ANU, a theatre company co-founded by Louise Lowe and Owen Boss, whose

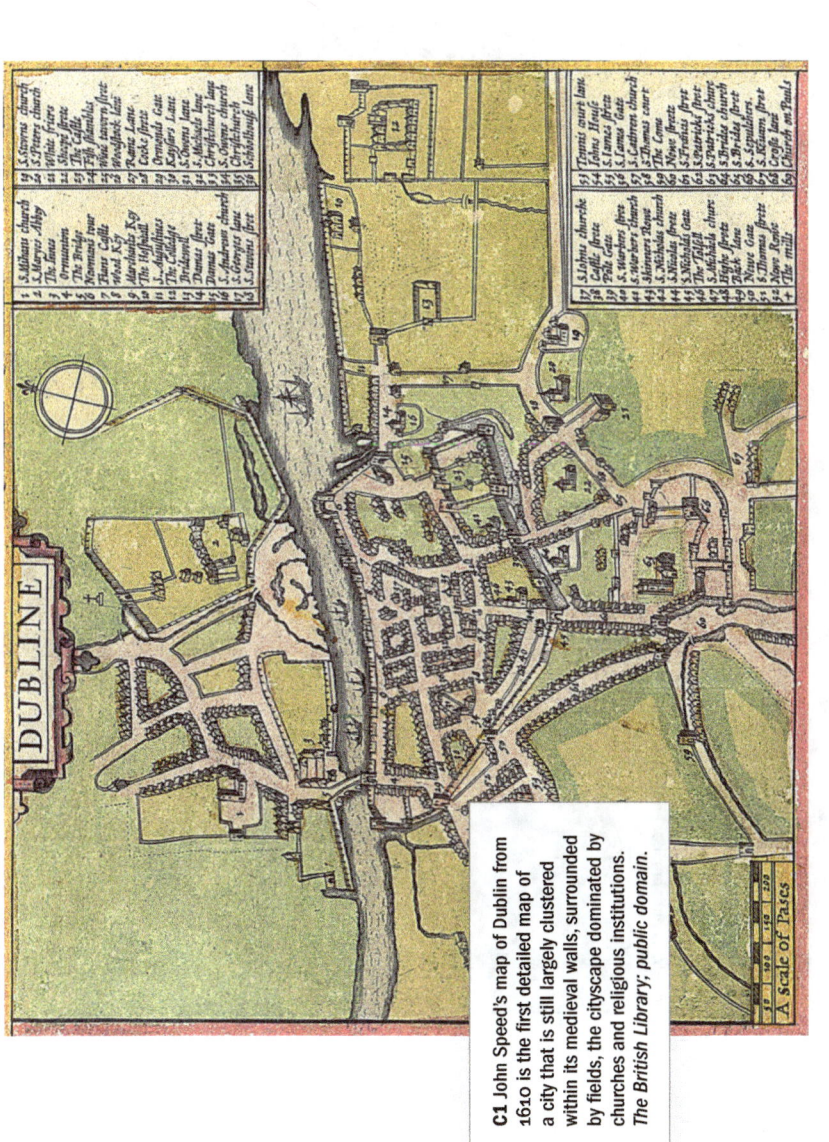

C1 John Speed's map of Dublin from 1610 is the first detailed map of a city that is still largely clustered within its medieval walls, surrounded by fields, the cityscape dominated by churches and religious institutions. *The British Library; public domain.*

C2 John Rocque's map of 1756 is the most detailed of the 18th-century maps of the city. Note the open fields beyond St. Stephen's Green in the bottom right, and ships in the mouth of the Liffey. The city it portrays,' writes poet Peter Sirr, 'is both familiar and alien.' *Public domain*.

C3 This map of Dublin from 1836 originally published by the Society for the Diffusion of Useful Knowledge shows a defined city core, and the effects of the Wide Streets Commission in laying out thoroughfares. However, even as late as this, the canals still define the city limits, both to the north and to the south, with fields and trees where there are now densely-populated suburbs. Society for the Diffusion of Useful Knowledge; public domain.

C4 *Plan of Dublin*, 1939. By the middle of the twentieth century, Dublin has moved beyond a city core defined by the ring of the canals. Note the Celtic cross streetscape of Crumlin just inside the city boundaries, and the extent to which the Phoenix Park still marks a western boundary. *Geographia Ltd., London, ca. 1935; public domain.*

C5 This portrait of Sydney Owenson, Lady Morgan, by the French painter René Théodore Berthon evokes the world of private libraries, correspondence and Kildare Street salons of her *Memoirs*. René Théodore Berthon. Public domain, via Wikimedia Commons.

C6 When it was first staged in 1926, Sean O'Casey's play about the 1916 Rising, *The Plough and the Stars*, provoked riots for a scene in which an Irish flag was unfurled in a pub – seen here in Wayne Jordan's 2016 centenary production at the Abbey Theatre. The actors (left to right) are Mark Fitzgerald (Lieutenant Langon), Barry Ward (Jack Clitheroe), Karl Quinn (The Figure in the Window), Tony Flynn (A Bartender), and Dara Devaney (Captain Brennan). *Photography by Fergus Bourke. Courtesy of The Abbey Theatre Archive.*

C7 On a gable end at 20 Richmond Cottages, not far from where he grew up on Russell Street, Shane Sutton's mural of Brendan Behan is as woven into the streetscape as Behan himself had been when he was one of Dublin's most celebrated and visible writers. *Alamy*.

C8 'Commemorate me where there is water, canal water …' Poets Brendan Kennelly and Paula Meehan, walking along the banks of the Grand Canal, near the statue of Patrick Kavanagh by John Coll (1991). The occasion was the launch of the collection of Dublin poetry, *If Ever You Go*, edited by Pat Boran and Gerard Smyth. *Photograph by Dara Mac Donaill. Courtesy of Irish Times.*

C9 For many years, novelist John Banville kept a small flat just opposite the Ha'penny Bridge in Dublin, where he claimed to find the rhythms of the city conducive to writing. Many of his Benjamin Black novels were written here. *Photograph by Brenda Fitzsimons. Courtesy of Irish Times.*

C10 'I don't know if writers ever are properly in the place where they live,' novelist Anne Enright told an interviewer in 2008. 'They're always in a slight state of exile.' She is pictured here on the beach at Bray, near where she lives at the very edge of the greater Dublin area. *Photograph by Fran Veale, Getty Images.*

C11 Sally Rooney's first two novels, *Conversations with Friends* and *Normal People* take place mostly in and around the centre of Dublin. Her 2021 novel, *Beautiful World, Where are You?*, centres around a successful writer who leaves Dublin for the west of Ireland. Rooney was photographed here on Grattan Bridge for an interview with *Elle* magazine in 2017. *Photograph by Patrick Bolger.*

C12 'We're very much in the realm of starchitects and designers who flit easily between cities across the globe,' Peter Sirr writes of Dublin's Docklands. The poet Thomas Kinsella (1928–2021) – one of the great chroniclers of the city's hidden histories – is here pictured in the redeveloped Grand Canal Square in 2010. *Courtesy of Irish Times.*

The conditions in Dublin's tenements in the early twentieth century were amongst the worst anywhere in Europe. In this rare photograph of a tenement room, the remnants of the original fireplace and wood panelling contrast sharply with the paucity of furnishing and general state of collapse. *Courtesy of the Royal Society of Antiquaries of Ireland.*

'Monto Cycle' of plays – *World's End Lane* (2010–2011), *Laundry* (2011), *The Boys of Foley Street* (2012), and *Vardo* (2014) – interrogated the history of the area through a series of site-specific performances, drawing heavily on oral histories. Staged in the buildings and on streets of the area, *World's End Lane* goes back to when the area was a red-light district at the beginning of the twentieth century ('World's End Lane' was the original name for what became part of Montgomery Street); the second play, *Laundry*, was staged in one of the Monto's unlikely neighbours, the Magdalene Laundry in Railway Street, in which nuns of the Sisters of Charity incarcerated so-called 'fallen women'. *The Boys of Foley Street*, staged on the street itself, and in a nearby Corporation flat, picks up the story from when heroin tore through the social fabric of the community in the 1970s and 1980s, while *Vardo* brings the story up to the present with the stories of the many migrant workers who now live in the area, and who help to 'fuel a thriving invisible economy'.[5] Collectively, these plays make up an epic cycle of a few narrow streets through which it would be easy to pass on the way from O'Connell Street to Connolly Station without paying much notice to the bookies, pubs, and small shops along the way.

We could go back further, however. The area that became the Monto (bordered by Gardiner Street, Summerhill, and Marlborough streets) began neither as a red light district nor as tenements. When it was first built in the eighteenth century, it was a new development for the wealthy and professional classes who wanted clean air and wide streets away from the dilapidation and congestion of the medieval city around St. Patrick's Cathedral. Indeed, there was a period during which some of the most impressive townhouses in the city were being built on the north side of the city. The jewel in the crown was Henrietta Street, begun in the 1730s, followed by the great mansion of Tyrone House on Marlborough Street in 1740 (which was a counterpart to Leinster House on the southside; it is still impressive as offices for the Department of Education). This in turn prompted planning of the spacious mall of Drogheda (later Sackville, and later again O'Connell) Street in the 1750s, which was also originally residential, followed by the development of Mountjoy Square, while the surrounding areas were populated in the 1780s by only slightly less prestigious homes for 'the merchant and official class'.[6]

> **Wide Streets Commission:** Created in 1757, but given enhanced authority and funding in 1782, the Wide Streets Commission was a planning body set up by the City that effectively redrew the map of Dublin, widening streets like Dame Street and Gardiner Streets, building Carlisle (later O'Connell) Bridge, and laying out new streets to create connecting thoroughfares and vistas. The walkable (and cyclable) city of today owes much to the Commissioners' foresight.

At the heart of this community of privilege was the world's first purpose-built maternity hospital, the Rotunda, on what is now Parnell Square, which was funded in part by its adjacent pleasure gardens. This became 'the unchallenged hub of city fashion'.[7] 'Here concerts, masquerades, card-parties and balls were held,' writes social historian Constantia Maxwell in *Dublin Under the Georges* (1937). 'There were walks and shrubberies, a spacious bowling-green and a grand terrace upon which an orchestra played.'[8] A little over two hundred years later, this would be the hospital in which Sharon Rabbitte would give birth in Roddy Doyle's *The Snapper* (1990). And, in the continued repurposing of buildings in this part of the city, the northern side of the square is where The Hugh Lane Gallery of modern art found a home in a former city mansion, and where Poetry Ireland, which publishes the major Irish poetry magazine, *Poetry Ireland Review*, is now based in a building whose fine plaster cornices are a reminder of a genteel past.

It may take some imagining now to picture this part of the city as a new, upmarket housing development, but that is precisely what it was.

Although usually associated with his home on Merrion Square, on the south side of the city, the gothic novelist Joseph Sheridan Le Fanu was born here, at 45 Lower Dominick Street, just as the area was going into decline in 1814. His unnerving 1872 story 'The Familiar' is partly set here a century earlier. In it, a retired sea captain, Captain Barton, finds himself constantly hearing footsteps as he walks around the city at night – a situation that escalates in terror. At one point, Barton is making his way home through streets still under construction in the north city: 'The road on either side was embarrassed by the foundations of a street, beyond which extended waste fields full of rubbish and neglected lime and brick-kilns, and all silent now as though no sound had ever disturbed their dark and unsightly solitude.'[9] It is worth speculating whether Le Fanu, who lived through the period during which the once-fashionable townhouses of Dominick Street were being turned into tenements, was prefiguring the area's decay in this uncanny story of a haunting. In 'The Familiar', it is in this wasteland of an unbuilt city that he first realizes that whatever he is hearing is not natural and wants to kill him.

The street in which Le Fanu was born was the same one in which Lady Morgan (who would later have her own impressive political and literary salon on the city's south side, not far from where the adult Le Fanu would live on Merrion Square) lived for a time, when she was still Sydney Owenson, as companion to Lady Steele in the 1790s. Lady Steele had moved into a 'fine, old-fashioned furnished house in Dominick Street' whose 'costume of the eighteenth century' included curtains of 'rich crimson satin damask' and 'a beautiful marble chimney-piece, finely sculptured, which reached half way to the ceiling, and was surmounted with a range of Etruscan vases.' However, as Owenson recalls in her memoirs, the ladies quickly decided that 'this antique splendour' needed to be 'replaced by the style of the furniture then in vogue' and the room was soon filled with late-Georgian chic: 'lemon-coloured calico hangings, highly glazed with dark chintz borders; the Etruscan vases were replaced by ornaments of Derbyshire spar, and pier tables painted and gilded.'[10]

This, then, was the world of the northside of Dublin at the end of the eighteenth century, and it would linger in pockets for a few years yet, with some of the more impressive Protestant churches of the time – always a good marker of prosperity – being built in the early nineteenth century: St. George's in 1815, St. Mary's (known as 'The Black Church') in 1830, and the Abbey Presbyterian Church (known as 'Findlater's',

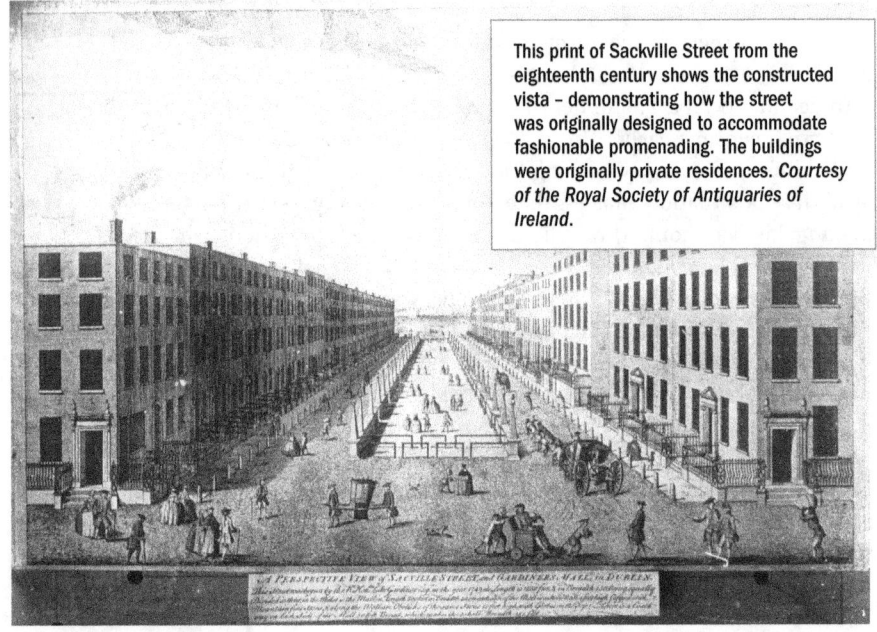

This print of Sackville Street from the eighteenth century shows the constructed vista – demonstrating how the street was originally designed to accommodate fashionable promenading. The buildings were originally private residences. *Courtesy of the Royal Society of Antiquaries of Ireland.*

after the wine merchant who sponsored it) in Rutland (later Parnell) Square, belatedly in 1864. Indeed, as late as 1878, when Oliver St. John Gogarty was born nearby at 5 Rutland Square East, it was still a fashionable address. In some parts of the north city, however, even as Owenson and Lady Steele were redecorating with lemon-coloured calico, the neighbourhood was declining.

This can be measured in various ways. David Dickson notes, for instance, that in 1800 there were six peers and eight Members of Parliament with addresses on Sackville Street; when Shelley arrived to rent rooms there twelve years later, there were none.[11] Property prices are also a useful indicator of such matters, and Kevin Kearns notes that city mansions on the northside that had sold for £8,000 in 1791 were selling for £2,500 by 1801, and £500 by 1849. At a time when the city's population was expanding rapidly, property speculators bought up these massive old houses at a fraction of their original value, and divided them up for rental to as many families as they could cram into each high-ceilinged room. By the 1870s, even the magnificent houses of Henrietta Street were slums; by the time of the 1911 Census, what had been fifteen single-family houses on the street were occupied by 835 people, including members of nineteen different families who were shoehorned into 7 Henrietta Street.[12] By any measure, these were horrific slums.

The north inner city, then, has long been shaped by the lives of people living and working in buildings that were meant for other purposes, and hence do not quite function as they were designed. The novelist Christine Dwyer Hickey captures this eloquently in her novel *The Cold Eye of Heaven* (2011), in which an elderly lawyer, Farley Slowey, his grip on reality receding, wanders around a contemporary Dublin in which the present is increasingly confusing, overlaid with memories. Wandering into his legal offices on the north quays, just down from the Four Courts, he finds it empty of living people, but inhabited nonetheless by 'past lives that have been lived in here, first as reception room for a family of merchants. Later a tenement flat for God knows how many. Later again a series of come-and-go offices before Slowey & Co. Legal and Town Agents, finally came to roost here. Chrissy [his receptionist] told him once that these two rooms were a ballet school in the twenties.'[13]

If small legal practices increasingly colonized the buildings around the Four Courts, closer to O'Connell Street what had originally been built as a residential district would become, by the middle of the nineteenth century, one of the city's main shopping areas. McSwiney, Delaney & Co., described as 'one of the first purpose-built department stores in the world', opened opposite the GPO in 1853,[14] becoming Clery & Co. in 1883. It remained a Dublin landmark until its closure in 2015, with its clock a well-established meeting point for both real and fictional inhabitants of the city. 'On the street of laughing gulls', writes Gerard Smyth in 'Clery's Clock' (2020), 'the shy and brazen stood in wait, / Eros met his Aphrodite; / the hands of Clery's Clock told us we were late.'[15] However, outside of the department stores and later the shopping arcades, this has long been a place for a different kind of shopping. The north inner city is bounded to the west by the wholesale food markets of Smithfield, and, at one point, cattle markets. At the area's heart is still the open-air fruit and vegetable market on Moore Street, a Dublin institution of which the writer Christy Brown declares, in his poem 'City Dweller' (1977): 'I've never looked down from the hills of Mourne / to the laughing sea at my feet / for the grandest of scents to my nostrils borne / came from the stalls in Moore Street.'[16] Paula Meehan, in 'Buying Winkles' (1991), remembers being sent as a child 'out into Gardiner Street', to find the woman selling periwinkles: 'She'd be sitting outside the Rosebowl Bar / on an orange-crate, a pram loaded / with pails of winkles before her.' It was, she writes, 'the sweetest extra winkle / that brought the sea to me. / "Tell yer Ma I picked them fresh this morning."'[17] In his memoir *Twice Round the Black Church* (1962), Austin Clarke makes a pilgrimage back to the small grocer's, the sweet shop, and the butcher's shop that he remembers from his childhood at 83 Manor Street, finding that 'as I came towards Capel Street, memories were jumping over the counters, and bounding out of shops that had changed their owners long since or had gone down in the world.' He recalls in particular the magical smokehouse behind the butcher's shop, with its 'glowing ashwood, and almost hidden in the gloom above hung the Limerick hams.'[18]

> **Cattle Markets:** Memoirs of growing up in Dublin in the late nineteenth and early twentieth centuries almost all mention cattle in the streets. From the end of the seventeenth century, sales of cattle in the city were common, and in 1863 a large cattle market was opened in Prussia Street. Within a few years, more than three-quarters of a million cattle were sold here every year, many of them herded down the North Circular Road to the docks for export. The markets continued to operate until the 1970s.

Geographically, this area rich with the memory of 'past lives lived' forms something of a ring with O'Connell Street as its core, bounded by the Royal Canal to the north, cut off from the Phoenix Park to the west by the Smithfield markets and Collins Barracks (now a museum), and from Dublin Bay to the east by the docks. Perhaps more than anything, what unites this wider north inner-city area is the memory of the tenements and their surviving traces. So when Clarke revisits the shops of his youth in the early 1960s he walks past 'the Georgian mansions that have been tenements for three-quarters of a century or more'. 'Now they have been condemned by the Corporation, being in too bad a state to be saved.' He walks down 'a dead street for the time being, windows concreted, floors ripped, sudden gaps of basement. A few of the tenements were still inhabited and I stared in a ground-floor window with a feeble greenish light within, perhaps from a broken gas mantle; cardboard patches against a few of the broken panes, the door wide open, the hallway pitch-black and ill-smelling.'[19] What Clarke was witnessing in the 1960s was the final act of a long-term housing crisis that had been taking shape since at least the 1790s, when the Reverend James Whitelaw's *Essay on the Population of Dublin* recorded people living 'crowded together to a degree distressing to humanity', at one point counting 108 people in a single tenement.[20]

> **Rev. James Whitelaw:** The Rev. James Whitelaw was the vicar of St. Catherine's Church, in the Liberties, when in 1798 he realized that it would be impossible to begin to help the poor without an accurate assessment of the total population of Dublin. He thus began the first door-to-door census of the city, along the way cataloguing at first hand the truly appalling living conditions of the poorest. His final tally – 182,370 – is the first accurate census of Dublin, while his eyewitness accounts are a unique record.

The tenements hold a paradoxical place in Dublin's literature. They are often thought of as having been ignored, as something deliberately unseen; and yet, at the same time, Dublin's literary culture would be very different without them. The sense that the inner-city slums were somehow overlooked is partly due to the rural and peasant focus of so many plays from the early Abbey Theatre, whether John Millington Synge's *The Playboy of the Western World* or the comedies of Lady Gregory. In fact, the first Abbey play to deal directly with tenement life was *Blight*, staged at the Abbey Theatre by Joyce's friend, Oliver St. John Gogarty, in 1917. 'With noise, misery, and vermin, rest is impossible, not to talk of sleep,' tenement-dweller Tully tries to explain to a well-meaning philanthropist, Lady Maxwell-Knox, who assumes that alcohol abuse is the root problem (as opposed to being a symptom) in the tenements. 'Why do we drink? Because we want to sleep,' Tully informs her, adding (with a typical Gogarty flourish), 'and because it's cheaper than chloroform!'[21]

Blight touches on something that features in all accounts of tenement life: the enforced intimacy of entire families living in a single room, and of multiple families in a single building – a situation by turns degrading, dangerous, exhausting, and at the same time fostering a rich sense of community. 'Eight families living in my tenement,' eighty-year-old Maggie Murray told Kearns in his oral history. 'I had four sisters and three brothers. Me mother's sister had twenty-one children! We grew up in one small room and six of us slept in one bed. [...] Sure, the bed was loaded with bugs and hoppers and you'd be scratching yourself.'[22] Likewise, the protagonist of James Stephens's novel *The Charwoman's Daughter* (1912) lives 'in a small room at the very top of a big, dingy house in a Dublin back street. As long as she could remember she had lived in that top back room. She knew every crack in the ceiling, and they were numerous and of strange shapes. Every spot of mildew on the ancient wall-paper was familiar.' Her window stayed firmly shut, because it was covered in grime, and every time she opened it, 'she was forced to wash herself, and as water had to be carried from the very bottom of the five-story house up hundreds of stairs to her room, she disliked having to use too much water.'[23] Stephens's novel, Paula Meehan would later recall when thinking of her own childhood in the north inner city, was one that 'deeply affected the way I read the city.'[24]

Again and again, Dublin's writers have been struck by the contrast between the extreme poverty of the occupants of these buildings when they were tenements, and the leisured lives of their original owners. In Maura Laverty's 1951 Gate Theatre play, *Liffey Lane*, one character, Billy, describes his room in the basement of a tenement on Hardwicke Street. 'My basement home even has running water … it trickles musically down the walls. Lying in bed at night, I'll imagine myself back in the days of good Lord Hardwicke. I'll torture myself by making believe that I'm listening to the decanting of the madeira and sack that were once cradled in my cellar.'[25] In a similar way, Christy Brown in *Down All the Days* (1970) remembers his mother telling the family stories of the dilapidated house on North King Street where she had lived before Christy was born, that was 'supposed to be haunted' by its earlier inhabitant, the notorious judge Lord Norbury, the so-called 'Hanging Judge' who had sentenced Robert Emmet to death. 'A house once elegant where men had lived elegant lives, frock-coated gentlemen with powdered wigs and aristocratic noses.'[26] Similarly, in James Joyce's *Finnegans Wake* (1939), this disorienting sense of an aristocratic past haunting the poverty of the present takes the form of a single, long unspooling sentence, jumping back and forth through time: '[…] floors dangerous for unaccompanied old clergymen, thoroughly respectable, many uncut pious books in evidence, nearest watertap two hundred yards away, fowl and bottled gooseberry frequently on table, man has not had boots off for twelve months, infant being taught to hammer flat piano, outwardly respectable, sometimes hears from titled connection, one foot of dust between bannister and cracked wall […]'.[27]

The tenements are also the setting for one of the most enduring Dublin novels, James Plunkett's *Strumpet City* (1969), set during the Dublin Lockout of 1913. The novel's main setting is a tenement at a fictional address, No. 3 Chandlers Court. 'The steps that led up to the hall were uneven, the fanlight was broken, the door stood wide open. The area showed a basement window stuffed with cardboard. From each window of the four storeys above poles stuck out and carried ropes which supported clothes.' However, Plunkett does make use of a real episode that ultimately prompted the clearing of the tenements, when, on 2 September 1913, two tenement buildings on Church Street collapsed, killing seven people. One of Plunkett's characters later witnesses 'the skeletons of two houses, their rooms and stairways laid naked by the collapse of the wall. Twisted beams and broken floors and masonry hung at dangerous angles. From time to time, pieces of brick and wood were wrenched loose by the wind and raised a cloud of dust as they fell.'[28] Fifty years later, in June 1963, the same thing would happen again, when within a few weeks of one another, Georgian buildings collapsed in Bolton Street and in Fenian Street, killing four Dubliners. In this instance, the tragedies were used to justify the demolition over the next decade of a further 1,200 historic buildings, which one city planner likened to 'a horde of silent zombies'.[29]

For all that has been written about the north inner city, the writer who has done most to shape the literary imagination of this part of Dublin has been Seán O'Casey. O'Casey was born in this part of Dublin in 1880, at 85 Upper Dorset Street. In the previous century, in 1751, when the street was newly built and fashionable, the playwright Richard Brinsley Sheridan, author of the phenomenally popular *School for Scandal* (1777), had been born at nearby 12 Dorset Street. Both Sheridan's mother, Frances Sheridan, and his father, Thomas Sheridan, were also playwrights, with Thomas Sheridan forever engrained in Dublin's memory as the manager of the Smock Alley Theatre who managed to provoke two theatre riots. 'The house in Dorset Street was modest and elegant at the same time,' writes R. B. Sheridan's biographer, Fintan O'Toole; 'a solid four-storey building in a newly developed part of Dublin, respectable but not ostentatious.'[30] If Sheridan was one of the most successful and enduring playwrights of the eighteenth century, the same is true for the nineteenth century of Dion Boucicault, who in 1820 was born around the corner, at the top of Gardiner Street. When, his play *The Colleen Bawn* opened in Dublin's Theatre Royal in 1861, it was one of the theatrical events of the century, and Dubliners pulled his carriage in triumph through the streets on its opening night. There are probably few other streets in the world in which there was a major playwright born in three successive centuries in what is effectively the same neighbourhood.

By the time O'Casey was born on Upper Dorset Street, the area had gone the way of so many surrounding streets, and No. 85 was listed as a tenement at the time of his birth. The family moved around the corner not long after to a smaller but more recently built residence, an artisan's cottage at 9 Innisfallen Parade, before moving to a terraced house in the docklands. O'Casey thus knew the world of the tenements well, and his first major play, *The Shadow of a Gunman* (first performed at the Abbey in 1923) was written while he was sharing a room in a Georgian tenement building at 35 Mountjoy Square. The stage directions for the play are precise. 'A Return Room in a tenement house in Hilljoy Square [O'Casey's thinly disguised name for Mountjoy Square]. To the back two large windows looking out into the yard; they occupy practically the whole back wall space. [...] Running parallel with the window is a stretcher bed; another runs at right angles along the wall at right.' The play hinges around those two 'stretcher beds' placed head-to-head: one is the bed of an aspiring writer, Donal Davoren, who lets it be imagined that he is a gunman, and the other is occupied by Seumas Shields, a pedlar. Davoren (in O'Casey's detailed stage directions) 'bears upon his body the marks of the struggle for existence and the efforts towards self-expression,' whereas the burly Shields 'frequently manifests the superstition, the fear and the malignity of primitive man.'[31] The constant abrasion of these two utterly incompatible personalities, thrown together by necessity and cramped living quarters, is what drives the play; and in that respect it sets the template for the rest of his *Dublin Trilogy.*

The Shadow of a Gunman was followed by *Juno and the Paycock* in 1924, and *The Plough and the Stars* in 1926. Collectively, the plays are usually linked as documents of the Irish revolution, set during the War of Independence, Civil War, and 1916 Rising respectively. However, they are also united by being set in tenements. *The Plough and the Stars*, for instance, opens with a workman attempting to fit a lock to the door of the rooms that the main characters, Jack and Nora Clitheroe, are trying to make into a respectable home. This aspiration for privacy is in constant conflict with the other tenement-dwellers, whose sense of

In Seán O'Casey's Dublin plays, characters live their lives on the streets as much as in their tiny tenement rooms. This vibrant street scene is from the 1976 Abbey production of *The Plough and the Stars*, with Bill Foley and Angela Newman as Uncle Peter and Mrs Gogan and Siobhán McKenna as Bessie Burgess. *Photograph by Fergus Bourke. Courtesy of the Abbey Theatre Archive.*

communal space has no place for locked doors. Of the character Mrs Grogan, for instance, we are told, 'a fly could not come nor go out of the house without her knowing.' Likewise, the Clitheroe's lodger, Uncle Peter, lives in a room in which he is unable to avoid the character known as The Covey, who takes delight in annoying him. 'Lemme out, lemme out', howls Uncle Peter. 'Isn't it a poor thing for a man who wouldn't say a word against his greatest enemy to have to listen to that Covey's twartin' animosities, shovin' poor, patient people into lashin' out of curses that darken the soul with th' shadow of th' wrath of th' last day?'[32] The trouble is, in a tenement, you have to listen: there is nowhere else to go.

In fact, collectively O'Casey's *Trilogy* also provides us with an anatomy of a tenement house, a kind of inhabited architectural cross-section of a single building. For instance, the opening act of *The Plough and the Stars* is set in 'the front and back drawing-rooms in a fine old Georgian house, struggling for its life against the assaults of time, and the more savage assaults of the tenants. The room shown is the back drawing-room, wide, spacious, and lofty.'[33] The identification of the rooms – 'front and back drawing-rooms' – is extremely precise here. In *Shadow of a Gunman*, Donal Davoren lives in the 'return room' – that is, the box room at the turn (or 'return') of the stairs, far less desirable than the ground floor where the Clitheroes live in the companion play. The character of Maisie Madigan, when she first appears in *Juno and the Paycock*, is introduced by the room she inhabits, as 'an oul' back-parlour neighbour'. Mrs Grigson, who appears in *Shadow of a Gunman*, is described as 'one of the cave-dwellers of Dublin, living as she does in a tenement kitchen' (which would have been in the basement), 'to which only an occasional sickly beam of sunlight filters through a grating in the yard.' At the top of the house, the character of Bessie Burgess, in *The Plough and the Stars*, lives in 'one of two small attic rooms; [...] the ceiling slopes up towards the back, giving to the apartment an air of compressed confinement.'[34]

Each room tells a story. Donal Davoren's 'return room' at the back of the house is a mark of his real inconsequentiality, while Bessie Burgess's rooms at the top of the house are a sign of her ability to rise above political differences, and so on. In *Juno and the Paycock*, 'the living-room of a two-room tenancy occupied by the Boyle family in a tenement house in Dublin' fills up with furniture (including a gramophone) on the expectation of an inheritance. However, when this hope evaporates, and even the modest furniture that had been on the stage at the beginning has been repossessed, the rooms return to their original poverty. His son abducted, his wife and daughter gone, it is into this empty tenement room that one of O'Casey's most memorable characters, Captain Boyle, the 'paycock' of the play's title, stumbles at the final curtain, rip-roaring drunk, and it is the room as much as the character that provides the play's lasting image. 'The counthry'll have to steady itself,' he announces to his equally drunken sidekick, Joxer. 'It's goin' … to hell … Where'r all … the chairs … gone to … steady itself, Joxer … Chairs'll … have to … steady themselves [...] I'm telling you … Joxer … th' whole worl's … in a terr … ible state o' … chassis!'[35]

In the word 'chassis' – Boyle's distinctive pronunciation of 'chaos' – O'Casey captures in a single word the ambivalent quality of life in the tenements. Tenement life unquestionably was chaotic, with no running water, no locks on the doors, and the constant fear of eviction. However, 'chassis' is not the same thing as 'chaos'. There is a certain affection contained in the word, much in the way that even though Captain Boyle drinks his family into penury, he is among O'Casey's most enduring and popular creations. There is a paradox here, also found in oral histories of the tenements. On one hand, while everyone who lived in a Dublin tenement speaks of the awful privations – dirt, disease, violence, addiction, and hunger – at the same time many remember with fondness their communal life. 'It was a hard life,' Mary 'Bluebell' Murphy told Kevin Kearns. 'But I wish I was back in the tenement again. We were all one family, all close. We all helped one another. If I had a tenement house now I'd go back and live in it. … yes, I would.'[36] We glimpse here what the sociologist of urban life Richard Sennett has called 'the uses of disorder'; he argues that attempts to iron out all of the inconveniences of city life in the name of efficiency ultimately destroy communities, because 'the most direct way to knit people's social lives together is through necessity, by making men need to know about each other in order to survive.'[37]

'Did you know that not a stone's throw from us was born Seán O'Casey, author of *The Plough and the Stars?*', Brendan Behan's mother, Kathleen, asked in her autobiography, *Mother of All the Behans*.[38] For fourteen years, through the 1920s and 1930s, the Behans lived at 14 Russell Street, 'in a Georgian House that had gone to rack and ruin as a tenement,' with one toilet for fourteen families, as Behan himself put it.[39] 'He was the first actual writer I saw', Paula Meehan recalls. 'My father pointed him out to me. He was staggering from Murray's public house in Seán Mac Dermott Street. "A great writer, but a terrible messer," was my father's verdict.'[40] 'I don't want to give the impression that Russell Street was the worst slum in Dublin,' Kathleen Behan would later note, giving us a sense of the fine distinctions that existed in tenement life. 'In fact, it was more on the fringes of Slumdom (though, Heaven knows, nobody today would put up with the conditions there). For all the overflowing lavatories and the fights between drunken old bowsies, I was living like a queen compared to the people in the Diamond.'[41]

When he was in his teens, however, Behan's family were moved from Russell Street to a house in the new southside suburb of Kimmage where it borders Crumlin,[42] as part of an initiative by Eamon de Valera's government to clear the tenements. 'He built those great housing estates like something you'd see in Siberia,' recalled Kathleen Behan. 'It was a terrible thing to move half the city out on to the sides of mountains, without schools, buses or shops. Out in the slums we lived a rebellious, anarchic life that didn't suit the new Ireland at all.'[43] Her son Brendan was also miserable. 'Again and again,' as one of his biographers put it, 'he wandered back to Russell Street looking for his old companions and for the warmth and camaraderie of his first fourteen

One of the great transformations of Dublin in the twentieth century was the replacement of tenements with social housing. In this photograph from 1933, bricks of the demolished eighteenth-century buildings on Mary Lane in the north inner city are being shovelled away, while the new flats lie ready for occupancy. In the background is the tower of St. Michan's Church, whose foundations date from 1095. *Courtesy of Dublin City Library and Archives.*

years.'[44] 'I remember, when we got our notice to get moving,' recalled Brendan Behan, 'hearing one oul' wan moaning to my mother: "Oh! Mrs. Behing, jewel and darling! don't go out to Kimmage – that's where they ate their young." Four miles away it was, and no more, where this cannibalism took place.'[45] For Behan, the streets in which he grew up remained his imaginative territory, and it would be here that he would set the plays on which his reputation rests.

Behan's play *The Quare Fellow*, which premiered at the Pike Theatre on Herbert Lane in 1954, takes place in Mountjoy Prison, signalled to the audience in the opening minutes when a prisoner sings of 'The Old Triangle', which goes 'jingle jangle / All along the banks of the Royal Canal'[46] – the Royal Canal that ran past the end of Russell Street, a few hundred yards up from the prison. His later play, *The Hostage* (1959) – which began life as an Irish-language play, *An Giall* (1958) – is set in Nelson Street (again, nearby), in what the stage directions describe simply as 'an old house in Dublin that has seen better days'.[47] While both of these plays are far from plotless – one is set the night before an execution in the prison and the other involves a British soldier taken hostage by the IRA – what really drives them is character and an exuberant delight in language. In this respect, Behan is precisely what many thought him to be at the time: a successor to O'Casey. 'The tenement plays of Seán O'Casey were wonderfully affirmative,' writes Paula Meehan, 'as I had lived amongst the children and grandchildren of his characters, and I never agreed with the notion that he wrote caricature – if people have nothing except their personalities then there is an art to being in the world which might come across as larger than life.'[48] Part of this sense of life as performance involves a certain extravagance of speech, an emblem of which might be the extra syllable that an inner city accent adds to 'Dublin': 'Dubbalin' (as in the collection of Behan's journalism, *The Dubbalin Man*). This is more than accent; it is an attitude to language, and it was forged in the tenements.

When stories matter – when they are all you have – and that is combined with life in an enclosed, tightly knit community, individuals can become their stories, and their identities are etched with the sharp definition of a stage light. One marker of this is the prevalence of nicknames, which become almost a form of street poetry, the wearable haiku of a life. So we have real-life individuals such as 'Duckegg' Kirwan and 'Bluebell' Murphy, who spoke to Kevin Kearns. Dominic Behan also recalls that 'Russell Street was a great place for meaningful nicknames'. One woman on the street who once offered her neighbour a less-than-generous bacon sandwich was known as 'Half-a-Rasher',[49] making her a cousin (or perhaps half-cousin) to Rashers Tierney, the protagonist of *Strumpet City*, or Cut-the-Rasher in Maura Laverty's *Liffey Lane*. Brendan Behan's writings are peppered with figures such as the German fishmonger from Summerhill 'who was known as Frankenstein for short', or the notably short ex-soldier known as 'Duck-the-Bullet'.[50] His early novel *The Scarperer* opens in a Dublin pub where Pig's Eye, the Goofy One, Nancy Hand, the Shaky Man, and Tralee Trembles are getting an early start on the day's drinking. 'Pig's Eye,' Nancy Hand tells him. 'You're the colour of a corpse that's not in its health.'[51] Pig's Eye gets a cameo again in *The Hostage*, which also includes a scene in which an inspector requests a list of tenants in the boarding house in which the play is set: 'Bobo, The Mouse, Ropeen ...'[52] Likewise, all of the principle characters in *Juno and the Paycock* – Juno, the Captain, and Joxer – have nicknames, while O'Casey's less memorable characters tend to have more pedestrian names like Johnny or Mary. Fluther Good, in *The Plough and the Stars*, was in fact named after a real Dubliner, a prodigious drinker from Foley Street, and when John Ford's film version of the play appeared in 1937, the real Fluther took legal proceedings against O'Casey for giving his name to a character who was an earnest, sober trade unionist.[53] Indeed, when one rare character from beyond the pale of the north city appears in O'Casey's *Plough and the Stars*, she has no name at all; in the script she is simply 'The Woman from Rathmines'.

If the tenements and their memory dominate Dublin's north city, it would be a mistake to think of this part of the city as being one unremitting expanse of poverty, even in the 1920s and 1930s. The poet Austin Clarke's family, for instance, were by no means destitute; he was educated in the early years of the century at the private Jesuit school, Belvedere College, where he began to acquire his scholarly understanding of early Irish-language poetic forms. When he looked out at Manor Street, what he later came to see was its etymology. 'Manor Street was a continuation of Stonybatter (Gaelic, *bother*: road), which was in ancient times part of the highway from Tara of the Kings to Cuala in Leinster.'[54] Likewise, although set largely in rural County Galway, Somerville and Ross's 1895 novel *The Real Charlotte* opens in a middle-class enclave in Mountjoy Square: 'An August Sunday afternoon in the north side of Dublin. Epitome of all that is hot, arid, and empty. Tall brick houses, browbeating each other in gloomy respectability across the white streets; broad pavements, promenaded mainly by the nomadic cat.'[55] At around the same time (in 1893 to be precise), James Joyce's family lived nearby, in what his brother Stanislaus describes as 'a large old sombre house in Fitzgibbon Street [No. 14] off Mountjoy Square, at that time a good residential quarter for well-to-do families. To judge by the size of the rooms, the house had seen better days.'[56]

It was also here, in one of the pockets of 'gloomy respectability', that the novelist and philosopher Iris Murdoch was born in 1919, at 59 Blessington Street. Although the house is still there, her family moved to England when she was very young. And yet, as her biographer Peter J. Conradi puts it, Murdoch had 'a lifetime's investment in Irishness, visible in every decade of her life: [...] a source of reassurance, a reference-point, a credential, somewhere to start out from and return to.'[57] In her 1965 novel *The Red and the Green*, set in Dublin during the Easter Rising in 1916, Murdoch makes Blessington Street home to one of her characters, Cathal Dumay, who is member of the Irish Volunteers:

> The Dumay's house stood at the upper end of Blessington Street, a wide, sad, dirty street due north of the Pillar, which crawled up the hill and ended at the railings of a melancholy little park. It had, under the pale bright sky, its own quiet air of dereliction, a street leading nowhere, always full of idling dogs and open doorways. Yet in form it closely resembled the other great Georgian arteries of Dublin, with its noble continuous façade of sombre, blackened red brick which seemed to absorb, rather than to be revealed by, the perpetual rainy light.[58]

Blessington Street runs parallel to Eccles Street. Only a few years after Murdoch was born, with the publication of Joyce's *Ulysses*, Eccles Street would become one of the most recognized addresses in modern fiction, as the home of Molly and Leopold Bloom, who live at No. 7. At this point, the unexpected conjunctions begin to accumulate and take on their own life, for Eccles Street is connected to Blessington Street by Nelson Street, the setting for Behan's *The Hostage* – which means we might imagine a parallel Dublin in which Molly Bloom, Cathal Dumay and Pig's Eye are neighbours, meeting one another on the street.

In the 'Calypso' episode of *Ulysses*, Joyce channels morning on Eccles Street through the consciousness of Leopold Bloom, as Bloom sees the sun 'nearing the steeple of George's Church.' Bloom later makes his way to nearby Hardwicke Street (where 1916 Rising leader Joseph Mary Plunkett had his Theatre of Ireland, and Billy in *Liffey Lane* had his damp basement), where he notes 'Larry O'Rourke's' pub. He then goes on to Dlugacz's butcher's shop, at 101 Upper Dorset Street, in a premises now occupied (with a nice touch of irony) by a restaurant offering a completely plant-based cuisine. Dorset Street was, of course, also where both Sheridan and O'Casey had been born. Later, in the novel's 'Cyclops' episode, when Bloom goes into Barney Kiernan's pub at 8–10 Little Britain Street (next to what is now a Chinese printing business), the Jewish Bloom is challenged on his nationality by a character who Joyce names only as 'the citizen':

– What is your nation if I may ask, says the citizen.
– Ireland, says Bloom. I was born here.

The citizen said nothing only cleared the spit out of his gullet and, gob, he spat a Red bank oyster out of him right in the corner.[59]

These streets are the heart of Joyce's Dublin, territory that he had been mapping since the short stories that make up *Dubliners* (1914). The first story in *Dubliners* opens with the narrator looking up at 'the lighted square' of the window of a house in Great Britain Street (which is now Parnell Street). In the second story, 'An Encounter', we are told in the first paragraph that the narrator's friend's parents 'went to eight-o'clock mass every morning in Gardiner Street, and the peaceful odour of Mrs. Dillon was prevalent in the hall of the house.'[60] The next story, 'Araby' begins with a description of a nearby street: 'North Richmond Street, being blind, was a quiet street except at the hour when the Christian Brothers' School set the boys free.'[61] The Joyce family lived at No. 17 North Richmond Street in 1894–1898 and they had earlier rented rooms on Hardwicke Street, where 'The Boarding House' is set. They later moved again to 32 Glengariff Parade, located behind Mountjoy Prison, which Joyce's brother, Stanislaus, recalls as 'a depressing neighbourhood'.[62] Collectively, the stories have long been recognized as creating an image of a city presided over by a sense of paralysis, with citizens as inward-looking as the houses on North Richmond Street, described in 'Araby' as gazing at one another 'with brown imperturbable faces',[63] (brown being the characteristic brick of Georgian Dublin).

However, there is a paradox here. In its long disintegration, the Georgian streets of North Dublin may seem to embody paralysis, but they are also monuments to change:

> *The damp, disintegrating houses*
> *Shuffle shoulder to shoulder through time*
> *Everything living its posthumous existence*
> *Hungering in me for an image*
> *That is not mere archaeology,*
> *The casual coupling of history and self.*[64]

So writes the poet Michael O'Loughlin of the streets around Parnell Square. 'If you blink you'd miss it', writes Paula Meehan in 'Window on the City' (2000):

> *your own life passing*
> *into memory, frame by frame.*
> *Sometimes you can't be sure of your own name.*
> *So fast, the changing*
> *face of the city.*

Elsewhere in the same sequence of poems, 'The Lost Children of the Inner City' (also 2000), she writes in the poem 'History Lessons':

> *We read our city like an open book –*
> *who was taken and what was took*
>
> *Spelt out in brick and mortar,*
> *a history lesson for every mother's daughter.*[65]

Dublin's north inner city is perhaps best understood, as Meehan intimates, as a kind of book, in which stories of changing lives are written in the bricks, with some lines scratched out, and others written on top of them, like a great palimpsest. If the major transformation of the nineteenth century was the end of the Anglo-Irish as a ruling class, and their absorption into the professional middle classes, this found an architectural expression in the repurposing of their townhouses as tenements or offices. By the same token, if one of the great social changes in the early twenty-first century has been the most substantial wave of inward migration to Ireland in its modern history, this, too, is visible as new communities move into the old buildings. Already, in a play like Sebastian Barry's *The Pride of Parnell Street* (2007), about a couple from the north inner city in the 1990s, torn apart by violence, drugs and poverty, there is a sense of a community changing. 'Sure a street is only a fucking film set, isn't it,' asks the character of Janet. 'There's new actors coming in all the time, new fucking stories. Thank God.'[66]

163 · THE NORTH INNER CITY

While the plans to replace derelict Georgian buildings (and in some cases restore them) have been carried out in phases since the 1920s, there still remain streets where the once elegant old townhouses have fallen into ruin. This photo was taken in the north inner city in 2021. *Photography by Seán Harrison.*

You are now as likely to find a Korean restaurant, a Polish grocery, or a Halal butcher on the ground floor of an old Georgian house as you would Barney Kiernan's pub. And as these new Dubliners find a literary voice, they, too, add to the layered memories of these streets. The São Paulo-born Dublin poet Rafael Mendes, in his poem '32 Kg Suitcase' tells us: 'before I left home / I packed a 32 kg suitcase.' He then asks: 'if I was to come back / what would I pack?'

> *a red brick from henrietta street*
> *a slang dictionary from the north inner city*
> *burdock's fish and chips*
> *bookshops: books upstairs and chapters*
> *fragments of stories from smokers*
> *huddled in doorways*[67]

1. Dartmouth Square
2. Paul Smith born, Charlemont Street
3. Portobello (La Touche) Bridge
4. Eavan Boland born, 17 Leeson Park
5. Joyce born, 41 Brighton Square
6. J.M. Synge born, 2 Newtown Villas
7. G.B. Shaw born, 3 Upper Synge Street
8. George Russell's home, 17 Rathgar Avenue
9. Maeve Brennan's house, 48 Cherryfield Avenue
10. Findrum, Pearse Hutchinson's house, 179 Rathgar Road
11. Yeats's home, Riversdale Avenue, Dundrum

South Dublin

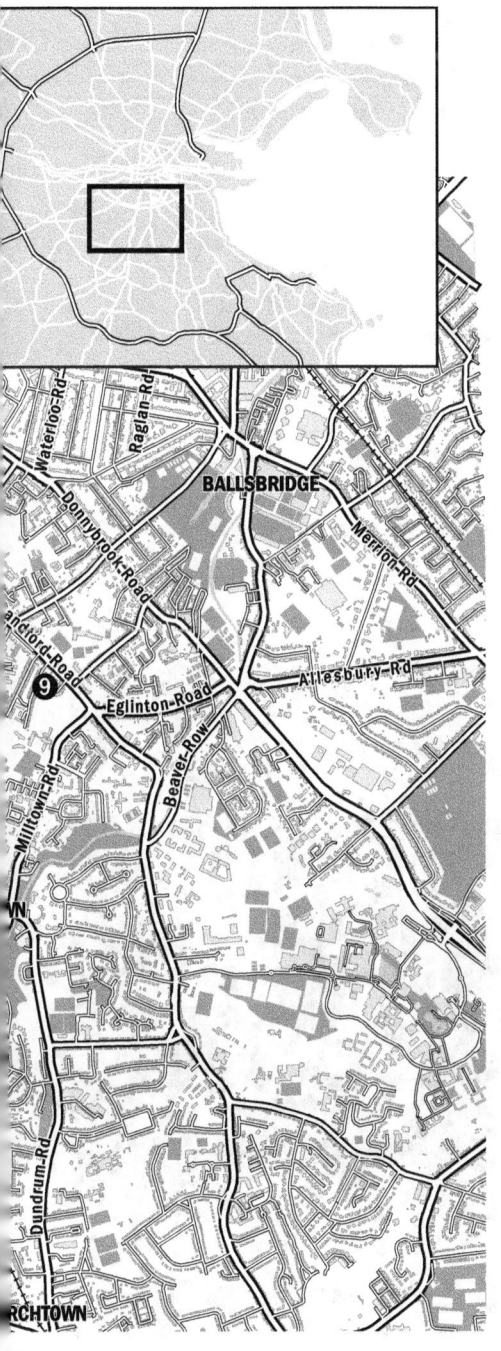

8

The headline reads, **Katherine O'Dell at Home**, and there is a second, smaller picture, of my mother with the new dishwasher, 'one of the first in Ireland, apparently!' with a bright look on her face that says, 'I have no idea how to work this thing.' **Katherine O'Dell enjoys her newly modernised kitchen, in Dublin's elegant Dartmouth Square.**[1]

Anne Enright's 2020 novel *Actress* opens in the summer of 1973 at a twenty-first birthday party for the narrator, Norah FitzMaurice, hosted by her mother Katherine O'Dell, the actress of the book's title. As she does so often, Enright here gauges the meaning of Dublin's geography with precision. Dartmouth Square is indeed (as the gossip columnist would have it) 'elegant', a row of substantial, two-storey-over-basement nineteenth-century redbrick houses set back from the street, wrapped around a private park, just back from the Grand Canal on the south side of the city in the inner suburb of Ranelagh. And in this scene of domesticity and security (which, as we might expect, the novel will gradually unravel) Enright captures the quality that defines the inner suburbs of the south city.

Looked at from the air, or on a map, Dublin north and south has a certain symmetry, with an inner core defined on south side by the Grand Canal and on the north side by the Royal Canal, both of which form arcs entering the Liffey more or less opposite one another. However, on the ground the two sides of the city around their respective canals look and feel quite different from one another. The houses around Dartmouth Square, for instance, almost all date from the

No. 17 Leeson Park, with 'its brass One and Seven. / Its flight of granite steps', was the house in which the poet Eavan Boland was born. The fictional address that is the setting for Anne Enright's *Actress*, nearby in Dartmouth Square, would be only slightly less grand and similar architecturally. *Photography by Seán Harrison.*

nineteenth century, when the bridges of the 1790s opened up an area beyond the Grand Canal that then marked the edge of the city. Originally, then, this was a residential district outside the dirt and congestion of the city centre, but still within an easy stroll of St. Stephen's Green. However, unlike the four- and five-storey city terraces that had been built on the north side in the eighteenth century in Henrietta Street, which required a sizeable staff of servants to run (and subsequently turned to other uses when the world of servants faded), most of the homes south of the Grand Canal were built as single-family houses for the prosperous middle classes. As such, these streets were never subjected to anything like the scale of improvised repurposing that turned so much of the northside into tenements. Certainly, some houses in this part of the city were converted into flats or offices over the years, while any available open ground has since been infilled by expensive architectural ingenuity. On the whole, however, the houses of Ranelagh, Rathmines, Rathgar, and further out to Terenure and Templeogue, are used today largely as they were intended: as homes for Dublin's middle classes.

Within this area there are nonetheless the kind of finely calibrated distinctions that are so important to members of the middle classes everywhere. In *Actress*, for instance, Dartmouth Square is located midway between Charlemont and Leeson Street bridges, one bridge west from Baggot Street Bridge, near where writers such as Patrick Kavanagh and Brendan Behan had lived in bedsits in the 1940s and 1950s. In his 2021 book *Intimate City*, poet Peter Sirr revisits Dartmouth Square, reflecting that he remembered 'how this used to be the kind of place an average citizen could afford to live in, in rented basement flats or rooms carved out of the original grandeur.' He goes on to recall that 'Luke Kelly, of the Dubliners, had lived at number 7. Micheál Mac Liammóir and Hilton Edwards [founders of the Gate Theatre] were in digs at number 30 before moving to the Regency opulence of Harcourt Terrace. Paul Durcan was born in number 57, and not far away from where I am sitting on my bicycle [poet] Michael Hartnett lived in a basement flat.'[2] In Anne Enright's novel, the fictional 'actress' of the title, Katherine O'Dell, 'posing, as though for *Life* magazine, with her new white goods' in 1973 would have had a career that peaked in the 1950s and 1960s, which meant that the crowd of folk musicians and Gate Theatre actors who show up for her daughter's party in one of the book's chapters were credibly neighbours, based on actors and musicians who had actually lived on the street. As such, she lives in what was a bastion of leafy respectability, but which at the time would have been on the borders of the bohemian wilds of Baggotonia. 'Dublin was a small town in those days,' muses Norah, 'even the bullies were small, but the gossip was stupendous, and I know it wasn't healthy, but I do miss it.'³

A fictional house on the real Dartmouth Square in the summer of 1973 in *Actress* makes a good starting point for reading the literature of Dublin's southside. It is, first and foremost, a home, and those rows of firmly closed front doors – in an area where some of the parks are still for residents' use only – make this part of Dublin quite different from, say, the public spaces of O'Connell Street or even from nearby St. Stephen's Green. It is also very different indeed from the north inner city, particularly if we go back to a time when tenement life would have spilled out from the open front doors on to the street. There is also a question of what we might call singularity. There is only one General Post Office or one façade of Trinity College, which means that when these public places figure in works of literature over the years, the layers of meaning accumulate, and characters from a Sally Rooney novel brush past the ghosts of Beckett or Burke as they go through Trinity's Front Gate, or Cuchulain stands beside Pearse in the Post Office while Beckett's character, Neary, bangs his head off his buttocks. By contrast, one house on Dartmouth Square looks more or less like any other, so it is not always easy to tell if your own house is haunted, or your neighbour's.

> **Governing Dublin:** Over the years, the jurisdictional definition of Dublin has changed. Initially confined to the walled area around Dublin Castle, it eventually came to include the area within the canals, but not townships like Rathmines, which remained independent until the Local Government Act (1929). Legislation in 1993 later split areas to the north and west (such as Blanchardstown and Balbriggan) into a new administrative county, Fingal, while the south coast, extending inland to Dundrum, is now administratively Dún Laoghaire-Rathdown.

Having said that, each of the south inner suburbs has its own identity. 'Suburbs have their local pride, and are each a joke to the others and to the city,' astutely observes the playwright Christine Longford in her 1936 book *Dublin*; 'the mention of any one of them is sure of a laugh on the Dublin stage.'⁴ These differences between adjacent areas have deep historical roots. William Duncan's 1821 map of the city shows Harold's Cross, Rathmines, and Ranelagh, closest to the canal, as distinct villages, with churches and shops at their centres, while further out the equally distinct villages of Rathgar, Templeogue, Terenure, Milltown, Dundrum, Clonskeagh, and Donnybrook more or less follow the course of the River Dodder. None is so large that it is not possible for a cartographer to record the larger houses by name. By 1847, Rathmines had grown large enough to be afforded township status in its own right, distinct from Dublin, later taking in Ranelagh, Rathgar, and Milltown, thereby creating what David Dickson calls 'the most enduring and

The town of Rathmines was incorporated in 1847, and remained separate from Dublin until 1930. The original town hall (whose clock tower is visible here) still stands. Note the tram lines, connecting Rathmines with the city centre. *Courtesy of the National Library of Ireland.*

combative of the suburban townships'.[5] Demand for an existing horse-drawn omnibus service to the city centre led to the building of the Harcourt Street Railway line from Rathmines in 1859, which introduced the phenomena of the suburban commuter to Dublin. The novelist Charles Lever provides us with a profile of Dublin's first commuters. 'The 8:30 train is filled with attorneys; the ways of Providence are inscrutable; it arrives safely in Dublin. With the 9:00 train come fresh jovial-looking sort of fellows with bushy whiskers and geraniums in buttonholes. They are traders. 9:30 the housekeeper train. 10 o'clock the barristers whose fierce faces look out at the weather. 11 o'clock men of wit and pleasure.'[6] By 1899, the township of Rathmines from which these commuters hailed had its own elaborate town-hall building, in use until it was absorbed into the city of Dublin in 1930. The building still stands, and we can think of it as an emblem of the relationship of these south inner suburbs and the wider city: a part, yet apart.

LUAS: In 2004, fifty-five years after the last tram, Dublin introduced a light rail system, the LUAS. Where the earlier DART followed the curve of the coast, the two lines of the LUAS intersect like an inland crosshair. The LUAS is already beginning to develop its own literature, such as Eileen Casey's poem 'Warriors', which images a man, 'swift as an antelope' running to catch a LUAS train, his winter coat dissolving 'to gorgeous Maasai colours'.

At the same time, if we want a reminder that south Dublin is not an undifferentiated expanse of treelined avenues, it is worth recalling that two of Dublin's most prominent writers of tenement fiction were both from the area around the Grand Canal, and both set their work here: Paul Smith, who was born just off Charlemont Street, and Lee Dunne, who was born in a block of flats in Ranelagh. Dunne became a public figure in Dublin in the 1970s, when in one of the last gasps of the Irish literary censorship, his semi-autobiographical novel about alcoholism, *Paddy Maguire is Dead* (1972) was banned. Dunne fought the order in a very public court case in which he was defended by the future Irish President, Mary Robinson, then a practising lawyer. The world of *Paddy Maguire* is that described in his most successful novel, *Goodbye to the Hill* (1966), set in a block of flats in Ranelagh that he describes as 'a scab, a kind of dry sore on the face of Dublin.'[7] Likewise, the 'grey rectangular block' of flats in his 1970 novel *Does Your Mother?* is a place where 'children played happily in the filth and dirt that had turned the roadway into a gigantic dustbin.'[8]

Paul Smith's major novels, *The Countrywoman* (1962) and *Annie* (1972), are set in the same area. He creates two fictional streets — Rock Road and Kelly's Lane — but the presence of the canal, the bridges, and the dome of the church in Rathmines place his work precisely. 'The room was quiet,' begins a passage early in *The Countrywoman*, 'but outside night fog from the Canal lay sodden and trapped in the well of the Lane, stuffing the yawns of the open doorways and the black stairs with a swirling swell of vapour, and leaving the naked laths of the ceilings and the red-raddled walls wringing wet.'[9] A later novel, *Annie*, revolves around a brothel in the area, its inhabitants continually conscious of the relative wealth that exists in such close proximity as they make their way through a nightmare Dublin in which 'bloated blossom-faced whores like Lilly Sherman sidestepped others [...], most of them hugging bottles of red biddy in a rigor-mortis clutch under flung coats, and all of them, like one-armed Hop-the-Twig, bewildered from being bullied too long into a life, as they made for the consoling dark of the canal and the shelter of elders and willows, and the randy, lusty men waiting under them.'[10]

The Grand Canal of Hop-the-Twig and Lilly Sherman is a leisurely twenty-minute walk down the canal from Baggot Street Bridge, and Patrick Kavanagh's 'leafy-with-love banks and green waters of the canal / Pouring redemption for me'[11] — and yet it seems a world away. More akin to Smith's Grand Canal than Kavanagh's, in Samuel Beckett's poem 'Eneug I', the overripe fecundity of the reeds and algae in the canal toward Portobello Bridge become a reminder of decaying life. Beginning with an image of 'my darling's red sputum / from the Portobello Private Nursing Home' (a small hospital that was located beside Portobello Bridge), the poem sets off inland down the canal, to towards the Parnell Bridge, which connects with Clogher Road:

> I trundle along rapidly now on my ruined feet
> flush with the livid canal
> at Parnell Bridge a dying barge
> carrying a cargo of timber and nails
> rocks itself softly in the foaming cloister of the lock[12]

Whether imagined as a ribbon of idyllic countryside, or as the decaying 'livid canal' of Beckett's poem, the Grand Canal marks a firm demarcation line between the south suburbs and the city core, just as the Dublin mountains (and, more recently, the ring road of the M50 motorway) mark its southern boundary. Between these limits (the pockets of desperation in Dunne's and Smith's novels aside), there is a large tract of Dublin that at first seems to be a sturdy but private bastion of middle-class domesticity, solid but lacking the anarchic literary energy of the north city – but which turns out to be as rich in literary resonance as any other part of the city.

Eavan Boland (1944-2020)'s work often explored the gap between her experience as a 'suburban woman' and narratives of history and politics. She is pictured here in the 1970s with her husband, novelist and playwright Kevin Casey, and their children at their home in Dundrum. *Courtesy of Irish Times.*

There are good reasons why this richness might not be immediately obvious, which become clear when we look at the work of the writer who has most fully made this part of the city her poetic territory: Eavan Boland. In a conversation with Paula Meehan in 2014, Boland spoke of her sense, while a student in Trinity in the 1960s, of there being 'two cities' in Dublin:

> One city gave a distinct feel of being the centre of the earth; that is, the bars, the theatres, the library, the conversations, the events. The Dublin of writers, journalists, artists. I won't say that it was smug. But it was definitely insular. And I picked up something that was almost disdain for this other Dublin, the place where I would end up living in a few years. Where meals were put on the table, and children had to go to school, and people had to catch the last bus, and pay their rates. It was deemed to be anti-intellectual.[13]

Boland was part of the Trinity generation of the mid-1960s; Derek Mahon and Michael Longley were fellow students, and Eiléan Ní Chuilleanáin and Brendan Kennelly had just joined the teaching staff; meanwhile, just outside the gates, the roaring generation of Patrick Kavanagh, Brendan Behan, and Flann O'Brien, who had lionized the literary pubs, theatres, and conversations, were tottering towards a boozy end. The differences between the two generations (although there would be mutual respect, as well) had as much to do with where they lived as it did with disputes over literary form.

Boland not only lived most of her life in the south Dublin suburbs; she immersed herself in that world with a poet's intense attention, first signalled in the title of an early collection, in 1967: *New Territory*. She was born at 17 Leeson Park, around the corner from the Dartmouth Square of Enright's *Actress*, in a house of which she would later ask:

> *where exactly*
> *was my old house?*
> *Its brass One and Seven.*
> *Its flight of granite steps*
> *its lilac tree whose scent*
> *stayed under your fingernails*
> *for days.*[14]

She later lived for a time as a student in a flat on Morehampton Road (which hardly counts as leaving home, for it runs parallel to Leeson

Park) and then married and settled slightly further out in Dundrum, near the foothills of the Dublin mountains. 'The last dark shows up the headlights / of the cars coming down the Dublin mountains. / Our children used to think they were stars.'[15]

'What happened,' Boland later told an interviewer, Jody Allen Randolph, 'was that, as far as poets were concerned, I went off the radar screen. I went to the suburbs. I married. I had two small children. And it was there I discovered, when I began to put the life I lived into the poems I wrote, that the relation between what went into the Irish poem and what stayed outside it was both tense and hazardous for an Irish woman poet.'[16] And so, beginning with poems such as 'Suburban Woman' and 'Ode to Suburbia' in her 1975 collection *The War Horse*, Boland uses the idea of the suburbs to put space between her private world and the public world of the city centre, with its monuments and history, much as the suburbs themselves were designed to do:

> **Dublin Mountains:** Dubliners often refer to upland to the south of the city as the Dublin Mountains, although by most measures they are really large hills. The peaks closest to Dublin – Three Rock, Kilmashogue, Tibradden – are all just over 400 metres, while the highest peak, Lughnaquilla in County Wicklow, is 925 metres. However, because they are largely open countryside, they remain a kind of wilderness frontier, and mark the city's southern boundary.

No magic here. Yet you encroach until
The shy countryside, fooled
By your plainness falls, then rises
From your bed changed, schooled
Forever by your skill,
Your compromises.[17]

Over the years, Boland would continue to find new ways of writing about what it meant to be both a woman and a poet, and to question the legacies of Irish history, using the suburbs as a place in which it was possible to think anew. By the time of her 2001 collection *Against Love Poetry*, in 'Suburban Woman: Another Detail', she imagines the cycle of life repeating itself. With her own family now grown, Boland finds 'another woman is living my life,' in a line that may consciously echo (and subvert) John Montague's from 'Herbert Street Revisited' ('someone is living our old lives'),[18] with its memories of his neighbour Brendan Behan staggering home. Boland's are very different 'old lives': 'She goes to my door and closes it. / Goes to my window and pulls the curtain slowly.'[19]

While Boland clearly felt that this suburban Dublin was off the literary radar, it would probably be more accurate to say that it was the ordinary lives lived here that were missing from the literary map. As for the place itself, a little excavation shows the south Dublin suburbs to be as much a site for the Irish Literary Revival as Abbey Street or the Aran Islands. For instance, George Bernard Shaw had been born at 3 (now 33) Synge Street, just north of the Grand Canal in 1856. Six years after Shaw left Ireland, the Joyce family's perambulations brought them to 41 Brighton Square, a short walk up the Rathmines and Rathgar roads from where Shaw had been born. It was here that James Joyce was born in 1882. Not surprisingly, this part of the city would resurface in his writing. For instance, in the 'Ithaca' episode of *Ulysses* (the novel's second-last chapter, which deals with homecoming, written in the form of a question-and-answer catechism), Bloom is asked (or asks himself): 'In what ultimate ambition had all concurrent and consecutive ambitions now coalesced?' The answer:

> [...] to purchase by private treaty in fee simple a thatched bungalowshaped 2 storey dwellinghouse of southerly aspect [...] at such a distance from the nearest public thoroughfare as to render its houselights visible at night above and through a quickset hornbeam hedge of topiary cutting, situate at a given point not less than 1 statute mile from the periphery of the metropolis, within a time limit of not more than 5 minutes from tram or train line (e.g. Dundrum, south, or Sutton, north) [...][20]

In the solidly middle-class world of *Ulysses*, this vision of commuter heaven is only partly tongue-in-cheek. Or, again, early in Book II of *Finnegans Wake*, we find: 'Red bricks are all hellishly good value if you trust to the roster of ads but we'll save up ourselves and nab what's nicest and boskiest of timber trees in the nebohood'[21] – which, in its own Wakean way, evokes the idea of the leafy suburb.

The poet, playwright, organizer, and mystic George Russell (who wrote as 'Æ') lived from 1900 to 1906 at 25 Coulson Avenue, around the corner from where the Joyces lived on Brighton Square. Next door to Russell lived Maud Gonne, a very prominent republican activist and playwright who provoked a police raid (and a minor riot) on the street in 1903 when she hung an old black petticoat on a stick outside her house to protest the visit to Ireland of Edward VII. Around the corner lived Countess Markiewicz, the first woman elected to the House of Commons, and her husband Casimir, a playwright and theatre director, who in 1910 founded his own Independent Theatre Company as a rival to the Abbey. Russell was very much the heart of this little clique, for although he is less well known today, in his own lifetime he was a pivotal figure who knew everyone, and was one of the great literary enablers of the age. 'What miracle,' asks Æ in a passage from his poem 'Transformations', 'was it made this grey Rathgar / Seem holy earth, a leaping place from star to star.'[22]

In part, the 'miracle' was the product of persistent hard work on Russell's part, for he was a practical and generous facilitator of the cultural activities of others. 'Dublin is waking up in a number of ways & about a number of things,' Yeats wrote to his sister Susan (or 'Lilly', as she was known) in 1898. 'Russell is doing a good part of the awakening. He is a most amazing person.'[23] He was, among other things, one of the people who kept alive the young Irish National Theatre Society (later the Abbey) at a critical phase. He also edited *The Irish*

You could walk past 17 Rathgar Avenue without noticing it. However, when George Russell (1867–1935) lived here in the early decades of the twentieth century, his weekly salon was a creative centre for more than one generation of Irish writers. Russell, who wrote as Æ, painted murals based on his mystical visions on the walls of the room facing the street. *Courtesy of Dublin City Library and Archives.*

Homestead from 1897, which was then incorporated in 1923 into *The Irish Statesman*, which he edited until 1930. Between them, these two magazines published just about every major Irish writer of the time, including Yeats, Joyce, Somerville and Ross, Katharine Tynan, Shaw, and O'Casey, as well as more than a hundred literary pieces by Russell himself, as part of what bibliographer Tom Clyde calls the *Homestead*'s 'dizzying mix, which gives us dairying next to drama, and beekeeping next to politics.'[24] 'Surely you have heard even in London that Dublin is growing alive steadily, with immense waves of new ideas,' Russell wrote to a friend in 1901. 'Gaelic Leagues, Literary Theatres, music, art, even business – the spirit of business – has opened a sleepy eye after a long slumber, and won't be allowed to go asleep again.'[25]

In 1906, Russell and his family moved to 17 Rathgar Avenue, to a single-storied redbrick terraced house, where he held a regular open house on Sunday evenings, and painted the walls with images from his mystical visions of supernatural beings. These salons became, in the words of his biographer, 'one of the nuclei' of the Irish Literary Revival.[26] The Abbey actress, Maire Nic Shiubhlaigh, in her memoir *The Splendid Years*, recalled those evenings, in a room in which Russell's paintings of pastel-tinted winged spirits and rays of light adorned the walls of the room (he would also paint elaborate murals on the walls of the offices of the Irish Theosophical Society, in Ely Place). 'Distinguished men of letters mingled with literary-minded clerks and shop assistants near the little fireplace,' she recalled, 'and first manuscripts frequently changed hands for publication.'[27] The poet and playwright Padraic Colum lived until 1911 about a ten-minute walk away, at the top of Upper Rathmines Road, near the poet and editor of the *Dublin Magazine*, Seumas O'Sullivan, who held his own salons on Sunday afternoons (whereas Russell's were on Sunday evenings). From 1923 until 1956 in 80 Upper Rathmines Road, O'Sullivan published the *Dublin Magazine*, which printed work not only by Russell and Colum, but also early poetry by Samuel Beckett ('Alba'), and the full script of Teresa Deevy's play, *The King of Spain's Daughter* (1935).

Also among the 'distinguished men of letters' who spent time in Russell's house on Rathgar Avenue in the early years of the century was the novelist and memoirist George Moore. 'I followed him [Russell] in imagination all the way up the long Rathmines Road,' writes Moore in his memoir *Hail and Farewell*. 'His definition of ideas are formless spiritual essences, and the room in 17, Rathgar Avenue is full of them, economic, pictorial, and poetic.'[28] The suburbs beyond Rathgar

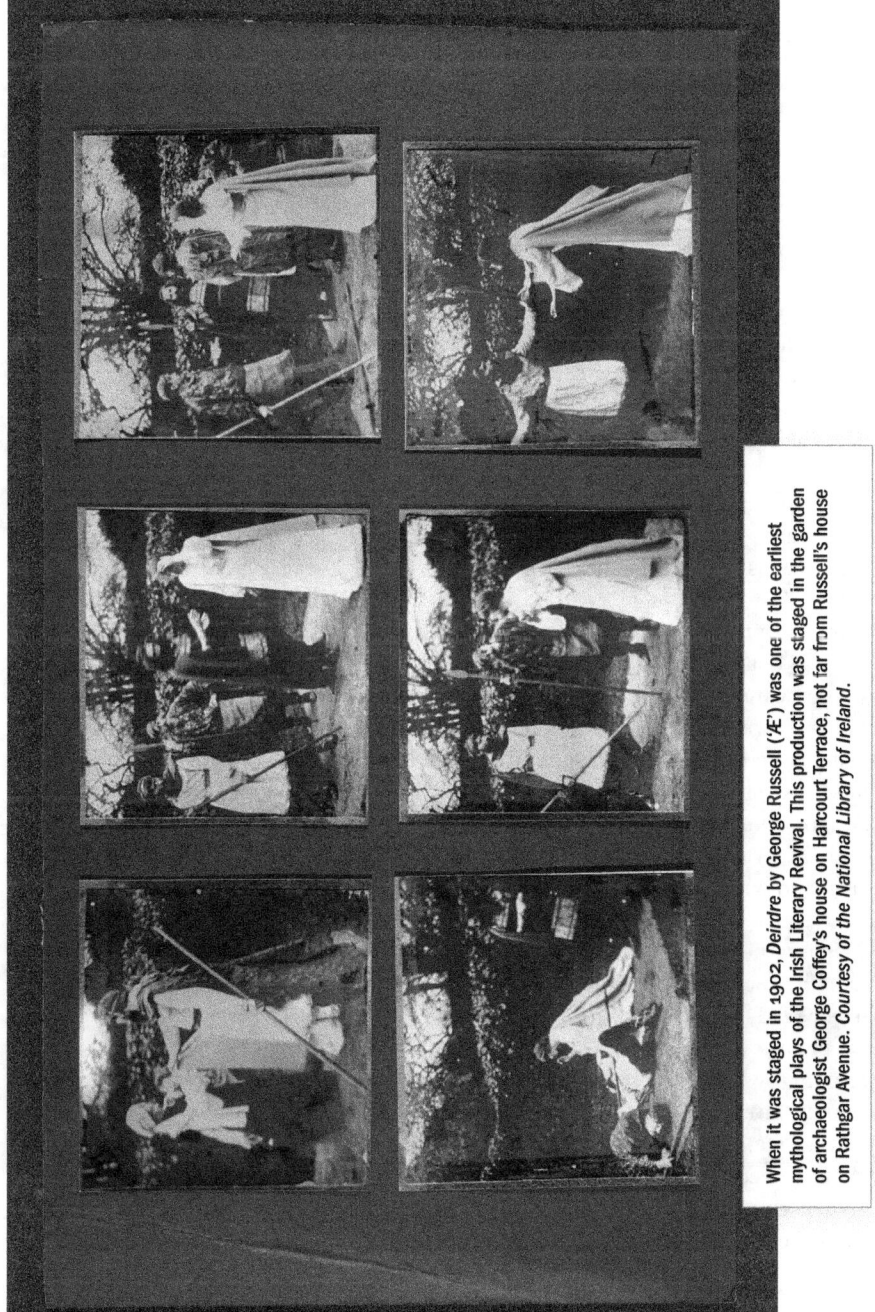

When it was staged in 1902, *Deirdre* by George Russell (Æ) was one of the earliest mythological plays of the Irish Literary Revival. This production was staged in the garden of archaeologist George Coffey's house on Harcourt Terrace, not far from Russell's house on Rathgar Avenue. *Courtesy of the National Library of Ireland.*

appear elsewhere in *Hail and Farewell* as a kind of unexpected pastoral, in which Moore wanders 'sometimes as far as Rathfarnham and Tallaght,'[29] where he encounters 'among cottages, and within sight of purple hills' a countryside 'nearly empty, only an occasional herdsman to remind me of myself in this drift of ruined suburb, with a wistful line of mountains enclosing it.'[30]

Although the land beyond Rathgar certainly was to some extent open countryside at the time, there may also be a sly inside joke in Moore's account of the peasants and herders of Rathfarnham, if we remind ourselves that the writer who perhaps did most to establish the Irish peasant as a literary figure at the time of the Irish Literary Revival was John Millington Synge, author of *Riders to the Sea* (1904) and *Playboy of the Western World* (1907). From his writing alone, it would be easy to imagine Synge growing up in a cabin in the Wicklow hills or on the Aran Islands, reared on potatoes and seaweed. His sole literary work that gives any indication he might actually have had any urban existence is a short poem from 1896, 'In the City Again', in which he writes: 'Wet winds and rain are in the street, / Where I must pass alone.'[31] In fact, however, Synge was very much a child of the suburbs. He was born in 1871 in what was then Rathfarnham (and is now considered Churchtown), in a substantial three-storey house then known as Newtown Little (now 2 Newtown Villas). The family moved a short distance across the River Dodder to Orwell Park in 1882, about ten minutes' easy stroll from where Joyce was born that same year at Brighton Square. There is every chance that, as infants, they passed one another in their perambulators. Synge later attended school at Leeson Park, the street on which Eavan Boland would be born in 1944.

If Synge began his life on the same suburban streets where two of Dublin's most archetypal chroniclers of urban life – Joyce and Boland – lived, W. B. Yeats would end his Dublin years in this area. Again, when we picture the Yeatses at home, the image that comes to mind is the remote tower of Thoor Ballylee in County Galway. However, in 1932, shortly after the death of their long-time friend, Lady Gregory, at whose estate, Coole Park, they spent so much time, W. B. and George Yeats moved to Riversdale, a house on its own grounds in Dundrum. 'The poet at first regretted the great rooms of Coole as he settled into the gracious but not grand suburbs,' writes his biographer, Terence Brown.[32] However, Yeats became very much at home here in his final years, in what he described to his friend Olivia Shakespear as a 'little creeper-covered farm-house [that] might be in a Calvert woodcut.

[...] There [are] apple trees, cherry trees, roses, smooth lawns,' he told her, '& no long climb upstairs.'[33]

Yeats knew the area because his sisters, Elizabeth and Susan, ran Cuala Industries in nearby Dundrum from 1908 until 1923, before moving to Merrion Square, and then to Baggot Street. With a name taken from the pre-medieval name for the territory south of the Liffey (Cuala) and inspired by the Arts and Crafts movement of William Morris, they produced Irish embroidery, and, more lastingly, ran a printing house that published prominent (and beautiful) editions of many Irish writers of the time (including the work of their brother). The area had other associations for Yeats, as well. In 'Easter 1916', he refers to one of the leaders of the rebellion, Patrick Pearse, as a man who 'kept a school'.[34] That school was the nearby St. Enda's, an experiment in education, initially housed in Cullenswood House, Ranelagh, before moving in 1910 to an eighteenth-century house, The Hermitage, off Grange Road in Rathfarnham. Another of the signatories of the 1916 Rising, the poet and playwright Thomas MacDonagh, lived in the lodge of the Hermitage, where he wrote his poem 'Dublin Tramcars': 'Calvin and Chaucer I saw to-day / Come into the Terenure car'.[35] In those same years, James Stephens, whose *The Insurrection in Dublin* (1916) is the classic eyewitness account of the Rising Pearse helped to lead, was living at 2 Leinster Square in Rathmines.

There is thus a direct route connecting the birthplace of one Nobel laureate (Shaw) that crosses a canal written about by another (Beckett), and which runs up the Rathmines Road and Rathgar Avenue to the final home of another (Yeats) with a stop along the way at the birthplace of the Irish writer who indisputably should have been a Nobel laureate (Joyce). Mix in Æ's literary salon, Pearse's school, a clutch of the leaders of the 1916 Rising, the Cuala Press, and two of the most important Irish literary magazines of their time, and the old cliché of redbrick suburbia as a kind of cultural wasteland with no history quickly dissipates.

What is more, this burst of activity is not confined to the first decades of the twentieth century. By 1917, after he had published his first collection of poems, *The Vengeance of Fionn*, Austin Clarke 'was a regular visitor to Æ's gatherings on Sunday nights.' Clarke continued to write throughout his long life, and his final collection appeared in the year of his death, 1974. Although born in the north inner city, he moved to Templeogue in 1937 while an elderly Yeats was still living about a fifteen-minute walk away at Riversdale. There, Clarke 'thought often of "The Wild Old

Man", a little more than a mile away in his house at Rathfarnham, knocking impatiently on his bedroom wall at seven o'clock in the morning for his cup of tea.'³⁶ Clarke himself later wrote in the poem 'Midnight in Templeogue' (1963) of the quality of light on the edge of the city: 'Here, after dark, is city-light, / Faint glow, advertisement in cloud, / Our frankincense, a grace reflected.' Apart from having Yeats as a neighbour, living in Templeogue during the 1940s and 1950s gave Clarke a distance from the hard-drinking world of literary pubs around Baggot Street and Grafton Street, for reasons he spells out in the poem 'Guinness Was Bad for Me'. 'Men elbow the counter in public houses, drink, / Their pints of plain, their chaser, or small one, / [...] Soon all are glorious, all are immortal / Beings of greater day, hierophants.'³⁷ In Templeogue, he could avoid the hierophants, keeping clear of the ferocious sociability of the literary pubs to concentrate on writing.

In fact, the closer one looks at the south suburbs, it would seem that for more than one generation, it could be a place both to define what it meant to be a Dublin writer, and, paradoxically, to escape from those definitions. For instance, Maeve Brennan's parents had both been very actively involved in the 1916 Rising and in the subsequent War of Independence. When Brennan was born in 1917, the family lived at 10 Belgrave Road, next door to the revolutionary (and doctor) Kathleen Lynn, who features as a character in Emma Donoghue's 2020 novel of the 1918 Spanish Flu pandemic, *The Pull of the Stars*. Brennan's family later moved to a smaller, newer house nearby, at 48 Cherryfield Avenue. In her biography of Brennan, *Homesick at The New Yorker*, Angela Bourke describes the house as 'a scaled-down version of Dublin's older terraced houses, they were shaped like piano keys, with a lower, narrower "return" projecting from the back of each pair, so that the kitchen and bathroom windows of adjacent houses faced each other across tiny paved yards and garden walls.'³⁸ When Brennan's father was subsequently appointed as Secretary to the Irish Legation in Washington, DC, the family moved to the US, and by 1952 Maeve Brennan was beginning to write, first for *Harper's Bazaar* and then for *The New Yorker*, where she wrote as 'The Long-Winded Lady' and established herself as a fixture of the New York literary scene. However, much of what she wrote was of Dublin.

Her first short story for *The New Yorker* – 'The Morning after the Big Fire' – opens in Cherryfield Avenue. 'From the time I was almost five until I was almost eighteen, we lived in a small house in a part of Dublin called Ranelagh,' writes Brennan in that early story. 'On our

'We lived in a small house in a part of Dublin called Ranelagh.' Maeve Brennan (1917-1993)'s family home at 48 Cherryfield Avenue (although not redbrick, as she remembers it). The design resembles a scaled-down twentieth-century version of the larger houses on Dartmouth Square or Leeson Park, closer to the canal. *Photography by Seán Harrison.*

street, all of the houses were of red brick and had small back gardens, part cement and part grass, separated from one another by low stone walls.'[39] Brennan continued to publish in *The New Yorker* until the early 1980s, although in later years she was troubled by mental illness, and the writing became less frequent. Nonetheless, in story after story, she returns to the Dublin neighbourhood in which she grew up, so that for regular *New Yorker* readers south Dublin was probably as familiar as Brooklyn. In her final story for *The New Yorker*, which appeared in 1981, there is a remarkable passage:

> Yesterday afternoon, as I walked along Forty-second Street directly across from Bryant Park, I saw a three-cornered shadow on the pavement in the angle where two walls meet. I didn't step on this shadow, but I stood a minute in the thin winter sunlight and looked at it. I recognised it at once. It was exactly the same shadow that used to fall on the cement part of our garden in Dublin, more than fifty-five years ago.[40]

The three-cornered shadow in Bryant Park (behind the New York Public Library) that fell on a garden in Ranelagh can stand as an emblem of the literary imagining of this part of Dublin. The shadow that Brennan saw could not, for instance, have fallen on the GPO, or on Dublin Castle. Their shadows are too specific, too laden with very public stories and memories to be transferable. On the other hand, comparatively speaking, one garden in Ranelagh is very much like another, and their stories and memories are, for the most part, kept firmly behind their closed front doors. So, while this is an area rich in literary associations, it wears them lightly, and can take the imprints of other shadows, and other stories, in ways not possible in the more public parts of Dublin.

Writing like Brennan's, then, which engages intensely with the world of the south Dublin suburbs, also involves a distinctive kind of distancing, which we do not find in the tenement literature of the north inner city, for instance. There is a lingering a sense that this could be elsewhere, and that here memories sit lightly on the surface. It is this tension that underlies Eavan Boland's writing. 'There is a duality to place,' she writes in a 2002 essay, 'The Woman, The Place, The Poet'. Some places, she writes, are saturated with 'the fiery shorthand of history', the insistent memory of 'violent and random events'. By contrast, 'the suburb is all about futures. Trees grow; a small car becomes a bigger one to accommodate new arrivals. Then again, there is little enough history, almost no appeal to memory.' Boland attempts to 'locate herself as a poet' between the two: 'not exactly the suburb, not entirely the hill covered with blue shrubs, but somewhere composed of both.' It is, she concludes, 'in the zone between them something happens. Ideas of belonging take on the fluidity of sleep'[41] – or, as Maeve Brennan discovered, the fluidity of shadows that can fall simultaneously on two continents.

The sense of being both here and elsewhere in these streets runs through the literature of south Dublin. For instance, the poet Pearse Hutchinson grew up at Findrum (as the house is named), at 179 Rathgar Road, and lived there until his death in 2012. Born in 1927, his mother was a close friend of Constance Markievicz, and he was one of the last pupils to attend Pearse's St. Enda's School, where he became fluent in Irish. However, shortly after publishing his first poem in 1945, he became fascinated with Spanish, Portuguese, and Catalan cultures, and his first collection, *Tongue Without Hands* (1963), takes its title from the Spanish epic El Cid; his next, *Faoistin Bhacach* (1968), was in Irish, and his third collection was composed of translations from Catalan. For Hutchinson, the streets of south Dublin extend far beyond the island of Ireland. So, he was capable of writing a poem such as 'Refusals' (1969), which takes place entirely within a Dublin bus passing down 'stone-trapped Richmond Street and Rathmines Road', crossing 'the blue calm water of the Grand Canal [...] and its unsurpassed / capacity to welcome light consoling';[42] and yet, this determinedly Dublin suburban poem sits side by side in the same collection with poems such as 'Spain 67' and translations of Spanish folk songs.

Hutchinson was the co-editor of *Cyphers* ('one of the most consistently satisfying of little poetry magazines' says one commentator),[43] along with the poets Eiléan Ní Chuilleanáin, Macdara Woods, and Leland Bardwell. While Bardwell moved around (living, variously, in a basement flat at 33 Lower Leeson Street, damp rooms in Hatch Street, and a house in Tallaght), Ní Chuilleanáin and Woods settled near Hutchinson in Manders Terrace, just across from Ranelagh Park. Ní Chuilleanáin is also a scholar of medieval and renaissance literature, and from her first collection, *Acts and Monuments* (1972), her work encompasses longer vistas of time while keeping in focus the people and things around her. By the same token, the poetry of her late husband, Macdara Woods, is both connected to worlds beyond (notably Umbria, in Italy, where the couple spent much of their time), and is immersed in the life of Ranelagh. In 'East Wall East Road', for instance, he imagines travelling to nearby Clonskeagh 'where my mother is slowly dying', 'across the river and city / across the Grand Canal', before finally seeing his own house in Ranelagh, which prompts him to counsel himself: '*hold onto this / I think / and that is where I was born / down there / in Upper Leeson Street.*'[44] In those few lines, Woods inscribes three generations of his family into the streetscape of south Dublin. 'It takes some time to make an epic,' Woods writes elsewhere in 'Stopping the Lights, Ranelagh 1986', 'or to see things for the epic that they are.'[45] Harry Clifton, who began publishing at the same time as Woods and Ní Chuilleanáin, has a similar sense of the epic in the suburban. In his 2017 collection *Portobello Sonnets*, he begins with the observation that the area around Portobello Bridge where he lives once had a large Jewish population, and he weaves this awareness into his lived experience the increasingly multi-ethnic population who live in the Upper Camden Street area today: 'Africans, Asian [...] Weird conflations / Of humanity, [...] brilliant as the Greeks / At deciphering fate, as powerless as myself.'[46]

Ní Chuilleanáin's brother writes as the crime novelist Cormac Miller, making him part of what has effectively become a crime wave in Irish fiction over the past twenty years, in which south Dublin plays a distinctive role. To take only two of many possible examples, in Gene Kerrigan's first crime novel, *Little Criminals* (2005), after establishing that Frankie Crowe and Martin Paxton are violent, impulsive criminals, we find them cruising around at night in south Dublin, where 'every house in this part of Ballsbridge cost at least two or three times the price of the average Dublin home.'[47] You just know this is not going to end well. Likewise, Tana French's 2018 novel *The Wych Elm* pushes the borders of the crime genre, by beginning with a protagonist, Toby, whose comfortable life in a south Dublin apartment is shredded when he is attacked during a burglary, leading him to move to his uncle's house, on an unnamed street of 'terraced Georgian grey-bricks [...]

with a double line of enormous oaks and chestnuts [...] giving the inside its own micro-climate, dim and cool and packed with a rich unassailable silence that comes as a shock after the boil of city noises.' Here, as ever, French is as elusive with Dublin addresses (she prefers the fictional to the real) as she is precise with a sense of place. In this treelined oasis, Toby finds no sanctuary, only the recognition that the thing he could not evade after the attack was 'myself, whatever that had become', going on to wonder 'whether everything since that night has been no more than a last burst of light from a dying star.'[48]

Crime fiction typically thrives in places and at times when there are suddenly unaccountable quantities of cash sloshing around – Los Angeles in the 1940s or Scandinavia in the 1990s are good examples – and in this respect Dublin is no different. In the early 1990s, the endemic poverty and underdevelopment that had shaped large areas of Dublin since the beginning of the nineteenth century began to be reversed, and by the end of the twentieth century, Ireland found itself with one of the most rapidly growing economies in the world. Perhaps the most obvious outward sign of this was an upward spiral in property prices, and Dublin's southern suburbs, which had never lost their social cachet, became the epicentre of an unprecedented property boom. Even after the market crashed spectacularly in 2008, this area of the city recovered quickly, producing the kind of cyclic reversal of fortunes ready-made for more than one kind of fiction.

For instance, the property rollercoaster provides the shape for Anne Enright's 2011 novel *The Forgotten Waltz*, which tracks the implosion of a marriage that begins during the heady years of the property boom in 2002, when Gina and Conor take out a large mortgage to buy a small house in a recently built housing estate in Clonskeagh, near the Dublin mountains: a 'house fitted Lego-like to its neighbour, which had the basement and split the middle floor.' 'This threw me a bit,' confesses Gina: 'the fact that it was only half a house until you went upstairs. It was like the place had suffered a stroke.'[49] Later in *The Forgotten Waltz*, when Gina is on her own, she moves back into her childhood home, in the older suburb of Rathmines. From here, in what feels like a redemptive moment towards the end of the novel, she walks towards the city centre. 'On Rathmines Road there is grit under my feet [...]. I pass the Observatory Lane, a shanty row of shops, Blackberry Lane; [...] the green dome of Rathmines church is still capped with white. The canal cuts a clean line under the bridges, the black water reflects the frozen water on its banks, and I am glad of the fresh air, my dreaming boots walking me into Dublin town.'[50] In some ways, Gina's walk encapsulates the movement of the novel itself, back to a place where houses are whole, and the world is more fully grounded, like the grit under her boots. What had been the anonymous, ephemeral suburbs are no emblems of stability.

The upward (if uneven) spiral of property prices in Ireland since the early 1990s has also had the effect of changing parts of south Dublin beyond recognition. As land becomes more valuable, older buildings are torn down, and adjoining countryside is swallowed up. This architectural amnesia registers in various ways in the fiction of this part of the city, but perhaps most strikingly in Deirdre Madden's 2013 novel *Time Present and Time Past*, where the character of Fintan, while simply having lunch one day, discovers that words and objects suddenly appear strange to him. He is particularly disoriented by a photograph of the first commuter line to connect the south suburbs to the city centre, the Harcourt Street line, of which Charles Lever had written back in the late nineteenth century. 'Dublin at the turn of the century looks cluttered and weirdly complex [...] He can no more imagine himself on the same streets alongside these people who had lived in the same city as him, than he can imagine himself as a figure on Grecian urn.'[51]

A similar anxiety over losing the past also surfaces in Eavan Boland's later collections, such as *Against Love Poetry* (2001), and *Woman Without a Country* (2014). In the poem 'Once in Dublin' she writes: 'Empty out the streets / Fit the cars easily / into their parking place. / Slow the buses down by thirty years.'[52] Over time, what had once been 'that nameless city'[53] of suburban Dublin has become for her a place full of memories, which are now themselves under threat. She finds an image of this in the residual village-like quality of the suburb of Dundrum being concreted over by a large shopping centre, the somewhat ironically named 'Town Centre': 'Here in our village of Dundrum / The Manor Laundry was once the Corn Mill. / The laundry was shut and became a bowling alley.' In Boland's earlier poetry, imagining the suburbs as a place without memory had been enabling; in her final poems there is a reversal, and instead we see her beginning to mourn the loss of a place now rich in memories that have been created and then erased within a lifetime:

> *I walk to the Town Centre,*
> *I stand listening to a small river,*
> *Closed in and weeping.*
> *Everyone leaving in the dusk with a single bag,*
> *The way souls are said to enter the underworld*
> *With one belonging,*
> *And no one remembering.*[54]

1. Dún Laoghaire pier
2. Sandymount Strand
3. Martello Tower, Sandycove
4. Seamus Heaney's home, Strand Road, Sandymount
5. Maeve Binchy's home, 4 Sorrento Road, Dalkey
6. Hugh Leonard's home, Pilot View, Dalkey
7. Frank McGuinness's home, Booterstown Avenue
8. Yeats's birthplace, 5 Sandymount Avenue
9. G.B. Shaw home, Torca Cottage, Torca Road
10. Montpelier Parade, Monkstown
11. Dalkey Island
12. Samuel Beckett birthplace, Cooldrinagh, Kerrymount Ave. and Brighton Road
13. Flann O'Brien's home, 21 Watersland Road

The South Coast

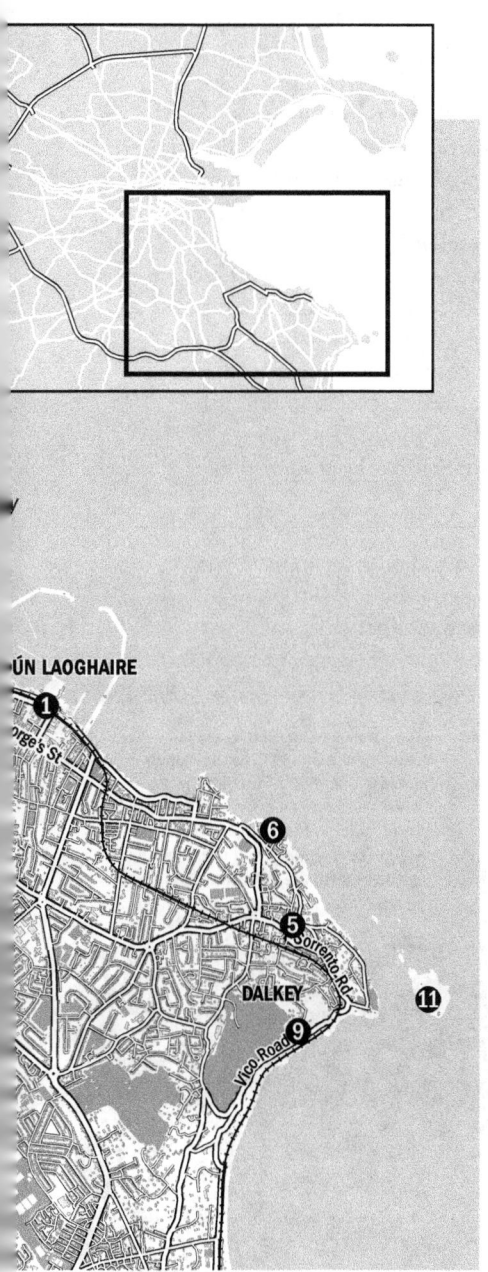

9

'Am I walking into eternity along Sandymount Strand?' Stephen Dedalus asks himself near the beginning of the 'Proteus' episode of *Ulysses* (1922) as he walks along the water's edge on the south side of Dublin Bay, 'his boots crush cracking wrack and shells.'[1] Joyce's character had walked this shore before. In his earlier novel, *A Portrait of the Artist as a Young Man* (1916), Stephen leaves the house of a Catholic religious order on the north side of the city, where he had been discussing the possibility that he might have a religious vocation, and walks out over Dollymount Strand, looking across Dublin Bay towards Sandymount, where 'the clouds were drifting above him silently and silently the seatangle was drifting below him; and the grey warm air was still: and a new wild life was singing in his veins.'[2] Alone on the sand, he sees a girl in the distance, also alone, looking out to sea, 'like one whom magic had changed into the likeness of a strange and beautiful seabird.' For Stephen, this moment of simple beauty is a kind of epiphany, the revelation that it is possible, as he puts it to 'recreate life out of life'; or, in other words, to become an artist who creates from the ordinary world around him – which in his case happens to be the city of Dublin.

When we meet Stephen walking along the strand once again in *Ulysses* (this time on the south side of the bay), his euphoria has settled into a more thoughtful mood of contemplation, as the expanse of sand, sea,

'Am I walking into eternity along Sandymount Strand?' The seemingly endless tidal flats of Dublin Bay are interrupted only by the iconic, and much loved, stacks of the Pidgeon House station (to the right) and much less loved incinerator (to the left). The hill is Howth Head. *Photography by Seán Harrison.*

and sky leads to him to speculate on the nature of world he sees around him. 'Ineluctable modality of the visible,' Stephen thinks to himself: 'at least that if no more, thought through my eyes. Signatures of all things I am here to read, seaspawn and seawrack, the nearing tide, that rusty boot. Snotgreen, bluesilver, rust: coloured signs.'³ That resonant phrase 'ineluctable modality of the visible' is not of Joyce's (nor, indeed of Stephen's) own making; it comes from Aristotle, who argues in his treatise *On the Soul* that colour is the one inescapable (or 'ineluctable') quality of the visible world – hence, the 'ineluctable modality of the visible'. However, Joyce is stretching the phrase's meaning in a slightly different direction here; it is not just colour, but the visible world itself that is 'ineluctable', or inescapable. No matter how often our thoughts might gravitate toward abstract ideas, we exist in a world of things: 'thought through my eyes'. To see the world – even if it is only seaweed, or a 'rusty boot' – is a form of thought: 'Signatures of all things I am here to read.'

That these pivotal passages in Joyce's work should take place amidst the 'seawrack' and high clouds on the shores of Dublin Bay tell us something we know from experience: everything is simplified when we are standing at the edge of a seemingly endless expanse of sea and sky. 'Gaineamhlach síoraí soir / go huiscí farraige i bhfad uaim / imeallbhord geal Bhleá Claith / ag nochtadh pobal gréine,' writes the poet Marcus Mac Conghail in his poem 'Dumhach Thrá' or 'Sandymount' ["To the east sand shimmers / infinitely towards the distant sea / Dublin's light-soaked coastline / lays bare the people of the sun"].⁴ This makes the south coast of Dublin a distinctive part of the city, particularly because it is so often possible elsewhere in Dublin to forget that Dublin is a coastal city. For instance, Dartmouth Square in Ranelagh, where Anne Enright's *Actress* is set, merges into the suburb of Ballsbridge; from Ballsbridge to the coast is only a twenty-minute walk (the distance is less than two kilometres). However, in the tree-shaded streets around Dartmouth Square, there is very little sense of the sea, no intimations of vast expanses of water and sky. It is only after you pass the mouth of the Grand Canal Basin at Ringsend, and travel along the coast, that the sea becomes a dominant presence, and you smell salt in the air (as opposed to the roasting barley of the Guinness brewery). Only when we reach the sea is there that sense of outward connection, of encounters. For the Nigerian-born Irish poet Chiamaka Enyi-Amadi, in her poem 'When' (2019), the train station in Dún Laoghaire is where, 'On a cold evening I wait for you, […] a faded figure rushing through / Autumn drizzle.'⁵ It is also where we confront something larger than ourselves. In one of his quietly understated poems about the harbour in Dún Laoghaire, near where he lives, the poet Gerald Dawe writes in his 2019 collection *The Last Peacock*:

> *swooping gulls fall*
> *upon a crab shell*
> *and play.* This is it.
> This be all.[6]

Likewise, Frank McGuinness, in his 1994 poem 'Booterstown', imagines the link between the street on which he lives – Booterstown Avenue – and the sea: 'Beneath my house a smugglers' tunnel carves / Its way from a cave that looks into the Irish Sea / And it ends outside the Catholic Church in Booterstown.'[7] His play *The Bird Sanctuary* (also 1994), takes its name from the preserved lands at the foot of Booterstown Avenue, which not only provide the play with its central metaphor but also connect the residential street to a wide open space where wilderness overcomes domesticity. Indeed, the sense of drama in this meeting of sea and land can sometimes spill over into ironic reflection. In Megan Nolan's 2021 novel *Acts of Desperation*, her protagonist tells us that 'when I tried one day to stand at the pier on Dún Laoghaire and look out to sea and reflect on my misfortune, I lasted only a few minutes before becoming self-conscious and retreating. [...] I felt in Dún Laoghaire comically cinematic, swaying there in the grey mist.'[8]

> **Dún Laoghaire Harbour:** One of the great engineering works of the nineteenth century was the creation of an artificial harbour at Dún Laoghaire (originally Kingstown), built over an extended period from 1820 until 1860. Originally named Kingstown, in honour of George IV sailing from the newly built port in 1821, it effectively created a focal point for the south coast, and a point of departure for England for many emigrants.

This, then, is a part of the city in which the world that is not made by human hands – the sea – is a constant presence, and this meeting produces encounters and revelations that run a full range of possibilities. Among such moments is one of the best-known (and perhaps most ironic) in modern literature in any language. In Samuel Beckett's play *Krapp's Last Tape* (1958), the elderly Krapp (the stage directions describe him as 'a wearish old man') is recording his thoughts on a reel-to-reel tape recorder, as he has done every year on his birthday, pausing to listen back to the tapes of past years. He is, we might say, haunted by the 'ineluctable modality of the temporal'. At one point, shuffling through the recordings of his younger self, Krapp finds a tape in which his ecstatic voice describes a moment recalled on the end of the pier at Dún Laoghaire:

Spiritually a year of profound gloom and indigence until that memorable night in March, at the end of the jetty, in the howling wind, never to be forgotten, when suddenly I saw the whole thing. The vision at last. [...] What I suddenly saw was this, that the belief I had been going on all my life, namely – [*Krapp switches off impatiently, winds tape forward, switches on again*] – great granite rocks the foam flying up in the light of the lighthouse and the windgauge spinning like a propeller, clear to me at last that the dark I have always struggled to keep under is in reality my most – [*Krapp curses, switches off tape ...*]⁹

Over the years, various critics and biographers have regarded this moment of revelation as something that actually happened to Beckett when he was visiting Dublin in 1945, and which turned out to be 'a pivotal moment in his entire career'. Beckett later told his biographer James Knowlson: 'I realised that Joyce had gone as far as one could in the direction of knowing more, [being] in control of one's material. [...] I realised that my own way was impoverishment, in lack of knowledge and in taking away, in subtracting rather than adding' – embracing 'the dark I have always struggled to keep under'. He also added, however, that 'Krapp's vision was on the pier in Dún Laoghaire; mine was in my mother's room. Let's make that clear once and for all.'¹⁰

Beckett's decision to relocate his own moment of ironic insight to this particular spot on Dublin's south coast was no accident. If he was defining his writing – which would take as its materials 'impoverishment', and 'subtracting rather than adding' – in

'... great granite rocks the foam flying up in the light of the lighthouse and the windgauge spinning like a propeller ...' The is the anemometer at the end of Dún Laoghaire Pier, where Samuel Beckett's Krapp has his moment of ironic revelation in *Krapp's Last Tape*. Photography by Seán Harrison.

opposition to James Joyce's writing, in which languages, mythologies, and voices are piled on top of one another in impossible profusion, he may well have decided that he needed a location from which Joyce was visible, as it were. So if you stand near the end of the East Pier in Dún Laoghaire beside the anemometer where Krapp has his revelation (now marked with its own Beckettian plaque), you can look across the water towards Sandycove (not to be confused with Sandymount). It was here that Joyce lived for a short time in the Martello Tower that stands beside the sea, a building described by Oliver St. John Gogarty (who shared it with Joyce), as looking 'like the muzzle of an old fashioned cannon, ringed around the top.'[11] And it is in this tower on a summer's day – 16 June 1904, to be precise – that *Ulysses* opens. 'Stately, plump Buck Mulligan [the character based on Gogarty] came from the stairhead, bearing a bowl of lather on which a mirror and a razor lay crossed. [...] He held the bowl aloft and intoned: – *Introibo ad altare Dei*.'[12]

Ulysses was published in 1922, and the Martello Tower in Sandycove has been accumulating meanings ever since. On 16 June 1954 Flann O'Brien, Patrick Kavanagh, Anthony Cronin and a few others decided to mark the fiftieth anniversary of the day in 1904 on which *Ulysses* is set by hiring a horse-drawn carriage to retrace the route taken by

John Ryan, Anthony Cronin, Brian O'Nolan (Flann O'Brien), Patrick Kavanagh, and A.J. Levanthal assemble in front of the Joyce Martello Tower at Sandycove, on 16 June 1954, in preparation for a boozy horse-drawn carriage ride into the city, on what would become the first Bloomsday celebration. *Courtesy of Irish Times.*

the character of Stephen Dedalus (loosely based on Joyce himself) from Sandycove into the centre of Dublin. Drink was, of course, involved. Cronin writes that while the horses were 'deep in their nosebags, Myles [Flann O'Brien] appeared to be deep in something else; while Paddy, even on the journey out, appeared to have been absorbing refreshment by some secret chemical process known only to himself.'[13] In the years since, what has come to be known as Bloomsday – 16 June – has become an annual celebration of the literary cultures of Dublin, centring around the Martello Tower in Sandycove, which is now a Joyce museum.

Almost fifty years later again, at the conclusion of his Oxford Lectures on Poetry, delivered on 23 November 1993 (on the eve of the Joint Declaration that ultimately opened the path to peace in Northern Ireland), Seamus Heaney placed the Martello Tower in Sandycove in a poetic configuration of five Irish towers that included Yeats's tower of Thoor Ballylee in County Galway. Collectively, Heaney suggested, they form a 'symbolic ordering of Ireland [...] tolerant of difference and capable of metamorphoses within all the multivalent possibilities of Irishness, Britishness, Europeanness, planetariness, creatureliness, whatever.' Within this imaginary geography, Heaney suggests that the tower in Sandycove is a symbol of 'Joyce's attempt to "Hellenize the island", to marginalise the [British] imperium which had marginalised him.' Joyce did so, claims Heaney, by placing Ireland within 'a more or less Mediterranean, European, classically endorsed world-view,' as opposed to a map with London at its centre. So, Joyce's tower in Sandycove, paired with Yeats's tower, becomes for Heaney 'an archetypal symbol, the *omphalos*, the navel of a reinvented order'.[14]

Seamus Heaney had a phrase for places such as Joyce's tower (or, indeed, Beckett's pier) – places where literature is possible: he called them 'places of writing'. In November 1976, the County Derry-born

'I felt that lift I used to sense at the seaside in Portstewart ...' For much of his writing life, Seamus Heaney worked in a small attic room in his home at Strand Road, Dublin. At one point, he installed a skylight, which just allowed a glimpse of Dublin Bay. *Getty Images*.

Heaney and his family moved to 191 Strand Road, in Sandymount, directly opposite to where Stephen Dedalus pondered the 'ineluctable modality of the visible'. In another of Dublin's clusters of Nobel laureates, the house where he would live for the rest of his life is about a ten-minute walk from where W. B. Yeats (who won the Nobel Prize for Literature in 1923) was born at what is now 5 Sandymount Avenue (and which was No. 1 George's Villas at the time of Yeats's birth in 1865). Heaney built a small study in the house's attic in which to write, 'in conscious resistance to the expectations of suburbia. It was a dis-place, if you like. Like most places of writing. And it has served me well.'[15] He later installed skylights in the roof, through which it was just possible to see the Strand and the waters of Dublin Bay.

There is a passage in one of Heaney's unpublished diaries (noted by Roy Foster in his 2020 book *On Seamus Heaney*), in which the poet records his own moment of epiphany looking out over Sandymount Strand in 1979:

> This morning the sea was bright with sunlight, the tide was in to the strand. [...] I felt the lift I used to sense at the seaside in Portstewart, or on the coast at Dingle or Donegal. I felt that the seven years since leaving Belfast had paid off, that perhaps steady inward effort would be possible. I felt I could trust. [...] I am now in the study upstairs. The trains rattle through the sunlit suburban morning. The birds chatter in the garden bushes, the red leaves of the creeper on the gable flutter.[16]

The ghost of Joyce makes an appearance on the Strand in the poem on which Heaney began work that morning, 'Station Island' (1984). He appears as a tall man, carrying an 'ash plant' walking stick, who pulls Heaney up by the arms from the strand to 'the tarmac among the cars', telling him: '"Your obligation / is not discharged by any common rite. / What you do must be done on your own."' This comes at the end of a decade in which Heaney had been constantly urged to be a public figure who engaged with the conflict in Northern Ireland. Instead, the ghost of Joyce – who himself had counselled 'silence, exile, and cunning' – advises Heaney that an artist's engagement need not always be direct: '"You lose more of yourself than you redeem / doing the decent thing. Keep at a tangent. / When they make the circle wide, it's time to swim."'[17] Some would say that this marks a turning point in Heaney's work, what he would call in his Nobel address, *Crediting Poetry* (1995), making 'space in my reckoning and imagining for the marvellous as well as the murderous'.[18] Elsewhere in the collection *Station Island*, in the poem 'In Illo Tempore', that sense of wonder at the world finds a home on Sandymount Strand:

Now I live by a famous strand
where seabirds cry in the small hours
like incredible souls

and even the range wall of the promenade
that I press down on for conviction
hardly tempts me to credit it.[19]

Later again, the figure of Joyce walking with his 'ash alongside the strand' melds with Heaney's own father in the enigmatic, three-line poem 'The Strand', from the collection that followed the Nobel Prize, *The Spirit Level* (1996):

The dotted line my father's ashplant made
On Sandymount Strand
Is something else the tide won't wash away.[20]

It may seem remarkable that Heaney, whose imagination was so deeply rooted in the rural farming landscape of his Ulster childhood, would find not just a home, but a 'place of writing' in suburban Dublin. However, as with Joyce and Beckett, the presence of the sea in this part of the city changes everything. As Heaney writes in another context, 'the visible sea at a distance from the shore' seems 'untrespassed still, and yet somehow vacated'. Always the connoisseur of the precise word, Heaney hits on the exact term for this point where the sea and sky seem to intimate the edge of the world: the 'offing'. 'Strange how things in the offing, once they're sensed, / Convert to things foreknown.'[21]

For more than one writer, then, the literature of Dublin's south coast is a literature of 'the offing' (keeping in mind that the word also carries the suggestion of something about to happen). For instance, while Elizabeth Bowen may have grown up in Herbert Place beside the Grand Canal, and was best known for her novel of an Irish country-house, *The Last September* (1929), her Irish short stories written during World War II seem to have a magnetic pull towards the Dublin coast. In the story 'Unwelcome Idea' from the collection *Look at All Those Roses* (1941), two women meet on the Dalkey tram travelling from Ballsbridge towards the coast. The 'unwelcome idea' that hovers over their desultory conversations about shopping, children, and trips to the beach, is that were the war to come to Ireland, their world would vanish forever. Bowen begins with the tram journey, written in that crystalline prose so characteristic of her writing. 'Along Dublin bay, on a sunny July morning, the public gardens along the Dalkey tramline look bright as a series of parasols', the story opens. 'Then at a point you see the whole bay open – there are nothing but flats of grass and the sunk railway between the running tram and the still sea. An immense glaring reflection floods through the tram.' From that point, Bowen quietly notes that houses become more weathered as you approach the sea, and 'stucco, slate and slate-fronts, blotched Italian pink-wash, dusty windows, lace curtains, and dolphin-lines seem to be the eternity of this tram route.' That word 'eternity', so casually dropped into the descriptive passage, sets up the next line: 'Quite soon the modern will sag, chip, fade. Change leaves everything at the same level. Nothing stays bright but mornings.'[22] We are, once again, walking into eternity on Sandymount Strand (or at least taking the tram).

There is an equally ambivalent sense of sailing into the offing in the darkly comic conclusion of Samuel Beckett's novel *Malone Dies* (1951), in which Lady Pedal takes a group from a local asylum on an ill-fated outing to Dalkey Island, just down the coast from Sandycove. 'The island. A last effort. The islet. The shore facing the open sea is jagged with creeks. One could live there, perhaps happily, if life was a possible thing, but nobody lives there.' In the novel's final paragraphs, Lady Pedal falls and her charges set out in the small boat on their own, but in the opposite direction from the shore: 'absurd lights, stars, the beacons, the buoys, the lights of earth and in the hills the faint fires of the blazing gorse.' There, in the open water, the character named Lemuel (echoing the first name of Jonathan Swift's Lemuel Gulliver) realizes:

> never there he will never
> never anything
> there
> any more

– at which point the novel ends, setting up the opening of *The Unnameable* (1953), the final novel of the trilogy of which *Malone Dies* is the second part: 'Where now? Who now?'[23]

As is so often the case in Dublin writing, while the presence of sea mists and receding horizons might suggest epiphanies and revelations, it also produces the countertendency to mock any such notions. Dalkey, Flann

Dalkey, writes Flann O'Brien (1911-1966) in *The Dalkey Archive*, 'is an unlikely town, huddled, quiet, pretending to be asleep.' In spite of the rapid growth of the city along the south coast, the main streets of the original villages – such Castle Street in Dalkey, pictured here – still retain their small-town character. *Photography by Seán Harrison.*

O'Brien writes, tongue firmly in cheek in his posthumously published novel *The Dalkey Archive*, 'is an unlikely town, huddled, quiet, pretending to be asleep. [...] It looks like an humble settlement which must, a traveller feels, be next door to some place of the first importance and distinction,' 'And it is – a vestibule of heavenly conspection.'[24] 'Behold it,' he continues in mock reverence. 'Ascend a shaded, dull, lane-like way, *per iter*, as it were, *tenebricosum*, and see it burst upon you as if a curtain had been miraculously whisked away. Yes, the Vico Road.' There is indeed a Vico Road in Dalkey, which seems to evoke Giambattista Vico, the late-seventeenth and early eighteenth-century Italian philosopher who argued that history was circular, spiralling into eternity. 'Is there to be recalled in this magnificence a certain philosopher's pattern of man's lot on earth – thesis, synthesis, chaos?' asks O'Brien grandly. His answer: 'Hardly.'[25] In fact, the names of the Vico Road or nearby Sorrento Terrace are not traces of some lost colony of Italian philosophers, but instead linger from the Italianate villas of the wealthy Anglo-Irish of the early nineteenth century, fresh from their European Grand Tours.

In spite of O'Brien sticking the pin of satire in any pretensions that Dalkey might have, it has a sense of its own literary heritage. For instance, George Bernard Shaw lived here from 1866 to 1874 in Torca Cottage, on Torca Road. Later, the playwright Hugh Leonard grew up and lived most of his life in Dalkey, and it is here that he set his Tony award-winning play, *Da* (1973). 'Six years after my father's death', he wrote in a memoir, *Out After Dark* (1989), 'I wrote a play in which I attempted to sort out my feelings for him and lay my anger to rest.'[26] *Da* centres on the character of Charlie (loosely based on Leonard himself), who returns to Dalkey to sift through his past life. The play is woven into the area's geography, its streets and lanes, and the sea is present in a very particular way. Charlie's mother has been absent throughout his life, but as a child he was told that this was because she kept the light on the Lambay Island lightship, moored in Dublin Bay:

CHARLIE: Me Aunt Bridie says it wasn't true what you told me when I was small, about me mother being on Lambay Island where she wasn't able to get hold of me, and living on pollack and Horny Cobblers. [...] My God ... my mother living on a lightship, trimming the wick and filleting Horny Cobblers. What a blazing, ever-fertile imagination you had – Cobblers aren't even edible!²⁷

Leonard followed *Da* with *A Life* (1979). The play opens with the character who has been Charlie's surrogate father, Drumm, conducting a guided tour of Dalkey, beginning with its park, 'remarkable for its views of sea and mountains':

This hillside is all that remains of what was called the Commons of Dalkey. Where the town – I speak in the Catholic sense: the Protestants call it a village – where it now stands there was once only gorseland and furze, moorland and wretched cabins. The coming of the railroad in 1834 turned the wilderness into a place of habitation for the well-to-do, who were closely followed by the tradespeople and members of the middle classes who knew their place and on that account lost no time in leaving it.²⁸

This is actually a reasonable potted history of the communities – call them towns, villages or suburbs – that punctuate this coast: Booterstown, Blackrock, Monkstown, Dún Laoghaire, Sandycove, and then beyond to Dalkey, Killiney, and so to Bray. As had happened with the inland southern suburbs of Rathmines, Rathgar, and Ranelagh, the south coast of Dublin was farmland in the early nineteenth century, in this case dotted with the seaside villas of Dubliners wealthy enough to afford a summer refuge from their Georgian townhouses. The poet Thomas Moore, for instance, wrote in his memoirs that as a boy in the 1790s, the family of one of his schoolfriends owned 'a very handsome country villa near Black-rock, at which I used to pass, with my young friend Beresford, the greater part of my vacations.'²⁹ This is a world we find in Maria Edgeworth's novel *The Absentee* (1812), where Mrs. Rafferty has a villa 'called Tusculum, situate near Bray', which she is rather too fond of displaying to visitors. The villa features 'a little conservatory, and a little pinery, and a little grapery, and a little aviary, and a little pheasantry, and little dairy for show, and a little cottage ditto, with a grotto full of shells, and a little hermitage full of earwigs, and a little ruin full of looking-glass, "to enlarge and multiply the effect of the Gothic".'[30] The poet Gerald Dawe, who lives in Dún Laoghaire, still senses the ghosts of this vanished world in his poem 'East Pier' (2019), in which he writes of 'our encampments – / villas wedged into cliff face, / the grand terraces / overlooking the bay; / an older order of things.'[31]

In his novel published in 2021 (but set just before the time of *The Absentee*), *The Ballad of Lord Edward and Citizen Small*, novelist and film-maker Neil Jordan also evokes one of these seaside villas with mock-Italian names. Frescati House, in Blackrock, was the actual childhood summer home of the novel's historical protagonist, Lord Edward Fitzgerald; his town residence was Leinster House, now the seat of government. Away from the city, Fitzgerald and his African American companion, Tony Small, look out across the water, 'where ships of the line sat out on the bay like painted toys on the horizon,' and together wander aimlessly 'around the lawns in front of the white-stuccoed building with each window shuttered, as if in search of something lost among plants that had withered with the winter.'[32] It is precisely this incongruous off-season quality to Dublin's seaside communities (in a climate seldom suited to sun-lounging) that has become a kind of motif for Jordan. His first novel, *The Past* (1980), is set largely in Bray during World War II, in a house with a view of 'a thin strip of the promenade resistant to the water hopping off it and the broader band of sea which accepts the rain, mottled by seagulls.'[33] In a later novel, *Sunrise with Sea Monster* (1994), his protagonist is living in present-day Bray with his father, when at one point a storm hits the town. 'The water covered everything, the telegraph poles sprouting from it, the railings, occasional cars, everything suffused in its greenish glow.'[34]

The sea may offer an horizon of possibility in the offing, but all it takes is one big storm or a rising sea level to remind us that it also holds the prospect of annihilation. Indeed, in his 2021 book *A Little History of the Future of Dublin*, architectural commentator Frank McDonald observes that 'although estate agents selling desirable period houses in Clontarf or Sandymount may not wish to acknowledge it', climate change is raising the level of Dublin Bay – 120mm in the twenty years between 2000 and 2020.[35] Eilís Ní Dhuibhne's first novel, *The Bray House* (1990), had already picked up on this intimation of the city's end in a rare dystopian Dublin novel, in which a team of Swedish archaeologists at some unspecified point in the future visit Bray to carry out excavations years after all of Ireland has been destroyed by a catastrophic accident in a nuclear power plant. 'Bray had been, when I'd last visited it, a strange combination of common garden suburb and splendid Victorian bathing resort: in it the doggedly modest and the magnificently pretentious met.' Excavating the remains of this world to assemble a meticulous catalogue of all the bits and pieces that made up life in Bray in the late twentieth century, Ní Dhuibhne's narrator is shocked to find that these remnants of lives lived are now purely of academic interest. No one is really interested in how an ordinary, secure town could sleepwalk its way to disaster: 'there is no longer anything new or startling about our finds.'

> **Beyond Bray:** Bray marks a kind of imaginary boundary for Dublin, if only because the open country of the Sugarloaf Mountain insulates it from the next community. However, further along the coast, the village of Greystones is very much within commuting distance, and beyond that again the village of Kilcoole is the location of an unpublished Samuel Beckett manuscript set in the seaside town where Beckett's father once had a house.

At one point Ní Dhuibhne writes of Bray that 'what lay behind the seafront then was a country market town and a huge suburban sprawl of housing estates.'[36] This 'suburban sprawl', extending from the original villages of the coast inland to the Dublin mountains, is a twentieth- and twenty-first-century phenomenon. Even as late as the early twentieth century, maps of the area show large stretches of farmland here; however, in the pattern that has repeated itself over and over in Dublin's history, it was precisely to this open countryside that Dubliners and Dublin institutions were attracted as older settled areas became crowded. So, it was here, in 1961, that the Irish broadcaster, RTÉ, relocated from the historically resonant General Post Office to a greenfield site about two kilometres inland from Sandymount Strand. Three years later, the new campus of University College Dublin, originally clustered in various historic buildings around St. Stephen's Green, opened in Belfield, inland from Blackrock. While this created something of a break with the generations of writers who were associated with UCD from earlier in the century – Flann O'Brien, Kate O'Brien, and Mary Lavin, for instance – by the end of the century it would produce a significant group of writers, including playwrights Conor McPherson and Marina Carr, and novelist Joseph O'Connor, who would be closely linked to the new, modernist campus, five kilometres south-east of its original city-centre site.

By the time UCD and RTÉ had moved into south Dublin, the area was effectively a well-established suburb. Among the first to begin building houses in this area had been Samuel Beckett's father, William, who had been a builder and property developer, and who built the family home, Cooldrinagh. It was here that Samuel Beckett was born in 1906, on the corner of Kerrymount Avenue and Brighton Road in the suburb of Foxrock, directly inland from Dún Laoghaire. Foxrock at that time was a place in which it was possible to have extensive grounds, and Beckett's family home had large trees and lemon verbena growing around the tiled porch. 'None but tranquil sounds,' muses the narrator of Beckett's novel *Molloy*; 'the clicking of mallet and ball, a rake on pebbles, a distant lawn-mower, the bell of my beloved church. And birds of course, blackbird and thrush, their song sadly dying, vanquished by the heat, and leaving dawn's high boughs for the bushes' gloom. Contentedly I inhaled the scent of my lemon verbena.'[37] Less palatial, but more typical of the wider area, is 21 Watersland Road, where Flann O'Brien lived in what was then a recently built bungalow through most of the 1950s and 1960s.

The houses in which Beckett grew up, or in which O'Brien lived may never have had 'little pheasantries' like Mrs. Rafferty's Tusculum, but this has nonetheless become one of the most expensive areas of the city in which to live. The house in which Samuel Beckett was born on Brighton Road, for instance, was on the market in 2013 for €4.75 million, after its property-developer owners need to sell in the wake of the financial crash of 2008. Even Flann O'Brien's more modest single-story suburban home at Watersland Road would today sell for about €750,000. As property – and the price of property – became one of the most abiding concerns in Irish society in the early twenty-first century, this part of Dublin became the axis around which the cycles of boom and bust pivoted. One writer who has been particularly attuned to the effects of this kind of concentration of wealth in property has been Maeve Binchy, who lived most of her life in Dalkey, and wrote in a room looking out over Dalkey Castle and Dublin Bay. However, her Dublin novels typically take as their territory the slightly more inland suburbs of south Dublin, such as *Tara Road* (1998), which takes its title from a fictional address for a reason: the plot revolves around the escalating value of real estate and its effect on neighbourhoods. So, the house on Tara Road in which the novel is set is described by one character as the 'fastest-moving bit of property in Dublin [...] a regular gold-mine.' By creating a fictional address, Binchy is able to use a single imagined location to bring together multiple aspects of the changing face of the city: 'This road stood out alone in Dublin,' she writes, dropping a broad hint as to what she is about:

Any other street was either up-market or down-market, this was the exception. There were houses in Tara Road which changed hands for fortunes. There were dilapidated terraces, each house having several bedsitters where the dustbins and the bicycles spelled out shabby rented property. There were red-brick middle-class houses where civil servants and bank officials lived for generations; there were more and more houses like their own, places that had been splendid once and were gradually coming back to the elegance that they had previously known.[38]

This world is familiar from Binchy's other Dublin novels, including *Evening Classes* (1996), *Scarlet Feather* (2000), and *Quentin's* (2002), where fictional places and characters intersect from one novel to the next. Part of what makes Binchy a novelist capable of selling more than 40 million books globally is that her fictional world is both specific enough to be a recognizable contemporary Dublin, to which she brings her sharp journalist's eye for underlying forces of change, and at the same time speaks to similar patterns of suburban living for a reader experiencing soaring property prices in the suburbs of Melbourne or Toronto.

Binchy's observation that the houses on Tara Road in 1998 were 'gradually coming back into their elegance' was made at a time when Ireland's economy was going through a period of unprecedented

'Why leave a good place?', Maeve Binchy (1939-2012) once asked. Born in Glenageary, on the south coast, novelist Binchy lived for most of her life in Dalkey. She is pictured here on the pier just across from Dalkey Island. *Getty Images.*

economic growth, in what became known as the Celtic Tiger. To a large extent, this was driven by a period of aggressive globalization, with the journal *Foreign Policy* ranking Ireland as the most globalized country in the world by 2002, well ahead of Singapore and Switzerland.[39] It has remained among the most globalized societies in the world ever since. Within a very short span of years, life in Ireland became much more like other parts of the developed world: a more ethnically diverse, connected world in which Starbucks was no longer exotic. And, as the novelist Kevin Power puts it, 'suddenly – overnight as it were – there was a new ruling class, a vast Catholic bourgeoisie, resident in a six-mile triangle of south County Dublin, who peopled the universities and the courts and the chambers of government with capable and confident women and men.'[40] This had a visible effect on the built fabric of the city, particularly in Power's 'six-mile triangle', as a disproportionate amount of the wealth generated in this period went into personal property, rapidly clearing from streets like Tara Road any traces of the bohemian bedsitters.

Binchy would be the precursor for a booming genre of popular fiction aimed at female readers who had more often than not found a home in the suburbs of Dublin's south coast, or in the south suburbs adjoining the Grand Canal. And, as was the case with crime fiction, behind the dust jackets featuring whimsical line drawings in pastel colours, there was often serious intent. For instance, in Marian Keyes's novel *This Charming Man*, published on the eve of the economic crash in 2008, the protagonist, an investigative journalist named Grace Gildee, lives in 'a redbrick terrace in the "upmarket suburb of Donnybrook". (Quote from estate agent.) A pretty house, very charming with original features. *Extremely* small. Of course it wasn't exactly in the heart of Donnybrook, [which is just inland from Sandymount] [...] Perhaps we didn't live in Donnybrook at all. Perhaps we'd been had by the estate agent and actually lived in Ranelagh, which wasn't half as nice.'[41] As the narrative of *This Charming Man* unravels, we glimpse a deeply misogynist political culture which suggests that under the façade of this middle-class world in which there is real estate but no community, all is far from well.

This period of unprecedented economic growth and its accompanying discontents opened the way for a flourishing of genre fiction in Ireland in more ways than one. Many of the distinctive features of Dublin – the Georgian tenements, the pub culture, the village-like intimacy of the original suburbs – were related, if not to poverty, at least to economic underdevelopment, and this in turn produced distinctively local ways of living. As large parts of Dublin came to look more and more like other cities, it was as if Dublin's peculiarities intruded less on literary forms equally at home in the hills above Los Angeles or in the suburbs of Helsinki. So, for instance, Keyes admits that in *This Charming Man* she renamed the two main Irish political parties (Fianna Fáil and Fine Gael) 'the Nationalist Part of Ireland and the Christian Progressives' not to avoid libel suits, but 'to make pronunciation, etc. a bit easier for non-Irish readers.'[42] When you have sold more than 30 million books worldwide, as Keyes has done, you need a fictional world that will be familiar to a global readership, even if comments about Donnybrook estate agents are very much aimed at a local reader. That kind of balancing act is much easier to manage on streets with a shallow historical memory.

There is something similar at work when the detective who makes his Philip Marlowesque way through Declan Hughes' Ed Loy novels arrives home in Dublin from Los Angeles. In the second Ed Loy novel, *The Colour of Blood* (2007), Loy drives through 'Sandyford and Kilgobbin' (two suburbs inland from Blackrock) and arrives at the house at the heart of his investigation. Loy thinks it 'looks like a Victorian merchant's idea of a baronial castle,' complete with 'castellated windows, battlements and a small octagonal flag tower';[43] as readers, we recognize it as the gothic *noir* mansion that could equally be the setting for Raymond Chandler's *The Big Sleep* in the hills above Los Angeles. Nor is this a coincidence. 'He is an insider because he was born and brought up in Dublin,' Hughes later wrote of Loy, 'and an outsider, because he has been away so long that the streets seem alien to him when he returns. [...] He feels there is here and here is there.'[44]

Hughes is part of a wave of crime novelists who have established themselves in Ireland in the first decades of the twenty-first century, and for whom it is precisely the fact that so many of the streets in south County Dublin are safe, prosperous, and awash with new wealth that they are ideal settings for crime. So, to take only a few of many possible examples, when the serial killer known as 'The Priest' strikes in Gerard O'Donovan's 2010 novel of that name, his first victim barely escapes with her life, and is found 'on the Lower Kilmacud Road [not far from Blackrock] in the early hours, half naked and in terrible distress'; not far away, reporter Siobhan Fallon only locks the shared outside door of her apartment building so as not to upset the neighbours, not because she feels any sense of threat. 'As far as she knew, there'd never been any actual intruders discovered in Ballsbridge Court. It was much too nice a block for that'[45] – an assumption she is about to find is badly mistaken.

Likewise, when Niamh O'Connor's detective Jo Birmingham in *Taken* (2011) begins investigating a child snatched from the back of a car in an inner-city petrol station with 'a Methadone clinic on one side, a homeless shelter on the other', she does not expect that a trail of cocaine and prostitution will lead her to a suspect living in Sandymount, whom she questions in Dalkey Garda Station, which 'operates out of a converted Edwardian house with sea views, at the end of a quiet cul-de-sac populated in the main by writers and artists. The joke was that if you got stationed here, you needed amphetamines to unwind.'⁴⁶ While this does not match the actual site of the Dalkey police station, it does sound remarkably like Sorrento Road, where Maeve Binchey lived, and it joins Sorrento Terrace, where the playwright Lennox Robinson lived in the 1940s and 1950s, and where Neil Jordan now lives, in what is considered some of the most exclusive real estate in the city.

It is not only crime novelists for whom the snug prosperity of south County Dublin has uses. Since 1998, south Dublin has had its own resident satirist, in Paul Howard's writing centring around the character of Ross O'Carroll Kelly. The (increasingly former) rugby-playing Ross, who works in his father's (fictional) real estate firm of Hook, Lyon and Sinker, was introduced to Irish readers in a weekly column in the *Sunday Tribune* newspaper in 1998, moving in 2007 to the *Irish Times*. Along the way, there has been a new Ross O'Carroll Kelly novel every year since 2000, including novels of the economic crash such as *This Champagne Mojito is the Last Thing I Own* (2008) and *Downturn Abbey* (2013). There is also a book of interviews with characters from Ross's fictional world, *We Need to Talk About Ross* (2009), and a mock travel guide to south Dublin, *Ross O'Carroll Kelly's Guide to (South) Dublin: How to Get by On, Like, €10,000 a Day* (2008). The *Guide* contains a detailed glossary of the distinctive south Dublin accent, in which the DART is pronounced 'dort', and almost every sentence is punctuated by 'like' or 'roysh [right]' – as in 'Ross is, like, a cultural phenomenon, roysh?'

It is not only accent that matters in Ross's world; it is the distinctions between Dublin suburbs that might be indistinguishable to outsiders. Indeed, Howard has admitted that Ross 'doesn't travel well, I think, because the humour, especially the cultural references, are a bit parochial'⁴⁷ – a sly dig at the part of Ireland that

> **The DART:** In 1984, the Dublin Area Rapid Transit (or DART) electric rail service began connecting Bray and Howth, running more or less along the coast, defining a new DART geography of the city. In 1987, the carriages began to feature a revolving selection of poems, beginning with Yeats's 'Beautiful Lofty Things'. The two hundred or so poems that made the journey were later collected as *Between the Lines: Poems on the Dart*, Jonathan Williams, ed. (Dublin: Lilliput, 1994).

would consider itself most cosmopolitan. So, in one of the newspaper columns, Ross's mother Fionnuala, who 'has, like, no day-to-day exposure to the kind of people who use public transport' is traumatized by watching a television documentary on Dublin's newest light-rail system, the Luas. 'I thought prosperity was a tide that was going to lift all boats,' she wails. 'Clearly not, from the way some of these tram people spoke and dressed. For the first ten minutes, I thought I was watching a rerun of *Strumpet City*.' When she later hears of a plan to connect her part of south Dublin to the rest of the city by joining the two Luas lines, she is outraged. '"Connecting [...] Leopardstown [an exclusive south Dublin enclave] to Fetter-bloody-cairn [Fettercairn, a working-class suburb]. And Fortunestown! There's a place out there called Fortunestown! It's like something from a cowboy movie!"'[48]

While the satiric note is not always as firmly to the fore as it is in Paul Howard's work, it has made itself felt in much of the literature of south Dublin over the past few decades. For instance, Paul Murray's *Skippy Dies* (2010) revolves around a fictional private, fee-paying boys' school in south County Dublin, Seabrook, where the boys spend their time watching internet porn and taking pills in a suburban world where 'the great pink hoop of the Ed's Doughnut House sign broadcasts its frigid synthetic light into the night, a neon zero that outshines the moon and all the constellations of infinite space beyond it.'[49] *Skippy Dies* manages to be both funny and disquieting at the same time; and, in its disquiet in the midst of prosperity, it hits a note heard in other fiction set in south County Dublin in these years. Something of that same disquiet is felt in Hugo Hamilton's *Dublin Palms* (2019), set in the early 1980s, when the narrator arrives back from Germany to a city where 'everybody in Dublin is back from somewhere.' Caught between languages, he finds himself increasingly unable to speak. Meanwhile, he and his wife move into a small house along the south coast where the sea can be glimpsed through an upstairs window. As their lives collapse into bankruptcy, he finds himself drawn to the sea at night, watching the wave and tide. 'I got so involved in watching this process of offering and retracting that I saw nothing but the emptying. It seemed to me that while everyone was asleep, the earth was steadily being depleted, everything was running out, the ground I stood on was bankrupt.'[50]

Similarly, in Karl Geary's *Montpelier Parade* (2017), Sonny, a character from a working-class part of Dublin finds himself doing work on a house that is part of 'the grand Georgian terrace of Montpelier Parade' in Monkstown. 'The hallway and the sitting room at the front of the house faced south and were brightly lit. You knew the sea lay beyond, at the bottom of a gentle hill, partially hidden behind rooftops.'[51] As a relationship develops between Sonny and the house's owner, Vera, he begins to find pill bottles around the house, and realizes that her world that he had envied so much is more dysfunctional than his own. When she dies of an overdose at the novel's end, Sonny walks to nearby Seapoint, where 'granite steps ran into the sea. [...] You plunged headlong into the brown-grey sea. Holding your breath, the sudden silence. You could taste the salt at your lips and held your breath for as long as you could, and for a moment you were between worlds, before being thrown from the water, fighting for that precious air.'[52]

This is the twenty-first-century Dublin version of Stephen Dedalus's 'walking into eternity'; and it is caught up in class and property. 'As the twentieth century ended, we were doing something that no one else in Irish history had ever done. We were figuring out how to be rich.'[53] Perhaps more than any of his contemporaries, Kevin Power precisely locates the profound social transformation that took place in Ireland at the turn of the twentieth to the twenty-first century in south County Dublin, initially in his first novel, *Bad Day in Blackrock* (2008), and subsequently in his satirical second novel, *White City* (2021). *Bad Day in Blackrock* is based on a real-life incident from 2000, in which a young man was kicked to death in a brawl outside a Dublin nightclub. The four young men charged with his killing all came from wealthy families from south County Dublin and attended fee-paying Blackrock College secondary school, but only one was ever successfully convicted of manslaughter. 'Even as I write this account,' writes Power's narrator, the older brother of the dead boy, ' – even as I labour over this attempt to impose form on the ineffable, on the defiantly formless – things still seem cosy, smooth, unendangered. Girls still wear their Ugg boots and their Prada perfume. Boys still play rugby for schools in leafy suburbs. Families still have two cars, utility rooms, wine cellars. Latvian maids to clean the kitchen. We do know it will end, of course, our golden age, our belle epoque.' For the narrator of *Bad Day at Blackrock*, that world both persists, and, at the same time, has already ended with his brother's killing – 'We just haven't realized it yet.' The novel ends with the parents of one of the young men charged with (and subsequently acquitted of) the killing leaving Sandymount, moving into what had been a holiday home off the Kerry coast, on the edge of a much wilder sea, 'alone on a bleak and emptying island, receding and alone at last where everything ends.'[54]

1. Greendale Community School, Briarfield Road, Kilbarrack
2. Glasnevin Cemetery
3. Griffith Park, Drumcondra
4. Strand Pub, North Strand Road
5. Séan O'Casey's home, 18 Abercorn Road
6. Bram Stoker's home, 15 Marino Crescent
7. Finglas
8. Howth Head

North Dublin

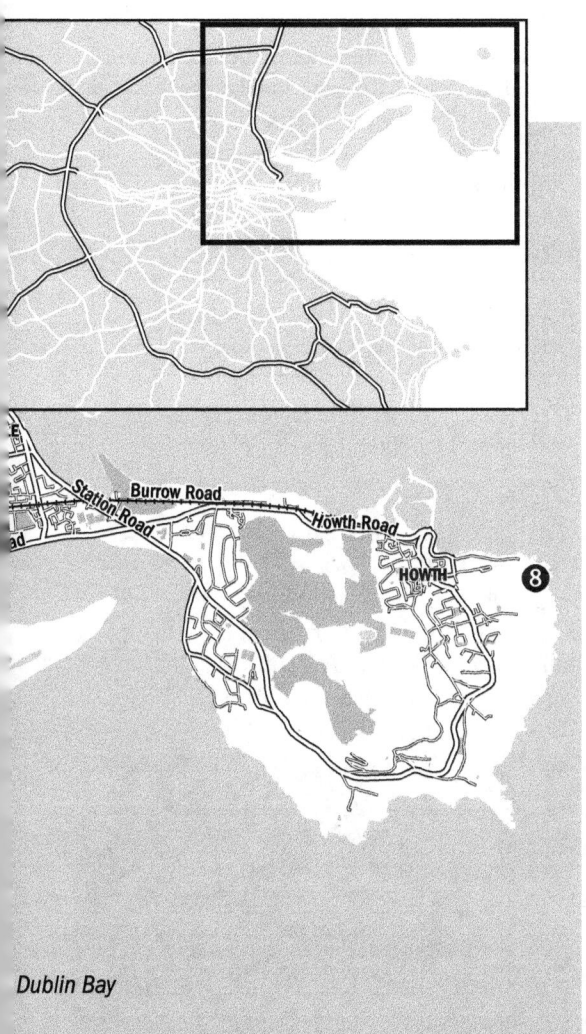

Dublin Bay

10

In Roddy Doyle's 1993 novel *Paddy Clarke Ha Ha Ha*, the ten-year-old narrator climbs to the top of a barn in the northside Dublin suburb where he lives in the 1960s, and looks out over the changing landscape around him. 'The barn became surrounded by skeleton houses. The road outside was being widened and there were pyramids of huge pipes at the top of the road, up at the seafront. The road was going to be a main road to the airport.'[1] Although *Paddy Clarke Ha Ha Ha* appeared immediately after Doyle's hugely popular *Barrytown Trilogy* of novels – *The Commitments* (1987), *The Snapper* (1990) and *The Van* (1991) – it is set earlier, when the north Dublin suburbs of the *Trilogy* were still being built. It is, in a sense, the (recent) prehistory of the earlier novels, and it marked the real intent of Doyle's larger project: to redraw Dublin's literary map to include the expanding suburbs of the north city, centring around Kilbarrack, where Doyle himself grew up and for a time taught at Greendale Community School.

If there are streets in the Liberties that follow tracks already well-trodden when the Vikings landed, and much of the streetscape of the inner city retains its original Georgian layout, there are large tracts of north Dublin beyond the Royal Canal that bear only topographical similarity to the landscape of small villages and country lanes that existed here less than a century ago. Along with Dermot Bolger in

One could drive past what was once Greendale Community School in Kilbarrack without taking much notice; however, it was here that Roddy Doyle was working as a teacher when he began writing in the late 1980s, and it is at the heart of the world of his Dublin novels. *Photography by Seán Harrison.*

Finglas, Roddy Doyle has been part of a generation who have insisted that streets only recently built – and the lives lived on them – could be literary worlds every bit as compelling as Winetavern Street or St. Stephen's Green. For Doyle, this social history of north Dublin is personal, as becomes apparent in his non-fictional memoir of his parents, *Rory and Ita* (2002). Doyle's parents were both born in the south suburbs, in Terenure, but moved after their marriage in the late 1950s to a newly built Dublin Corporation house in Kilbarrack. 'The house was in the City of Dublin but across the road was County Dublin. We went out the gate, and we were in a field that dropped down to the ditch, a great big ditch that flooded every time there was a shower of rain. [...] Our houses were built in a straight line, anticipating the new road.'[2] As he put it later in an interview. 'And it wasn't just me, it was the whole country. Modernity was coming up the road as the cement was drying.'[3]

When the redbrick terraces of the south suburbs of Rathmines and Rathgar were being laid out in the nineteenth century, the Dublin hills marked a southern limit, beyond which the city ended. Likewise, as individual villas and villages blended into the suburbs of Foxrock or Sandyford along the south coast, they formed an area bounded by the Dublin mountains on one side, and the sea on the other. To the north of the city – and, indeed, to the west – the situation was quite different. Here, where land stretches away to the north and the west, topography offers nothing to stand in the way of adding a new row of houses or a new industrial estate. As a result, there was a period in the early nineteenth century when the two sides of inner-city Dublin seem to mirror one another, like two sides of the concentric rings of a tree. By mid-century, each side of the city had its own circular canal separating the medieval and Georgian cores from a third ring of Victorian suburbs: the Grand Canal (1779) on the southside, and the Royal Canal (1817) on the northside. So, at the same time that southside middle-class suburbs such as Ranelagh, Ballsbridge, and Terenure were being built, on the northside there were parallel Victorian developments in Phibsborough and Drumcondra, where just over a hundred redbrick houses were built in 1879, in what David Dickson calls 'the last of the satellite townships'.[4] However, where in the twentieth century the south city eventually hit the limits of the Dublin Mountains, the north city remained open to the rest of the country; and that, in turn, would eventually make the north city distinct. That sense of a fluid boundary registers in the two major north Dublin landmarks of the nineteenth century: the Midland Great Western Railway's Broadstone Terminus, built in

1847; and, nearby, the city's largest Catholic burial place, Glasnevin Cemetery (originally Prospect Cemetery), which opened in 1832. It is here that many of Dublin's writers – including Maura Laverty, James Clarence Mangan, and Brendan Behan – are buried. The Catholic cemetery was built here in the nineteenth century for the same reason that the terminus for a national rail network ended here at the same time, or that Dublin Airport would be built further out in the twentieth century: this was one of the moveable edges of the city, unimpeded by geography.

The other feature of north Dublin that differentiates it from the south city is its relationship to the sea. Where the south coast is largely residential from Ringsend to Bray, on the north side of the Liffey the coastline is broken by the industrialized area of the docks, and much of its connection to open water is blocked by the long strip of Bull Island, a feature that formed when the North Bull Wall, a breakwater, was built in 1842 to keep the mouth of the Liffey from silting up. So, while the prosperous residential area of Clontarf was first built in the nineteenth century because of its sea views, and further out Howth has its own fishing fleet, between them much of the city is cut off from the kind of direct contact with the expanse of the sea that you find all along the south coast. In fact, if there was any natural boundary marker in the north city, it was the relatively small River Tolka, whose significance Seán O'Casey recalls puzzling over as a child. 'Take the Tolka. That was what was called a river, yet it was only the size of a brook, for he had paddled in it, and had filled a jar with minnows out of it. Yet it was the river Tolka. Puzzle, puzzle, puzzle. Of course he remembered the time it flooded the rotting little white-washed cottages on its bank, and swept away swift the statue of the Blessed Virgin standing in the muddy space beside the river.'[5]

> **Rivers of Dublin:** Apart from the Liffey, there are more than forty named streams and rivers in Dublin. Some watercourses, once important to the development of the city, are now almost or completely covered over, such as the Poddle (which runs beneath Dublin Castle and once provided water to industries in the Liberties) or the Stein, which runs under Trinity College. Others, like the Dodder on the southside and the Tolka on the northside, have become like linear parks through heavily populated suburbs.

The area north of the Royal Canal can thus seem like a place of unfixed boundaries, and Dublin's writers have responded to this. For instance, when Leopold Bloom travels with the funeral cortège from Newbridge Avenue (not far from Sandymount, where Stephen wonders if he is walking into eternity) in James Joyce's *Ulysses* (1922) to Paddy Dignam's burial in Glasnevin, he is effectively going to what

The 'slow weedy waterway' of the Royal Canal. This is the Crossguns Bridge, over which Joyce's Leopold Bloom passes on his way to Glasnevin Cemetery. The canal marks the division between the older Georgian core, and the Victorian suburbs of the north city (and in the 'Hades' episode of *Ulysses*, evokes the River Styx). *Photography by Seán Harrison.*

was then the edge of city. On its way, the funeral cortège crosses the Royal Canal – which, in an episode known as 'Hades', makes the canal into Dublin's River Styx from Greek mythology. 'In silence they drove along Phibsborough Road. An empty hearse trotted by, coming from the cemetery: looks relieved.' Bloom then muses: 'Crossguns Bridge: the Royal Canal'.[6] The Royal Canal, connecting the city with the midlands, and ultimately going as far as the Shannon River, carries Bloom in his imagination beyond the city limits, and he has a vision of the bargeman's journey, how 'on the slow weedy waterway he had floated on his raft coastward over Ireland drawn by a haulage rope past beds of reeds, over slime, mudchoked bottles, carrion dogs.'[7] With these images of decay and dying here (the 'slime' and 'carrion dogs'), the barge he sees might be on its way not from the Irish midlands, but from the land of the dead – which is precisely what the episode is about. For Joyce, what was in 1904 the shifting outer boundary of the city could serve as a boundary between worlds.

The Royal Canal acted as a boundary in other ways, as well. As the middle-class terraces of Drumcondra were being built, only a few streets away the tenements of north inner-city Dublin were continuing their long decline, and this would also shape the longer development of the entire north side. For Brendan Behan, growing up in the 1920s and 1930s in Russell Street, in a Georgian tenement not far from Crossguns Bridge, and only a few hundred metres away from the single-family homes of Drumcondra, the division between the two parts of the city was not the Canal or the Tolka: it was class. 'Our street was a tough street,' he later wrote, 'and the last outpost of toughness you'd meet as you left North Dublin for the redbrick respectability of Jones' Road, Fitzroy Avenue, Clonliffe Road and Drumcondra generally. Kids from those parts we despised, hated and resented. [...] It was suspected that some of them took piano lessons and dancing lessons, while we of the North Circular Road took anything we could lay our hands on which was not nailed down.'[8] And yet, even as Behan was a child playing in the streets of the old north inner city, on either side of Drumcondra two new working-class garden suburbs were being laid out on greenfield sites in Cabra and in Marino, where 1,400 homes would be constructed by the time the Behan family left Russell Street in the 1930s for a similar new development in the south-west of the city, in Crumlin.[9]

In her 2007 Booker-winning novel *The Gathering*, Anne Enright maps these layers from the north city map on to three successive generations of social mobility in ways that illuminate the subtle distinctions that sweeping generalizations such as 'northside' and 'southside' can easily mask. In the wake of her brother Liam's suicide, the novel's narrator, Veronica Hegarty, obsessively reimagines her grandmother's house in Broadstone: 'a world unto itself; a little enclave of artisan's cottages close to the centre of Dublin, that fitted together like Lego.' Ada's world is still very much a Victorian city house: her hall door was 'flat against the street. There was no garden or path up to it so people passed by very close'. It was here that Veronica thinks she remembers Liam being abused, and as she tries to understand his lost life, she revisits the area. 'The streets are tiny,' she thinks. 'These are toy houses. We could not have lived here.' The house in which Veronica grew up is nearby, but in a very different neighbourhood, at 4 Griffith Way. This is a fictional address, but its name is carefully chosen, for there is a Griffith Walk and a Griffith Place in Marino, the major northside development of corporation terraced houses from the 1920s; and Griffith Avenue would be one of the defining northern boundary roads in the expanding city, 'arguably the finest achievement of mid-twentieth century planning in Dublin,' according to Frank McDonald.[10] Ada's artisan cottage may have been 'just a few miles from where we lived – I know that now, of course, but when we were children it might as well have been Timbuctoo.' Further away again, the adult Veronica lives in an unnamed suburb in 'a new five-bedroom detached', in the south coastal suburb of Booterstown. 'It's all a bit Tudor and red brick with Queen Anne overtones.' When she visits her mother's house, she finds that it, too, now seems 'always smaller than it should be. [...] The place is all extension and no house.'[11] Between these three houses – Broadstone, Drumcondra, and Booterstown – *The Gathering* uses the map of Dublin as a kind of topographical language to explore generational memory and class mobility.

> **Dublin Docks:** Dublin's docks were on the Liffey quays until in 1767 the South Wall, ending in the Poolbeg Lighthouse, defined the harbour mouth, creating a port on the southside at Ringsend. In 1842, its counterpart, the North Bull Wall, was added (causing the silting which produced Bull Island), and a deepwater port was built in the Alexandra Basin opposite. For more than a century, the docks provided one of the main sources of employment in Dublin's inner city, until containerization vastly diminished the number of dockworkers in the 1970s.

It is not coincidental that Anne Enright sets so much of *The Gathering* on the north side of Dublin, for this is not just a place of memory; it is a place where constant change threatens to erase memory. One example can stand for the multiple ways in which the north city is marked by a particular kind of flux. William Duncan's 1821 map of the city shows the East Wall area, which juts out into Dublin Bay just east of Connolly Station, laid out as The North Lotts, with perfectly aligned – but empty – roads, waiting to be developed in the first wave of industrialization. Fifty years later, the Ordnance Survey map of 1876 shows only a few rows of terraced houses with small front gardens, among them Hawthorn Terrace; a few years later Seán O'Casey's family would live at No. 25 for ten years, before moving to 18 Abercorn Road, almost directly behind it, just off Upper Sheriff Street. As O'Casey's biographer Christopher Murray describes it, 'bounded by the northern railway line on one side, [...] and the docklands on the other, East Wall is a veritable world in itself, even today.'[12] By the early 1980s, however, the tightly knit community that had grown up around the docks was fragmenting, as much of the shipping moved to a container port further up the coast, cutting the demand for labour, and the world of the dockers began to vanish – a moment Dermot Bolger captures in his 2019 Abbey Theatre play, *Last Orders at the Dockside*, set in 1980. Today, elements of the old neighbourhood of Abercorn Road remain, but the end of the street looks directly into a steel-and-glass office block that is part of the new financial services district that has sprouted on the old docklands over the past two decades. So, in Sebastian Barry's *Pride of Parnell Street*, set in 1999, when

'A pygmy Manhattan', is how Paul Murray's narrator in *The Mark and the Void* describes the cluster of new buildings that have been built in the twenty-first century in the old north docks. Among the most prominent is the sloping cannister of the Convention Centre. *Photography by Seán Harrison.*

Janet finally meets her estranged husband, Joe, at the play's end, she tells him that one of their sons is about to get a job on a building site. Joe asks if that means he will have to emigrate to England. "'No, Joe. Dublin. The Financial Services Centre. The docklands and all." "The what?" I says. "The docklands," she says. "Oh," says I. "Like your da before him." "Yeh," she says, "like the da, only not working the ships. Buildin' the new offices and all."'[13]

For Dublin's writers, this new shining city-within-a-city that has emerged in the space of a generation has become something of an emblem of the profound transformation that took place within Ireland as a whole during the economic boom years of the late 1990s and early 2000s. Paul Murray's 2015 novel *The Mark and the Void* is set entirely in this world, with a protagonist – a Frenchman named Claude – who works for the fictional offshore Bank of Torabundo, lives in an apartment overlooking his office, and has lunch every day in a coffee shop on the ground floor of the same building. 'What's it like to be alive in the twenty-first century?' he asks at one point. 'Look at this place, for example. We're in the middle of Dublin, where Joyce set *Ulysses*. But it doesn't look like Dublin. We could be in London, or Frankfurt, or Kuala Lumpur. There are all these people, but nobody's speaking to each other, everyone's looking at their phones. And that's what this place is for. It's a place for being somewhere else. Being here means not being here. And *that's* modern life.'[14] Similarly, Alan Glynn's 2009 political thriller *Winterland* hinges on shady dealings surrounding the construction of a vast office tower in the Docklands, the (once again fictional) Richmond Plaza. 'Tribune Tower, the Chrysler, the Empire State, *on* and *on*, the World Trade, Sears, whatever the next one's going to be. No one cares anymore,' declares the novel's corrupt developer to the reporter who is about to expose him. 'But what's happening now in Dublin, with *this* [...] well it makes the whole thing exciting again' – and moments later everything erupts in gunfire.[15]

When novelists come to deal with place, it is almost as if when somewhere has been transformed beyond recognition once, it becomes possible to imagine that process of change going on indefinitely. In his 2018 novel *The Earlie King and The Kid in Yellow*, Danny Denton conjures up a dystopian future Docklands as a place of collapse. His Dublin, set in a not-so-distant future, is based on the premise (by no means unreasonable, given Irish weather and climate change) that it has not stopped raining in living memory, added to which there has been an unspecified 'digital catastrophe'. In this city where 'rain is the constant moment', Dublin is an all-but submerged city. 'Six vast leaking blocks, the Croke Park Flats, were the oldest accommodation in the slums north of the city. The lower-ground floor had been all shops in the old days but that was under four feet of water now.' Observing this drowned world is a detective/reporter named (not coincidentally) O'Casey, who lives in a damp apartment near where the real Seán O'Casey lived in East Wall, the floorboards warping. This part of the city has been 'empty since the bust times, sad and spooky were those industrial places.' The only part of the city even remotely habitable is 'the chrome and glass and marble of the Financial District',[16] where Dubliners go when they need to be dry for a few minutes. Further north, only the odd house fortunate enough to be on higher ground survives. From a pre-industrial wasteland to a tightly knit working class community, to a steel and glass post-industrial zone, and – in Denton's imagining – back again to wasteland; this history of the transformations (real and imagined) of the Docklands area tells us something about the wider north city outside the Georgian core. This is a place of shifting boundaries, where one city is constantly erasing what came before it.

Sometimes in the literature of north Dublin, this sense of incipient formlessness materializes as a pervasive sea-fog. For instance, the sole cluster of Georgian houses north of the Royal Canal is Marino Crescent, in Clontarf, adjacent to where the suburb of Marino would be built in the 1930s, but looking out over Dublin Bay. Constructed in 1792 (ostensibly to block another landowner's view of the bay), it is rich in literary associations. The Tyrone-born writer known for his stories of the Irish peasantry, William Carleton, lived here for a time during the peak of his writing career. Elizabeth Bowen's mother's family home was nearby at Mount Temple. In 1947, Mount Temple became a school, attended both by the writer Christopher Nolan, author of *Under the Eye of the Clock* (1987) and by the members of the band U2. But it was at 15 Marino Crescent in 1847 that Bram Stoker, the author of *Dracula*, was born; Florence Balcombe, whom he would marry, was born at 1 Marino Crescent in 1878. In *Shadowplay*, Joseph O'Connor's 2019 novel based on the life of Stoker, O'Connor imagines the young Stoker running along the seawall in front of his house in Clontarf, alone in the early morning, and feeling that sense of living at the edge of an uncertain world. 'The bay looms in his mind, the surge of the breakers, the lugubrious moan of the lighthouse foghorn. The ghost of a drowned sailor chained to the mast of an ice-caked ship with a sail stitched from hanged men's shrouds. An image from a play he's been trying to write. But he doesn't have a shape for it yet.'[17]

O'Connor is here resituating in Clontarf one of the uncanniest moments in *Dracula* (1897) when the vampire first arrives in England. The passage begins with an account of a massive storm hitting the English coastline outside the town of Whitby, followed by a strange calm and 'a

'Strange horrors seemed to gather round him …' Bram Stoker (1847–1912) grew up in one of earliest residential streets in Clontarf, at 15 Marino Crescent. The writer William Carleton lived on Marino Crescent for a while, and Elizabeth Bowen's family on her mother's side owned the nearby estate of Mount Temple. *Photography by Seán Harrison.*

rush of sea-fog, greater than any hitherto – a mass of dank mist, which seemed to close on all things like a grey pall,' out of which materializes a black schooner, on the deck of which 'lashed to the helm was a corpse, with drooping head, which swung horribly to and fro at each motion of the ship.'[18] This image actually goes back to when Stoker lived in Clontarf, to a little-known story, 'Buried Treasure', that he published in a Dublin magazine, *The Shamrock*, in 1875 when he was still a twenty-eight-year-old civil servant in Dublin Castle. In this early story, set in Clontarf, the story's protagonist, Robert, lacking the money to propose to the woman he loves, becomes convinced that there is treasure in the hold of a half-sunken ship that he sees during an exceptionally low tide 'towards Dollymount, [...] over Crab Lake, [...] on the North Bull' – just along the coast from Marino Crescent. Robert becomes obsessed with the wreck, and almost dies when he ventures out on the tidal flats beyond Dollymount Strand to retrieve the treasure. 'Strange horrors seemed to gather round him, borne on the wings of the blast. [...] All the dead that he had ever known circled round him in a weird dance. As the stormy gusts swept by, he heard amid their screams the lugubrious tolling of bells.'[19] This may be the coast of Dublin's northside; but it is also recognisably the world of cold fear and swirling mists that we know from *Dracula*.

Perhaps it is the sea-fog, the dampness, or the lack of definition, but a sense of the closeness of some other world along Dublin's north coast haunts more than just Stoker. In Neil Jordan's novel *Mistaken* (2011), Stoker himself is a kind of vampiric presence in Clontarf. The novel's narrator, Kevin Thunder, grows up in 14 Marino Crescent, where 'the house next door bore a brass plaque announcing to whoever was interested that Bram Stoker, creator of *Dracula*, had once inhabited it.' Having seen his first vampire film 'in the Scouts hall on the Howth Road,' Kevin is haunted by the sound of 'the humming of bats' or vampires' wings, like the humming of high-voltage electricity wires.' Fairview Park, which faces the Crescent, becomes 'a garden of horror [...]. The sound was everywhere, in the mud-soaked basin of the Tolka river, the cement walkway above it, the metal bridge that crossed it to the East Wall. It moaned round the gantries of the dock cranes beyond, round the swans weaving their circles in whatever water was left in the mud.'[20] In her 2019 crime novel *The Killer in Me*, Olivia Kiernan sets a whole series of grisly murders in Clontarf, including one in which a body turns up on the shoreline. 'Up along the promenade, the road is quiet. Thin clouds of mist twirl in the orange streetlight. Beyond the silence, the occasional drunken shout as people tumble out of the local yacht club. Behind me, the fat moon rolls on the shining black sea.'[21] As the examples multiply, it is remarkable how often the north coast of Dublin, from Clontarf to Howth, appears in literature at night, with a cold sea mist in the air – whereas in fiction set only a few kilometres away across Dublin Bay, the sun almost invariably shines, and Killiney Bay is compared to the Bay of Naples. It is as if each had its own literary micro-climate, in logical defiance of the meteorological realities of shared weather.

That same sense of haunted dread hangs over the plays of Conor McPherson, who has made this part of Dublin his own. McPherson came to international prominence after *The Weir* opened at the Royal Court in London in 1997. *The Weir* looks like a classic rural Irish play. Set in a remote country pub in 'Leitrim or Sligo' (according to the non-committal stage directions), it is a play of storytelling, in which a small group of regulars gather around the bar to tell one another ghost stories – of the fairy fort in a nearby field or of the man who reputedly attended his own funeral. However, the story that truly troubles them – and the audience – is told by a visitor to the area, Valerie, who lives in north Dublin (we are told she works in Dublin City University, on Collins Avenue), and whose daughter, Niamh, has drowned in the swimming pool in Clontarf. Valerie tells a story about the time, at home on her own after her daughter has been buried, the phone rings. 'The line was very faint. It was like a crossed line. There were voices, but I couldn't hear what they were saying. And then I heard Niamh. She said, "Mammy?" And I ... just said, you know, "Yes."'[22] For an Irish theatre tradition that has long located the pure wellspring of folklore and of the supernatural in the rural West of Ireland, *The Weir* reverses this imaginary geography; here, the play's most unnerving encounter with the dead is centred in Clontarf, narrated by a Dubliner to a group of west of Ireland farmers.

A number of McPherson's plays map this area of Dublin that runs up North Strand Road to Howth, typically involving a group of male characters, confused by life and alcohol, who inhabit a kind of limbo in which they are tormented by their pasts and dread the future. This is also a world in which the tattered traces of the Catholicism that was once such a dominant element in Irish life is more a source of angst than of consolation. *Dublin Carol* (2000), for instance, is set in a funeral parlour on the Strand Road, across from the Strand pub (actual Dublin pubs are perhaps the most important geographical markers in McPherson's stage world), where Noel explains why he drinks. 'Boredom. Loneliness. A feeling of basically being out of step with everybody else. Fear. Anxiety. Tension. And of course, a disposition to generally liking the whole fucking thing of drinking until you pass out.' He talks about the one woman who loved him, and how her care, rather than redeeming his life, simply enabled him to spend his days 'sneaking around pubs all up in Raheny and Killester and Harmonstown,' until he came to believe that 'God had sent me like a drink-angel. Like I believed in God and he'd sent this to take care of me.'[23] In the tormented world of these plays, love (including the love of God) is what enables a kind of living hell to continue, with only glimpses of redemption.

McPherson's 2006 play, *The Seafarer*, moves further north along the coast road, to Baldoyle, which McPherson describes as 'a suburb of the city with a church and a few pubs and shops at its heart. From the coast one is looking at the north side of Howth peninsula.' Here, over the course of a Christmas Eve, a group of alcoholic men find themselves playing cards with a stranger named Lockhart, who may or may not be the devil. There are certainly enough indications to lead one character, Sharkey, to ask him: 'What's Hell?' 'Well, you know, Sharkey,' replies Lockhart, 'when you're walking round and round the city and the street lights have all come on and it's cold.' The play takes its title from the eighth-century Anglo-Saxon poem 'The Seafarer', which McPherson uses as an epigraph. 'He knows not / Who lives most easily on land, how I / Have spent my winter on the ice-cold sea / Wretched and anxious'. 'That's where I really am,' Lockhart tells Sharkey. 'Out on that sea'[24] – but a sea that is indistinguishable from a city at night.

In Conor McPherson's plays, it is not so much the place that haunts his characters; they haunt themselves. In fact, it is almost as if the provisional feel of the built environment in this part of the north city is what allows him to make the inner lives of his characters his terrain. Nor is he alone. In *Mistaken*, for instance, Neil Jordan describes the carpark in Beaumont Hospital, not far from where his narrator grows up in Marino Crescent, looking as if it had 'fallen from an aeroplane bound for Frankfurt or Moscow.'[25] Pat Boran's poem 'Place Names' (2012) opens with a car breaking down 'Where the M50 crosses the M1 / to join the N32,' and the poet trying to give directions, 'in which confusion the names / I might have

The movement of population from older and often derelict buildings in the inner city continued into the 1960s and 1970s. This later wave of social housing initially took the form of high-rise apartments, much like those found elsewhere in Europe – and very unlike the close, communal world of the tenements. The largest of these was Ballymun, near Dublin Airport, seen here in a 1971 photograph. *Courtesy of Dublin City Library and Archives.*

chanced meant little – / Clonsaugh or Collinstown, / Belmayne or Darndale – / all borders lost within the web of lights.'[26] In Fiona Scarlett's 2021 novel *Boys Don't Cry*, set in a public housing scheme in Ballymun, the narrator at one point describes the flats in which he lives looking into what 'was supposed to be a garden – well, according to Da anyway – and there was a remnant of a burned-out bench to prove his point. But I was glad the council got bored and decided to leave it as it is. You wouldn't get much football done in a garden.'[27] For more than one writer, this is a place of unfinished spaces.

This sense of living in an urban environment only partly completed also makes its way into recent crime fiction, perhaps most vividly in Tana French's 2012 novel *Broken Harbour*. The years immediately preceding the financial crash of 2008 marked a period of frenzied housing construction in Ireland, so that when the economy imploded and builders declared bankruptcy, the retreating economic tide left behind the skeletons of hundreds of partially built housing developments. These became known as 'ghost estates' – and they are the ideal place for a crime scene. French's fictional Broken Harbour is along the coast at Dublin's northern extremity, beyond Howth. 'As we got deeper into the estate, the houses got sketchier, like watching a film in reverse. Pretty soon they were random collections of walls and scaffolding, with the odd gaping hole for a window; where the house-fronts were missing the rooms were littered with broken ladders, lengths of pipe, rotting cement bags. [...] "Jaysus," [detective] Richie [Curran] said; in the silence his voice was loud enough that both of us jumped. "The village of the damned."'[28]

Often, Dublin crime writing will work with the tension between the anonymous spaces of urban sprawl, and the memories attaching to older neighbourhoods, much in the way that Enright does with *The Gathering*. Gene Kerrigan's writing, for instance, mixes real, identifiable Dublin locations such as the North Strand with locations such as the fictional Glencara estate, which recurs throughout his writing, 'all terraced houses with well-tended front gardens. They were of a standard municipal design that was duplicated throughout the Glencara estate and across similar council-built estates throughout Dublin – Finglas, Cabra West, Drimnagh, Crumlin, Ballyfermot. Small and narrow, most of the houses now bristled with extensions.'[29] An attempted shooting in the (fictional) Blue Parrot pub in (fictional) Glencara sparks the events in Kerrigan's *Dark Times in the City* (2009), which links the new estate with two very different (real) parts of the north city. The story centres on the Mackendrick crime family, who live on the summit of Howth, a peninsula that juts out into Dublin Bay. 'There was a time when you just needed to be well off to live here – now the very seriously rich were all over the place. It was far from this that the Mackendricks had been raised' – in Ballybough, an old working-class district between Drumcondra and East Wall, where some of Dublin's real organized crime families still have roots. A later Kerrigan novel, *The Rage* (2011), returns to the area around Ballybough, where the small, redbrick terraced houses 'look directly onto the street, no garden, the pavement just inches away.'[30] In this novel, both Kerrigan's fictional crime family, and his fictional detective, Bob Tidey, come from the same streets. For crime novelists such as Kerrigan, it is the interconnectedness of Dublin – the proximity of criminals and police, rich and poor, old and new – that makes it such a fertile ground for crime fiction.

The complexity, flux, and interconnectedness of Dublin north of the Royal Canal, then, offer Dublin writers something very different from the old medieval or Georgian core. And it is this territory that Roddy Doyle has mapped out – almost in real time – over the course of a career of more than thirty years. Basing his writing on Kilbarrack, where he grew up, Doyle has created a fictional suburb, Barrytown, which takes its name from a Steely Dan song that begins: 'I'm not one to look behind / I know that times must change'. In his first novel, *The Commitments*, the novel's protagonist, the teenaged Jimmy Rabbitte Jr., is trying to convince his friends to form a soul band. 'Where yis from?' he asks them. '(He answered the question himself)':

> Dublin. (He asked another one.) – Wha' part o' Dublin? Barrytown. Wha' class are yis? Workin' class. Are yis proud of it? Yeah, yis are. (Then a practical question.) – Who buys the most records? The workin' class. Are yis with me? (Not really.) Your music should be abou' where you're from an' the sort o' people yeh come from.[31]

From that starting point, over the years Doyle has created a complete world, a fictional Dublin suburb that overlays the real city, where the city centre of College Green or O'Connell Street is almost irrelevant, and where his characters speak a language every bit as distinctive (and far more inventively expletive-filled) as that of Ross O'Carroll Kelly's satirical southsiders, who require their own glossary. He has built up this world by following the comedy of the Barrytown Trilogy with a much darker novel of domestic abuse, *The Woman Who Walked into Doors* (1996), about a woman named Paula Spencer who works as a cleaner in the more middle-class neighbouring northside suburbs, 'Clontarf, Sutton, Killester and Raheny; they're the houses I clean. Raheny is the worst. You're only in the gate, you haven't looked up at the house yet, and you know: kids.'[32] Many of Doyle's later novels track characters from his first novels of the 1990s as they age, the city changes, the cement dries, neighbourhoods once filled with small children are increasingly populated by pensioners, and markers of class shift. In *The Guts* (2013), for instance, a now-retired Jimmy Rabbitte Jr. meets up with an old friend from his band days, Des. 'Des was southside. *Rednecks and southsiders need not apply*. But that kind of shite didn't seem to matter much any more.'[33]

Jimmy Rabbitte Jr. reappears again in *The Deportees*, a story sequence that Doyle wrote originally in 2006 for a Dublin newspaper aimed at new migrants to Ireland, *Metro Eireann*. 'It happened, I think, some time in the mid-1990s,' Doyle later commented. 'I went to bed in one country and woke up in a different one.' In that resounding passage from *The Commitments* back in 1987, Jimmy goes on to identify first the Irish, then Dubliners, and then specifically northside Dubliners, with African Americans (and with James Brown in particular, whose music their soul band is going to play). 'Twenty years on, there are thousands of Africans living in Ireland,' Doyle remarked in his introduction to *The Deportees*, 'and, if I was writing that book [*The Commitments*] today, I wouldn't use that line. It wouldn't actually occur to me, because Ireland has become one of the wealthiest countries in Europe and the line would make no sense.'[34]

The more mature, 2006 version of Jimmy Rabbitte puts together a new band, this time made up not exclusively of working-class Dubliners, but of the new Irish, with an African drummer (on 'djembe drum and scream'), Portuguese and African American back-up singers, a Romanian horn and accordion section, a Russian drummer, and a Nigerian singer, King Robert. When King Robert auditions for Jimmy, he sings 'Many Rivers to Cross' 'so well and so convincingly that, for three great minutes, Jimmy had forgotten that the nearest river to them was actually the Liffey.' That same year, 2006, Doyle wrote a sequel to *The Woman Who Walked Into Doors*, entitled *Paula Spencer*, in which, 'ten years later, [...] Paula Spencer was still cleaning offices but now she went to work alone and the other cleaners were men from Romania and Nigeria.'[35] Meanwhile, some of those new migrants were themselves beginning to write their experience of the city, such as Melatu Uche Okorie, who in 2018 published her first collection of stories, *This Hostel Life*. While not set in a specific location in Dublin, Okorie introduces into Dublin writing the new, distinctive voice of asylum seekers who live in the legal limbo of what is known as 'direct provision', which can go on indefinitely, so that they are not even able to work alongside the real-life Paula Spencers in cleaning offices. 'In my last hostel,' says one of her narrators, 'dey give you provision any day, but's gonna be one month since you collect last.'[36]

There is a similar sense of living in an urban world that can change beyond recognition in a lifetime in the work of Dermot Bolger, whose fiction, poetry, and drama is deeply rooted in the north Dublin suburb of Finglas. Where Doyle's fiction maps change into the future, Bolger more often looks to the past of a changed world. For instance, in Bolger's 1987 novel *The Woman's Daughter* a character recalls first moving from the city centre to Finglas. 'It felt like we were out in Meath or Wicklow. [...] And as I swung my head round to see this street with muck and stones from builders all over the road and every second house still empty, I got so excited I almost cried out with so much space everywhere.'[37] As with Roddy Doyle in Kilbarrack, for Dermot Bolger the experience of being a writer growing up in Finglas presented a challenge that has since defined his writing: to create a sense of place for an area whose rural identity had been buried in pavement, and whose urban self is still taking shape. Recalling a period in the early 1980s when he drove a mobile library around the outer suburbs, Bolger once wrote: 'I grew to know and love Dublin in all its diversity, and yet it is the strange world of those new housing estates that remains most vividly in my head. [...] I, too, had been born in such an invisible place – a country village populated by an influx of families from both the old city and the country.'[38]

The point here about the Irish families who moved to the new suburbs in the 1950s and 1960s is worth noting. While many were from the demolished tenements of the inner city, as many again were internal émigrés escaping a rural Ireland that was undergoing its own economic crisis. 'They planted trees in the image of their lost homeland,' observes the narrator, Hano, in Bolger's 1990 novel *The Journey Home*, 'put down potato beds, built timber hen-houses. [...] *The children of limbo* was how Shay [a character whose family have moved from the Liberties] called us once. We came from nowhere and found we belonged nowhere else.' In *The Journey Home*, when the two characters – one whose family is originally from the Liberties, the other whose family had moved from County Kerry – return to Finglas at the novel's end, the moment marks a true homecoming. 'And I realized that it wasn't the bright streets of the city centre that had brought him home, but this invisible, unofficial city which we had both inherited.'[39] For Bolger (as for Doyle), writing becomes a way of making the invisible city visible.

When Hano and Shay at last recognize Finglas as home, they remind us that there has always been a sense in which the edge of the city has been the edge of possibility, where something new can be created. Running through the literature of north Dublin, whose defining piece of physical infrastructure is now the airport, is also a fragile thread of the utopian, a certain weightless feeling of lift, as if from here the world can always be remade anew. This counterbalances those works of literature of the north city that would write it as a kind of limbo, a place of displaced origins experienced as loss. For some writers, it can also be a place where something new begins. That sense of possibility is conjured up vividly in one of Paula Meehan's best-loved poems, 'My Father Perceived as a Vision of St. Francis' (1994), where the image of her father feeding the birds in the family's back garden in Finglas takes on a quality of wonder:

> They came then: birds
> of every size, shape, colour; they came
> from the hedges and shrubs,
> from eaves and garden sheds,
> from the industrial estate, outlying fields,
> from Dubber Cross they came
> and the ditches of the North Road.
> The garden was a pandemonium
> when my father threw up his hands
> and tossed the crumbs to the air. The sun
> cleared O'Reilly's chimney
> and he was suddenly radiant,
> a perfect vision of St. Francis,
> made whole, made young again,
> in a Finglas garden.[40]

Beyond Howth: The limits of Dublin along the north coast are less clearly defined than on the south coast, and urban development is now more or less constant as far as the village of Malahide. Beyond Malahide is Portrane, which is where St. Ita's Hospital is located – or 'The Portrane Lunatic Asylum', as Belacqua calls it in Samuel Beckett's short story 'Fingal', in *More Pricks than Kicks*. It also features in Anne Enright's novel *The Gathering*.

That same sense of transcendent possibility in the ordinary is there in one of Yeats's final poems, 'Beautiful Lofty Things' (1938), which brings us back again to the north coast, to the peninsula that juts out furthest into Dublin Bay: Howth. In a final look back in a poem written shortly before he died, Yeats summons a lifetime of memories, from 'O'Leary's noble head', to Lady Gregory seated at 'her great ormolu table', but ending with a vision of Maud Gonne, in a very precise location:

> *Maud Gonne at Howth station waiting a train*
> *Pallas Athene in that straight back and arrogant head:*
> *All the Olympians; a thing never known before.*[41]

There is a similar mixture of resignation and possibility in one of Derek Mahon's great poems, 'Beyond Howth Head' (1970), which he ends by looking out to the Baily Lighthouse, which sits at the eastern tip of Howth Head:

> *across*
> *dark waves where the bell-buoys dimly toss,*
> *the Baily winks beyond Howth Head*
> *and sleep calls from the silent bed;*
> *while the moon drags her kindred stones*
> *among the rocks and the strict bones*
> *of the drowned, and I put out the light*
> *on shadows of the encroaching night.*[42]

And, finally, what is perhaps the great affirmation in Irish literature, the final chapter of Joyce's *Ulysses*, the 'Penelope' episode, builds to its conclusion with Molly Bloom's memory of an afternoon on Howth Head. After carrying us across the city, through its myriad stories and lives, the novel ends with a single very long sentence, in which Molly Bloom lets her thoughts wander over life, sex and love:

> [...] the day we were lying among the rhododendrons on Howth head in the grey tweed suit and his straw hat the day I got him to

' ... across / dark waves where buoys dimly toss, / the Baily winks beyond Howth Head.' For poet Derek Mahon (in these lines from 'Beyond Howth Head'), the Baily Lighthouse marks the outer limits of Dublin, the point beyond which there is only sea. *Courtesy of Dublin City Library and Archives.*

propose to me yes first I gave him the bit of seedcake out of my mouth and it was leapyear like now yes 16 years ago my God after that long kiss I near lost my breath yes he said I was the flower of the mountain yes so we are flowers all a womans body yes that was the one true thing he said in his life and the sun shines for you today yes.[43]

1. Mullingar House Pub, 9 Chapelizod Road, Chapelizod
2. St. Laurence's Church, Church Lane, Chapelizod
3. Phoenix Park
4. Thomas Kinsella born, 37 Phoenix Street, Kilmainham
5. Áras an Uachtaráin, Phoenix Park
6. Behan family home, 70 Kildare Road, Kimmage (Crumlin)
7. Christy Brown's home, 54 Stannaway Road, Kimmage
8. Stone Boat Pub, 35 Sundrive Road, Kimmage
9. Limekiln Lane, Tallaght
10. Clondalkin

Riverrun

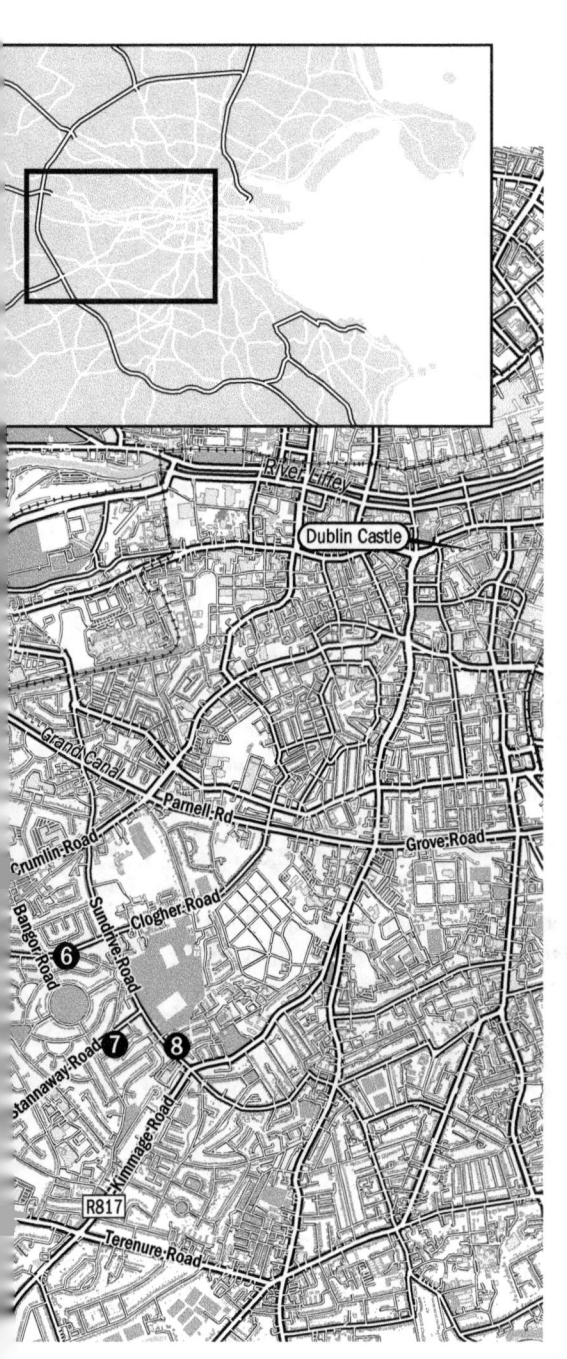

11

I praise
The gifts of the river.
Its shiftless and glittering
Re-telling of a city,
Its clarity as it flows,
In the company of runt flowers and herons,
Around a bend at Islandbridge
And under thirteen bridges to the sea.
Its patience at twilight –
Swans nesting by it,
Neon wincing into it.

Eavan Boland's 1994 poetry collection *In a Time of Violence*, ends with a sequence of poems entitled 'Anna Liffey' in which she meditates on the River Liffey as a 'Spirit of Water, / Spirit of place.' These are poems about: 'The city where I was born. / The river that runs through it. / The nation which eludes me.'[1] The Liffey is very much Dublin's 'spirit of place', although there are substantial areas of the city – any of the inland suburbs, for instance – where it is possible to live with very little awareness of the river. Even along its banks, there are stretches in which it would be possible to mistake the river for a wide canal, hemmed in on either side with quays and buildings. Travelling downstream, when the river reaches the more expansive skyline around O'Connell Bridge, the seagulls and intimation of open water remind us that this is a tidal estuary. It is only in following the river in the opposite direction, upstream, 'around a bend at Islandbridge', that the Liffey takes shape as a freshwater river that twists into the country's interior. Here we travel back not only to the city's origin, but to Boland's origins as a poet, to her first collection, *23 Poems* (1962), and the poem 'The Liffey Beyond Islandbridge': 'Past town, the Liffey breaks from iron into grass, / Then wanders, with swans preening / In the shaken warmth of early March.' As the poem develops, she touches on the paradox of this part of the city: it is both Dublin's origin, and, at the same time, as the city expands westward, its future: 'Look well. Further beyond that river bend / Are spaces teemed with cities which must / Strike a destiny.'[2]

The point at which the river narrows, somewhere between what is now Islandbridge and Usher's Island, at the western end of Dublin's quays, was the original point of human activity in what would become Dublin. Long before the Vikings landed and settled further downstream where the river is still tidal and they could moor their longboats in the dark pool, Dubh Linn, there had been human activity on the banks of the Liffey at the point where the river narrows and grows shallower. At the river crossing, several tracks leading across the island intersected before meandering up the hill on the south bank. There is little known about these first river people, whether they settled or were just passing through. We do know, however, that it was here that someone sunk into the riverbed a set of wooden frames to provide some footing in the silt. This made it possible to wade across the Liffey, and gave the place its name, Áth Cliath, or the ford of the hurdles. 'I understand that the hurdles involve woven rods of willow or hazel, but they seem too flimsy, too haphazard,' observes the poet Peter Sirr in his reflections on Dublin, *Intimate City* (2021), 'too much exactly like the kind of unlikely artefact you expect the past to concoct to test your credulity.'[3]

In some ways, this flimsy but effective human structure can stand as a kind of image for the city in all its vulnerability and endurance: woven rods wedged in the mud against the flow of the river. It is certainly the case that the paradox of the river as both origin and constant change is one to which Dublin's writers return repeatedly. In 'Aston Quay: January 2008', Macdara Woods enjoins himself to 'Look closely at this streetscape / now / to underline it / see it as it is,' even if images of 'drays and barges / and the smell and taste of big copper pennies' and ghosts of long-gone buildings keep intervening. 'My breath tightens / along the river / *Wind and gulls / May it not be lost / May it not be lost forever.*'[4] Likewise, Oliver St. John Gogarty's poem 'Liffey Bridge', from his 1924 collection, *An Offering of Swans*, opens with the poet gazing 'along the waters at the West, / Watching the low sky colour into flame,' picking up a feature of the Liffey that adds yet another element to its symbolic suggestiveness; its east-west alignment means that when standing on any of its bridges at close of day, looking upstream is to see the city silhouetted against the setting sun. For Gogarty, that darkening sky to the west is a primordial image of 'that desolation back again, / Which reigned when Liffey's widening banks were bare; / Before Ben Edair gazed upon the Dane, / Before the Hurdle Ford, and long before / Finn drowned the young men by its meadowy shore.'[5]

> **Liffey Bridges:** The earliest wooden bridge across the Liffey was where what is now Liam Mellows Bridge is now located, connecting Usher's Quay and Arran Quay. The oldest surviving bridge is the Anna Livia Bridge (1753) in Chapelizod, originally called Dodson's Bridge, but renamed in 1982 to mark the strong associations of Joyce's *Finnegans Wake* with the area. Of the twenty-four bridges now crossing the Liffey in the Dublin area, three are named for writers: the James Joyce Bridge (2003); the Seán O'Casey Bridge (2005) and the Samuel Beckett Bridge (2009).

For all of these writers, the River Liffey powerfully evokes a sense not only of a place, but of old time, and of time passing. So it makes sense that a work that is obsessed with time should circle obsessively around this part of Dublin: James Joyce's *Finnegans Wake* (1939). Joyce's densest and most complex novel opens in mid-sentence, with the portmanteau word 'riverrun': 'riverrun, past Eve and Adam's, from swerve of shore to bend of bay, brings us by a commodious vicus of recirculation back to Howth Castle and environs.' In that first sentence, taking us in a majestic sweep down the river, out towards 'Howth Castle and environs', Joyce's final novel might seem to be picking up where *Ulysses* ends, on Howth Head. But it sweeps back in from Dublin Bay 'by a commodious vicus of recirculation', past the Church of the Immaculate Conception (known as 'Adam and Eve's'), located on the banks of the River Liffey just past Winetavern Street, on the site of the first Viking settlement of Dublin. In the *Wake*'s world of associational logic, the Viking origins of a city and Adam and Eve as mythic originators of the human race echo one another as stories of origin. And so the novel continues, until the missing start of that opening sentence finally appears more than six hundred pages later, with the novel's final word: 'the'. 'A way a lone a last a loved a long the [riverrun, past Eve and Adams' ...]'.[6] In other words, the opening sentence is not really an opening sentence at all, but the continuation of a sentence that begins on the final page, and flows on, like a river.

For all of its mind-bogglingly labyrinthine games with language and sense, *Finnegans Wake* is a Dublin novel. And it is a book in which the River Liffey is as much a presence as the river is in the city itself. At one point, in one of Joyce's best-known passages, the 'Anna Livia Plurabelle', the voice of the river itself speaks. As Joyce wrote to his patron, Harriet Weaver Shaw in 1924, 'I have finished the *Anna Livia* piece. [...] It is a chattering dialogue across the river by two washerwomen [...]. The river is named Anna Liffey':[7]

> O
> *tell me all about*
> *Anna Livia! I want to hear all*
> *about Anna Livia. Well, you know Anna Livia? Yes, of course, we all*
> *know Anna Livia. Tell me all. Tell me now.*

In *Finnegans Wake*, the voices of the city become a kind river of words, returning time and again to a single point on the riverbank, near where the river narrows, and the original hurdles were set in the mud.

Insofar as it has a plot, *Finnegans Wake* is a Dublin version of the myth of the Fall, transplanted to the suburb of Chapelizod, adjacent to the Phoenix Park in the west of the city, at the point where the Liffey is no longer tidal. Here, in the Mullingar House pub, live the Earwicker family, made up of a mother, her sons Shem and Shaun, daughter Issy, and her husband, Humphrey Chimpden Earwicker, or HCE, 'only and long and always good Dook Umphrey for the hunger-lean spalpeens of Lucalizod [combining the place names of adjacent Chapelizod and Lucan] and Chimbers to his cronies it was equally certainly a pleasant turn of the populace which gave him as sense of those normative letters the nickname Here Comes Everybody.' As with so much in *Finnegans Wake*, Chapelizod is both a real place, and a site for Joyce's games with language and meaning. So, for instance, at one point he puts together a passage made up entirely of actual house names from the area, both poking gentle fun at the practice of giving suburban houses fanciful names, and at the same time using them to reveal a hidden poetry in the ordinary world. 'By this riverside, on our sunnybank, how buona the vista, by Santa Rosa! A field of May, the very vale of Spring. Orchards here are lodged; sainted lawrels evremberried. You have a hoig view ashwald, a glen of marrons and of thorns. Gleannaulinn, Adreevin; purty glint of plaising height. This Norman court at boundary of the ville, yon creepered tower of a church of England [...].'[8] Gently buried in this sentence are the names of actual house names in Chapelizod, most of which still exist today: Riverside House, Sunnybank, Buena Vista, Santa Rosa, Mayfield House, Springvale, Orchard Lodge, St. Laurence Lodge, Hillview, Ashview, Glenmaroon, Norman Court and Boundaryville. Glennaulin and Ardreevin are street names that still exist.

The 'creepered tower of a church of England' of St. Laurence's Church, with its fifteenth-century tower, also features in Joseph Sheridan Le Fanu's gothic novel, *The House by the Churchyard* (1863), which in turn haunts Joyce's novel in various guises, as 'the old house by the churpelizod', or as the '*Old House by the Coachyard*', 'the ghastcold tombshape of the quick foregone on, the loftleaved elm Lefanunian abovemansioned'.[9] Le Fanu first came to prominence with his *Ghost Stories of Chapelizod* (1851), which had first appeared serially in the *Dublin University Magazine* (which he would later edit) the previous year. Like his earlier stories of the area, even though *The House by the Churchyard* was published in 1863, it is set in 1767, at a time when 'Chapelizod was about the gayest and prettiest of the outpost villages in which old Dublin took a complacent pride.' Writing to his wife, George, in 1919, W. B. Yeats recounts a day in which, after 'two days headache, fit for

St. Laurence's Church, in Chapelizod, provides the setting for J. S. Le Fanu's *The House by the Churchyard*, and continues to haunt Joyce's *Finnegans Wake*. The original Norman tower is clearly visible in this photo from 1865. *Courtesy of the National Library of Ireland.*

nothing else I spent yesterday evening wandering about Chapel-Izod looking for the ruins of the great house of the Ormonds [to whom he was distantly related] – a tower was still left in 1830 – but there is not a trace. [...] hardly even a trace of Lefanu's world remaining.'[10]

However, if he had looked closely in 1919, Yeats would have found that there were indeed traces of Le Fanu's world. *The House by the Churchyard* describes the village thus: 'The jolly old inn, just beyond the turnpike at the sweep of the road, leading over the buttressed bridge by the mill, was first to welcome the excursionist from Dublin, under the sign of the Phoenix'. It is this pub, Mullingar House, that became the setting for *Finnegans Wake* in 1939. You can still drink a pint there today. In Le Fanu's novel, what starts out as a tale of village life soon gives way to 'a weight in the atmosphere, and a sort of undefined menace brooding over the little town, as if unseen crime or danger – some mystery of iniquity – was stealing into the heart of it.' Before long, that atmosphere takes over the novel, so that as a character named Mervyn is walking homewards up the 'lonely track, with great bushes and hedgerows overhanging it' of the Ballyfermot Road, he looks back and sees 'traced against the dark horizon the still darker outline of the ivied church tower of Chapelizod' and it conjures up for him 'thought of the dead that lay there, and of all those sealed lips might tell.'[11]

Chapelizod differs from the other villages of Dublin in that it effectively forms the southern boundary of one of the city's defining features: the Phoenix Park. If the Georgian streetscapes, squares, and public buildings are Dublin's great eighteenth-century legacy, and the southern suburbs and docks its Victorian legacy, the Phoenix Park is arguably the off-centre centrepiece of the seventeenth-century city. This area to the west of the city had been a priory demesne in the sixteenth century, but in the frantic landgrab that followed the Restoration of the 1660s, the Duke of Ormond (whose family name was Butler, hence Yeats's interest), decided to build a royal residence with extensive hunting grounds on a large rise of land to the north-west of the city. David Dickson has called the resulting park 'Ormond's great legacy to the city', arguing that it would probably have been impossible to create a parkland on such a scale at any other time.[12] The resulting public space has survived insurrections, famines, and (equally dangerously) property booms, and is today just over 700 hectares, making it more than twice as large as Central Park in New York.

If James Joyce's *Finnegans Wake* can be said to have a location, it is the Mullingar House pub, dating from 1694, on the edge of the Phoenix Park, in Chapelizod, where in Joyce's novel the publican HCE lives with his family. *Photography by Seán Harrison.*

From the outset, the Phoenix Park formed Dublin's western boundary; and, even today, only the suburb of Castleknock stands between the Park's western edge and the M50 ring-road, which marks a kind of outer edge for the twenty-first-century city. And yet, if it was geographically peripheral, the Phoenix Park has been a focal point of Dublin life since it was built in the seventeenth century, initially as a counterbalance to St. Stephen's Green at what was then the city's southern limits. The Phoenix Park's sheer size, its herd of free-roaming deer, and its woodlands always contrasted sharply with the manicured gravelled walks and flowerbeds of the Green. From the outset, then, the Phoenix Park has been a kind of tamed wilderness, both part of the city, and the place where Dubliners go when they want to escape the city. This paradox is present in the earliest known poem about the Park (and one of Ireland's earliest pieces of topographical writing in English), James Ward's 'Phoenix Park' from 1718. The poet begins by making his 'heedless way' through the Park: 'Intent on Nature's Works my wondring Mind, / Shakes off the busy Town she left behind'. The contrast between the comforts of nature and the pressures of the city leads him to equate the city with sin, and the parklands with redemption. 'While thus retir'd, I on the City look, / A Grouppe of Buildings in a Cloud of Smoak, / [...] I learn her Vice and Follies to despise, / And love that Heav'n, which in the Countrey lies.'[13]

Ward is not being wildly original here; the equation of the natural world with something like religious redemption is the main reason that there are so many shepherds and woodlands in eighteenth-century poetry. However, in Dublin this set of associations would evolve into what would effectively become a thriving local subgenre of Phoenix Park pastoral poetry. In part, this was because the presence of the large and impoverished Irish-speaking tenant population in the rest of the country meant that using actual Irish countryside as an image of pristine goodness was always going to be tricky for Anglo-Irish poets. By contrast, the neatly walled – and more importantly, depopulated – Park provided a pastoral landscape wiped clean of any awkward historical baggage. And so, from 1770, we have 'Phoenix Park: A Poem', published by 'A Ranger': 'Where gentle Ana Liffey smoothly glides, / To bathe Eblana with her azure Tides, / Fast by her banks, behold a lovely scene, / Rich in the beauties of the grove and plain.'[14] A few years later, in the same vein, John Leslie published a poem in which 'the Liffey's winding charms / Awake the rural strain!', prompting a panegyric in which the Park offers a vista of the entire city as far as Dublin Bay, using the nearby estate of Palmerstown House as an imagined vantage point: 'Lo! Modern Tully's villa, midst yon bow'rs / Commands the scene.'[15]

The Phoenix Park also loomed large in the imagination of eighteenth-century Dublin for reasons other than how well it could be slotted into the conventions of pastoral poetry. Leslie's poem, for instance, was dedicated to the most senior figure in British rule in Ireland, the Lord Lieutenant of the time, Simon Harcourt. Although it would not be until the 1780s that the Lord Lieutenant would begin to use one of the houses in the Park as an official residence (and initially only as a summer retreat), Dublin Castle's patronage and the presence of a large army barracks within the Park meant that for those for whom the presence of a beneficent Lord Lieutenant and a strong garrison of British soldiers was a source of comfort, the tranquillity of the parklands became an emblem of the benefits of effective colonial rule. For Irish men and women less comforted by men in red uniforms, the meaning of

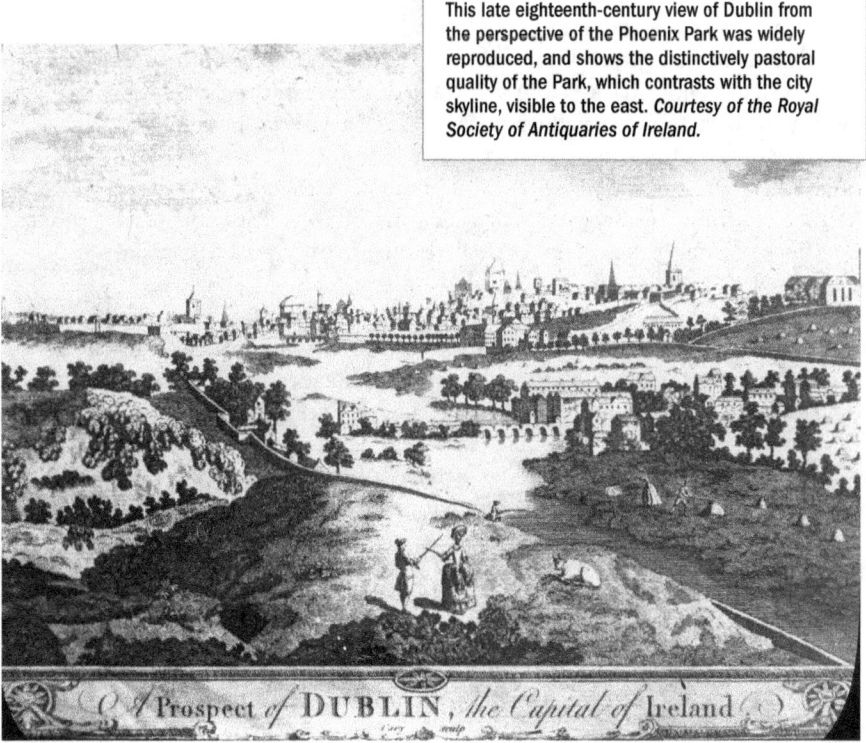

This late eighteenth-century view of Dublin from the perspective of the Phoenix Park was widely reproduced, and shows the distinctively pastoral quality of the Park, which contrasts with the city skyline, visible to the east. *Courtesy of the Royal Society of Antiquaries of Ireland.*

the Park took on a different significance. As early as 1737, in one of his final poems, Jonathan Swift typically took a more satirical view, writing a four-line epigram on the extensive gunpowder magazine that had recently been built there:

> *Behold! a proof of* Irish *sense!*
>   *Here* Irish *wit is seen!*
> *When nothing's left, that's worth defense,*
>   *We build a magazine.*[16]

For writers of the time less critical of their world than Swift (which was more or less everyone), the presence of the viceregal court in the Park assured that it would feature in novels of fashionable life, a genre of writing that would become both increasingly popular and increasingly numerous throughout the century. So, to take one of many possible examples, in Matilda Fitz John's exclamatory *Joan!!!*, from 1796, the heroine, Elizabeth, is delighted when her companion, the wealthy widow Lady Jemima, 'extended her indulgence so far as to take her with her, when, with all the state of widowhood, she went for her airings on the circular road, and among the beautiful varieties of the Phoenix Park.'[17] For fashionable Dublin in the eighteenth and nineteenth centuries, walking, horseback-riding and carriage drives in the Park were the counterpart to promenading in the Green: it was *the* place (or at least one of the places) to see and to be seen.

At the same time, the activity with which the Phoenix Park was perhaps most strongly linked in Irish literature in this period had an entirely darker relation to promenading widows: duelling. 'People took out their pistols for all sorts of provocations – some of them petty and ridiculous,' comments the social historian Constantia Maxwell in *Dublin Under the Georges* (1937), noting that the manager of the Theatre Royal, Richard Daly, fought nineteen duels in two years at one point.[18] There were other places in Dublin in which it was possible to fight a duel, but the Park was by far the favourite. In his *Personal Sketches* (published in 1830, but largely dealing with the period before 1800), Sir Jonah Barrington recalls getting into a dispute with Leonard M'Nally (who was later involved in the 1798 Rebellion), during which things very quickly escalated:

> In forty-five minutes we were regularly posted in the middle of the review-ground in the Phoenix park, and the whole scene, to any person not so seriously implicated, must have been irresistibly

ludicrous. [...] My second having stepped nine paces, then stood at the other side, handed me a case of pistols, and desired me to '*work* away, by J—s!' M'Nally stood before me very like a beer-barrel on its stillings, [...] so I thought it best to lose no time on my part. The poor fellow staggered, and cried out, 'I am hit!' – and I found some twitch myself at the moment which I could not at the time account for.[19]

Likewise, in Charles Lever's first novel, *The Confessions of Harry Lorrequer* (1839) (published serially in the *Dublin University Magazine*) the hero returns to Dublin after an absence to find little has changed in his native city. 'An occasional letter from Mr. O'Connell, and now and then a duel in the "Phaynix" constituted the current pastimes of the city.' Lorrequer himself narrowly avoids Barrington's fate, waking up in his rooms in Trinity after a particularly drunken night to find himself committed both to a duel and to a college exam that morning:

It is truly unpleasant, on rubbing your eyes and opening your ears, to discover that the great bell is ringing the half-hour before your quarterly examination at college, while Locke, Lloyd and Lucian are dancing a reel through your brain, little short of madness; scarcely less agreeable is it to learn that your friend Captain Wildfire is at the door in his cab, to accompany you to the Phoenix, to stand within twelve paces of a cool gentleman [...] that he may pick you out 'artist-like'.[20]

Lorrequer (unlike Barrington) does the sensible thing; he skips both exam and duel, and boards the first boat to Paris.

The association of the Phoenix Park with the ritualized mayhem of duelling gave way to an altogether more serious form of violence in 1882. On 6 May, the Chief Secretary for Ireland, Lord Frederick Cavendish, and the Under-Secretary, Thomas Henry Burke, were stabbed to death by members of a secretive militant republican group, the Invincibles, just outside the Viceregal Lodge. Dublin was fascinated by the details of these particularly gruesome killings – surgical knives were used – and within days ballad-sellers were hawking more than thirty different broadside ballads on what became known as the 'Phoenix Park Murders'.[21] Usually anonymously written, printed on a single sheet of cheap paper, and sold in the streets for a few pennies, broadside ballads were in constant circulation in Dublin throughout the late eighteenth and nineteenth centuries. Many were part of a genre of murder ballads, reporting luridly on crimes, trials, and executions in four-line rhyming stanzas. However, Ireland's long history of insurrection meant that not every murder was necessarily viewed as a crime by the wider populace, so we also find a subgenre of informer ballads, where the sympathy is very much with the perpetrators. In the case of the Phoenix Park Murders, the odium of the informer was directed at James Carey, who had been part of the conspiracy, but who later turned state's evidence. Among those he convicted was a cab driver who drove the getaway vehicle, the wonderfully named James 'Skin-the-Goat' Fitzharris, who gives his name to a ballad composed entirely of wildly inventive curses: 'Skin-the-Goat's Curse on Carey'. 'May his toes fill with corns like a puckawn's horns / Till he can neither wear slippers or shoes, / With a horrid toothache may he roar like a drake / And jump like a mad kangaroo.' Skin-the-Goat will later make an appearance in *Ulysses*, where the cabman's shelter by Butt Bridge in which Bloom and Stephen take shelter in the 'Eumaeus' episode is said to be kept by 'the famous Skin-the-Goat, the invincible, though he wouldn't vouch for the actual facts.'[22]

By the 1880s, then, the pastoral imaginings of the previous century had been overlaid by darker associations. These are present in Le Fanu's *The House by the Churchyard*, when the character of Dr. Sturk is found in the Park with horrific head wounds, and 'blood coming from one ear and his mouth'.[23] And it is also in the Phoenix Park that HCE in *Finnegans Wake* is alleged to have committed the unnamed act for which he is repeatedly and phantasmagorically arraigned and tried, over and over again. Later again, Conor Brady's 2012 historical crime novel *A June of Ordinary Murders* revisits the site of the 1882 murders when two more (unrelated) bodies are found. 'It was here,' the novel begins, 'where the boundary wall of the Phoenix Park met the granite pillars of the Chapelizod Gate, and where beech and pine trees formed a small, dense copse close by [...] that a keeper found the two bodies on the third morning of the extraordinary heatwave that settled on the island of Ireland in the third week of June, 1887.' When Joe Swallow of the Dublin Metropolitan Police is sent to investigate, he quickly realizes that he 'had been to this place before', and that 'five years earlier the copse was one of dozens of locations in the park he had searched' after the murders of Cavendish and Burke.[24]

Mixing in with its complex literary legacy as a pastoral idyll, duelling ground, and site of political assassination, ever since the first Lord Lieutenant took up residence in the Viceregal Lodge, the Phoenix Park has been associated with a certain kind of ceremonial power. After Irish

Independence in 1922, the building became for a time the official residence of Ireland's Governor-General (Ireland was still a member of the British Commonwealth until 1949); from 1938 onwards, it became the official residence of the Irish President, Áras an Uachataráin. It was here that an increasingly elderly and deeply conservative third president, Eamon de Valera – a veteran of the 1916 Rising – lived while he held office from 1959 until 1973, when he retired at the age of 90. In his 1978 poem 'Making Love Outside Áras an Uachataráin', Paul Durcan imagines the ageing president, peering out at an Ireland he no longer recognizes:

When I was a boy, myself and my girl
Used bicycle up to the Phoenix Park;
Outside the gates we used lie in the grass
Making love outside Áras an Uachtaráin.

Often I wondered what de Valera would have thought
Inside in his ivory tower
If he knew that we were in his green, green grass
Making love outside Áras an Uachtaráin.[25]

The symbolic significance of the Phoenix Park was compounded yet again in 2004. If Durcan's poem commemorated a point in the 1960s when the generation who had founded the state were overtaken by a new generation, in 2004 the Áras was the location for the formal ratification of the treaty creating the largest ever expansion of the European Union – admitting countries including Poland, Slovenia, and Hungary. The effects of that expansion would be far-reaching. Among them, for the first time since the Huguenot migrations of the seventeenth century, Dublin became a destination for new migrants, particularly from Eastern Europe. Within a decade, Polish would overtake Irish as the second most widely spoken language in the country, and there would be more than 120,000 Polish people living in the country by 2016.[26] Marking the moment, Seamus Heaney read a poem commissioned for the event, 'Beacons at Beltaine', which traces back the Irish words that lie behind the name 'Phoenix': 'fionn uisce' ('clear water'). 'So on a day when newcomers appear / Let it be a homecoming and let us speak / [...] From middle sea to north sea, shining clear / As phoenix flame upon *fionn uisce* here.'[27]

If the Phoenix Park is very much a public space – whether for ceremonies of state, or for settling affairs of honour with a brace of pistols –

the streets immediately surrounding it still have a Victorian flavour, more distinctly urban on the eastern side towards the city, while some residential streets on the Park's western edge retain the cottages and trees of an earlier countryside. The redbrick Victorian terraces on the eastern side carry over to the south bank of the Liffey, in areas such as Inchicore and Kilmainham.

> *Now, in Inchicore*
> *my cigarette smoke rises*
> *– like lonesome pub-talk.*[28]

So writes the poet Michael Hartnett, in one of his *Inchicore Haiku* (1983). It was in Kilmainham, at No. 37 Phoenix Street, that the poet Thomas Kinsella lived as a child, and this is a remembered world to which his mature poetry returns, again and again. *'There are established personal places / that receive our lives' heat / and adapt to their mass, like stone,'* he writes in his 1990 collection *Personal Places*. 'Phoenix Street,' he later mused, 'seemed an imaginative name. But the next street was Park Street. And I can see the planner idling over his map, looking Northward from his site across the Liffey, at the Phoenix Park.' He would later describe his poem '38 Phoenix Street' – the address of his next-door neighbour – as 'my first encounter as an infant with people outside our family [...] staring at the stranger; at the other': 'Look. / I was lifted up / past rotten bricks weeds / to look over the wall.'

This part of the city has been one of Kinsella's 'personal places' for many years, not just in his memory but in his poetry, as well. Going back to his 1968 collection *Nightwalker and Other Poems*, we find a long poem entitled 'Phoenix Park'. Here, in a complex meditation on morality, sickness, and love, the Park and its small tuberculosis hospital, St. Mary's, become both a place where the poet and his wife are utterly together and a 'point of departure' for a return to the city:

> *The tyres are singing, cornering back and forth*
> *In our green world again; into groves of trees,*
> *By lake and open park, past the hospital.*
> *The west ignites behind us; round one more turn*
> *Pale light in the east hangs over the city.*[29]

Neither fully city, nor fully country, the Phoenix Park continues to occupy a place between the two. It is part of what defines Dublin, but also a reminder of an Ireland to the west of the city where even the light is different.

That light, however, is a changing light. Immediately to the south and to the west of the Phoenix Park and Kilmainham, the development of Dublin is not unlike areas such as Finglas or Ballymun to the north of the city, in that there are no natural boundaries to contain the urban spread. Kinsella, who worked for a time in the Department of Finance just as the city began to swallow up the surrounding countryside, would later write scathingly in *One Fond Embrace* (1988) of the city moving 'southward into the foothills / to where the transplanted can trudge / from Kennedy's Villas and Cherryfield Heights / to Shangri-La for a bottle of milk.'[30] Initially at least, the reason for this development to the south-west was the same as for places on the northside such as Marino, and later Kilbarrack and Ballymun: to find space for better public housing for the thousands of Dubliners living in the tenements in the inner city. So, from the 1930s onwards, Dublin began to expand rapidly not

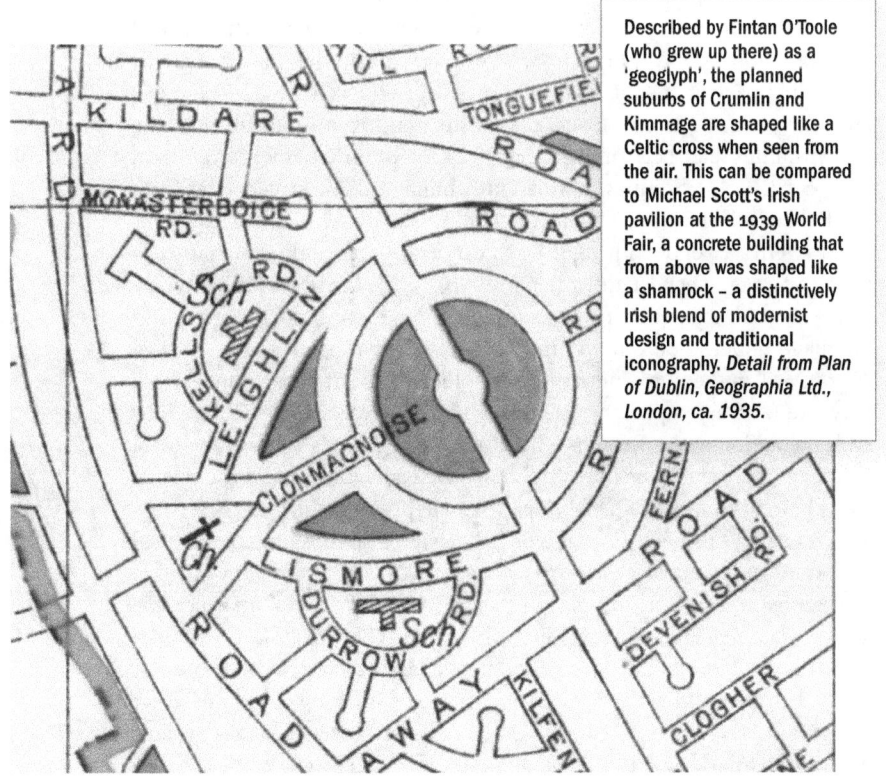

Described by Fintan O'Toole (who grew up there) as a 'geoglyph', the planned suburbs of Crumlin and Kimmage are shaped like a Celtic cross when seen from the air. This can be compared to Michael Scott's Irish pavilion at the 1939 World Fair, a concrete building that from above was shaped like a shamrock – a distinctively Irish blend of modernist design and traditional iconography. *Detail from Plan of Dublin, Geographia Ltd., London, ca. 1935.*

only towards northwards, but also to the south-west, transforming the villages and farmlands of Crumlin, Kimmage, and Ballyfermot. These new suburbs, in geographer Joseph Brady's description, were 'built in short terraces of ten or fewer houses with good front gardens and substantial rear gardens. Pebbledash was the preferred facing.'[31] From the air, the streets of Crumlin form a gigantic Celtic cross. The writer and journalist Fintan O'Toole, who grew up in the area, once described his 'home terrain' as 'a geoglyph, like the Nazca Lines of Peru or the white horses and giants cut into the chalk downs of England.' 'The thing was, though,' observes O'Toole, 'that on the ground level, where we were, you couldn't see this at all.'[32]

So when Brendan Behan's tenement-owning grandmother died in 1936, and it was discovered when her will was read that the building on Russell Street in the north inner city where they lived had been condemned to be torn down, the thirteen-year-old Behan's family were moved to newly built public housing at 70 Kildare Road, where Kimmage meets Crumlin, in a house that is currently painted a vivid shade of lilac. This is both a twenty-minute walk and a world away from where George Russell had held his salons at 17 Rathgar Road. Although Behan did not write much about this part of the city (apart from two radio sketches, *Moving Out* and *The Garden Party* in 1950), one of his neighbours did. In 1924, the Brown family had been moved out of a two-room tenement on North King Street to 54 Stannaway Road in Kimmage, a few streets over from the Behans. Christy Brown was the twelfth surviving member of a family of twenty-two, born in 1932 with cerebral palsy, and (as he put it in a letter to publisher Liam Miller in 1963), 'until the age of seventeen I could not talk except by my eyes and foot and a queer sort of grunting language understood only by my family.'[33] Brown's first book, *My Left Foot* (1954), is the powerful autobiographical account of how he learned to write (and later paint) with the only limb over which he had control. Behan knew the Browns, and after *My Left Foot*'s success the local Kimmage pub, the Stoneboat on Sundrive Road, would stand them both free pints of Guinness, in the hope that the presence of famous writers would attract business. Brown would later develop his autobiographical memories in his novel *Down All the Days* (1970), a book immersed in the sensations of this working-class suburban world, with its 'innumerable backyards of corporation dwellings, an ironclad heritage of broken bedsteads, rusty bicycle frames, crumbling sheds, rotten mattresses, lines of washed clothes gathering up soot and grime of smoking chimneys – and occasional green rows of cabbages and mad improbable blazes of geraniums and dahlias flowering like manna in the desert.'[34]

While probably not featuring on calendars of famous Irish literary pubs, the Stoneboat on Sundrive Road, Crumlin, has a good claim to be just that. It was the local for both Brendan Behan and Christy Brown, where the owner undertook the not inconsiderable burden of standing both writers drinks. *Photography by Seán Harrison.*

Brown is unusual, however, in writing about Dublin's western suburbs with the kind of retrospective longing and imagining that we find in older parts of the city, such as Kinsella's Kilmainham. Instead, much of the writing of the western suburbs takes a kind of paradoxical sustenance from its sense of placelessness. Sometimes, this is explicit. For instance, one of the stories in Christine Dwyer Hickey's *The House on Parkgate Street*, entitled 'Absence', is set in Ballyfermot, a large working-class estate west of Kimmage, and built at the same time as Finglas in the 1950s. The story opens with the character of Frank returning home to Ballyfermot, looking out of the window of a taxi. 'As far as he can see, nothing much has changed, apart from one modern-looking lump of a building further down the road. It looks like the same old, bland old Ballyer that it always was. Rows of concrete-grey shops under a dirty-dishcloth sky.'[35] Likewise, after having lived at the heart of the bohemian literary culture of Baggotonia in the 1960s (a period she documents in all its creative squalor in her 2008 memoir, *A Restless Life*),[36] the poet Leland Bardwell had one too many run-ins with a landlord, and found herself living in Killinarden, in Tallaght, a full eight kilometres beyond Crumlin. 'What is this place called Tallaght now?' Bardwell asks. 'The name, roughly translated, means The Land of the Plague. There used to be a monastery there, which presumably tried to succour the dying. A mere thirty years ago, the old village, built on a rise, well above the soggy foothills, consisted of a solitary street. It was a "pretty village", marginally forgotten.'[37] Later, she declares in her poem 'The Bingo Bus': 'In Killinarden there was nothing – / Nothing – but in the nearer town / There was the Bingo Bus.'[38]

The extent to which areas such as Tallaght or Ballyfermot have completely overwritten their earlier shape can be registered by turning to one of Ireland's most prolific novelists of the 1880s and 1890s, Katherine Tynan. In the final decades of the nineteenth century, Tynan lived about the same distance from the city centre as Bardwell a century later, in a house known as Whitehall, in Clondalkin: 'a small cottage building with little windows under immense overhanging eaves of thatch and a hall door within a porch of green trellis.' In her memoirs, she recalls visiting her neighbours, who lived in nearby Belgard Castle: 'Belgard is surrounded by an ancient buttressed wall. As it is so very old, it is always crumbling in one piece or another. [...] From an Italian balustrading in front of the house you look down into a tangled orchard with a well in it.'[39] A century later this idyllic countryside has changed beyond recognition; rather than crumbling castles and thatched cottages, there are now large housing estates, punctuated by undeveloped wasteland and industrial units. 'Maybe Jesus is wandering these roads tonight,' muses Dermot Bolger in his poem 'Jesus of Clondalkin' (2006). 'Unrecognised, unacknowledged, utterly alone, / Passing half built apartment blocks investors own, / Passing burnt-out cars, glass shards, twisted chrome, / Threading a path through Neilstown and Quarryvale.'[40]

> **Irish Place Names:** Throughout Ireland as a whole, many Irish place names are anglicized versions of Irish-language names. In this respect, Dublin is different from the rest of the country. Because much of the city was not initially settled by Irish-speakers, Irish-based names are relatively rare in the city centre. It is only on the outer edges that we find Tallaght (from the Irish *támhleacht*, or 'plague pit'), Drimnagh (*druimneach*, or 'land with ridges'), or Ballyfermot (from *baile*, or 'town' or 'farm' and an Old Norse name, *Þormundr*, or *Thormaid*).

One writer who has created a fictional world from this part of Dublin is playwright Mark O'Rowe, who is from Tallaght and writes about what he has called 'a Tallaght of the mind'. His plays, such as *Crestfall* (2003) and *Howie the Rookie* (1999) are typically written as a series of interlocking monologues (suggesting his characters' separation from one another) that weave a world of violence, addiction, sexual abuse, and constant threat. Here, the landscape seems familiar, but the voices are stylized by rhyme and rhythm, and place names are often fictional or do not appear on any map. In *Crestfall*, for instance, which deals with sexual violence, there is a Beacon Street and a Rowney Street, neither of which exist, and there are places that have local names not to be found on any official map, such as The Boneland or Mick McGillacuddy's Field. However, in *Howie the Rookie*, made up of the interlocking monologues of two young men on the edges of a chaotic world of violent crime, there is a real location – Limekiln Lane – that is both anonymous and recognizable:

> Headin' through The Close, spot The Howie Lee, Peaches' mate 'cross the green, sittin' on a bench, smokin'. Howie that held me for a batterin'. He spots me, stands up, he shouts.
> I turn.
> He calls me name.
> I'm gone.
> I'm gone up The Limekiln Lane.[41]

The writer Karl Whitney, who is also from Tallaght, writes about growing up in the area. 'I didn't hate Tallaght,' he writes, 'but I knew it wasn't like the towns and cities I saw on TV or read about in books.' The point for O'Rowe is in fact the opposite: the western suburbs of Dublin look very much like a kind of suburban landscape found across twenty-first-century Europe, and, as such look like places that populate the globalized imaginations of people everywhere. Considered in this way, the western edges of Dublin are, like its northern frontier, places of blurred boundaries in more than one respect. Whitney, returning to the area where he grew up 'on the very edge of the city,' notes that 'the location isn't by any means unpleasant, but there is an unavoidable feeling of isolation, and I could easily see how one could feel stranded here.'[42] Springfield, for instance, where Mark O'Rowe grew up, is well past the M50 ring-road, which acts as a kind of porous twenty-first-century boundary marker for Dublin.

In fact, it is increasingly difficult to say where Dublin ends at its western extremities. As long ago as 1967 there was a municipal plan for a Greater Dublin Area, taking in north Wicklow, north Kildare, and south Meath, centred around four ex-urban satellite towns of Tallaght, Clondalkin, Lucan, and Blanchardstown. By 1971, the population of the entire Greater Dublin Area passed the million mark, at which point, as David Dickson writes, 'the city could claim to be a European megalopolis.'[43]

The absence of strong place memory can be a form of freedom. Although the script makes it clear that the setting is Tallaght, Mark O'Rowe's *Howie the Rookie* (Abbey Theatre, 2006) creates its own almost abstract stage world. The actor here is Aidan Kelly. Photograph by Ros Kavanagh. Courtesy of the Abbey Theatre Archive.

Well before this milestone was reached, however, Flann O'Brien, in one of his 'Cruiskeen Lawn' columns for the *Irish Times*, was spinning his own surreal version of the expanding city:

> Some fine day the inhabitants of Leixlip [about 15 kilometres west of the Phoenix Park] will notice something unusual about the horizon and, sending forth scouts to investigate, will find it is Dublin. Dublin just down the road today. Tomorrow? The tide will have engulfed ancient Leixlip [...] People in Athlone [more than 100 kilometres away] will say 'You saw what happened in Leixlip. They thought they were safe, that their unborn sons would never be Dublin men. *Hodie Leixlip, Cras nobis* [today Leixlip, we tomorrow]. Let us menfolk take to the hills, let our women-folk be instructed in the art of baking cakes containing keys. To arms!'⁴⁴

A City of Commuters: While it is possible to map the physical growth of Dublin in the twenty-first century, there has also been invisible growth in the form of a growing number of commuters from beyond the city. According to the Central Statistics Office, a quarter of Dublin workers in 2016 – or more than 130,000 people – live outside the city or suburbs, mostly, but not exclusively, in the neighbouring counties of Kildare, Meath, and Louth, from where they commute into the city each day for work.

In the years ahead, as Dublin expands northwards and westwards, eluding definition with every new housing estate that swallows up another field, it may become increasingly difficult to counter placelessness. 'The point is their sameness,' Fintan O'Toole wrote of Dublin's outer suburbs when Roddy Doyle's Barrytown novels set in Kilbarrack first appeared in the early 1990s. 'Like it or not, it is where we live now, and we need fictions that do it justice.'[45] Over the past half century, finding a literary language for the reality that most Dubliners now inhabit in the city's suburbs has been acknowledged by some of the city's leading writers, among them Anne Enright, Roddy Doyle, Paula Meehan, and Eavan Boland. It is equally a challenge taken up less self-consciously (but often with a much larger readership) by writers of genre fiction, such as Tana French, Gene Kerrigan, or Marian Keyes. At the same time, even as the centre of Dublin has become more of a walking and cycling city, the continuing rise in the cost of property means that the urban villages of writers that once existed in the city centre, drawn together by creative companionship and low rents, are unlikely to return, at least in the form in which they once existed.

In facing this task of the imagination, we can, perhaps find an image from literature itself. At the conclusion to James Joyce's great short story, 'The Dead', the character of Gabriel Conroy stands at the window of the Gresham Hotel, in the very centre of Dublin, where the snow tapping at the window lulls him into a moment of reverie. 'He watched sleepily the flakes, silver and dark, falling obliquely against the lamplight. The time had come for him to set out on his journey westward. Yes, the newspapers were right: snow was general all over Ireland. [...] His soul swooned slowly as he heard the snow falling faintly through the universe and faintly falling, like the descent of their last end, upon all the living and the dead.'[46] If for Gabriel Conroy in 'The Dead' the challenge was to let his imagination expand westwards towards another life, it may be that the parallel challenge for Dublin's writers in the future will be to find forms for the literary imagination to embrace the western and northern peripheries of a city that has for centuries lived through its literature.

Read On ...

George Bernard Shaw was once asked if Ireland would ever stop producing great actors, to which he reputedly replied: 'I'm afraid not.' The same could be said of Dublin and writers.

To put that continuing deluge of words in context, history makes a good place to start. While there have been histories of Dublin since at least John T. Gilbert's epic three volume tome (1854–1859), David Dickson's *Dublin: The Making of a Capital City* (London: Profile, 2014) is the lively, authoritative, standard work, and is likely to remain so for many years; the book you are reading is much indebted to it. The same author's *The First Irish Cities: An Eighteenth-Century Transformation* (New Haven: Yale University Press, 2021) makes a useful supplement. Dickson's bibliography is where to go for an exhaustive listing of decades of academic writing on the topic, ranging from the studies by Seán Duffy on medieval Dublin, to Jacqueline R. Hill on civic politics in the eighteenth and nineteenth centuries, or geographer Joseph Brady's comprehensive *Making of Dublin* series of books, which track its twentieth-century development in detail. Taking a more visual approach to the topic, John Gibney's *Dublin: A New Illustrated History* (Cork: Collins Press, 2017) makes excellent use of photos, illustrations, and maps to tell the story of the city. Peter Somerville-Large's *Dublin: The First Thousand Years* (Belfast: Appletree Press, 1988) is worth finding for its trove of anecdotes, while further back on the second-hand bookshelves, architectural historian Maurice Craig's *Dublin 1660–1860* (1952; Dublin: Allen Figgis, 1980) still holds its own, as does Constantia Maxwell's wonderfully readable *Dublin Under the Georges: 1714–1830* (London: Faber and Faber, 1937).

Boosted by centenary fever, you could fill a decent-sized library with books on the period between the 1913 Dublin Lockout and the Irish

Civil War in the early 1920s, with a library-within-a-library filled with books on the 1916 Rising in Dublin. Probably the best way through the thickets and ambushes is the beautifully produced and fiendishly heavy *Atlas of the Irish Revolution*, edited by John Crowley, Donal Ó Drisceoil, and Mike Murphy (Cork: Cork University Press, 2017). More portable is Maurice Walsh's compelling *Bitter Freedom: Ireland in a Revolutionary World 1918–1923* (London: Faber, 2015). If you were going to choose one book on the 1916 Rising among the dozens that have appeared, perhaps the most vivid is the day-by-day account of Clair Wills's *Dublin 1916: The Siege of the GPO* (Cambridge, MA: Harvard University Press, 2009).

More specialized aspects of Dublin life are also worth exploring. Kevin C. Kearns's *Dublin Tenement Life: An Oral History* (Dublin: Gill and Macmillan, 1994) has become a classic. So, too, has *Dublin: An Urban History: The Plan of the City* (Dublin: Anne Street Press, 2007), a masterclass in image-based narrative by architect Niall McCullough. McCullough's book is part of a growing interest in Dublin's built environment that includes Yvonne Whelan's *Reinventing Modern Dublin: Streetscape, Iconography, and the Politics of Identity* (Dublin: University College Dublin Press, 2003). The Royal Irish Academy have produced some very attractive small volumes in their map-based Irish Historic Towns Atlas series: Colm Lennon and John Montague, *John Rocque's Dublin: A Guide to the Georgian City* (Dublin: Royal Irish Academy, 2010) and Frank Cullen, *Dublin 1847: City of the Ordinance Survey* (Dublin: Royal Irish Academy, 2015). Also useful is Neal Doherty's *The Complete Guide to the Streets of Dublin City* (Orpen Press: Dublin, 2016), the most recent book to provide a street-by-street listing of Dublin street names and their origins. Finally, for a reminder that there is a landscape beneath the city, Clair L. Sweeney's *The Rivers of Dublin* (rev. ed. Dublin: Irish Academic Press, 2019) has become an unexpected Dublin favourite, going through multiple editions.

In terms of literary Dublin, Vivien Igoe's *A Literary Guide to Dublin* (London: Methuen, 1994) is a useful and accurate alphabetical listing of the places where ninety-one writers lived and worked in the city. Siobhán Kilfeather's *Dublin: A Cultural and Literary History* (Oxford: Signal Books, 2005) is a highly readable short history from pre-Viking settlement to the present, while Thomas and Valerie Pakenham's *Dublin: A Traveller's Reader* (London: Constable and Robinson, 1988) is a rich and often surprising anthology of writings of all sorts about the city from Holinshed's *Chronicles* in 1577 onwards to the mid-twentieth century.

Literary biographies provide a more focused view of Dublin, and there are many from which to choose. The relevant sections of any of the classic biographies of the major writers are all brimming with detail; particularly recommended are Leo Damrosch, *Jonathan Swift: His Life and His World* (New Haven: Yale University Press, 2013); Richard Ellmann's *James Joyce* (rev. ed. Oxford: Oxford University Press, 1982) and his *Oscar Wilde* (London: Hamish Hamilton, 1987); James Knowlson's *Damned to Fame: The Life of Samuel Beckett* (London: Bloomsbury, 1996); or R. F. Foster's magisterial two-volume *W. B. Yeats: A Life* (Oxford: Oxford University Press, 1997 and 2003); and while George Bernard Shaw did not write much about Dublin, he grew up in the city, where Fintan O'Toole clearly places him in *Judging Shaw* (Dublin: Royal Irish Academy, 2017). For a more portable approach to biography, reading Colm Tóibín's *Mad, Bad, Dangerous to Know: The Fathers of Wilde, Yeats & Joyce* (London: Penguin, 2018) is like being led around the city by a gifted conversationalist who has read everything.

Dublin produces author memoirs by the shelfload, but it is difficult to match the distilled, luminous quality of Elizabeth Bowen's *Seven Winters*, published as *Bowen's Court & Seven Winters: Memories of a Dublin Childhood* (London: Vintage, 2017). At the opposite end of the stylistic spectrum, Seán O'Casey's *Autobiographies* (New York: Carroll & Graf, 1984) fill six volumes of overripe prose, where an army of arrestingly alliterative adjectives is always preferred to a single descriptor. Between these two poles, Dublin's great wits and talkers have produced some memorable accounts of the city, but start with George Moore's acerbic *Hail and Farewell*, made up of three volumes: *Ave*, *Salve* and *Vale*. There is a well-edited edition from Catholic University Press (Washington, 1985). In the same vein is Oliver St. John Gogarty's *As I Was Going Down Sackville Street* (1937; Dublin: O'Brien Press, 1997). Gogarty and Moore's modern contemporary, with respect to dry wit, is John Banville, with his much gentler *Time Pieces: A Dublin Memoir* (Dublin: Hachette Books, 2016). Memoirs of the Dublin of McDaid's pub era are a subgenre in their own right, but the best is Anthony Cronin's unsentimental *Dead as Doornails* (Dublin: Dolmen Press, 1976); equally clear-eyed and more wide-ranging is Leland Bardwell's *A Restless Life* (Dublin: Liberties Press, 2008). Perhaps the most remarkable memoir as *bildungsroman* is Christy Brown's *My Left Foot* (1954; London: Minerva, 1991). And for memoirs at a tangent, as it were, Stanislaus

Joyce's memoir, *My Brother's Keeper: James Joyce's Early Years* (New York: Viking, 1958) has become a classic in its own right, while for an insight into two ordinary Dublin lives in the middle of the last century, read Roddy Doyle's warm account of his parents, *Rory and Ita* (London: Vintage, 2002). Finally, Fintan O'Toole's *We Don't Know Ourselves: A Personal History of Ireland Since 1958* (London: Head of Zeus, 2021) is precisely what it says: a personal history (and hence one very much based in Dublin) by one of Ireland's most astute commentators.

James Joyce holds a place all his own in Dublin literature. The global scholarly industry around Joyce is famously vast, so there is no shortage of commentary on his writing about Dublin. A summation of that work can be found in Catherine Flynn's magnificent annotated centenary edition of *Ulysses* (Cambridge: Cambridge University Press, 2022), which is a kind of non-linear encyclopaedia of Dublin. It draws on earlier work, also rich in maps (and old photographs) such as Ian Gunn and Clive Hart's *Dublin: A Topographical Guide to the Dublin of Ulysses* (London: Thames and Hudson, 2004), and the earlier Bruce Bidwell and Linda Heffer's *The Joycean Way: A Topographic Guide to* Dubliners & A Portrait of the Artist as a Young Man (Baltimore: Johns Hopkins University Press, 1981). If you want a set of maps more likely to fit in your pocket, look for *The Ulysses Guide: Tours Through Joyce's Dublin* (London: Methuen, 1988) by Robert Nicholson, the long-time curator of the Joyce Martello Tower in Sandycove; also a former curator of the Joyce Tower was Vivien Igoe, author of *James Joyce's Dublin Houses & Nora Barnacle's Galway* (Dublin: Lilliput, 1998). On a related note, if you thought that all of Samuel Beckett's works were set in a rubbish-filled no-man's-land, your mind will be changed by Eoin O'Brien's illustrated *The Beckett Country* (Blackcat/Faber: Dublin and London, 1986), which firmly locates the writer in Dublin.

Finally, there are a few books that simply fall into the category of the indispensable when it comes to Dublin literature. Each year, Dublin City Libraries choose a single book about Dublin to celebrate in an annual event known as One City, One Book. In 2014, instead of choosing a novel, the Library commissioned poets Pat Boran and Gerard Smyth to compile an anthology of Dublin poetry. The result, *If Ever You Go* is precisely what the subtitle promises: *A Map of Dublin in Poetry and Song* (Dublin: Dedalus Press, 2014), made up of nearly three hundred poems arranged by area. More personal is Eavan Boland's *A Poet's Dublin*, edited by Paula Meehan and Jody Allen Randolph (Manchester: Carcanet, 2014), which mixes poems, Boland's own photographs, and a conversation between Boland and Meehan to sketch a uniquely personal portrait of the city. Its counterpart is Thomas Kinsella's *A Dublin Documentary* (Dublin: O'Brien Press, 2006), a mixture of poetry, prose, and photographs. Finally, poet Peter Sirr's *Intimate City: Dublin Essays* (Oldcastle: Gallery Press, 2021) is a series of beautifully observed essays on the city and its writers that will make you want to walk through Dublin all over again.

Notes

Introduction The Imagined City in Time of Pandemic
1. Berryman, *Dream Songs*, 322.
2. Joyce, *Ulysses*, 64.
3. Kinsella, *Collected Poems*, 60.
4. Beckett, *Selected Works*, 102, 111.
5. Yeats, *Collected Works VIII*, 148–149
6. Bowen, *Collected Impressions*, 180.
7. Joyce, *Ulysses*, 120.
8. Boran and Smyth, *If Ever You Go*, 226
9. Casey, 'Between Geography and Philosophy', 684.
10. Mahon, *Poems*, 500.

1 Mapping the City
1. Boland, *Collected Poems*, 204.
2. MacNeice, *Collected Poems*, 163.
3. Dickson, *Dublin*, 43.
4. Sirr, *Intimate City*, 48–49.
5. Gwynn, *Ireland Old and New*, 8
6. Woolf, 'Scandinavian Intervention', 114.
7. Dickson, *Dublin*, 21, 25.
8. Berryman, *Dream Songs*, 329.
9. Dickson, *Dublin*, 92.
10. Leerssen, *Hidden Ireland*, 31, 36.
11. McDonald, *Future of Dublin*, 1.

12. Craig, *Poems*, 34.
13. Dickson, *Dublin*, 141.
14. McParland, 'Wide Street Commissioners', 21.
15. Jordan, 'Whitelaw's "Essay"', 141.
16. Bowen, *Shelbourne*, 41
17. Bartlett, 'Ireland During Revolutionary Wars', 90.
18. Edgeworth, *Absentee*, 83.
19. Edgeworth, *Absentee*, 83–84
20. Owenson, *Memoirs*, 172.
21. Boland, *Journey with Two Maps*, 45–46, 49, 51.
22. Hourihan, 'Cities and Towns', 232, 236.
23. O'Neill, 'Bourgeois Ireland', 518
24. Edgeworth, *Absentee*, 83.
25. Crowe, 'Urban and Rural Living Conditions', 63.
26. Dickson, *Dublin*, 372.
27. Longford, *Dublin*, 141
28. Yeats, *Autobiographies*, 169.
29. Foster, *Vivid Faces*, xxii.
30. McGarry, 'Easter Rising', 242.
31. Robinson, Letter to Lady Gregory, 1924; NYPL.
32. Behan, *Brendan Behan's Island*, 14.
33. O'Sullivan, *Brendan Behan*, 245.
34. Central Statistics Office, 'Population and Vital Statistics', 2003.
35. Smyth, *Sundays of Eternity*, 63.
36. Central Statistics Office, 'Migration and Diversity', 2017.
37. Glynn, 'Migration and Integration', 572.
38. Boran and Enyi-Amadi, *Writing Home*, 146
39. Meehan, *Mysteries of the Home*, 46–47.

2 Baggotonia

1. McGahern, *Collected Stories*, 357–358.
2. McGahern, *Collected Stories*, 66.
3. McGahern, *Collected Stories*, 360.
4. Kiberd, 'City in Irish Culture', 223.

5. Dickson, *Dublin*, 537.
6. Ryan, *Remembering How We Stood*, 28.
7. Montague, *Company*, 77.
8. Cronin, *Dead as Doornails*, 3.
9. Kavanagh, *Poet's Country*, 308.
10. Montague, *Company*, 65.
11. Cronin, *Dead as Doornails*, 7.
12. Mahon, *Poems*, 207
13. Fallon, *Age of Innocence*, 234
14. Cronin, *Dead as Doornails*, 78.
15. B. Behan, *Scarperer*, 9.
16. Cronin, *Dead as Doornails*, 70.
17. O'Brien, *Collected Letters*, 29
18. O'Brien, *Best of Myles*, 18–19; 256.
19. Kavanagh, *Poet's Country*, 241.
20. Donleavy, *Ginger Man*, 272.
21. O'Brien, *Complete Novels*, 168.
22. Kavanagh, *Collected Poems*, 169.
23. Ryan, *Remembering How We Stood*, 98.
24. Kavanagh, *Collected Poems*, 191.
25. Igoe, *Literary Guide*, 125.
26. Kavanagh, *Collected Poems*, 130.
27. Kavanagh, *Collected Poems*, 130; Meehan, *Mysteries of the Home*, 89.
28. Kavanagh, *Poet's Country*, 272.
29. Kavanagh, *Collected Poems*, 227, 224.
30. Kennelly, *Essential*, 33.
31. Banville, *Time Pieces*, 48–49.
32. Berryman, *Dream Songs*, 366.
33. Montague, *Company*, 34.
34. Montague, *Collected Poems*, 111.
35. Montague, *Company*, 30.
36. Simpson, *Beckett and Behan*, 1.
37. Swift, *Stage by Stage*, 107.

38. 'Waiting for Godot', *Pike Newsletter*, 1.
39. Beckett, *Letters*, II: 418.
40. Simpson, *Beckett and Behan*, 124.
41. Beckett, *Selected Works*, III: 69, 74. See also Beckett, 'Waiting for Godot'; and Morash, *Irish Theatre*, 199–208.
42. Simpson, *Beckett and Behan*, 124.
43. Beckett, *Letters*, II: 560–561.
44. Mercier, 'Uneventful Event', 6.
45. Kavanagh, *Poet's Country*, 226.
46. Behan, *Confessions*, 288.
47. Beckett, *Letters*, II, 207
48. Beckett, *Selected Works*, III, 222.
49. Clifton, *Portobello Sonnets*, 13.
50. Banville, *Time Pieces*, 93.
51. Cronin, *Dead as Doornails*, 197.
52. Bardwell, *Restless Life*, 246, 288, 247, 256.
53. Woods, *Collected Poems*, 357.
54. Montague, *Company*, 44.
55. McGahern, *Letters*, 138, 98–99, 107.
56. Kinsella, *From City Centre*, 69.
57. Kinsella, *Dublin Documentary*, 81.
58. Banville, *Time Pieces*, 1, 14.
59. Banville, *Mephisto*, 143, 217.
60. Banville, *Book of Evidence*, 129, 167.
61. Banville, *Time Pieces*, 66.
62. Banville [Black], *Christine Falls*, 27.
63. Banville [Black], *Elegy for April*, 4–5.

3 Around St. Stephen's Green

1. Bowen, *Seven Winters*, 467, 471.
2. Bowen, *Seven Winters*, 479.
3. Bowen, *Seven Winters*, 483.
4. O'Brien, *My Ireland*, 110.
5. Kavanagh, *Collected Poems*, 167.

6. 'Women Writers' Club Function', 6.
7. Deevy, Letter to Patricia Lynch.
8. Deevy, Letter to Florence Hackett.
9. Tóibín, 'Mary Lavin', 97.
10. Lavin, *In a Café*, 185, 201.
11. Tóibín, 'Mary Lavin', 109.
12. Bowen, *Seven Winters*, 477–478.
13. Bowen, *Seven Winters*, 492.
14. Jordan, *Lord Edward and Citizen Small*, 102.
15. Dickson, *Dublin*, 166–167, 230–231.
16. Murdoch, *Red and Green*, 86
17. Igoe, *Literary Guide*, 172.
18. Yeats to Oliver St John Gogarty (1 February, 1922) [Accession 4062]; Yeats to Olivia Shakespear (17 February, 1922) [Accession 4071]; *Collected Letters* [Intelex].
19. White, *The Devil You Know*, 10.
20. Joyce, *Echoland*, 4–5.
21. Odin, *Last Speech*, 1.
22. Dickson, *Dublin*, 85.
23. Philips, *St. Stephen's Green*, 12.
24. Bickerstaffe, *Stephen's Green*, 1.
25. Newburgh, *Essays*, 215.
26. Bowen, *Collected Impressions*, 180.
27. Bowen, *Shelbourne*, 11, 157, 161.
28. Glendinning, *Elizabeth Bowen*, 226; the passage from *The Shelbourne* is on page 172.
29. Owenson, *Memoirs*, 29.
30. Owenson, *O'Donnel*, vii.
31. Bowen, *Shelbourne*, 68.
32. Frazier, *George Moore*, 299.
33. Bowen, *Shelbourne*, 110.
34. Frazier, *George Moore*, 273–274.
35. Frazier, *George Moore*, 300. The story is also in Yeats, *Autobiographies*, 328.

36. Yeats, *Autobiographies*, 329.
37. Frazier, *George Moore*, 310.
38. Russell, *Letters*, 63.
39. Yeats, *Autobiographies*, 327.
40. Moore, *Salve*, 115–116, 187.
41. Gogarty, *Sackville Street*, 1, 7.
42. Joyce, *Ulysses*, 135, 5, 140–141.
43. *Dublin: Explorations and Reflections*, 167, 172.
44. O'Brien, *Country Girls*, 195.
45. Stephens, *Charwoman's Daughter*, 148.
46. Meehan, *By Magic*, 73.
47. Boland, *Historians*, 49.
48. Tóibín, *Mad, Bad and Dangerous*, 21.
49. Whaley, *Memoirs*, 34–35.
50. Joyce, *Portrait*, 184. Actually, Buck Egan was an Irish politician famous for fighting duels, and friend of Thomas 'Buck' Whaley; and Richard 'Burnchapel' Whaley was Thomas Whaley's father, so-called for having burnt Catholic chapels during the 1798 rebellion. Joyce conflates all three here.
51. Joyce, *Portrait*, 188, 189.

4 Trinity College

1. Stephens, *Charwoman's Daughter*, 20–21.
2. Bowen, *Seven Winters*, 473.
3. Hinkson, *Student Life*, 3.
4. Joyce, *Portrait*, 1980.
5. Joyce, *Ulysses*, 121.
6. Nealon, *Snowflake*, 13.
7. Lever, *O'Donoghue*, 209.
8. Birmingham, *Hyacinth*, 14.
9. Mahaffy, *Conversation*, 1.
10. Yeats, *Early Articles*, 144.
11. Beckett, *Selected Works*, IV: 127.
12. Tóibín, *Mad, Bad and Dangerous*, 3.
13. Mahaffy, *Conversation*, 23–24.

14. W. B. Yeats, *Poems*, 486.
15. Tone, *Autobiography*, 10.
16. Whitbread, *Land They Loved*, 97.
17. Davis, *Prose and Poetry*, 305.
18. Quinn, *Young Ireland*, 12.
19. Davis, *Prose and Poetry*, 185.
20. Yeats, *Poems*, 289.
21. Brady, *Ordinary Murders*, 62.
22. Brown, *Irish Times*, 175.
23. Ó Cadhain, *Cré na Cille*, vii.
24. Harris, 'Edmund Burke'.
25. Burke, *Sublime*, 35.
26. Gibbons, *Burke*, 2.
27. Rooney, 'Even if You Beat Me', 5.
28. Rooney, *Conversations*, 34.
29. Rooney, *Normal People*, 221–222.
30. Dawe, *Last Peacock*, 46.
31. Boran and Smyth, *If Ever You Go*, 152.
32. Boland, *Collected Poems*, 20, 15.
33. Longley, 'Empty Holes of Spring', 53.
34. McCrea, *First Verse*, 16.
35. Longley, *Collected Poems*, 236.
36. Madden, *Authenticity*, 11.

5 Around the Liberties
1. McCullough, *Dublin*, 5.
2. Dickson, *Dublin*, 4.
3. Hudson, 'Knúte and Viking Dublin', 319.
4. Archeology World Team, 'Extraordinary Viking Village'.
5. Sirr, *Intimate City*, 34.
6. Smyth, *Sundays of Eternity*, 11.
7. Brady, *Dark River*, 33.
8. French, *Faithful Place*, 18, 433–434.
9. Yeats, *Poems*, 420.

10. Heaney, *Death of a Naturalist*, 13.
11. Heaney, *North*, 38.
12. Heaney, *North*, 22; Brandes and Durkan, *Heaney*, C202.
13. Friel, *Collected Plays*, II:121.
14. Friel, *Collected Plays*, II:113.
15. Fletcher, *Performance and Polity*, 280–283.
16. Fletcher, *Performance and Polity*, 293, 300. Translations by Alan J. Fletcher.
17. Fletcher, *Performance and Polity*, 92–93.
18. Beckwith, 'Drama', 83.
19. Fletcher, *Performance and Polity*, 136.
20. Burnell, *Landgartha*, np.
21. Hitchcock, *Historical View*, 13.
22. Simpson, *Smock Alley*, 31.
23. Pollard, *Dublin's Trade in Books*, 66–74.
24. Clyde, *Irish Literary Magazines*, 73.
25. Munter, *Dictionary of Print Trade*, 214–217.
26. *The Gentlemen*, 15.
27. Cibber, *Dublin Miscellany*.
28. Burke, *Riotous Performances*, 229–240. For the text of *Mahomet*, translated by James Miller and John Hoadley, that was playing at Smock Alley, see Miller and Hoadley, *Mahomet*, 2.
29. Burke, *Riotous Performances*, 230–231.
30. *Mr. Sh—n's Apology*. The advertised date of publication on the title-page is the year 2754, clearly as fictitious as the authorship.
31. Sheridan, *Humble Appeal*, 34.
32. Pilkington, *Memoirs*, 78.
33. Pilkington, *Memoirs*, 67.
34. Swift, *Letter*, 1.
35. Swift, *Modest Proposal*, 5, 9.
36. Pilkington, *Memoirs*, 137.
37. Swift, *Collected Poems*, 730.
38. Swift, *Gulliver's Travels*, 233.
39. Swift, *Collected Poems*, 737.

40. Clarke, *Collected Poems*, 328, 460.
41. Yeats, *Plays*, 942.
42. Lydon, 'Medieval City', 27.
43. Boran and Smyth, *If Ever You Go*, 235.
44. Ó Neachtain, *Éamuinn Uí Chléire*.
45. Carleton, *Life*, I:194–196.
46. LeFanu, *Cock and Anchor*, 1, 97.
47. Le Fanu, *Best Ghost Stories*, 262, 264.
48. Boran and Smyth, *If Ever You Go*, 242.
49. Boran and Smyth, *If Ever You Go*, 242.
50. McElligott, *Stoker*, 3, 53–54.
51. O'Donoghue, *Mangan*, 91.
52. Mangan, *Autobiography*, 21.
53. Mangan, *Poems*, 453.
54. O'Donoghue, *Mangan*, 82.
55. Mangan, *Prose*, xi.
56. Mangan, *Prose*, 306–307.
57. Yeats, *Poems*, 138.
58. Kinsella, *Collected Poems*, 18.
59. Boran and Smyth, *If Ever You Go*, 239.
60. Joyce, *Critical Writings*, 178–179.
61. Ellmann, *Joyce*, 259, 264.
62. Joyce, *Critical Writings*, 176, 186.
63. Joyce, *Dubliners*, 175, 215, 220, 225.

6 O'Connell Street and the Abbey Theatre

1. Holloway, *Abbey Theatre*, 178
2. *Proclamation of Independence*.
3. Doyle, *Star Called Henry*, 110.
4. Stephens, *Insurrection*, 1
5. McGarry, 'Easter Rising', 249, 240.
6. Stephens, *Insurrection*, 24.
7. Barry, *Long Long Way*, 87.
8. Murphy, *Brave Time*, 169

9. Donoghue, *Pull of the Stars*, 6
10. Boran and Smyth, *If Ever You Go*, 42, 44; trans. by Louis de Paor.
11. Murdoch, *Red and Green*, 413.
12. O'Flaherty, *Short Stories*, 89, 93.
13. Mills, *Fallen*, 122.
14. Stephens, *Insurrection*, 84–85.
15. O'Flaherty, *Insurrection*, 8, 28.
16. MacDonagh, *Dawn is Come*, 43.
17. Plunkett, *Circle and Sword*, np.
18. Pearse, *Plays, Stories, Poems*, 338.
19. Connolly, *Which Flag*, 105.
20. Moran, *Staging Easter Rising*, 15.
21. Yeats to Elizabeth Yeats (30 April, 1916) [Accession 2935], *Collected Letters* [Intelex].
22. Yeats, *Poems*, 391–394.
23. O'Casey *Collected Plays*, I:217.
24. Pearse, *Plays, Stories, Poems*, 323.
25. Yeats, *Poems*, 611.
26. Yeats, *Plays*, 1063.
27. Beckett, *Selected Works*, I: 2.
28. Smyth, *Sundays of Eternity*, 72.
29. Doherty, *Complete Guide*, 63–64.
30. Bowen, *Seven Winters*, 13.
31. O'Brien, *My Ireland*, 114.
32. Joyce, *Echobeat*, 17–18, 54.
33. O'Brien, *Country Girls*, 131.
34. Doyle, *Love*, 102.
35. Joyce, *Ulysses*, 88.
36. Joyce, *Ulysses*, 107–110.
37. Yeats, *Poems*, 460.
38. MacNeice, *Collected Poems*, 163.
39. Gogarty, *Sackville Street*, 263.
40. O'Casey, *Autobiographies*, I:327.

41. Clarke, *Collected Poems*, 209.
42. Murphy, *Price of Stone*, 46.
43. Banville, *Time Pieces*, 115.
44. Lally, *Eggshells*, 19.
45. Gray, *Citysong*, 16.
46. Hickey, *Cold Eye of Heaven*, 44.
47. Boran and Smyth, *If Ever You Go*, 51.
48. Rooney, *Beautiful World*, 15–16.
49. Moore, *Ave*, 120, 116.
50. O'Casey, *Autobiographies*, I, 299.
51. Moore, *Ave*, 116.
52. Gregory, *Our Irish Theatre*, 140–141.
53. W. B. Yeats, *Autobiographies*, 169.
54. W. B. Yeats, *Irish Dramatic Movement*, 56.
55. Foster, *Vivid Faces*, xxiii, 75.
56. Shelley, *Address*, 7.
57. Kennelly, *Shelley in Dublin*, 10.
58. Hunt, *Abbey*, 128.
59. 'Send Out O'Casey', 7.
60. Yeats, *Irish Dramatic Movement*, 418.
61. Robinson, Letter to Lady Gregory, NYPL.
62. O'Brien, *Best of Myles*, 38.
63. Kavanagh, 'Graftonia', 5.
64. O'Neill, 'Noble Call'.

7 The North Inner City

1. Wingfield, *Collected Poems*, 146.
2. Boland, *Poet's Dublin*, 97, 103–104.
3. Kearns, *Tenement Life*, 68–70.
4. Joyce, *Ulysses*, 308.
5. ANU Productions; as site-specific works, the plays do not have published texts.
6. Somerville-Large, *Real Charlotte*, 227.
7. Dickson, *Dublin*, 160.

8. Maxwell, *Dublin Under the Georges*, 115.
9. Le Fanu, *In a Glass Darkly*, 46–47.
10. Owenson, *Memoirs*, 172.
11. Dickson, *Dublin*, 278.
12. Crowe, 'Poverty and Health'.
13. Hickey, *Cold Eye of Heaven*, 50.
14. Rains, *Commodity Culture*, 14, 93.
15. Smyth, *Sundays of Eternity*, 74.
16. Boran and Smyth, *If Ever You Go*, 55–56.
17. Meehan, *Mysteries of the Home*, 16–17.
18. Clarke, *Twice Round the Black Church*, 33.
19. Clarke, *Twice Round the Black Church*, 29.
20. Whitelaw, *Essay*, 50.
21. Gogarty, *Poems and Plays*, 514.
22. Kearns, *Tenement Life*, 61.
23. Stephens, *Charwoman's Daughter*, 1–2.
24. Boland, *Poet's Dublin*, 102.
25. Laverty, *Liffey Lane*, 51.
26. Brown, *Down All the Days*, 47.
27. Joyce, *Finnegans Wake*, 544; Joyce actually took the passage from an account of tenements in York by S. Seebohm Rowntree, *Poverty: A Study of Town Life*, London: Macmillan & Co., 1902, 155. I am indebted to my colleague Sam Slote for this reference.
28. Plunkett, *Strumpet City*, 235, 446.
29. McDonald, *Little History*, 42–43.
30. O'Toole, *Traitor's Kiss*, 17–18.
31. O'Casey, *Plays: I*, 93–94.
32. O'Casey, *Plays: I*, 163, 166, 174.
33. O'Casey, *Plays: I*, 161.
34. O'Casey, *Plays: I*, 239.
35. O'Casey, *Plays: I*, 3, 89.
36. Kearns, *Tenement Life*, 5.
37. Sennett, *Uses of Disorder*, 138.
38. Kathleen Behan, *Mother of All the Behans*, 60.

39. Behan, *Brendan Behan's Island*, 148–149.
40. Boland, *Poet's Dublin*, 100.
41. Kathleen Behan, *Mother of All the Behans*, 83.
42. The house to which the Behans moved after Russell Street was on the border between Crumlin and Kimmage; various biographers use both designations.
43. Kathleen Behan, *Mother of All the Behans*, 77.
44. O'Sullivan, *Brendan Behan*, 32.
45. Behan, *Brendan Behan's Island*, 14.
46. Behan, *Complete Plays*, 39.
47. Behan, *Complete Plays*, 130. The identification of the setting as Nelson Street is contained in Behan, *Brendan Behan's Island*, 14–15.
48. Boland, *Poet's Dublin*, 100.
49. Dominic Behan, *Tell Dublin I Miss Her*, 44.
50. Behan, *Dubbalin Man*, 70.
51. Behan, *Scarperer*, 14.
52. Behan, *Complete Plays*, 159.
53. Aherne, *D'You Remember*, 63–64.
54. Clarke, *Twice Round the Black Church*, 15.
55. Somerville and Ross, *Real Charlotte*, 1.
56. Stanislaus Joyce, *Brother's Keeper*, 51.
57. Conradi, *Murdoch*, 29.
58. Murdoch, *Red and Green*, 65.
59. Joyce, *Ulysses*, 240.
60. Joyce, *Dubliners*, 11.
61. Joyce, *Dubliners*, 21.
62. Stanislaus Joyce, *Brother's Keeper*, 123.
63. Joyce, *Dubliners*, 21.
64. O'Loughlin, *Poems*, 50.
65. Meehan, *By Magic*, 138, 137.
66. Barry, *Parnell Street*, 28.
67. Boran and Enyi-Amadi, 93–94.

8 South Dublin

1. Enright, *Actress*, 9.
2. Sirr, *Intimate City*, 156.
3. Enright, *Actress*, 11, 12.
4. Longford, *Dublin*, 142.
5. Dickson, *Dublin*, 329.
6. Cited without attribution in Somerville-Large, *Dublin*, 226.
7. Dunne, *Goodbye to the Hill*, 8.
8. Dunne, *Does Your Mother?*, 7.
9. Smith, *Countrywoman*, 20.
10. Smith, *Annie*, 126.
11. Kavanagh, *Poems*, 224.
12. Beckett, *Selected Works*, IV: 10–11.
13. Boland, *Poet's Dublin*, 99.
14. Boland, *Collected Poems*, 224.
15. Boland, *Collected Poems*, 138.
16. Boland, 'Interview', 118–119.
17. Boland, *Collected Poems*, 66.
18. Montague, *Collected Poems*, 111.
19. Boland, *Collected Poems*, 306.
20. Joyce, *Ulysses*, 502.
21. Joyce, *Finnegans Wake*, 235.
22. Boran and Smyth, *If Ever You Go*, 327.
23. Yeats, *Collected Letters II*, 326.
24. Clyde, *Irish Literary Magazines*, 142.
25. Mathews, *Revival*, 34
26. Summerfield, *Myriad-Minded Man*, 104.
27. Nic Shiublaigh, *Splendid Years*, 28–29.
28. Moore, *Vale*, 245.
29. Moore, *Salve*, 175–176.
30. Moore, *Ave*, 8–9.
31. Synge, *Collected Works*, I: 16.

32. Brown, *Yeats*, 337.
33. Yeats, *Letters*, 799, 798.
34. Yeats, *Poems*, 391.
35. Boran and Smyth, *If Ever You Go*, 326.
36. Clarke, *Penny in the Clouds*, 51, 206.
37. Clarke, *Poems*, 281, 277.
38. Bourke, *Maeve Brennan*, 61.
39. Brennan, *Springs of Affection*, 3.
40. Brennan, *Long-Winded Lady*, 267.
41. Boland, 'The Woman, The Place, The Poet', 222.
42. Hutchinson, *Poems*, 46.
43. Clyde, *Irish Literary Magazines*, 274.
44. Woods, *Poems*, 218–219.
45. Woods, *Poems*, 83.
46. Clifton, *Portobello Sonnets*, 24.
47. Kerrigan, *Little Criminals*, 58–59.
48. French, *Wych Elm*, 92, 83.
49. Enright, *Forgotten Waltz*, 20.
50. Enright, *Forgotten Waltz*, 247.
51. Madden, *Time Present*, 1, 11–12.
52. Boland, *Poems*, 295.
53. Boland, *Poet's Dublin*, 97.
54. Boland, *Woman Without a Country*, 75, 77.

9 The South Coast

1. Joyce, *Ulysses*, 30.
2. Joyce, *Portrait*, 170.
3. Joyce, *Ulysses*, 30.
4. Translation by Paddy Bushe; in Boran and Smyth, *If Ever You Go*, 299.
5. Boran and Enyi-Amadi, *Writing Home*, 27.
6. Dawe, *Last Peacock*, 15.
7. McGuinness, *Booterstown*, 14.

8. Nolan, *Acts of Desperation*, 105.
9. Beckett, *Selected Works*, III: 222.
10. Knowlson, *Damned to Fame*, 351, 352.
11. Gogarty, *It Isn't This Time of Year*, 69.
12. Joyce, *Ulysses*, 5.
13. Cronin, *Dead as Doornails*, 124.
14. Heaney, *Redress of Poetry*, 199–200.
15. O'Driscoll, *Stepping Stones*, 194, 231.
16. Foster, *On Seamus Heaney*, 96–97.
17. Heaney, *Station Island*, 92–94.
18. Heaney, *Crediting Poetry*, 20.
19. Heaney, *Station Island*, 118.
20. Heaney, *Spirit Level*, 63.
21. Heaney, *Seeing Things*, 107, 108.
22. Bowen, *Collected Stories*, 641.
23. Beckett, *Selected Works*, II: 279–280, 285.
24. O'Brien, *Complete Novels*, 610.
25. O'Brien, *Dalkey Archive*, 7–8.
26. Leonard, *Out After Dark*, 168.
27. Leonard, *Selected Plays*, 200.
28. Leonard, *Selected Plays*, 305
29. Moore, *Memoirs*, 19.
30. Edgeworth, *Absentee*, 89.
31. Dawe, *Last Peacock*, 13.
32. Jordan, *Lord Edward*, 103.
33. Jordan, *The Past*, 95.
34. Jordan, *Sunrise with Sea Monster*, 121.
35. McDonald, *Little History*, 128.
36. Ní Dhuibhne, *Bray House*, 66–67, 167, 254.
37. Beckett, *Selected Works*, II: 88. See also, E. O'Brien, *The Beckett Country* (1986), 3–7.
38. Binchy, *Tara Road*, 163, 150.
39. 'Globalization's Last Hurrah?', 38.
40. Power, *Bad Day*, 34.

41. Keyes, *Charming Man*, 141.
42. Keyes, *Charming Man*, viii.
43. Hughes, *Colour of Blood*, 66.
44. Hughes, 'Irish Hard-Boiled Crime', 168.
45. O'Donovan, *Priest*, 9, 11.
46. O'Connor, *Taken*, 40, 158.
47. Howard, 'Ten Things', 3.
48. Howard, *RO'CK of Ages*, 123, 129.
49. Murray, *Skippy Dies*, 40, 6.
50. Hamilton, *Dublin Palms*, 226.
51. Geary, *Montepelier Parade*, 69, 16.
52. Geary, *Montpelier Parade*, 232.
53. Power, *Bad Day*, 35.
54. Power, *Bad Day*, 235.

10 North Dublin

1. Doyle, *Paddy Clarke*, 13.
2. Doyle, *Rory and Ita*, 245.
3. Crown, 'Roddy Doyle'.
4. Dickson, *Dublin*, 346.
5. O'Casey, *Autobiographies*, 174.
6. Joyce, *Ulysses*, 124.
7. Joyce, *Ulysses*, 75.
8. Behan, *Hold Your Hour*, 149.
9. Ethington and McManus, 'Suburbs in Transition', 332.
10. McDonald, *Little History*, 36.
11. Enright, *Gathering*, 150, 36, 4.
12. Murray, *Seán O'Casey*, 38. Addresses at which O'Casey lived: pp. 19–20, 40, 129.
13. Barry, *Pride of Parnell Street*, 63.
14. Murray, *Mark and the Void*, 15.
15. Glynn, *Winterland*, 383, 387.
16. Denton, *Earlie King*, 46–47, 73.
17. O'Connor, *Shadowplay*, 16.

18. Stoker, *Dracula*, 104–105.
19. Stoker, 'Buried Treasure', 406.
20. Jordan, *Mistaken*, 17–18.
21. Kiernan, *Killer in Me*, 146.
22. McPherson, *The Weir*, 57.
23. McPherson, *Dublin Carol*, 34, 44.
24. McPherson, *Seafarer*, 1–2. 77–78.
25. Jordan, *Mistaken*, 389.
26. Boran and Smyth, *If Ever You Go*, 142.
27. Scarlett, *Boys Don't Cry*, 7.
28. French, *Broken Harbour*, 15.
29. Kerrigan, *Dark Times*, 7.
30. Kerrigan, *The Rage*, 181, 29, 2.
31. Doyle, *Barrytown*, 13.
32. Doyle, *Woman Who Walked Into Doors*, 94–95.
33. Doyle, *Guts*, 51, 54.
34. Doyle, *Deportees*, xii.
35. Doyle, *Deportees*, 50, 41, xi.
36. Okorie, *Hostel Life*, 3.
37. Bolger, *Woman's Daughter*, 10.
38. Bolger, *Invisible Cities*, 12.
39. Bolger, *Journey Home*, 6–7, 207.
40. Meehan, *Mysteries of the Home*, 44–45.
41. Yeats, *Poems*, 577–578.
42. Mahon, *Poems*, 60.
43. Joyce, *Ulysses*, 551.

11 Riverrun

1. Boland, *Collected Poems*, 231.
2. Boland, *Collected Poems*, 3.
3. Sirr, *Intimate City*, 15.
4. Woods, *Poems*, 355, 356.
5. Gogarty, *Poems and Plays*, 70.
6. Joyce, *Finnegans Wake*, 3, 628.

7. Joyce, *Letters*, 212–213.
8. Joyce, *Finnegans Wake*, 196, 32, 264.
9. Joyce, *Finnegans Wake*, 96, 213, 265.
10. Yeats, George and Yeats, W.B., *Letters*, 35–36.
11. Le Fanu, *House by the Churchyard*, 3, 4, 158.
12. Dickson, *Dublin*, 83–84.
13. Ward, *Miscellany*, 28, 32.
14. *Phoenix Park*, 3.
15. Leslie, *Phoenix Park*, 1.
16. Swift, *Poems*, 427.
17. Fitz John, *Joan!!!*, 75.
18. Maxwell, *Dublin Under the Georges*, 105.
19. Barrington, *Personal Sketches*, 313.
20. Lever, *Harry Lorrequer*, 116, 216.
21. O'Donnell, '"Skin-the-Goat's Curse"', 243–244.
22. Joyce, *Ulysses*, 437.
23. Le Fanu, *House by the Churchyard*, 397.
24. Brady, *June of Ordinary Murders*, 3, 5.
25. Durcan, *Snail in My Prime*, 41.
26. Central Statistics Office, 'Migration and Diversity', 2017.
27. Heaney, 'Beacons at Beltaine'.
28. Boran and Smyth, *If Ever You Go*, 266.
29. Kinsella, *Collected Poems*, 283, 63, 65, 92.
30. Kinsella, *Collected Poems*, 274.
31. Brady, *Dublin 1930–1950*, 213.
32. O'Toole, *Don't Know Ourselves*, 55.
33. Hambleton, *Christy Brown*, 11.
34. Brown, *Down All the Days*, 18.
35. Hickey, *House on Parkgate Street*, 17–18.
36. Bardwell, *Restless Life*, 2008
37. Bardwell, 'Tallaght II' in Bolger, *Invisible Cities*, 141.
38. Boran and Smyth, *If Ever You Go*, 351.
39. Tynan, *Twenty-Five Years*, 31, 235

40. Boran and Smyth, *If Ever You Go*, 342.
41. O'Rowe, *Howie the Rookie*, 36.
42. Whitney, *Hidden City*, 28, 22.
43. Dickson, *Dublin*, 536.
44. O'Brien, *Best of Myles*, 392–393.
45. O'Toole, 'Sound of the Suburbs', A8.
46. Joyce, *Dubliners*, 225.

Bibliography

Aherne, Bobby. *D'You Remember Yer Man? A Portrait of Dublin's Famous Characters.* Dublin: New Island, 2014.

anon. *The Gentlemen: An Heroic Poem in Two Cantos.* Dublin: np, 1747.

ANU Productions. 2020. http://anuproductions.ie/past-work/.

Archeology World Team. 'Archeologist "Extraordinary" Viking Village Find in Dublin'. 12 March 2020. *Archeology World.* https://archaeology-world.com/archaeologist-hails-extraordinary-viking-village-find-in-dublin/.

Banville, John. *Mephisto.* London: Paladin, 1986.

The Book of Evidence. London: Secker and Warburg, 1989.

Time Pieces: A Dublin Memoir. Dublin: Hachette Books, 2016.

[Benjamin Black]. *Christine Falls.* London: Picador, 2006.

[Benjamin Black]. *Elegy for April.* London: Picador, 2010.

Bardwell, Leland. *A Restless Life.* Dublin: Liberties Press, 2008.

Barrington, Jonah. *Personal Sketches of his Own Times.* New York: Redfield, 1856.

Barry, Sebastian. *A Long Long Way.* London: Faber and Faber, 2005.

The Pride of Parnell Street. London: Faber and Faber, 2007.

Bartlett, Thomas. 'Ireland During the Revolutionary and Napoleonic Wars, 1791–1815'. Ed. James Kelly. *The Cambridge History of Ireland: Vol. III, 1730–1880.* Cambridge: Cambridge University Press, 2018: 74–101.

Beckett, Samuel. 'Waiting for Godot'. Pike Theatre Collection. 1953. TCD Ms 10730.

The Selected Works of Samuel Beckett, 4 Vols. New York: Grove, 2010.

The Letters of Samuel Beckett 1941–1956. Vol. II. Ed. Martha Dow Fehsenfeld, Dan Gunn, Lois More Overbeck, and George Craig. Cambridge: Cambridge University Press, 2011.

Beckwith, Susan. 'Drama'. *Cambridge Companion to Medieval English Literature 1100–1500*. Ed. Larry Scanlon. Cambridge: Cambridge University Press, 2009: 83–94.

Behan, Brendan. *Hold Your Hour and Have Another*. Boston: Little, Brown, and Co., 1954.

    Brendan Behan's Island: An Irish Sketchbook. London: Hutchinson, 1962.

    Confessions of an Irish Rebel. New York: Lancer Books, 1965.

    The Complete Plays. London: Methuen, 1978.

    The Scarperer. London: Arena, 1987.

    The Dubbalin Man. Dublin: A. & A. Farmar, 1997.

Behan, Dominic. *Tell Dublin I Miss Her*. New York: G. P. Putnam's Sons, 1962.

Behan, Kathleen. *Mother of All the Behans: The Autobiography of Kathleen Behan as Told to Brian Behan*. Dublin: Poolbeg, 1994.

Berryman, John. *The Dream Songs*. New York: Farrar, Straus and Giroux, 1969.

Bickerstaffe, Isaac. *Stephen's Green: A Rhapsody, Exhibiting the Characters of the Belles, Beaux, Bucks, Bloods, Flashes, Fribbles, Jemmies, Jessamies, &c. of All Ranks and Professions that frequent the Beau-Walk*. Dublin: Printed for the Booksellers, 1763.

Binchy, Maeve. *Tara Road*. London: Orion, 1998.

Birmingham, George. *Hyacinth*. London: Edward Arnold, 1906.

Black, Benjamin. *See, Banville, John*.

Boland, Eavan. 'An Interview with Eavan Boland by Jody Allen Randolph'. *Irish University Review* 23.1 (1993): 117–130.

    'The Woman, The Place, The Poet'. *The Georgia Review* 55/56.1 (2001): 211–223.

    New Collected Poems. London: W. W. Norton, 2008.

    A Journey with Two Maps: Becoming a Woman Poet. Manchester: Carcanet, 2011.

    A Poet's Dublin. Ed. Paula Meehan and Jody Allen Randolph. Manchester: Carcanet, 2014.

    A Woman Without a Country. New York: W. W. Norton, 2014.

    The Historians. Manchester: Carcanet, 2020.

Bolger, Dermot. *The Woman's Daughter*. London: Penguin, 1987.

The Journey Home. London: Penguin, 1990.

'Introduction'. *Invisible Cities: A Journey Through Dublin's Suburbs*. Ed. Dermot Bolger. Dublin: Raven Arts Press, 1991.

Boran, Pat and Chiamaka Enyi-Amadi, eds. *Writing Home: The 'New Irish' Poets*. Dublin: Dedalus Press, 2019.

Boran, Pat, and Gerard Smyth, eds. *If Ever You Go: A Map of Dublin in Poetry and Song*. Dublin: Dedalus Press, 2014.

Bourke, Angela. *Maeve Brennan: Homesick at The New Yorker*. New York: Counterpoint, 2004.

Bowen, Elizabeth. *Collected Impressions*. New York: Alfred A. Knopf, 1950.

The Shelbourne: A Centre of Dublin Life for More than a Century. London: George G. Harrap, 1951.

Bowen's Court & Seven Winters: Memories of a Dublin Childhood. London: Vintage, 2017.

The Collected Stories of Elizabeth Bowen. London: Vintage, 1999.

Brady, Conor. *A June of Ordinary Murders*. New York: Minotaur, 2012.

The Dark River. Dublin: New Island Books, 2018.

Brady, Joseph. *Dublin 1930–1950: The Emergence of the Modern City*. Dublin: Four Courts Press, 2014.

Brandes, Rand and Michael J. Durkan. *Seamus Heaney: A Bibliography 1959–2003*. London: Faber and Faber, 2008.

Brennan, Maeve. *The Springs of Affection: Stories of Dublin*. London: Flamingo, 1997.

The Long-Winded Lady: Notes from The New Yorker. New York: Houghton Mifflin, 1998.

Brown, Christy. *Down All the Days*. Greenwich: Fawcett Crest, 1970.

My Left Foot. (London: Minerva, 1990).

Brown, Terence. *The Life of W. B. Yeats: A Critical Biography*. Dublin: Gill & Macmillan, 1999.

The Irish Times: 150 Years of Influence. London: Bloomsbury, 2015.

Burke, Edmund. *The Harvard Classics: On Taste; On the Sublime and Beautiful; Reflections on The French Revolution; A Letter To a Noble Lord*. New York: P. F. Collier, 1937.

Burke, Helen M. *Riotous Performances: The Struggle for Hegemony in Irish Theater, 1712–1784*. South Bend: University of Notre Dame Press, 2003.

Burnell, Henry. *Landgartha: A Tragie-Comedy as it was Presented in the New Theater in Dublin with Good Applause, being an Ancient Story.* Dublin: n.p., 1641.

Carleton, William. *The Life of William Carleton: Being his Autobiography and Letters.* 2 Vols. Ed. David J., O'Donoghue. London: Downey & Co., 1896.

Casey, Edward S. 'Between Geography and Philosophy: What Does It Mean to Be in the Place-World?' *Annals of the Association of American Geographers* 91.4 (2001): 683–693.

Central Statistics Office. 'CSO Population and Vital Statistics 2003'. 2003. www.cso.ie/en/media/csoie/releasespublications/documents/otherreleases/2003/populationandvitalstatistics.pdf.

'Census 2016 Profile 7: Migration and Diversity'. 2017. www.cso.ie/en/csolatestnews/presspages/2017/census2016profile7-migrationanddiversity.

Cibber, Theophilus. *Cibber and Sheridan: Or the Dublin Miscellany Containing all the Advertisements, Letters, Addresses, Apologies, Verses, &c. &c, &c. lately publish'd on Account of the Theatric Squabble, To Which are Added, Several Prologues and Epilogues, spoke at the Theater.* Dublin: Peter Wilson, 1743.

Clarke, Austin. *Twice Round the Black Church: Early Memories of Ireland and England.* Dublin: Moytura Press, 1962.

Collected Poems. Dublin: Dolmen Press, 1974.

A Penny in the Clouds: More Memories of Ireland and England. Dublin: Moytura Press, 1990.

Clifton, Harry. *Portobello Sonnets.* Hexham, Northumberland: Bloodaxe, 2017.

Clyde, Tom. *Irish Literary Magazines: An Outline History and Descriptive Bibliography.* Dublin: Irish Academic Press, 2003.

Connolly, James. *Under Which Flag? In Four Irish Rebel Plays.* Ed. James Moran. Dublin: Irish Academic Press, 2007. 105–132.

Conradi, Peter J. *Iris Murdoch: A Life.* London: Harper Collins, 2001.

Craig, Maurice. *Poems.* Ed. Andrew Carpenter. Dublin: Liberties Press, 2011.

Cronin, Anthony. *Dead as Doornails.* Dublin: Dolmen Press, 1976.

Crowe, Caitriona. Ed. 'Ireland in the Early Twentieth-Century: Poverty and Health'. National Archives of Ireland. 2011. www.census.nationalarchives.ie/exhibition/dublin/poverty_health.html.

'Urban and Rural Living Conditions Before the Revolution'. Ed. John Crowley, Donal Ó Drisceoil, and Mike Murphy. *Atlas of the Irish Revolution*. Cork: Cork University Press, 2017. 60–65.

Crown, Sarah. 'Roddy Doyle: A Life in Writing'. *The Guardian* (18 April 2011). www.theguardian.com/books/2011/apr/18/roddy-doyle-life-writing-profile.

Davis, Thomas. *Selections from his Prose and Poetry*. Ed. T. W. Rolleston. Dublin: Phoenix Publishing, n.d.

Dawe, Gerald. *The Last Peacock*. Oldcastle, County Meath: Gallery Press, 2019.

Deevy, Teresa. 'Letter to Florence Hackett'. TCD Ms. 10722. undated [1941].

'Letter to Patricia Lynch'. NLI Ms 40327/2 Lynch and Fox Papers. [1953]. Ms Letter, undated.

Denton, Danny. *The Earlie King and the Kid in Yellow*. London: Granta, 2018.

Dickson, David. *Dublin: The Making of a Capital City*. Dublin: Profile, 2015.

Doherty, Neil. *The Complete Guide to the Streets of Dublin*. Rathcoole: Orpen Press, 2016.

Donleavy, J. P. *The Ginger Man*. New York: Grove, 2010.

Donoghue, Emma. *The Pull of the Stars*. London: Picador, 2020.

Doyle, Roddy. *Paddy Clarke Ha Ha Ha*. London: Minerva, 1993.

The Woman Who Walked into Doors. London: Penguin, 1996.

A Star Called Henry: Volume One of The Last Roundup. London: Penguin, 1999.

Rory and Ita. London: Vintage, 2003.

The Deportees. London: Vintage, 2008.

The Barrytown Trilogy. London: Vintage, 2013.

The Guts. London: Viking, 2013.

Love. London: Penguin Random House, 2020.

Dublin: Explorations and Reflections by an Englishman. Dublin: Maunsel & Co., 1917.

Dunne, Lee. *Goodbye to the Hill*. Boston: Houghton Mifflin, 1966.

Does Your Mother? London: Arrow Books, 1970.

Durcan, Paul. *A Snail in My Prime: New and Selected Poems*. London: Harvill, 1993.

Edgeworth, Maria. *The Absentee.* Ed. W. J. McCormack and Kim Walker. Oxford: Oxford University Press, 1988.

Ellmann, Richard. *James Joyce: New and Revised Edition.* Oxford: Oxford University Press, 1983.

Enright, Anne. *The Gathering.* London: Jonathan Cape, 2007.

The Forgotten Waltz. London: W. W. Norton, 2011.

Actress. London: Jonathan Cape, 2020.

Etherington, Philip J., and McManus, Ruth. 'Suburbs in Transition: New Approaches to Suburban History'. *Urban History* (2007): 317–337.

Fallon, Brian. *An Age of Innocence: Irish Culture 1930–1960.* Dublin: Gill & Macmillan, 1998.

Fitz John, Matilda. *Joan!!! A Novel in Four Volumes.* London: Hookam and Carpenter, 1796.

Fletcher, Alan J. *Drama, Performance and Polity in Pre-Cromwellian Ireland.* Cork: Cork University Press, 2000.

Foster, R. F. *Vivid Faces: The Revolutionary Generation in Ireland 1890–1923.* London: Allen Lane, 2014.

On Seamus Heaney. Princeton: Princeton University Press, 2020.

Frazier, Adrian. *George Moore, 1852–1933.* New Haven: Yale University Press, 2000.

French, Tana. *Faithful Place.* London: Hodder and Stoughton, 2010.

Broken Harbour. Dublin: Hachette, 2012.

The Wych Elm. London: Viking, 2018.

Friel, Brian. *Collected Plays.* Vol. II. Ed. Peter Fallon. Oldcastle: Gallery Press, 2016.

Geary, Karl. *Montpelier Parade.* London: Vintage, 2017.

The Gentlemen: An Heroic Poem in Two Cantos. Dublin: np, 1747.

Gibbons, Luke. *Edmund Burke and Ireland: Aesthetics, Politics and the Colonial Sublime.* Cambridge: Cambridge University Press, 2003.

'Globalization's Last Hurrah?' *Foreign Policy* Jan.-Feb. 2002: 38–51.

Glendinning, Victoria. *Elizabeth Bowen.* New York: Alfred A. Knopf, 1978.

Glynn, Alan. *Winterland.* London: Faber, 2009.

Glynn, Irial. 'Migration and Integration since 1991'. *The Cambridge Social History of Modern Ireland.* Ed. Eugenio Biagini and Mary E. Daly. Cambridge: Cambridge University Press, 2017: 566–585.

Gogarty, Oliver St John. *As I Was Going Down Sackville Street: A Phantasy in Fact.* London: Rich & Cowan, 1937.

It Isn't This Time of Year At All! An Unpremeditated Autobiography. London: Sphere, 1983.

The Poems and Plays of Oliver St John Gogarty. Ed. A. Norman Jeffares. Gerrards Cross: Colin Smythe, 2001.

Gray, Dylan Coburn. *Citysong and Other Plays.* London: Nick Hern Books, 2019.

Gregory, Augusta. *Our Irish Theatre: A Chapter of Autobiography.* Gerrards Cross: Colin Smythe, 1972.

Gwynn, Stephen. *Ireland Old and New.* Dublin: Browne and Nolan, 1937.

Hambleton, Georgina Louise. *Christy Brown: The Life That Inspired My Left Foot.* London: Mainstream, 2007.

Hamilton, Hugo. *Dublin Palms.* London: 4th Estate, 2019.

Harris, Ian. 'Edmund Burke'. *Stanford Encyclopedia of Philosophy.* https://plato.stanford.edu/entries/burke/.

Heaney, Seamus. *Death of a Naturalist.* London: Faber, 1966.

North. London: Faber, 1975.

Station Island. London: Faber, 1984.

Crediting Poetry. Oldcastle, County Meath: Gallery Press, 1995.

The Redress of Poetry: Oxford Lectures. London: Faber, 1995.

The Spirit Level. London: Faber and Faber, 1996.

'Beacons at Beltaine'. *Irish Times* (1 May 2004). www.irishtimes.com/news/beacons-at-bealtaine-phoenix-park-may-day-2004-1.978088.

Hickey, Christine Dwyer. *The Cold Eye of Heaven.* London: Atlantic Books, 2011.

The House on Parkgate Street. Dublin: New Island Books, 2013.

Hinkson, H. A. *Student Life in Trinity College, Dublin.* Dublin: J. Charles & Son, 1892.

Hitchcock, Robert. *An Historical View of the Irish Stage, from the Earliest Period Down to the Close of the Season, 1788.* Dublin: William Folds, 1794.

Holloway, Joseph. *Joseph Holloway's Abbey Theatre: A Selection from his Unpublished Journal Impressions of a Dublin Playgoer.* Ed. Robert Hogan and Michael J. O'Neill. London: Southern Illinois University Press, 1967.

Hourihan, Kevin. 'The Cities and Towns of Ireland, 1841–1851'. John Crowley, William J. Smyth, and Mike Murphy. *Atlas of the Great Irish Famine, 1845–52*. Cork: Cork University Press, 2012. 228–239.

Howard, Paul. 'Ten Things I've Learned Writing Ross O'Carroll-Kelly'. *Irish Times* (3 April 2021), 3.

RO'CK of Ages: From Boom Days to Zoom Days: Ross O'Carroll Kelly (as told to Paul Howard). Dublin: Sandycove/Penguin, 2021.

Hudson, Benjamin. 'Knúte and Viking Dublin'. *Scandinavian Studies* 66.3 (1994): 319–335.

Hughes, Declan. *The Colour of Blood*. London: John Murray, 2007.

'Irish Hard-Boiled Crime: A 51st State of Mind'. In *Down These Green Streets: Irish Crime Writing in the 21st Century*, ed. Declan Burke. Dublin: Liberty Press, 2011. 161–168.

Hunt, Hugh. *The Abbey: Ireland's National Theatre: 1904–1978*. New York: Columbia University Press, 1979.

Hutchinson, Pearse. *Collected Poems*. Oldcastle: Gallery Press, 2002.

Igoe, Vivien. *A Literary Guide to Dublin*. London: Methuen, 1994.

Jordan, Neil. *The Past*. London: Jonathan Cape, 1980.

Sunrise with Sea Monster. London: Vintage, 1996.

Mistaken. London: John Murray, 2011.

The Ballad of Lord Edward and Citizen Small. Dublin: Lilliput Press, 2021.

Jordan, Thomas E. 'Whitelaw's "Essay on the Population of Dublin": A Window on Late Eighteenth-Century Housing'. *New Hibernia Review*. 15:3(Autumn, 2011): 136–145.

Joyce, James. *The Letters of James Joyce*. Ed. Stuart Gilbert. London: Faber and Faber, 1957.

The Critical Writings of James Joyce. Ed. Ellsworth Mason and Richard Ellmann. New York: Viking, 1959.

A Portrait of the Artist as a Young Man. Harmondsworth: Penguin, 1976.

Finnegans Wake. London: Penguin, 1992.

Dubliners. Ed. Terence Brown. Harmondsworth: Penguin, 1993.

Ulysses. Ed. Sam Slote. Richmond, Surrey: Alma, 2012.

Joyce, Joe. *Echobeat*. Dublin: New Island, 2017.

Echoland. Dublin: New Island, 2017.

Joyce, Stanislaus. *My Brother's Keeper*. New York: Viking, 1958.

Kavanagh, Patrick. 'Graftonia'. *Kavanagh's Weekly* (26 April 1952), 5.

   A Poet's Country: Selected Prose. Ed. Antoinette Quinn. Dublin: Lilliput, 2003.

   Collected Poems. Ed. Antoinette Quinn. Harmondsworth: Penguin, 2005.

Kearns, Kevin C. *Dublin Tenement Life: An Oral History*. Dublin: Gill and Macmillan, 1994.

Kennelly, Brendan. *Shelley in Dublin*. Dublin: Egotist Press, 1977.

   The Essential Brendan Kennelly: Selected Poems. Ed. Terence Brown and Michael Longley. Tarset, Northumberland: Bloodaxe Books, 2011.

Kerrigan, Gene. *Little Criminals*. London: Vintage, 2005.

   Dark Times in the City. London: Harvill-Secker, 2009.

   The Rage. London: Harvill-Secker, 2011.

Keyes, Marian. *This Charming Man*. London: Penguin, 2008.

Kiberd, Declan. 'The City in Irish Culture'. *City* 6.2 (2002): 219–228.

Kiernan, Olivia. *The Killer in Me*. London: Riverrun, 2019.

Kinsella, Thomas. *From City Centre*. Oxford: Oxford University Press, 1976.

   Collected Poems. Winston-Salem: Wake Forest University Press, 2006.

   Dublin Documentary. Dublin: O'Brien Press, 2006.

Knowlson, James. *Damned to Fame: The Life of Samuel Beckett*. London: Bloomsbury, 1996.

Lally, Caitriona. *Eggshells*. London: Borough Press, 2018.

Laverty, Maura. 'Liffey Lane'. Manuscript. Abbey Theatre Archive. 1951.

Lavin, Mary. *In a Café*. Dublin: Town House and Country House, 1995.

Le Fanu, Joseph Sheridan. *The Cock and the Anchor: Being a Chronicle of Old Dublin City*. Dublin: W. Curry, 1845.

   Best Ghost Stories. New York: Dover, 1964.

   The House by the Churchyard. Belfast: Appletree Press, 1992.

   In a Glass Darkly. Ware, Hertfordshire: Wordsworth, 1995.

Leerssen, Joseph Theodoor. *Hidden Ireland, Public Sphere*. Galway: Arlen House for the Centre of Irish Studies, 2002.

Leonard, Hugh. *Out After Dark*. London: Andre Deutsch, 1989.

Selected Plays. Ed. S. F. Gallagher. Gerrards Cross: Colin Smythe, 1992.

Leslie, John. *Phoenix Park: A Poem*. Dublin: William Wilson, 1772.

Lever, Charles. *The O'Donoghue*. London: Ward, Lock and Co., n.d. (1845).

The Confessions of Harry Lorrequer. London: Dent, 1907.

Longford, Christine. *Dublin*. London: Methuen, 1936.

Longley, Michael. 'The Empty Holes of Spring: Some Reminiscences of Trinity and Two Poems Addressed to Derek Mahon'. *Irish University Review* 24.1 (1994): 51–57.

Collected Poems. Winston-Salem: Wake Forest University Press, 2007.

Lydon, James. 'The Medieval City'. Ed. Art Cosgrove. *Dublin Through the Ages*. Dublin: College Press, 1988. 25–45.

MacDonagh, Thomas. *When the Dawn is Come*. In *Four Irish Rebel Plays*. Ed. James Moran. Dublin: Irish Academic Press, 2007. 43–81.

MacNeice, Louis. *Collected Poems*. Ed. E. R. Dodds. London: Faber and Faber, 1966.

Madden, Deirdre. *Authenticity*. London: Faber, 2002.

Time Present and Time Past. London: Faber and Faber, 2013.

Mahaffy, John Pentland. *The Principles of the Art of Conversation*. London: Macmillan & Co., 1887.

Mahon, Derek. *The Poems (1961–2020)*. Ed. Peter Fallon. Loughcrew: Gallery Press, 2021.

Mangan, James Clarence. *Poems*. New York: P.M. Haverty, 1859.

The Autobiography of James Clarence Mangan. Ed. James Kilroy. Dublin: Dolmen, 1968.

The Prose Writings of James Clarence Mangan. Ed. D.J. O'Donoghue. Dublin: M.H. Gill & Co., 1904.

Mathews, P.J. *Revival: The Abbey Theatre, Sinn Fein, The Gaelic League and the Co-operative Movement*. South Bend, Indiana: Field Day, 2003.

Maxwell, Constantia. *Dublin Under the Georges: 1714–1830*. London: Faber and Faber, 1937.

McCrea, Barry. *The First Verse*. Dingle: Brandon, 2008.

McCullough, Niall. *Dublin: An Urban History*. Dublin: Anne Street Press, 2007.

McDonald, Frank. *A Little History of the Future of Dublin*. Dublin: Martello Publishing, 2021.

McElligott, Jason. *Bram Stoker and the Haunting of Marsh's Library*. Dublin: Marsh's Library, 2019.

McGahern, John. *The Collected Stories*. London: Faber and Faber, 1992.

The Letters of John McGahern. Ed. Frank Shovlin. London: Faber, 2021.

McGarry, Fearghal. 'The Easter Rising'. Ed. Crowley, John, Donal Ó Drisceoil and Mike Murphy. *Atlas of the Irish Revolution*. Cork: Cork University Press, 2017. 240–257.

McGuinness, Frank. *Booterstown*. Oldcastle: Gallery Books, 1994.

McParland, Edward. 'The Wide Street Commissioners'. *Quarterly Bulletin of the Irish Georgian Society* XV.1 (1972): 1–32.

McPherson, Conor. *Dublin Carol*. London: Nick Hern Books, 2000.

The Weir. London: Nick Hern Books, 2000.

Shining City. London: Nick Hern Books, 2004.

The Seafarer. London: Nick Hern Books, 2006.

Meehan, Paula. *Mysteries of the Home*. Dublin: Dedalus Press, 2013.

As If By Magic: Selected Poems. Dublin: Dedalus, 2020.

Mercier, Vivian. 'The Uneventful Event'. *Irish Times* (18 February 1956), 6.

Miller, James, and John Hoadley. *Mahomet (the Imposter). A Tragedy. As it is Acted at the Theatre-Royal in Drury-Lane by His Majesty's Servants* (London: 1744).

Mills, Lia. *Fallen*. Dublin: Penguin Ireland, 2014.

Montague, John. *Collected Poems*. Oldcastle: Gallery Press, 1998.

Company: A Chosen Life. London: Duckworth, 2001.

Moore, George. *Hail and Farewell: Salve*. New York: Appleton, 1912.

Hail and Farewell: Ave. London: William Heinemann, 1921.

Hail and Farewell: Vale. London: William Heinemann, 1926.

Moore, Thomas. *Memoirs, Journal and Correspondence of Thomas Moore*. Ed. John Russell. London: Longmans, Brown, and Green, 1853.

Moran, James. *Staging the Easter Rising: 1916 as Theatre*. Cork: Cork University Press, 2005.

Morash, Christopher. *A History of Irish Theatre 1601–2000.* Cambridge: Cambridge University Press, 2001.

Mr. Sh—n's *Apology to the Town, With the Reasons Which Unfortunately Induced Him to His Late Misconduct.* Dublin: np, 1754.

Munter, Robert. *A Dictionary of the Print Trade in Ireland, 1550–1775.* New York: Fordham University Press, 1988.

Murdoch, Iris. *The Red and the Green.* London: Viking Penguin, 2000.

Murphy, Jimmy. *Of This Brave Time. Contemporary Irish Documentary Theatre.* Ed. Beatriz Kopschitz Bastos and Shaun Richards. London: Methuen Drama, 2020. 147–176.

Murphy, Richard. *The Price of Stone.* London: Faber, 1985.

Murray, Christopher. *Seán O'Casey: Writer at Work: A Biography.* Dublin: Gill and Macmillan, 2004.

Murray, Paul. *Skippy Dies.* London: Penguin, 2010.

The Mark and the Void. London: Penguin, 2015.

Nealon, Louise. *Snowflake.* London: Manilla Press, 2021.

Newburgh, Thomas. *Essays Poetical, Moral and Critical.* Dublin: Alex. M'Culloch, 1769.

Ní Dhuibhne, Eilís. *The Bray House.* Dublin: Attic Press, 1990.

Nic Shiublaigh, Maire. *The Splendid Years.* Dublin: Duffy, 1955.

Nolan, Megan. *Acts of Desperation.* London: Jonathan Cape, 2021.

O'Brien, Edna. *The Country Girls Trilogy.* New York: Farrar Straus Giroux, 1986.

O'Brien, Eoin. *The Beckett Country: Samuel Beckett's Ireland.* Dublin: Black Cat Press, 1986.

O'Brien, Flann. *The Best of Myles: A Selection from 'Cruiskeen Lawn'.* Ed. Kevin O'Nolan. London: Picador, 1975.

The Dalkey Archive. London: Picador, 1976.

The Complete Novels. London: Everyman, 2007.

The Collected Letters of Flann O'Brien. Ed. Maebh Long. Dublin: Dalkey Archive Press, 2018.

O'Brien, Kate. *My Ireland.* London: B.T. Batsford, 1962.

Ó Cadhain, Máirtín. *Cré na Cille (The Dirty Dust).* Trans. Alan Titley. New Haven: Yale University Press, 2015.

O'Casey, Seán. *Autobiographies.* Vol. I. New York: Carroll & Graf, 1984. 2 vols.

Collected Plays: Volume One. London: Macmillan, 1967.

O'Connor, Joseph. *Shadowplay.* London: Harvill Secker, 2019.

O'Connor, Niamh. *Taken.* London: Transworld Ireland, 2011.

Odin, John. *The Last Speech, Confession and Dying Words of Surgeon John Odin, Who Is to be Executed Near St. Stephen's Green.* Dublin: S. Harding, 1728.

O'Donnell, Teresa. '"Skin the Goat's Curse" on James Carey: Narrating the Story of the Phoenix Park Murders Through Contemporary Broadside Ballads'. *Crime, Violence and the Irish in the Nineteenth Century.* Ed. Kyle Hughes and Donald MacRaild. Liverpool: Liverpool University Press, 2018. 243–263.

O'Donoghue, D. J. *The Life and Writings of James Clarence Mangan.* Dublin: M. H. Gill, 1897.

O'Donovan, Gerald. *The Priest.* London: Sphere, 2010.

O'Driscoll, Dennis. *Stepping Stones: Interviews with Seamus Heaney.* London: Faber, 2008.

O'Flaherty, Liam. *Insurrection.* Dublin: Wolfhound Press, 1998.

— *The Short Stories of Liam O'Flaherty.* London: Jonathan Cape, 1937.

Okorie, Melatu Uche. *This Hostel Life.* Dublin: Skein Press, 2018.

O'Loughlin, Michael. *Poems 1980–2015.* Dublin: New Island, 2017.

Ó Neachtain, Seán. *Stair Éamuinn Uí Chléire.* Ed. Eoghan Ó Neachtain. Dublin: M. H. Gill, 1918.

O'Neill, Ciaran. 'Bourgeois Ireland, or, on the Benefits of Keeping One's Hands Clean'. Ed. James Kelly. *The Cambridge History of Ireland: Vol. III, 1730–1880.* Cambridge: Cambridge University Press, 2018. 517–541.

O'Neill, Rory. 'Panti's Noble Call at the Abbey Theatre'. 2 February 2014. www.youtube.com/watch?v=WXayhUzWnl0.

O'Rowe, Mark. *Howie the Rookie.* London: Nick Hern Books, 2000.

O'Toole, Fintan. 'The Sound of the Suburbs'. *Irish Times* (31 August 1991), A8.

— *A Traitor's Kiss: The Life of Richard Brinsley Sheridan.* London: Granta, 1997.

— *We Don't Know Ourselves: A Personal History of Ireland Since 1958.* London: Head of Zeus, 2021.

Owenson, Sydney. *O'Donnel: A National Tale.* London: Henry Colburn, 1814.

— *Lady Morgan's Memoirs.* 2nd ed. 3 Vols. London: W. H. Allen & Co., 1863.

Pearse, Patrick. *Plays, Stories, Poems*. Dublin: Helicon, 1980.

Philips, William. *St. Stephen's Green; or, The Generous Lovers, as it is Acted at the Theatre Royal, Dublin*. Dublin: John Brocas, 1700.

Phoenix Park: A Poem: By A Ranger. Dublin: Oliver Nelson, 1770.

Pilkington, Lætitia. *Memoirs of Mrs. Lætitia Pilkington*. Dublin: R. Griffiths, 1748.

Plunkett, James. *Strumpet City*. London: Hutchinson, 1969.

Plunkett, Joseph Mary. *The Circle and the Sword*. Dublin: Maunsell and Company, 1911.

Pollard, Mary. *Dublin's Trade in Books, 1550–1800*. Oxford: Oxford University Press, 1989.

Power, Kevin. *Bad Day in Blackrock*. Dublin: Lilliput, 2008.

'Proclamation of Independence'. 19 November 2018. Department of the Taoiseach. www.gov.ie/en/publication/bfa965-proclamation-of-independence/.

Quinn, James. *Young Ireland and the Writing of Irish History*. Dublin: University College Dublin Press, 2015.

Rains, Stephanie. *Commodity Culture and Social Class in Dublin 1850–1916*. Dublin: Irish Academic Press, 2010.

Robinson, Lennox. *Ireland's Abbey Theatre: A History 1899–1951*. London: Sidgwick and Jackson, 1951.

'Letter to Lady Gregory, Ms. Letter'. In The Henry W. and Albert A. Berg Collection of English and American Literature, The New York Public Library, Astor, Lenox and Tilden Foundations. 8 July 1924.

Rooney, Sally. *Conversations with Friends*. London: Faber and Faber, 2017.

Normal People. London: Faber and Faber, 2018.

'Even if You Beat Me'. Spring 2015. *The Dublin Review*. 8 June 2020. https://thedublinreview.com/article/even-if-you-beat-me/.

Beautiful World, Where Are You. London: Faber and Faber, 2021.

Russell, George (Æ). *Letters from Æ*. Ed. Alan Denson. London: Abelard-Schuman, 1961.

Ryan, John. *Remembering How We Stood: Bohemian Dublin at Mid-Century*. Dublin: Lilliput Press, 1987.

Scarlett, Fiona. *Boys Don't Cry*. London: Faber, 2021.

'Send Out O'Casey'. Irish Independent (12 February 1926), 7.

Sennett, Richard. *The Uses of Disorder: Personal Identity and City Life.* New Haven: Yale University Press, 1970.

Shelley, Percy Bysshe. *An Address to the People of Ireland.* Ed. Thomas J. Wise. London: Reeves and Turner, 1890.

Sheridan, Peter. *44.* London: Macmillan, 1999.

Sheridan, Thomas. *An Humble Appeal to the Publick, Together with Considerations on the Present Critical and Dangerous State of the Stage in Ireland.* Dublin: George Faulkner, 1758.

Simpson, Alan. *Beckett and Behan and a Theatre in Dublin.* London: Routledge and Kegan Paul, 1962.

Simpson, Linzi. *Smock Alley Theatre: The Evolution of a Building.* Dublin: Temple Bar Properties, 1996.

Sirr, Peter. *Intimate City: Dublin Essays.* Oldcastle, County Meath: Gallery Press, 2021.

Smith, Paul. *Annie.* London: Picdor, 1987.

The Countrywoman. London: Picador, 1987.

Smyth, Gerard. *The Sundays of Eternity.* Dublin: Dedalus, 2020.

Somerville, Edith Œ. and Ross, Martin. *The Real Charlotte.* London: Longmans, Green and Co., 1919.

Somerville-Large, Peter. *Dublin: The First Thousand Years.* Belfast: Appletree Press, 1988.

Stephens, James. *The Insurrection in Dublin.* New York: Macmillan, 1916.

The Charwoman's Daughter. London: Macmillan and Co., 1917.

Stoker, Bram. 'Buried Tresure'. *The Shamrock* (13–20 March 1875), 376–379; 403–406.

Dracula. London: Penguin, 1993.

Sullivan, Michael. *Brendan Behan: A Life.* Dublin: Blackwater Press, 1999.

Summerfield, Henry. *That Myriad-Minded Man: A Biography of George William Russell 'A.E.', 1867–1935.* Totowa: Rowan and Littlefield, 1975.

Swift, Carolyn. *Stage by Stage.* Dublin: Poolbeg, 1985.

Swift, Jonathan. *A Letter to The Shop-Keepers, Tradesmen, Farmers, and Common People of Ireland, Concerning yhe Brass Half-Pence Coined by Mr. Woods, With A Design to Have Them Pass in This Kingdom Wherein is shewn the Power of the said Patent, the Value of the*

Half-Pence and how far every Person may be oblig'd to take the same in Payments, and how to behave in Case such an Attempt shou'd be made by Woods or any other Person. (Very Proper to be kept in every Family.) By M.B. Drapier. Dublin: J. Harding, 1724.

A Modest Proposal for Preventing the Children of Poor People from Being a Burthen to their Parents or Country, and for Making them Beneficial to the Publick. Dublin: J. Harding, 1729.

Collected Poems of Jonathan Swift. 2 Vols. Ed. Joseph Horrell. London: Routledge and Kegan Paul, 1958.

Gulliver's Travels. Ed. Paul Turner. Oxford: Oxford University Press, 1998.

Synge, John Millington. *Collected Works: Volume I: Poems.* London: Oxford University Press, 1962.

Tone, Theobold Wolfe. *The Autobiography of Theobold Wolfe Tone.* 2 Vols. London: T. Fisher Unwin, 1893.

Tóibín, Colm. 'Mary Lavin: Context and Character'. *American Journal of Irish Studies* 10 (2013): 94–113.

Mad, Bad and Dangerous to Know: The Fathers of Wilde, Yeats and Joyce. London: Penguin, 2018.

Tynan, Katharine. *Twenty-Five Years: Reminiscences.* London: John Murray, 1913.

Ward, James. *A Miscellany of Poems.* Dublin: Edwin Sandys, 1718.

'Waiting for Godot'. *Pike Newsletter* (nd), 1.

Whaley, Buck. *Buck Whaley's Memoirs: Including His Journey to Jerusalem.* Ed. Edward Sullivan. London: Alexander Moring, 1906.

Whitbread, J. W. *Wolfe Tone.* In *For that Land They Loved: Irish Political Melodramas 1890–1925.* Ed. Cheryl Herr. Syracuse: Syracuse University Press, 1991.

White, Jack. *The Devil You Know.* Dublin: Allen Figgis, 1962.

Whitelaw, James. *An Essay on the Population of Dublin.* Dublin: Graisberry and Campbell, 1805.

Whitney, Karl. *Hidden City: Adventures and Explorations in Dublin.* Dublin: Penguin Ireland, 2014.

Wingfield, Sheila. *Collected Poems 1938–1983.* New York: Hill and Wang, 1983.

'Women Writers' Club Function'. *Irish Press* (8 June 1939), 6.

Woods, Macdara. *Collected Poems*. Dublin: Dedalus, 2012.

Woolf, Alex. 'The Scandinavian Intervention'. *The Cambridge History of Ireland: Volume I 600–1550*. Ed. Brendan Smith. Cambridge: Cambridge University Press, 2018. 107–130.

Yeats, George and Yeats, William Butler. *W. B. Yeats and George Yeats: The Letters*. Ed. Ann Saddlemyer. Oxford: Oxford University Press, 2011.

Yeats, William Butler. *The Letters of W. B. Yeats*. Ed. Allan Wade. London: Rupert Hart-Davis, 1954.

The Variorum Edition of the Poems of W. B. Yeats. Ed. Peter Allt and Russell K. Alspach. New York: Macmillan, 1957.

The Variorum Edition of the Plays of W. B. Yeats. Ed. Russell K. Alspach. London: Macmillan, 1966.

'Four Lectures by W. B. Yeats, 1902–1904'. Ed. Richard Londraville. *Yeats Annual* 8 (1991): 99–124.

The Collected Letters of W. B. Yeats, Volume II: 1896–1900. Ed. Warwick Gould, John Kelly, and Deirdre Toomey. Oxford: Oxford University Press, 1997.

Autobiographies: Collected Works, Vol. III. Ed. William H. O'Donnell and Douglas N. Archibald. New York: Scribners, 1999.

The Irish Dramatic Movement: Collected Works, Vol. VIII. Ed. Mary Fitzgerald and Richard J. Finneran. New York: Scribner, 2003.

Early Articles and Reviews: Collected Works, Vol. IX. Ed. John P. Frayne and Madeleine Marchaterre. New York: Scribner, 2004.

The Collected Letters of W. B. Yeats. Intelex Past Masters: Electronic Edition. 2021. www.nlx.com/collections/130.

Acknowledgements

I started writing this book more or less as a global pandemic began in the spring on 2020, and because I live just outside Dublin, this meant that it was written in rather curious circumstances, almost as a kind of imaginary rebuilding of a city from which I was temporarily exiled. That the terms of that exile made writing possible and pleasurable are due to my wonderful family, as always: Ann, Christopher, Dara, Aoife and Lindsay, with moral support from our dogs. That I was able to write it at all owes much to the staff of the Library in Trinity College Dublin for making materials available with generosity and ingenuity. I owe an immense debt of gratitude to David Dickson, who will always know vastly more about Dublin's history than I ever will, who read the manuscript and whose insights have improved the book; and to Declan Kiberd, who likewise read it, and whose wisdom has made it a better book. I have been extremely fortunate in being able to explore the ideas in this book with my students in Trinity, both undergraduate and postgraduate, for whom literary mapping and the injunction to 'go for a walk' at the end of a class has been a learning experience for all of us. My colleagues Philip Coleman and Sam Slote also deserve thanks, for their expert guidance on John Berryman and *Finnegans Wake*, respectively, while Victoria White was good enough to send me her father's novels during lockdown. My understanding of so many Dubliners' deep interest in their city has been enriched by my association with Dublin City Libraries, for whom some of the ideas here have been presented in the context of my annual UNESCO Dublin City of Literature lectures over a number of years. If the idea of Dublin as a city of literature has a home for me, it is in the city library on Pearse Street, and among the audiences I have met there. I would also like to thank those who have granted permissions to use photographs: the Royal Society of Antiquaries in Ireland, the National Library of Ireland, Dublin City Libraries and Archives, Pat Bolger, the *Irish Times*,

295 · ACKNOWLEDGEMENTS

Mairead Delaney, and the Abbey Archives, as well as Getty and Alamy. However, a very special round of applause goes to the photographer who worked with me on the book, Seán Harrison. One of my abiding images is a photo of Seán's father, Pat, having shinnied up the statue of W. B. Yeats in St. Stephen's Green just after sunrise, to scrub bird droppings from the poet's head in preparation for the photo included here. This book is much the richer for his dedication and for his eye. The look of this book owes much to the talent and commitment of the people at Cambridge University Press, including Sharon McCann, Sarah Lambert, Ian McIver, and Melissa Ward. A special thanks to Charles Phillips for his eagle-eyed copy-editing, and to my indexer, Alicia McAuley. Likewise, Joe LeMonnier's cartography gave life to the maps I had imagined when writing the book. However, the original idea for a book about Dublin and literature came from my friend and editor, Dr. Ray Ryan. From our first speculative conversations (including one in the Dublin House pub on West 79th Street in New York), through each step in the development of the series, Ray's commitment has been total, and I continue to learn from him.

Photo credits: Abbey Theatre Archive, Hardiman Library, NUI Galway: 5.2, 6.2, 7.3, 11.6; Alamy Images: 3.3, C6; Patrick Bolger, C7; Dublin City Library and Archives: 1.3, 5.6, 6.3, 7.4, 8.4, 10.5, 10.6; Getty Images: 0.2, 0.3, 0.4, 2.1, 2.3, 6.7, 9.4, 9.6; Seán Harrison: 0.5; 2.2, 2.4, 2.5, 3.1, 3.6, 3.7, 4.3, 4.4, 5.1, 5.3, 5.4, 6.6, 7.5, 8.1, 8.6, 9.1, 9.2, 9.5, 10.1, 10.2, 10.3, 10.4, 11.2, 11.5; Irish Times: 3.2, 4.5, 8.3, 9.3, C8, C9, C10; The Library, Trinity College Dublin and the Brendan Kennelly Private Collection: 4.6; National Library of Ireland: 0.1, 1.2, 3.5, 4.2, 6.1, 6.4, 6.5, 8.2, 8.5, 11.1; Public domain; 11.4, C1, C2, C3, C4, C5; Royal Society of Antiquaries of Ireland: 1.1; 3.4, 4.1, 5.5, 7.1, 7.2, 11.3.

Index

1641 rebellion, 104
1798 rebellion, xii, 21, 23, 86, 139, 240
1916 Rising. *See* Easter Rising
37, the, 59

Abbey Presbyterian Church, Parnell Square, 147
Abbey Street, 174
Abbey Theatre, Abbey Street Lower, xiii, xiv, xv, xvi, 6, 27, 59, 63, 68, 101, 102, 121, 124, 128, 136, 137–141, 151, 154, 175, 176, 215, 250
Abercorn Road, 215
Adam and Eve's Church, Merchant's Quay, 234
Æ. *See* Russell, George
Alexandra Basin, 215
Anglesea Road, 29, 30
Anna Livia Bridge, 233
Antient Concert Rooms, Pearse Street, 6, 7, 68
ANU Productions, xvi, 144
  Boys of Foley Street, The, 145
  Laundry, 145
  Monto Cycle, xvi
  Vardo, 145
  World's End Lane, 145
Aran Islands, 174
Áras an Uachtaráin, Phoenix Park, 241, 242–243
architecture, 8, 14–15, 21, 23, 25, 28–29, 30
  Georgian, ix, 14, 19–20, 21, 22, 24, 25, 26, 28, 30, 56, 57, 61, 62, 68, 112, 146, 148, 150, 155, 156, 160, 163, 183, 206, 210, 213, 214, 217, 237, *See also* Wide Streets Commission, tenements
  modern, 8, 15, 29, 30, 98, 157, 204, 215–217, 221–223, 226, 245, 246, 250
  tenements, xiii, xiv, 25–26, 28, 31, 144, 145, 147, 150–153, 155–157, 162, 213
  Victorian, ix, 15, 21, 25, 26, 57, 166–167, 211, 213, 214, 237, 244
Ardreevin, Chapelizod, 235
Aristotle
  On the Soul, 189
Arran Quay, 90, 233
Ashview, Chapelizod, 235
Athlone, County Westmeath, 250
Aungier Street, 23
Aviva Football Stadium, Lansdowne Road, 30

Baggot Lane, 42
Baggot Street, 28, 29, 42, 45, 51, 52, 56, 59, 179, 180, *See also* Baggotonia
  Lower, 43, 44, 60, 61
  Upper, 42, 56, 62
Baggot Street Bridge, 44, 51, 56, 62, 167, 170
Baggotonia, 33, 44–46, 51, 72, 167, 247
Bailey, the, Duke Street, 37, 45, 49
Baily Lighthouse, Howth, 228
Balbriggan, 168
Balcombe, Florence, 218
Baldoyle, 221
Ballsbridge, 25, 29, 183, 189, 195, 211
Ballsbridge Court, 204
Ballybough, 223

Ballyfermot, 28, 223, 246, 247, 248
Ballyfermot Road, 236
Ballymun, 28, 222, 245
Banville, John, 49, 51–53, 63
  Book of Evidence, The, 52
  Christine Falls, 52
  Elegy for April, 52–53
  Mephisto, 51–52
  Time Pieces, 44, 135
Barcelona, Spain, 20
Bardwell, Leland, 50, 92, 183, 248
  Restless Life, A, xvi, 49–50, 247–248
Barnacle, Nora, 5
Barrington, Sir Jonah, 241
  Personal Sketches, xii, 240–241
Barry, Sebastian
  Long, Long Way, A, xvi, 124
  Pride of Parnell Street, The, 162, 215–216
Bartlett, Thomas, 21
Baudelaire, Charles, 94
Beaumont Hospital, Beaumont Road, 221
Beaux Walk, St. Stephen's Green, 64
Beckett, May, 48
Beckett, Samuel, xv, 4, 5–6, 7, 47, 49, 83–84, 87, 168, 179, 193, 195, 200, 201
  'Alba', 176
  'Eneug I', 170–171
  'Fingal', 227
  'Wet Night, A', 83–84
  Krapp's Last Tape, xiv, 48–49, 190–192
  Malone Dies, 196
  Molloy, 201
  More Pricks Than Kicks, 5, 83–84, 227
  Murphy, xiv, 84, 128, 129–130
  Unnameable, The, 196
  Waiting for Godot, xiv, 47–48, 57
  Watt, 37
Beckett, William, 201
Beckwith, Susan, 103
Bective, County Meath, 59, 60
Behan, Beatrice, 29
Behan, Brendan, 28–29, 30, 36, 37, 38, 40, 43, 44, 46, 48, 49, 50, 56, 57, 58, 59, 63, 88, 89, 156–158, 167, 172, 173, 212, 214, 246, 247

Borstal Boy, 40
Dubbalin Man, The, 158
Garden Party, The, 246
Hostage, The, 29, 40, 158, 159, 160
Moving Out, 246
Quare Fellow, The, xiv, 29, 40, 47, 158
Scarperer, The, 38, 159
Behan, Dominic, 43, 158–159
Behan, Kathleen
  Mother of All the Behans, 156, 157
Belfast, 14, 93, 194
Belfield, 200
Belgard Castle, Clondalkin, 134, 248
Belgrave Road, 180
Bell, The, 37
Bellaghy, County Derry/Londonderry, 100
Belmayne, 222
Belton, Neil
  Game with Sharpened Knives, A, 64
Belvedere College, 159
Bergson, Henri, 83
Berkeley, George, 85, 91
Berryman, John, 4, 17
Bewley's, Grafton Street, 60
Bickerstaffe, Isaac
  Stephen's Green: A Rhapsody …, 65
Binchy, Maeve, 201–202
  Evening Classes, 202
  Quentin's, 202
  Scarlet Feather, 202
  Tara Road, 201–202
Birmingham, George
  Hyacinth, 81–82
Bishop Street, 98
Black, Benjamin. *See* Banville, John
  Elegy for April, xvi
Blackberry Lane, 184
Blackpitts, 100, 114
Blackpitts Lane, 112, 115
Blackrock, 78, 133, 198, 199, 200, 204
Blackrock College, 207
Blanchardstown, 168, 249
Blessington Street, 160
Bliss, Panti, 141
Bloomsday, 192–193
Boke of Common Praier, xi, 17

Boland, Eavan, 24, 92–93, 94, 166, 171, 172–174, 178, 185, 251
  'Anna Liffey', 232
  'Becoming an Irish Poet', 23–24
  'Belfast vs. Dublin', 93
  'Flight of the Earls, The', 93
  'Liffey Beyond Islandbridge, The', 232
  'Ode to Suburbia', 173
  'Once in Dublin', 185
  'Our Future Will Become the Past of Other Women', 94
  'Statue 1916', 73
  'Suburban Woman', 173
  'Suburban Woman: Another Detail', 173
  'That the Science of Cartography is Limited', 14
  'Woman, the Place, the Poet, The', 182
  'Writing in Time of Violence', 14
  23 Poems, 92, 232
  Against Love Poetry, 173, 185
  In Time of Violence, xv, 232
  New Territory, xiv, 92, 93, 172
  Poet's Dublin, A, xvi, 144
  War Horse, The, xv, 173
  Woman Without a Country, 185
Bolger, Dermot, 210, 225–226
  'Jesus of Clondalkin', 248
  Journey Home, The, xv, 226
  Last Orders at the Dockside, 215
  Woman's Daughter, The, 225–226
Bolton Street, 153
Book of Kells, 92
Booterstown, 190, 198, 215
Booterstown Avenue, 190
Boran, Pat
  'Place Names', 221–222
  'Spire (10 Years On), The', 136
Boss, Owen, 144
Boucicault, Dion, 153
  Colleen Bawn, The, 153
Boundary-ville, Chapelizod, 235
Bourke, Angela
  Homesick at the New Yorker, 180
Bow Lane, 98

Bowen, Elizabeth, 6, 9, 21, 56, 57–58, 66, 68, 75, 84, 91, 218
  'Unwelcome Idea', 195–196
  Bowen's Court, 56
  Death of the Heart, The, 57
  Last September, The, 56
  Look at All Those Roses, 195–196
  Seven Winters, xiv, 56, 61–62, 63, 78, 131
  Shelbourne, The, 66, 67, 68
Bowens Court, County Cork, 56, 61
Brady, Conor, 88
  Dark River, The, 99
  June of Ordinary Murders, A, 242
Brady, Joseph, 246
Bray, County Wicklow, 25, 198, 199–200, 205, 212
Brecht, Bertolt, 94
Brennan, Maeve, 180–182
  'Morning after the Big Fire, The', 180
  Springs of Affection, The: Stories of Dublin, xv
Brian Boru, 16
Bridgefoot Street, 112, 113
Brighton Road, 201
Brighton Square, 174
Broadstone, 214, 215
Broadstone Terminus, 211
Broderick, Edna, 93
Brown Thomas, Grafton Street, 88
Brown, Christy, 246–247
  'City Dweller', 149
  Down All the Days, xv, 152, 246
  My Left Foot, 246
Brown, Terence, 88, 178
Bruxelles, Harry Street. *See* Grafton Mooney, Harry Street
Budgen, Frank, 5
Buena Vista, Chapelizod, 235
Bull Island, 212, 215
Burke, Edmund, 85, 89–90, 91, 168
  Philosophical Enquiry into the Origin of our Ideas of the Sublime and Beautiful, A, xii, 89
Burke, Thomas Henry, 241, 242
Burnell, Henry, xi
  Landgartha, xi, 104

Bush Theatre, London, xv
Butt Bridge, 242

Cabra, 214, 223
Cambridge, University of, 81
Camden Street
    Upper, 183
Capel Street, 150
Carey, James, 242
Carleton, William, 113, 114, 218
Carlisle Bridge. *See* O'Connell Bridge
Carr, Marina, 200
Carter, Cornelius, 106
Casey, Edward, 8
Casey, Eileen
    'Warriors', 169
Casey, Kevin, 171
Castle Street, Dalkey, 197
Castle Street, Dublin, 106
Castleknock, 238
Catholic Emancipation, 22, 130
Catholic University of Ireland. *See*
    University College Dublin
Cavendish, Lord Frederick, 241, 242
Ceannt, Éamonn, 122
Cecilia Street, 73
Celtic Tiger, xv, 30, 184, 201, 202–203, 216, 222
Celtic Twilight. *See* Irish Literary Revival
censorship, xiv, 37, 58, 88, 170
Chancery Lane, 116
Chandler, Raymond
    Big Sleep, The, 204
Chapelizod, 233, 235–237, 242
Charlemont Bridge, 167
Charlemont Street, 170
Cherryfield Avenue, 180
Cherryfield Heights, 245
Christ Church Cathedral, Christchurch
    Place, 98, 99, 103, 106, 113
Christchurch Place, 20, 21, 106, 112
Christchurch Yard, 106
Church of the Immaculate Conception,
    Merchant's Quay. *See* Adam and Eve's
    Church, Merchant's Quay

Church Street, xiii, 26, 28, 152
Cibber, Theophilus, 107
Civil War, Irish, xiii, 27, 28, 66, 125, 128, 140, 154
Clare Street, 84
Clarence Mangan Road, 115
Clarke, Austin, 37, 111, 159, 179–180
    'Guinness Was Bad for Me', 180
    'Midnight in Templeogue', 180
    'Nelson's Pillar, Dublin', 135
    'Sermon on Swift', 111
    Mnemosyne Lay in Dust, xiv, 111
    Twice Round the Black Church, xiv, 150
    Vengeance of Fionn, The, 179
Clarke, T.J., 122
Clery's, O'Connell Street, 149
Clifton, Harry, 183
    Portobello Sonnets, 49, 183
Clogher Road, 171
Clondalkin, 248, 249
Clonliffe Road, 214
Clonsaugh, 222
Clonskeagh, 133, 168, 183, 184
Clontarf, 131, 199, 212, 218–220, 224
Clontarf, Battle of, xi, 16
Clyde, Tom, 176
Clyn, John, 17
Cnut the Great, 99
Coffey, George, 177
Coll, John, 43
College Green, xii, 19, 78, 79, 85, 93, 95, 104, 117, 224
Collins Avenue, 220
Collins Barracks, 150
Collinstown, 222
Colum, Padraic, 176
Connolly Station, 145, 215
Connolly, James, 27, 122, 126, 127, 139
    Under Which Flag?, 127
Conradi, Peter J., 160
Convention Centre, Spencer Dock, 30, 216
Cooldrinagh, Foxrock, 201
Coole Park, County Galway, 27, 65, 178
Coombe, the, 98, 114
Copper Alley, 100

Corkery, Daniel, 19
Coulson Avenue, 174
Country Shop, St. Stephen's Green, 58, 60
COVID-19 pandemic, xvi, 3, 4, 7, 9, 10, 11, 124
Craig, Maurice
   'Merrion Square', 19
Crane, Hart, 94
crime fiction, 52–53, 88, 99–100, 183–184, 203, 204–205, 219–220, 222–223, 242
Crist, Gainor, 36, 41
Croke Park, 27, 28
Cronin, Anthony, 37, 38, 44, 49, 192, 193
   Dead as Doornails, xv, 36, 37, 58
Crossguns Bridge, 213, 214
Crown Tavern, Fishamble Street, 107
Crumlin, 57, 157, 214, 223, 245, 246, 247
Cuala Industries, 179
Cullenswood House, Ranelagh, 179
Cumann na mBan, 123
Cumberland Place, 5
Cumberland Street North, 132
Cummings, E.E., 94
Curran, C.P., 5
Custom House, North Dock, ix, 19
Cyphers, 182

D'Olier Street, 88, 126
Daily Express, 70
Dalkey, 133, 195, 196–198, 201, 202, 205
Dalkey Castle, 201
Dalkey Island, 196, 202
Daly, Richard, 240
Dame Street, 19, 23, 106, 117, 122, 146
Dana, 71
Danes. *See* Vikings
Darndale, 222
Dartmouth Square, 60, 166, 167–168, 172, 181, 189
Dartry, 131
Davis, Thomas, 62, 87, 89, 117
   'Nation Once Again, A', 87
Davy Byrne's, Duke Street, 45, 80
Dawe, Gerald, 92
   'East Pier', 199

'Plinth, Berkeley Library, Trinity College', 92
Last Peacock, The, 190
Dawson Street, 20, 37, 57, 72, 80, 112
Dawson, Joshua, 20, 57
de Clare, Richard, 16
de Valera, Eamon, 38, 157, 243
Deevy, Teresa, 58–60
   Katie Roche, 58, 60
   King of Spain's Daughter, The, 59, 176
Derry/Londonderry, 141
Derry/Londonderry, County, 193
development. *See* architecture
Dick's Coffee House, Skinner's Row, 21, 107
Dickens, Charles, x
Dickson, David, 16, 18, 20, 64, 148, 168, 211, 237, 249
Dillon, John Blake, 87
Dingle, County Kerry, 194
Dirty Lane. *See* Bridgefoot Street
Dodder, River, 168, 212
Dodson's Bridge. *See* Anna Livia Bridge
Dollymount, 188, 219
Dolmen Press, xiv, 46, 49, 59
Dolphin Hotel, Essex Street, 58
Dominick Street, 20, 23, 26, 28, 62, 147
   Lower, 147
Donegal, County, 194
Donleavy, J.P., 36
   Ginger Man, The, xiv, 40–41, 44
Donnelly, Donal, 101
Donnybrook, 99, 131, 168, 203, 204
Donoghue, Emma
   Pull of the Stars, The, xvi, 124, 125, 126, 180
Donore, 99
Dorset Street, 153
   Upper, 153, 161
Doyle, Roddy, 29, 210–211, 224–225, 226, 251
   Barrytown Trilogy, xv, 210, 251
   Commitments, The, 210, 224, 225
   Deportees, The, 224–225
   Guts, The, 224
   Love, 132
   Paddy Clarke Ha Ha Ha, xv, 210

Paula Spencer, 225
Rory and Ita, 211
Snapper, The, 146, 210
Star Called Henry, A, 122
Van, The, 210
Woman Who Walked into Doors, The, 224, 225
Drapier, M.B. *See* Swift, Jonathan
Drimnagh, 223, 248
Drogheda Street. *See* O'Connell Street
Drogheda, Co. Louth, 17
Drumcondra, 25, 74, 131, 211, 213, 214, 215, 223
Drury Lane Theatre, London, 106
Dubber Cross, 227
Dublin Airport, 212, 222
Dublin Castle, 15, 16, 17, 18, 21, 23, 98, 99, 103, 104, 106, 115, 116, 168, 181, 212, 219, 239
Dublin City University, 220
Dublin Journal, 108
Dublin Magazine, xiii, 37, 176
Dublin mountains, 171, 173, 184, 211
Dublin University Magazine, xii, 62, 117, 235, 241
Dublin Weekly Journal, 106
Dubliners, the, 43, 167
Duffy, Charles Gavan, 87
Duke Street, 80
Duke, the, Duke Street, 45
Dún Laoghaire, xii, 25, 78, 133, 189–191, 192, 198, 199, 201
Dún Laoghaire-Rathdown, 168
Duncan, William, 168, 215
Dundrum, 42, 168, 171, 173, 174, 178, 179, 185
Dunne, Lee, 170, 171
  Does Your Mother?, 170
  Goodbye to the Hill, xiv, 170
  Paddy Maguire is Dead, 170
Durcan, Paul, 50, 167
  'Making Love Outside Áras an Uachtaráin', 243

Earl Street, 131
Earlsfort Terrace, 73
East Wall, 215, 217, 219, 223
Easter Rising, xiii, 27, 66, 88, 122–125, 126–129, 138, 140, 154, 160, 179, 180, 243
Eccles Street, 160
Edgeworth, Maria, 25
  Absentee, The, xii, 22, 25, 198–199
Edward VII, 174
Edwards, Hilton, 167
Eglinton, John, 71
El Cid, 182
Ellmann, Richard, 4, 118
Ely Place, 20, 63, 67, 68, 69, 70, 176
  Upper, 68
Emmet, Robert, 22, 86, 152
  rebellion, xii, 21–22
Empire Theatre, 122
Enright, Anne, 251
  Actress, xvi, 166, 167–168, 172, 189
  Forgotten Waltz, The, 184–185
  Gathering, The, xvi, 214–215, 223, 227
Envoy, xiv, 36, 37, 50
Enyi-Amadi, Chiamaka
  'When', 189
Essex Street, 106
  East, 104, 105
Examiner, The, xii, 106
Exchange Street, 106

Faddle Alley, 114
Fairview Park, 219
Famine, Great, xii, 24, 29, 66, 116
Farquhar, George, 84, 106
  Love and a Bottle, 106
Faulkner, George, 106, 109
Fenian Street, 153
Ferguson, Samuel, 117
Fettercairn, 206
Fianna Éireann, Na, 123
Fianna Fáil, 204
Fine Gael, 204
Fingal, 31, 168
Finglas, 9, 28, 30, 211, 223, 225–226, 227, 245
Finn's Hotel, South Leinster Street, 5
Fishamble Street, 23, 100, 102, 106, 112, 115, 116, 118

Fitz John, Matilda
    Joan!!!, 240
Fitzgerald, Lord Edward, 62, 199
Fitzgibbon Street, 160
Fitzharris, James 'Skin-the-Goat', 242
Fitzroy Avenue, 214
Fitzwilliam Place, 44
Fitzwilliam Square, 29, 44, 50, 59, 63
Fletcher, Alan, 102
Foley Street, 159
Foley, Bill, 154
Ford, John, 159
Foreign Affairs, xv
Foreign Policy, 203
Fortunestown, 206
Foster Avenue, 42
Foster, Roy, 26–27, 138
    On Seamus Heaney, 194
Four Courts, Inns Quay, 19, 27, 123, 149
Foxe, John
    Acts and Monuments, 115
Foxrock, 201, 211
Francis Street, 98
Frazier, Adrian, 68
Freeman's Journal, 133
French, Tana, 251
    Broken Harbour, 222–223
    Faithful Place, xvi, 99–100
    Wych Elm, The, 183–184
Frescati House, Blackrock, 199
Friel, Brian, 100
    Freedom of the City, The, 141
    Volunteers, xv, 101, 102
Fumbally Lane, 114, 134

Gaiety Theatre, Dame Street, 48
Galway, County, 119, 159
Gardiner Street, 20, 57, 146, 149, 153, 161
Gardiner, Luke (Jr), 20, 57
Gardiner, Luke (Sr), 20
Gate Theatre, Cavendish Row, xiv, 48, 152, 167
Geary, Karl
    Montpelier Parade, 206–207
General Post Office, O'Connell Street. *See* GPO, O'Connell Street

Gentleman, The, 107
George IV, 190
George's Church, Hardwicke Place, 160
George's Villas. *See* Sandymount Avenue
Germany, 206
Gibbons, Luke, 90
Gill, T.P., 70
Glasnevin, 131
Glasnevin Cemetery, 212, 213
Glenageary, 202
Glendinning, Victoria, 66
Glengariff Parade, 161
Glenmaroon, Chapelizod, 235
Glennaulin, Chapelizod, 235
Gloucester Diamond, Mountjoy Square, 144
Gloucester Street. *See* Seán McDermott Street
Glynn, Alan
    Winterland, 217
Gogarty, Oliver St. John, 63, 68, 70, 71, 82, 84, 148, 192
    'Liffey Bridge', 233
    As I Was Going Down Sackville Street, xiv, 70, 82, 134
    Blight, 151
    Offering of Swans, An, 233
Goldsmith, Oliver, 85
Goncourt, Edmond de, 68
Gonne, Maud, 174, 227
GPO, O'Connell Street, 27, 123, 124–125, 126, 128, 129–130, 131, 133, 139, 141, 168, 181, 200
Grafton Mooney, Harry Street, 34, 35, 45
Grafton Street, 10, 21, 22, 31, 34, 36, 37, 40, 41, 45, 49, 52, 60, 70, 74, 78, 80, 83, 100, 117, 180
Grand Canal, xii, 9, 15, 24, 25, 41–44, 51, 56, 62, 114, 123, 166, 167, 170–171, 174, 179, 181, 183, 184, 189, 203, 211
Grand Canal Basin, 8
Grand Canal Docks, 8
Graves, Robert, 94
Gray, Dylan Coburn
    Citysong, xvi, 133, 135–136
Great Britain Street. *See* Parnell Street

Great Brunswick Street. *See* Pearse Street
Green Cinema, Grafton Street, 41
Greendale Community School, Kilbarrack, 210
Greene's, Clare Street, 44
Gregory, Lady, 6, 27, 65, 68, 69, 137, 138, 140, 151, 178, 227
Gresham Hotel, O'Connell Street, 58, 119, 131, 132, 251
Greystones, County Wicklow, 200
Griffith Avenue, 214
Griffith Place, 214
Griffith Walk, 214
Guinness brewery, St. James' Gate, 26, 112, 189
Gwynn, Stephen
  Dublin Old and New, 16, 66

Haddington Road, 57
Haddington Road church, 51
Hamilton, Hugo
  Dublin Palms, 206
Harcourt Street, 169
Harcourt Terrace, 167, 177
Harcourt, Simon, 239
Hardie, Raymond, 101
Hardwicke Street, 126, 152, 160, 161
Hardwicke, Lord, 152
Harmonstown, 221
Harold's Cross, 133, 168
Harper's Bazaar, 180
Harris, Ian, 89
Hartnett, Michael, 50, 167
  Inchicore Haiku, 244
Hatch Street, 183
Hawthorn Terrace, 215
Head, Richard
  Hic et Ubique, 105–106
Heaney, Seamus, xv, 85, 100–102, 193–195
  'Beacons at Beltaine', 243
  'Digging', 100
  '*In Illo Tempore*', 195
  'Station Island', 194
  'Strand, The', 195
  'Viking Dublin: Trial Pieces', 100–102

Crediting Poetry, 194
Death of a Naturalist, 100
North, xv, 100–102
Spirit Level, The, 195
Station Island, 195
Henrietta Street, xii, 20, 26, 62, 112, 146, 148, 149, 163, 167
Henry Street, 131, 132
Herbert Lane, 46, 48, 57, 158
Herbert Park, 45
Herbert Place, 44, 52, 56, 57
Herbert Street, 29, 46, 48, 50, 57
Hermitage, the, Rathfarnham, 179
Hibernian Hotel, Dawson Street, 51, 59
Hibernian Magazine, 106
Hickey, Christine Dwyer
  Cold Eye of Heaven, The, xvi, 136, 149
  House on Parkgate Street, The, 247
Higgins, Aidan, 37
Hillview, Chapelizod, 235
Hitchcock, Robert
  Historical View of the Irish Stage, 104
Hodges Figgis, Dawson Street, 21, 44
Hoey's Alley, 109
Hoey's Court, 18
Hoggen Green. *See* College Green
Holloway, Joseph, 122, 126
Hopkins, Gerard Manley, 73
Howard, Paul, xv, 205–206, 224
  Downturn Abbey, 205
  Ross O'Carroll Kelly's Guide to (South) Dublin: How to Get by On, Like, €10,000 a Day, 205
  This Champagne Mojito is the Last Thing I Own, 205
  We Need to Talk About Ross, 205
Howth, 188, 205, 212, 220, 221, 223, 227–229
Howth Castle, 234
Howth Road, 219
Huband Bridge, 9
Hugh Lane Gallery, Parnell Square North, 146
Hughes, Declan, 204
  Colour of Blood, The, 204

Hughes, Ted, 94
Hume Street, 52
Hungary, 243
Hutchinson, Pearse, 182, 183
   'Refusals', 182
   'Spain 67', 182
   Faoistin Bhacach, 182
   Tongue Without Hands, 182
Hyde, Douglas
   Tincéar agus an tSídheog, An, 69

Inchicore, 244
Independent Theatre Company, 175
Innisfallen Parade, 153
Inniu, 36
Institute for Advanced Studies, Merrion Square, 64
Invincibles, 241
IRA, 102, 134, 141, 158
Irish Agricultural Organisation Society, 63, 71
Irish Citizen Army, 66, 123
Irish Homestead, xiii, 71, 176
Irish language, 9, 18–19, 36, 69, 112–113, 125, 158, 159, 238, 248
Irish Literary Revival, 74, 174, 176, 178
Irish Literary Theatre, xiii, 6, 68, 137,
   See also Abbey Theatre
Irish National Theatre Society. *See* Abbey Theatre, Abbey Street Lower
Irish Press, 38
Irish Republican Brotherhood, 123
Irish Statesman, 176
Irish Theosophical Society, 68, 176
Irish Times, xiii, xiv, 38, 39, 48, 88–89, 140, 205
Irish Volunteers, 123, 125, 160
Irish Women Writer's Club, 58
Island Street, 112
Islandbridge, 98, 232
Italy, 183

James I, xi, 17
James Joyce Bridge, 233
James Joyce Street, 144

Jameson distillery, Bow Street, 123
Jammet's, Nassau Street, 58
Johnson, Lionel, 117
Jones, Henry, 92
Jones' Road, 214
Jordan, Neil, 62, 199, 205
   Ballad of Lord Edward and Citizen Small, The, 199
   Lord Edward and Citizen Small, xvi
   Mistaken, 219, 221
   Past, The, 199
   Sunrise with Sea Monster, 199
Joyce, James, ix, 4, 5, 7, 37, 39, 65, 73, 117–119, 135, 159, 160–161, 174, 176, 178, 179, 191–194, 195, *See also* Bloomsday
   'Dead, The', 118–119, 251
   Dubliners, xiii, 118, 161
   Finnegans Wake, xiv, 118, 135, 152, 174, 233, 234–235, 236, 237, 242
   Portrait of the Artist as a Young Man, A, xiii, 71, 74–75, 79, 188
   Ulysses, ix, xiii, 5, 7, 70–71, 80, 118, 133–134, 144, 160–161, 174, 188–189, 192–193, 207, 212–213, 216, 228–229, 234, 242
Joyce, Joe
   Echobeat, 131
   Echoland, 64
Joyce, Stanislaus, 160, 161

Kavanagh, Patrick, 34, 35, 36, 37, 38, 40, 42–43, 44, 45, 46, 48, 49, 50, 56, 57, 58, 63, 88, 140, 167, 170, 172, 192
   'Adventure in the Bohemian Jungle', 57
   'Bank Holiday', 42
   'Canal Bank Walk', 43
   'From Monaghan to the Grand Canal', 43
   'Goat Tethered Outside the Bailey, A', 40
   'Lines Written on a Seat on the Grand Canal, Dublin', 43
   'Monaghan Hills', 35
   'On Raglan Road', 42–43
   'Paddiad, The', 42
   'Shancoduff', 35

'Spraying the Potatoes', 35
Come Dance with Kitty Stobling, xiv
Soul for Sale, A, xiv
Kavanagh's Weekly, 38, 45
Kearns, Kevin, 144, 148, 151, 156, 158
Kelly, Aidan, 250
Kelly, Luke, 43, 167
Kennedy's Villas, Bow Lane, 245
Kennelly, Brendan, 7, 92, 93, 172
   'Begin', 43–44
   'Shelley in Dublin', 139
   My Dark Fathers, 92
Kernoff, Harry, 37
Kerrigan, Gene, 223, 251
   Dark Times in the City, 223
   Little Criminals, 183
   Rage, The, 223
Kerry, County, 207
Kerrymount Avenue, 201
Kevin Street, 98
Keyes, Marian, 251
   This Charming Man, xvi, 203, 204
Kiberd, Declan, 35
Kiernan, Olivia
   Killer in Me, The, 219–220
Kilbarrack, 29, 210, 224, 226, 245, 251
Kilcoole, County Wicklow, 200
Kildare Road, 28, 246
Kildare Street, xiii, 23, 38, 66, 67, 68, 70, 71, 72
Kildare, County, 15, 80, 249, 250
Kildare, Earl of, 62
Kilgobbin, 204
Killester, 221, 224
Killinarden, 247, 248
Killiney, 198, 220
Kilmacud Road Lower, 204
Kilmainham, 244, 245, 247
Kilmashogue, 173
Kiltimagh, County Mayo, 38
Kimmage, 28, 157, 158, 245, 246
Kingstown. *See* Dún Laoghaire
Kinsella, Thomas, 4, 5, 50, 51, 244, 247

'38 Phoenix Street', 244
'Baggot Street Deserta', 51
'Bell, The', 51
'Clarence Mangan', 117
'Open House', 51
'Phoenix Park', 244
'Stable, The', 51
Another September, xiv, 51
Dublin Documentary, A, xvi
Nightwalker and Other Poems, 244
One Fond Embrace, 245
Personal Places, 244
Poems from the City Centre, xv, 51
Kippure, 15
Kirwan, Tommy 'Duckegg', 144, 158
Knowlson, James, 191

Lad Lane, 59, 60
Lally, Caitriona
   Eggshells, 135
Lambay Island, 198
Lantern Theatre Club, Mount Street Lower, 46
Larkin, Philip, 94
Laverty, Maura, 212
   Liffey Lane, xiv, 152, 159, 160
Lavin, Mary, 59, 60–61, 200
   'In a Café', 60–61
   Collected Stories, xv
   Tales from Bective Bridge, 60
Lawrence, D.H., 94
Le Fanu, Joseph Sheridan, 62, 114, 117, 147
   'Account of Some Strange Disturbances in Aungier Street, An', 114
   'Familiar, The', 147
   Cock and the Anchor, The, xii, 114
   Ghost Stories of Chapelizod, 235
   House by the Churchyard, The, xiii, 235–237, 242
Leerssen, Joep, 19
Leeson Park, 166, 172, 173, 181
Leeson Street, 61, 92
   Lower, 49, 183
   Upper, 42, 183

Leeson Street Bridge, 44, 167
Leinster House, Kildare Street, 62, 66, 72, 74, 146, 199
Leinster Lawn, 64
Leinster Square, 179
Leinster, Duke of, 28, 72, 74
Leitrim, County, 35, 220
Leixlip, County Kildare, 250
Leonard, Hugh
  Da, xv, 198
  Life, A, 198
  Out After Dark, 197
Leopardstown, 206
Leslie, John, 238–239
Levanthal, A.J., 192
Lever, Charles, 84, 169
  Harry Lorrequer, xii, 241
  O'Donoghue, The, 81
Liam Mellows Bridge, 233
Liberties, 26, 27, 98–119, 134, 150, 210, 212, 226
Liffey, River, xi, 8, 15, 18, 20, 26, 27, 30, 62, 78, 90, 91, 98, 102, 103, 134, 147, 166, 179, 183, 212, 215, 225, 235–237, 238, 244
Limekiln Lane, 249
Limerick, 56
Lincoln Place, 4, 63, 83, 84
Lisbon, x
literary magazines. *See* print culture
Little Britain Street, 161
Littlewood, Joan, 40
London, x, xiv, xv, 5, 22, 39, 47, 48, 61, 65, 68, 83, 104, 105, 106, 108, 109, 127, 176, 193, 220
Longford, Christine, 168
Longinus, 90
Longley, Edna. *See* Broderick, Edna
Longley, Michael, 93–95, 172
  'River & Fountain', 94–95
  New Territory, 93
  Ten Poems, 93
Los Angeles, USA, 184, 204
Louth, County, 250
Lowe, Louise, 144
Lowell, Robert, 94

Luas, xvi, 79, 132, 137, 169, 206, *See also* railways
Lucan, 235, 249
Lughnaquilla, 173
Lynch, Patricia, 59
Lynn, Kathleen, 180
Lynott, Phil, 34
Lyster, Thomas William, 70

M50, 171, 238, 249
M'Nally, Leonard, 240, 241
Mabbot Street. *See* James Joyce Street
Mac Conghail, Marcus
  'Dumhach Thrá', 189
Mac Diarmada, Seán, 122
Mac Liammóir, Micheál, 167
mac Murchada, Máel Mórda, 16
MacArthur, Malcolm, 52
MacBride, John, 127
MacDonagh, Thomas, 122, 126, 127
  'Dublin Tramcars', 179
  When the Dawn is Come, 126
MacNeice, Louis, 14, 15, 94
  'Dublin', 14, 18, 134
Madden, Deirdre
  Authenticity, 95
  Time Present and Time Past, xvi, 185
Mahaffy, John Pentland, 82, 83
  Principles of the Art of Conversation, The, 82, 83, 84
Mahomet, xii, 108
Mahon, Derek, 93, 172
  'Beyond Howth Head', 227–228
  'Fox in Grafton Street, A', 10
  'shiver in your tenement', 37
  Twelve Poems, 93
Malahide, 227
Malton, James, 65
Manders Terrace, 183
Manet, Édouard, 68, 69
Mangan, James Clarence, 73, 115–118, 119, 212
  'Extraordinary Adventure in the Shades, An', 117
  'Nameless One, The', 116
  'Sixty-Drop Dose of Laudanum, A', 116
  Autobiography, xiii, 116

Manor Street, 150, 159
Marcus, David
Midnight Court, The, 59
Marino, xiii, 28, 214, 218, 245
Marino Crescent, 218, 219, 221
Markievicz, Casimir, 174
Markievicz, Constance, 66, 73, 174, 182
Marlborough Street, 146
Marsh's Library, St. Patrick's Close, 114–115
Martyn, Edward, 6, 63, 68, 69, 137
Heather Field, The, 68
Mary Lane, 157
Maturin, Charles Robert
Melmoth the Wanderer, 115
Maxwell, Constantia, 146
Dublin Under the Georges, 240
Mayfield House, Chapelizod, 235
Mayor Street Bridge, 9
McArdle, Dorothy, 58
McCrea, Barry
First Verse, The, 94
McCullough, Niall, 98
Urban History of Dublin, 78
McDaid's, Harry Street, 34, 35, 36, 37, 45, 49, 50, 57, 58
McDonald, Frank, 19, 214
Little History of the Future of Dublin, 199
McGahern, John, 35, 37, 50–51
'Bank Holiday', 34–35, 42
'My Love, My Umbrella', 34
Amongst Women, 35
Nightlines, xv, 34
That They May Face the Rising Sun, 35
McGarry, Fearghal, 27
McGuinness, Frank, 190
Bird Sanctuary, 190
Observe the Sons of Ulster Marching towards the Somme, 141
McKenna, Siobhan, 154
McParland, Edward, 20
McPherson, Conor, 200, 220–221
Dublin Carol, 220–221
Seafarer, The, 221
Weir, The, 220

Meath, County, 4, 36, 60, 226, 249, 250
Meath, Earls of, 99
Meehan, Anna, 144
Meehan, Fr C.P., 116
Meehan, Paula, 144, 151, 156, 158, 162, 172, 251
'Buying Winkles', 149–150
'Child's Map of Dublin, A', 31, 72
'History Lessons', 162
'Home', 43
'Lost Children of the Inner City, The', 162
'My Father Perceived as a Vision of St. Francis', 227
'Night Walk', 114
'Window on the City', 162
Pillow Talk, xv
Mendes, Rafael
'32 Kg Suitcase', 163
Mercier, Vivian, 48
Merrion Square, 5, 24, 27, 44, 60, 62–63, 64, 68, 71, 72, 73, 75, 78, 81, 82, 147, 179
Mespil Road, 56
Metro Eireann, 225
Mhac an tSaoi, Máire
'Fód an Imris: Ard Oifig an Phoist 1986', 124
Middle Abbey Street, 137, 139
Miller, Cormac, 183
Miller, Liam, xiv, 59, 246
Milliken, John, 21
Mills, Lia
Fallen, 126
Milltown, 168
Moira House, Usher's Island, 147
Molesworth Street, 70
MoLI. *See* Museum of Literature Ireland, St. Stephen's Green
Monaghan, County, 35, 42, 56
Monkstown, 198, 207
Montague, John, 36, 46, 50
'Herbert Street Revisited', 46, 173
Montgomery Street, 144, 145
Monto, the, 136, 144–146

Montpelier Parade, 206
Moore Hall, County Mayo, 68
Moore Street, 131, 132, 133, 149
Moore, Brian
  Mangan Inheritance, The, 117
Moore, George, 20, 63, 67, 68–70, 71, 137
  Drama in Muslin, A, xiii, 68
  Esther Waters, 69
  Hail and Farewell, xiii, 69–70, 137, 176–178
  Salve, 69, 70
  Vale, 69
Moore, Henry, 73
Moore, Henry, Earl of Drogheda, 131
Moore, Thomas, 23, 68, 198
Moran, James
  Staging the Easter Rising: 1916 as Theatre, 127
Moran, Michael J. *See* Zozimus
Morehampton Road, 58, 172
Morgan, Alexander Campbell, 80
Morgan, Lady, 23, 26, 28, 66–68, 147, 148
  Memoirs, xiii
  O'Donnel, 67
  Wild Irish Girl, The, 23
Morgan, Sir Charles, 67
Morris, William, 179
Mount Street
  Lower, 44, 46, 51, 52
  Upper, 42, 44, 49, 52, 61, 62
Mount Street Bridge, 123
Mount Temple, Clontarf, 218
Mountjoy Prison, 40, 158, 161
Mountjoy Square, 60, 63, 144, 153, 159, 160
Mullingar House, Chapelizod, 235, 236, 237
Murdoch, Iris, 63, 160
  Red and the Green, The, xiv, 63, 125, 160
Murphy, Jimmy
  Of This Brave Time, 124
Murphy, Mary 'Bluebell', 156, 158
Murphy, Richard
  'Nelson's Pillar', 135
Murphy, Tom
  Gigli Concert, The, 141
Murray, Christopher, 215

Murray, Maggie, 151
Murray, Paul
  Mark and the Void, The, 216–217
  Skippy Dies, 206
Murray's, Seán McDermott Street, 156
Museum of Literature Ireland, St. Stephen's Green, xvi, 30, 73

na gCopaleen, Myles. *See* O'Brien, Flann
Nassau Hotel, South Frederick Street, 65
Nassau Street, 5, 58, 78, 81
Nation, The, xii, 24, 62, 87, 88, 117
National Gallery of Ireland, Merrion Square, 64, 68, 72
National Library of Ireland, Kildare Street, xiii, 23, 38, 60, 68, 70, 71, 72
National Museum of Ireland – Natural History, Merrion Street Upper, 72
National Museum of Ireland, Kildare Street, 72
Nealon, Louise
  Snowflake, 80
Neary's, Chatham Street, 37
Neilstown, 248
Nelson Street, 158, 160
Nelson, Admiral Horatio, 132, 133, 134
Nelson's Pillar, O'Connell Street, 123, 130, 131, 132, 133–135, 136, 160
New Orleans, USA, x
New Writers Press, 115
New York, USA, x, 20, 48, 180, 181, 237
New Yorker, 60, 180, 181
Newbridge Avenue, 212
Newman, Angela, 154
Newman, John Henry, 23, 73
News-Letter, xi, 18
newspapers. *See* print culture
Ní Chuilleanáin, Eiléan, 50, 92, 172, 183
  'Trinity New Library', 92
  Acts and Monuments, 183
Ní Dhuibhne, Eilís
  Bray House, The, xv, 199–200
Nic Shiublaigh, Maire
  Splendid Years, The, 176

Nolan, Christopher
    Under the Eye of the Clock, 218
Nolan, Megan
    Acts of Desperation, 190
Norbury, Lord, 152
Norman Court, Chapelizod, 235
Normans, 16, 99
North Bull Island, 219
North Bull Wall, 212, 215
North Circular Road, 150, 214
North Earl Street, 135
North King Street, 152, 246
North Lotts, The, 215
North Richmond Street, 161
North Road, 227
North Strand, 223
North Strand Road, 220
North Wall, 26

Ó Cadhain, Máirtín
    Cré na Cille, 89
    Eochar, An, 72
Ó Criomhthain, Tomás
    An tOileánach, 40
Ó Neachtain, Seán, 112–113
    Stair Éamoinn Uí Chléirigh, 112
Ó Neachtain, Tadhg, 112
Ó Nualláin, Ciarán, 36
O'Brennan, Kathleen, 138
O'Brien, Edna
    Country Girls, The, 131
    Lonely Girl, The, 72
O'Brien, Flann, 36, 37, 38–40, 44, 49, 58, 88, 172, 192, 200, 201
    'Cruiskeen Lawn', xiv, 39–40, 41, 88, 140, 250
    At Swim-Two-Birds, xiv, 38–39, 41–42, 57
    Béal Bocht, An, 39, 40
    Dalkey Archive, The, 197, 198
    Third Policeman, The, 39
O'Brien, Kate, 37, 51, 56–57, 58, 59, 200
    Land of Spices, 58
    My Ireland, 131

O'Carroll Kelly, Ross. *See* Howard, Paul
O'Casey, Seán, xiii, 137, 153–156, 158, 159, 161, 176, 212, 215, 217
    Autobiographies, 134–135
    Juno and the Paycock, 128, 154, 155–156, 159
    Plough and the Stars, The, xiii, 128–129, 139, 154–155, 156, 159
    Shadow of a Gunman, The, 128, 153–154, 155
O'Connell Bridge, xii, 122, 124, 125, 126, 130, 131, 137, 146, 232
O'Connell Street, xii, 20, 27, 31, 58, 59, 72, 78, 121, 122–137, 138, 144, 145, 146, 148, 149, 150, 168, 224
O'Connell, Daniel, 62, 130, 134
O'Connor, Joseph, 200
    Shadowplay, 218–219
O'Connor, Niamh
    Taken, 205
O'Dea, Jimmy, 48
O'Doherty, Éamonn, 135
O'Donoghue's, Lower Baggot Street, 43
O'Donovan, Gerard
    Priest, The, 204
O'Faoláin, Seán, 37
O'Flaherty, Liam, xiv
    'Sniper, The', 125
    Insurrection, xiv, 126
O'Loughlin, Michael, 162
O'Neill, Ciaran, 25
O'Nolan, Brian. *See* O'Brien, Flann
O'Rowe, Mark, 248–249
    Crestfall, 248, 249
    Howie the Rookie, xv, 248, 249, 250
O'Shannon, Cathal, 37
O'Sullivan, Seamus, xiii, 176
O'Sullivan, Sean, 36
O'Toole, Fintan, 153, 245, 246, 251
Observatory Lane, 184
Okorie, Melatu Uche
    This Hostel Life, 225
Olympia Theatre, xv
Orchard Lodge, Chapelizod, 235
Ormond, Duke of, 18, 19, 236, 237

Orpen, William, 69
Osborne, Danny, 62
Óttar *svarti*, 99
Owenson, Robert, 23
Owenson, Sydney. *See* Morgan, Lady
Oxford, University of, 81

Palace Bar, Fleet Street, 88–89
Palmerstown, 133
Palmerstown Park, 133
pamphlets. *See* print culture
Paris, 47, 68, 69, 241
Park Street, Kilmainham, 244
Parliament House, College Green, xii, 19, 85
Parliament Street, 106
Parlour Window, The, 106
Parnell Bridge, 171
Parnell Square, 146, 162
    East, 148
Parnell Street, 161
Parnell, Charles Stewart, 130, 134, 138
Parsons, Baggot Street, 44, 45
Pearl Bar, Fleet Street, 88
Pearse Street, 5–6, 15, 85, 130
Pearse, Patrick, 6, 27, 122, 126–127, 139, 168, 179, 182
    'I am Ireland', 129
Pembroke, 28
Pembroke Road, 42, 44, 45, 49, 57
Pembroke Street, 58
    Upper, 50
Pembroke, Earls of, 57
Pepper Canister Church, Mount Street, 51
Percy Lane, 51
Percy Place, 44, 49, 51
Pessoa, Fernando, x
Phibsborough, 25, 211
Phibsborough Road, 213
Philips, Katharine
    Pompey, 105
Philips, William, xi
    St. Stephen's Green: Or, the Generous Lovers, xi, 64–65, 106

Phoenix Park, xi, 18, 60, 150, 235, 237–245, 250
Phoenix Park Murders, 241–242
Phoenix Street, Kilmainham, 244
Pigeon House, 188
Pike Newsletter, 47
Pike Theatre, Herbert Lane, xiv, 40, 46–48, 49, 57, 59, 158
Pilkington, Lætitia, 109, 110
Pitt, William, 21
plague, 100, 104, 112, 114, 247, 248
    1348 (Black Death), 17
    1575, xi
Plunkett, James
    Risen People, The, 141
    Strumpet City, xiv, 141, 152–153, 159, 206
Plunkett, Joseph Mary, 122, 126, 160
    Circle and the Sword, The, 126
Poddle, River, xi, 15, 98, 99, 212
Poetry Ireland Review, xv, 146
Poland, 243
Poolbeg Lighthouse, 215
Portobello Bridge, 171, 183
Portobello Private Nursing Home, 171
Portrane, 227
Portstewart, County Derry/Londonderry, 193, 194
Powell, Humphrey, 17
Powell, Stephen, 106
Power, Kevin, 203
    Bad Day in Blackrock, xvi, 207
    White City, 207
Praeger, Robert Lloyd, 59
Pride of Life, The, xi, 103
print culture, 17, 18, 19, 21, 37–38, 88–89, 106–107, 109–110, 113, 179
    literary magazines, xii, xiii, xiv, 36, 37, 106, 175–176, 179, 182, 219
    newspapers, 39–40, 87–89, 108
    pamphlets, 107–110
'Proclamation of an Irish Republic', 122, 126, 130, 140
Prospect Cemetery. *See* Glasnevin Cemetery
Prussia Street, 150
pubs (literary), ix, 34–37, 38, 40, 51, 56, 57, 58, 88–89, 91, 107, 172, 180, 247

Quarryvale, 248
Queen's Theatre, Pearse Street, 6, 85–87
Quinn, James, 87

Raglan Road, 42, 45
Raheny, 221, 224
Railway Street, 145
railways, xii, 5, 25, 169, 174, 185, 196, 198, 211, 212, 215
   DART, xv, 169, 205, *See also* Luas
Randolph, Jody Allen, 173
Ranelagh, 25, 166, 167, 168, 170, 180, 181, 183, 189, 198, 203, 211
Ranelagh Park, 183
'Ranger, A'
   'Phoenix Park: A Poem', 238
Rathfarnham, 127, 131, 178, 179, 180
Rathgar, 133, 167, 168, 174, 175, 178, 198, 211
Rathgar Avenue, 175, 176, 177, 179
Rathgar Road, 182, 246
Rathmines, xiv, 25, 28, 30, 131, 133, 159, 167, 168, 169, 170, 174, 179, 184, 198, 211
Rathmines Church, 184
Rathmines Road, 176, 179, 184
   Upper, 176
Reeve, Alan, 88, 89
Remoundou, Natasha, 31
Richmond Street, North, 161
Rilke, Rainer Maria, 94
Rimbaud, Arthur, 94
Ringsend, xii, 26, 133, 189, 212, 215
Riversdale, Dundrum, 178, 179
Riverside House, Chapelizod, 235
Robinson, Lennox, 27, 140, 205
Robinson, Mary, 170
Rocque, John, xii, 20, 62
Rooney, Sally, 90–92, 168
   Beautiful World, Where Are You, 137
   Conversations with Friends, 90, 91
   Normal People, xvi, 91–92
Roscommon, County, 112
Rosebowl Bar, Gardiner Street, 149
Rotunda Hospital, Parnell Square East, 146
Royal Canal, xii, 9, 15, 25, 150, 158, 166, 210, 211, 212, 213, 214, 218, 224

Royal Court, London, xiv, 220
Royal Dublin Society, Kildare Street, 72
Royal Irish Academy, Dawson Street, 72
RTÉ, 200
Russell Street, 28, 38, 156, 157, 158, 214, 246
Russell, George, xiii, 50, 63, 68, 69, 71, 174–176, 179, 246
   'Transformations', 175
   Deirdre, 177
Russell, Thomas, 86
Rutland Square, 63, *See* Parnell Square
Ryan, John, 37, 42, 192
   Remembering How We Stood, 35–36, 58

Sackville Street. *See* O'Connell Street
Saint Michael and Saint John, Church of.
   See also Smock Alley Theatre
Salkeld, Blanaid, 58
Salmon, George, 80
Samuel Beckett Bridge, 233
Sandycove, 192, 193
   Martello tower, 192–193, *See also* Joyce, James
Sandyford, 204, 211
Sandymount, 131, 133, 188, 189, 194–195, 196, 199, 200, 203, 205, 207, 212
Sandymount Avenue, 194
Santa Rosa, Chapelizod, 235
Scarlett, Fiona
   Boys Don't Cry, 222
Schrödinger, Ernest, 64
   What is Life?, 64
Scott, Michael, 245
Seán McDermott Street, 130, 144
Seán O'Casey Bridge, 233
Seapoint, 207
Searsons', Baggot Street, 56
Sennett, Richard, 156
Shades Tavern, College Green, 117
Shakespear, Olivia, 63, 178
Shamrock, The, 219
Shannon, River, 213
Shaw, George Bernard, xiii, 37, 72, 174, 176, 179, 197

Shaw, Harriet Weaver, 234
Sheehy-Skeffington, Hanna, 139
Shelbourne Hotel, St. Stephen's Green, 21, 23, 65, 66, 68
Shelley, Percy Bysshe, 148
　Address to the Irish People, 139
Sheppard, Oliver, 128, 129
Sheridan, Frances, 153
Sheridan, Richard Brinsley, 153, 161
　School for Scandal, The, 153
Sheridan, Thomas, 108–109, 153
　Mr. Sh—n's Apology to the Town, 108
　Sighs and Groans of Mr. Sh——n, The, 108
Sheriff Street Upper, 215
Ship Street, 98
Shirley, James
　St. Patrick for Ireland, 104
Silicon Docks. *See* Grand Canal Docks
Simpson, Alan, 46, 47, 48
Simpson, Linzi, 105
Sinn Féin, 70, 127
Sinnott's, South King Street, 37
Sirr, Peter, 99
　'Poet and the Mapmaker, The', 15
　Intimate City, xvi, 167, 233
Sitriuc Silkenbeard, 16
Skinner's Row. *See* Christchurch Place
Sligo, County, 91, 220
Slovenia, 243
Smith, Michael
　'Long Lane', 117
Smith, Paul, 170, 171
　Annie, 170
　Countrywoman, The, xiv, 170
Smithfield, 149, 150
Smock Alley, 106
Smock Alley Theatre, xi, xii, 19, 22, 64, 104–106, 107, 110, 153
Smyllie, Robert 'Bertie', 39, 88, 89
Smyth, Gerard
　'Clery's Clock', 149
　'Cúchulainn in the GPO', 130
　'Hot Bread of St. Catherine's, The', 112
　'Taken', 30
　Sundays of Eternity, The, 99

Somerville and Ross, 176
　Real Charlotte, The, 159
Sorrento Road, Dalkey, 205
Sorrento Terrace, Dalkey, 197, 205
South Circular Road, 131
South Dublin Union poorhouse, James Street, 123
South Earl Street, 112
South Great George's Street, 78
South Wall, 215
Speed, John, xi, 15, 17, 78
Speranza. *See* Wilde, Lady Jane
Spire, the, O'Connell Street, 133, 135–136, 137
Spirit of the Nation, The, 87
Springfield, 249
Springvale, Chapelizod, 235
St. Andrew's Church, Suffolk Street, 78
St. Catherine's Church, Meath Street, 150
St. Enda's School, Rathfarnham, 122, 126, 179, 182
St. George's Church, Hardwicke Place, 147
St. Ita's Hospital, Portrane, 227
St. James's Gate, 26
St. John the Evangelist, Church of, xi, 102, 105
St. Laurence Lodge, Chapelizod, 235
St. Laurence's Church, Chapelizod, 236
St. Martin de Pole, Church of, 98
St. Mary's Church, Haddington Road, 57
St. Mary's Church, St Mary's Place, 147
St. Michael and St. John, Church of, Essex Street East, 104–105
St. Michael le Pole, Church of, Chancery Lane/Ship Street, 15
St. Michan's Church, Arran Quay, 157
St. Patrick's Cathedral, St. Patrick's Close, 15, 16, 99, 108, 109, 110, 112, 114, 116, 117, 146
St. Patrick's Hospital, Bow Lane, 111
St. Sepulchre, Manor of, 99
St. Stephen, Church of (near) St. Stephen's Green, 18
St. Stephen's Church, Mount Street. *See* Pepper Canister Church, Mount Street

St. Stephen's Green, xi, xvi, 18, 20, 22, 23,
    27, 30, 41, 44, 45, 52, 55, 58, 60, 61, 63,
    64–65, 66, 70, 72, 73–74, 79, 81, 123,
    167, 168, 200, 211, 238, 240
St. Werburgh's Church, Werburgh Street,
    104
Stag's Head, Dame Court, 91
Standard, The, 38
Stanley, Lady, 66
Stannaway Road, 246
Steele, Lady, 147, 148
Steely Dan, 224
Stein, River, 212
Stephens, James, 138
    Charwoman's Daughter, The, xiii, 72,
        77–78, 151
    Insurrection in Dublin, The, xiii, 122–123,
        124, 126, 179
Stevens, Wallace, 94
Stoker, Bram, xiii, 68, 84, 114–115, 218–219
    'Buried Treasure', 219
    Dracula, xiii, 114, 115, 219
Stoker, Sir Thornley, 68, 70
Stone Boat, Sundrive Road, 246, 247
Stoneybatter, 159
Strabane, County Tyrone, 36
Strand (pub), Strand Road, 220
Strand Road, 193, 194, 220
Strongbow, 16
Studies, 43
Suffolk Street, 78, 79
Sugarloaf Mountain, County Wicklow, 200
Summerhill, 146, 159
Sunday Tribune, xv, 205
Sundrive Road, 246, 247
Sunnybank, Chapelizod, 235
Sutton, 174, 224
Sweny's Chemist Shop, Westland Row, 4,
    5, 7
Swift, Carolyn, 46, 47, 48
Swift, Jonathan, xii, 18, 84, 85, 106, 108,
    109–112, 196, 240
    'Plain Story of the Fact, The', 109
    'Verses on the Death of Dr. Swift,
        D.S.P.D.', 110, 111

Gulliver's Travels, xii, 109, 111
Modest Proposal, A, xii, 109–110
Synge Street, 174
Synge, John Millington, 178
    Playboy of the Western World, 139, 151

Talbot Street, 132
Tallaght, 28, 178, 183, 247–249
Temple Bar, 73, 106
Templeogue, 167, 168, 179, 180
Terenure, 133, 167, 168, 179, 211
Theatre of Ireland, Hardwicke Street, 126,
    160
Theatre Royal, Crow Street, 240
Theatre Royal, Hawkins Street,
    23, 153
Thingmote, 78
Thomas Court, 99
Thomas Street, 98, 99, 112
Thomas, Dylan, 94
Thoor Ballylee, County Galway, 63,
    178, 193
Three Rock, 173
Tibradden, 173
Tóibín, Colm, 7, 50, 60, 61, 73, 84
    Mad, Bad, Dangerous to Know, 7
Tolka, River, 212, 214, 219
Tonduff, 15
Tone, Wolfe, 86, 87, 89
    *Argument on behalf of the Catholics of
        Ireland*, 86
Torca Road, Dalkey, 197
Trafalgar, Battle of, 134
Trieste, Italy, 117, 118
Trinity College Dublin, xi, 4, 5, 6, 7, 9, 15,
    17, 18, 21, 22, 24, 52, 77, 78–87, 100, 104,
    106, 107, 140, 168, 172, 212, 241
    Botany Bay, 83, 94
    Front Square, 94, 95
    Graduate Memorial Building, 94
    Library, xii, 17, 19, 81, 82, 89, 92
    Library (Berkeley), 91, 92
    New Square, 83, 87
    Rubrics, 95
Trinity Street, 87

Troubles (Northern Ireland), xv, 100–102, 141
Tubbermore Road, Dalkey, 205
Tynan, Katharine, 134, 176, 248
Tyrone House, Marlborough Street, 146
Tyrone, County, 218

U2, 218
United Ireland, 83
United Irishmen, xii, 21
University College Dublin, xiii, 23, 60, 73–74, 79, 118, 200
USA, 180
Usher's Island, 118, 119, 232
Usher's Quay, 233

Viceregal Lodge, Phoenix Park. *See* Áras an Uachtaráin, Phoenix Park
Vico Road, Dalkey, 197
Vico, Giambattista, 197
Vikings, xi, 9, 15–16, 31, 78, 98–99, 100–102, 210, 232, 233, 234
Visitatio Sepulcri, xi, 102–103, 105

Waldron, Lady, 70
War of Independence, xiii, 27, 125, 128, 154, 180
War of the Three Kingdoms, 17
Ward, James
    'Phoenix Park', 238
Washington, D.C., USA, 180
Waterford, 58, 60
Waterloo Road, 45, 59, 60
Watersland Road, 201
Webb's, Aston Quay, 44
Werburgh Street, 18
Werburgh Street Theatre, xi, 17, 104, 109
Westland Row, ix, xii, 4–5, 7, 8, 9, 82
Westmoreland Street, 117
Wexford, County, 36, 49
Whaley, Thomas 'Buck', 74
Whistler, James Abbott McNeill, 68
Whitbread, J.W.
    Wolfe Tone, 86–87

Whitby, Yorkshire, 218
White, Jack
    Devil You Know, The, 63–64
Whitehall, Clondalkin, 248
Whitelaw, Rev. James, 21, 150
    Essay on the Population of Dublin, xii, 150
Whitney, Karl, 249
Whyte's Academy, Grafton Street, 22
Wicklow Lounge, Wicklow Street, 37
Wicklow, County, 15, 16, 226, 249
Wide Streets Commission, xii, 19, 146
Wilbur, Richard, 94
Wilde, Lady Jane, 7, 24, 62
Wilde, Oscar, ix, 4, 5, 7, 24, 62, 82–83, 84
    Importance of Being Earnest, The, 83
    Lady Windermere's Fan, 83
    Lord Arthur Saville's Crime and Other Prose Pieces, 83
Wilde, Sir William, 62
William of Orange, 106
Williamite war, 18
Williams, Jonathan
    Between the Lines: Poems on the Dart (ed.), 205
Wilton Place, 42
Wilton Square, 59
Winetavern Street, 102, 112, 211, 234
Wingfield, Sheila
    'Melancholy Love, A', 144
Wood Quay, 16, 102
Woods, Macdara, 50, 183
    'Aston Quay: January 2008', 233
    'East Wall East Road', 183
    'Leland, PS from Yalta', 50
    'Stopping the Lights, Ranelagh 1986', 183
    Stopping the Lights in Ranelagh, xv
World War I, 124, 125, 126
World War II, 14, 27, 39, 64, 131, 134, 195, 196, 199

Yeats, Elizabeth, 127, 179
Yeats, George, 63, 178, 235
Yeats, Jack B., 45, 59
Yeats, Susan, 175, 179

Yeats, W.B., xiii, 6, 7, 26, 39, 50, 63, 65, 68, 69, 73, 83, 94, 127, 137, 138, 139, 176, 178–179, 180, 193, 194, 235–236, 237
'After Parnell', 138
'Beautiful Lofty Things', 205, 227
'Easter 1916', xiii, 127–128, 179
'September 1913', 88
'Seven Sages, The', 85
'Statues, The', 129
'Three Monuments, The', 134
'To Ireland in the Coming Times', 117

Countess Cathleen, The, xiii, 6, 67, 68
Death of Cuchulain, The, 128, 129
Dramatis Personae, 69
Words Upon the Window-Pane, The, xiv, 111
York Street, 115
Young Ireland movement, 87
Young Ireland rebellion, xii, 24

Zola, Émile, 68, 69
Zozimus, 114

For EU product safety concerns, contact us at Calle de José Abascal, 56–1º, 28003 Madrid, Spain or eugpsr@cambridge.org.

www.ingramcontent.com/pod-product-compliance
Lightning Source LLC
LaVergne TN
LVHW021946060526
838200LV00043B/1941